PENGUIN BOOKS

AFRICA'S CHOICES

Michael Barratt Brown was Principal of Northern College, Barnsley, from its founding in 1977 to 1984. Before that he was Senior Lecturer in Economics and Industrial Studies at the Extramural Department of Sheffield University. He is now the Chair of TWIN Ltd and of Twin Trading Ltd. For a time he worked with the United Nations and in the film industry. He has been a Visiting Professor at the Universities of Aligarh (1972). Hitotsubashi (1976), Papua New Guinea (1979), the University of California in Los Angeles (1987), the University of Alicante (1989), the University of Madrid (1993) and the University of Victoria in Vancouver (1994). He has written regularly for the *New Left Review, Tribune, Spokesman* and *European Labour Forum.* His books include *After Imperialism* (1963), *What Economics is About* (1970), *From Labourism to Socialism* (1972), *The Economics of Imperialism* (1974), *Information at Work* (1978), *Models in Political Economy* (1984; revised 1995), *European Union: Fortress or Democracy?* (1991), *Short Changed: Africa and World Trade* (with Pauline Tiffen, 1992) and *Fair Trade: Reform and Realities in the International Trading System* (1993). He is married with four grown-up children, lives in Derbyshire and grows fruit and vegetables as a hobby.

AFRICA'S CHOICES:

AFTER THIRTY YEARS OF THE WORLD BANK

Michael Barratt Brown

PENGUIN BOOKS

PENGUIN BOOKS

Published by the Penguin Group
Penguin Books Ltd, 27 Wrights Lane, London w8 5TZ, England
Penguin Books USA Inc., 375 Hudson Street, New York, New York 10014, USA
Penguin Books Australia Ltd, Ringwood, Victoria, Australia
Penguin Books Canada Ltd, 10 Alcorn Avenue, Toronto, Ontario, Canada M4V 3B2
Penguin Books (NZ) Ltd, 182–190 Wairau Road, Auckland 10, New Zealand

Penguin Books Ltd, Registered Offices: Harmondsworth, Middlesex, England

Published in Penguin Books 1995
10 9 8 7 6 5 4 3 2 1

The Acknowledgements on pages xi–xiv constitute an extension of this copyright page

Filmset in Monophoto Baskerville
Printed in England by Clays Ltd, St Ives plc

CONTENTS

'Redistribution through Growth'. The Case of Kenya
and the ILO Report. The Informal Sector. Basic
Human Needs: 'Strong' and 'Weak' Versions.
'Poverty is Natural'.

What were African Governments Doing Wrong? The
IMF and World Bank Policy Conditions. Ghana's
Economic Recovery Programme: A Case Study. The
Results of Structural Adjustment Policies. The Failure
of Export-led Growth.

The Fraser Report on Africa's Commodity Problems.
Debt Reduction, Diversification and Regionalization.
The World Bank's Performance Assessed. The Case
of Malawi. Changing Food 'Entitlement'.

Debt and Violence in Africa. The Case of Sudan –
Misuse of the Land. Hunger and Land Capacity.
Famine and War. Armed Intervention from Outside.

PART II WHAT AFRICANS ARE SEEKING

ACKNOWLEDGEMENTS

This book is dedicated to my colleagues in TWIN and Twin Trading and to the organizations of farmers and craft workers which are TWIN's partners in Africa. The pioneering practical work of development upon which they are engaged is not only the source of much of the information in this book but is its *raison d'être*. Their successes – and also their struggle with failures – have been the inspiration in its writing. At the same time, they must not be held responsible for what is written here. Like all practical people, they are chary of generalization – especially from such a small body of experience.

The words in the book are mine, but I regard myself only as a channel for the thinking of Africa's writers and the practice of Africa's farmers and workers, women and men, so that they shall gain a wider understanding, especially among readers outside Africa.

The debt I owe Adebayo Adedeji will be clear from the text but I wish to express here my gratitude to him for the encouragement he gave me for embarking on this project. It will also be clear to the reader in proceeding through the following pages how much Professor Adedeji has contributed to the new model of African political economy which is described.

I owe a special debt of gratitude to my old friend and comrade, Basil Davidson, who read through the whole text at an early stage and made invaluable comments and suggestions. It will be obvious from the textual references how much I have depended upon his historical work on Africa but, more than that, I wish to record how far the completion of the book depended upon his encouragement that I should persist in what at times seemed a Herculean task.

I am also deeply grateful to Victoria Bawtree, who read through the chapters one by one as they were written and not only criticized the writing but also drew on her wide knowledge of Africa to suggest sources of African writing, especially the non-anglophone sources, which

I have drawn upon. Peter Robbins was the third person to read the whole text and I was greatly helped both by his comments and by his enthusiastic belief in the book. Vella Pillay and Richard Day also read particular chapters and shared with me their deep knowledge of Africa. Lionel Cliffe read the first part of the book and made valuable comments and kindly made available to me a whole dossier of reports on grass roots initiatives in Southern Africa and directed me towards African sources that I would not otherwise have come across. I am deeply consious of the debt which I owe to those who have gone before me, in exploring Africa's voices and interpreting them for English readers – in particular, Paul Harrison, Bill Rau and Lloyd Timberlake.

Donald Wilson of Penguin Books deserves my particular thanks for his meticulous copy editing of my text. Apart from correcting my grammar and more involved sentences, he was able to correct many of my facts and give me great assistance with several of the Tables, drawing upon his very considerable knowledge of Africa. Any mistakes that remain are mine. Finally, I owe a particular debt to Mark Handsley of Penguin Books for persisting in his belief that the book was worth publishing.

I have to acknowledge the kind permission of the respective publishers for reproducing the two maps: the first on 'Africa's Vegetation' from Paul Harrison's *The Greening of Africa*, published by Paladin in 1987; the second on 'African States in 1976' from Basil Davidson's *Africa in Modern History*, published by Allen Lane in 1988. The latter is one of the few which shows Eritrea and also comprises *all* the African off-shore islands within the frame of a single page, thanks to James Davidson's clever revolving of the continent from its north–south axis. I am particularly grateful to Claude Aké and the Council on Foreign Relations for permission to quote from a paper prepared by Claude Aké for an African Studies Seminar of the Council in February 1994. I have quoted from the writings of so many people – Africans and students of Africa – in order to prepare this book. I am painfully aware of my ignorance beside their deep knowledge and experience, and I only hope that I have always made due acknowledgement of my debt in both the text and the references.

Grateful acknowledgement is made to the authors and publishers listed below for kind permission to quote passages from the following works:

Dele Olowu and J.S. Wunsch, *The Failure of the Centralized State*, Westview Press, 1990, p. 246.

Colin Leys, *Underdevelopment in Kenya: The Political Economy of Neo-colonialism*, Heinemann, 1975, pp. 220–21.

Ben Wisner, *Power and Need in Africa: Basic Human Needs and Development Policies*, Earthscan, 1988, p. 23.

Dan Smith, 'Conflict and War' in Susan George (ed.), *The Debt Boomerang: How Third World Debt Harms Us All*, Pluto Press, 1992, pp. 141–2.

Ibbo Mandaza, 'Perspectives on Economic Cooperation and Autonomous Development in Southern Africa' in Samir Amin, et al. (eds), *SADCC: Prospects for Disengagement and Development in Southern Africa*, Zed Books, 1987, pp. 212–13.

Claude Aké, 'Sustaining Development on the Indigenous' in World Bank, Long-term Perspective Study of Sub-Saharan Africa, Background Papers, 1990, vol. 3, pp. 9–12.

George Ayittey, 'Indigenous African Systems' in World Bank, Long-term Perspective Study of Sub-Saharan Africa, Background Papers, 1990, vol. 3, p. 27.

Chapter 11, pages 190–91, 194, 211: Samuel Wangwe, 'Building Indigenous Technological Capacity in African Industry' in Frances Stewart, Sanjaya Lall and Samuel Wangwe (eds.), *Alternative Development Strategies in Sub-Saharan Africa*, Macmillan, 1992, pp. 238, 267–8 and 272ff.

Chapter 11, page 204, Lynn Mytelka, 'Ivorian Industry at the Crossroads' in Frances Stewart, Sanjaya Lall and Samuel Wangwe (eds), *Alternative Development Strategies in Sub-Saharan Africa*, Macmillan, 1992, pp. 262–3.

Roger C. Riddell, *Manufacturing Africa*, James Currey, 1990, pp. 119 and 243.

Scott Tiffin and Fola Osotimehin for OECD, *New Technologies and Enterprise Development in Africa*, OECD, 1992, pp. 11–13 and 31–33.

George J.S. Dei, 'A Ghanian Rural Community in the 1980s' in D.R. Fraser Taylor and Fiona Mackenzie, *Development from Within*, Routledge, 1992, pp. 71–3.

Janet MacGaffey, *The Real Economy of Zaire*, James Currey, 1991, p. 35.

Chinua Achebe, et al., *Beyond Hunger in Africa: Africa 2057 – Conventional Wisdom and an African Vision*, James Currey, 1991, pp. 5–6.

Margaret Joan Anstee, 'Social Development in Africa: Perspective, Reality and Promise' in James Pickett and Hans Singer, *Towards Economic Recovery in Sub-Saharan Africa*, Routledge, 1990, p. 200.

Paul Harrison, *The Greening of Africa*, Paladin, 1987, p. 59.

David Siddle and Ken Swindell, *Rural Change in Tropical Africa*, Blackwell, 1990, pp. 159ff.

Piet Konings, 'The Political Potential of Ghanaian Miners: A Case Study of the AGC Workers at Obuasi' quoted in Piet Konings, *Labour Resistance in Cameroon*, James Currey, 1993, pp. 178–9.

Lloyd Timberlake, *Africa in Crisis*, Earthscan, 1991, p. 188.

Faber and Faber for W.H. Auden, lines from 'In Time of War: Commentary' from *Journey to a War*, 1939.

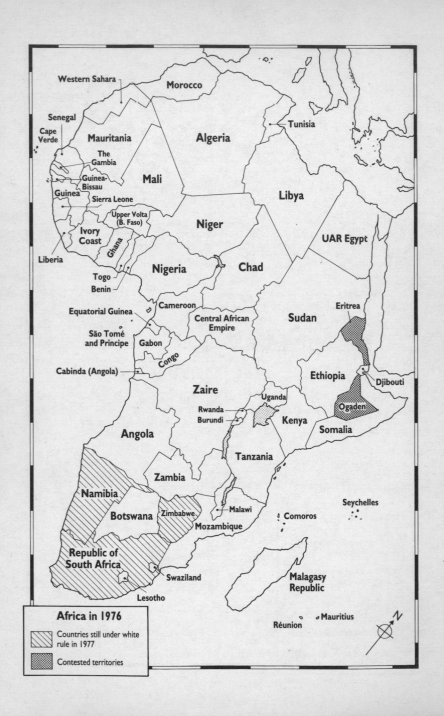

Western Sahara
Morocco
Senegal
Cape Verde
Mauritania
Tunisia
Algeria
The Gambia
Guinea-Bissau
Mali
Guinea
Sierra Leone
Upper Volta (B. Faso)
Niger
Libya
Ivory Coast
Ghana
Liberia
Nigeria
Chad
UAR Egypt
Togo
Benin
Cameroon
Eritrea
Equatorial Guinea
Central African Empire
Sudan
São Tomé and Principe
Gabon
Congo
Ethiopia
Djibouti
Cabinda (Angola)
Zaire
Ogaden
Rwanda
Uganda
Burundi
Kenya
Somalia
Angola
Tanzania
Zambia
Seychelles
Namibia
Malawi
Comoros
Botswana
Zimbabwe
Mozambique
Republic of South Africa
Malagasy Republic
Swaziland
Lesotho
Réunion
Mauritius

Africa in 1976

Countries still under white rule in 1977

Contested territories

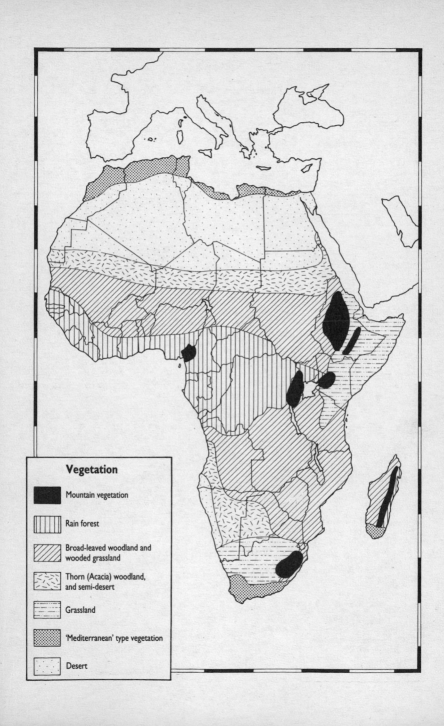

Vegetation

- Mountain vegetation
- Rain forest
- Broad-leaved woodland and wooded grassland
- Thorn (Acacia) woodland, and semi-desert
- Grassland
- 'Mediterranean' type vegetation
- Desert

Something New out of Africa

What has become embarrassingly clear, after three decades and more
after the attainment of independence by the majority of African countries,
is that the generality of our people have been excluded from any
significant contribution to the determination of national directions.

> Professor Adebayo Adedeji, formerly Executive Secretary of the United
> Nations Economic Commission for Africa.[1]

Where is the Voice of Africa?

The much-quoted aphorism of the Roman general, Scipio Africanus,
that 'There is always something new out of Africa' has in the past few
decades been turned on its head. There has always been something new
being offered *to* Africa. Indeed, there has been an absolute tidal wave of
books appearing about Africa's 'crisis', ranging from the flood of volumi-
nous official reports by the International Monetary Fund (IMF) and
the World Bank, with almost equally lengthy counter-reports from
academic institutions, to a mass of smaller books and pamphlets on
particular countries and aspects of what is perceived as the crisis. The
Notes at the end of this book are proof, if proof is needed, of this rising
tide. The intelligent general reader is by now in need of a guide through
such troubled waters. Fortunately, among the successive waves, there is
an increasing number of studies from Africans trying to make their
voices heard.

This book reflects my strong conviction that it is time that those
outside who are concerned about Africa should stop offering answers to
our perceptions of Africa's problems and just listen to Africans for a
change. The book is, therefore, the result of listening to, and of reading,
what Africans have to say. The first part of the book briefly reviews
what has successively been proposed from outside, and takes into

account actual African experience and African criticisms. The second and longer part looks directly at what Africans have themselves been proposing. Sometimes it has been possible to find the words of Africans, but African publications, although they are rapidly growing in number and range, are not yet so numerous; and it has often been necessary to rely on those like Basil Davidson, René Dumont, Paul Harrison, Bernard Lecomte, Fiona Mackenzie, Terry Ranger and Ben Wisner, who have sought to bring the authentic voices of Africa to us.

The book owes its origin to the combination of two powerful influences on my thinking as I became increasingly involved with development projects in Africa. The first was the publication in 1992 of the latest of Basil Davidson's pioneering studies of African history, *The Black Man's Burden: Africa and the Curse of the Nation-State*.[2] The second was the requirement in my work that I should study in depth the structure of Africa's foreign trade. Davidson was an old friend, whom I had come to rely on in trying to understand African development. His new book did not deal with Africa's economic problems – that was not its purpose – but it gave me the clue to their explanation. African society was different and apparently immune to the economic rationality which is the basic assumption of European political economy. Davidson tells the terrible story of the monstrous incubus that descended upon the African people when an insubstantial dream of a European-style 'national liberation' turned into the very real nightmare of the 'vampire state'.[3] Colonial rule was relatively short-lived but it left behind fifty-six so-called nation-states which were smothering the very life-support systems of the African peoples. Davidson looked back to the roots of traditional democracy in African society. He quoted the Nigerian professor of politics, Delo Oluwe, saying that 'what will get Africa out of her present food and fiscal crises is not the clamping down of more government controls, but the release of the people's organizational genius at solving community problems'.[4]

In *Black Man's Burden* Davidson drew upon his earlier historical studies to show the depth and extent of popular participation in traditional African society – traditions enshrining an 'organizational genius' that had been denigrated and well-nigh obliterated by European colonial rulers. Encouraged by the 1990s' movements of revolt throughout Africa against the 'pirates in power', Davidson felt able to support the concluding words of Roland Oliver, the doyen of British academic historians of Africa, in his latest book, *The African Experience*. Oliver had written in 1991 that 'The era of mass participation in the political process was about to begin.'[5] A new era, perhaps, but what was left of those traditions of popular participation on which to build? It seemed important to find out. I offer this attempt as a modest sequel to Davidson's splendid work.

Avoiding Cultural Imperialism

My approach to Africa's problems is that of a political economist, but political economy has to be studied within a wider framework of culture, and this becomes of special importance when cultures are as different as those of African and European peoples. Agronomists from the North have had to learn that agricultural techniques appropriate to northern soils and climates are not necessarily at all appropriate in Africa, and that African resistance to changing traditional techniques is often soundly based and not in any way stupid.[6] Economists and political scientists have to adopt a similar humility before criticizing African approaches to political economy and proposing their own solutions to problems as if these were of universal application. This is all the more necessary because educated Africans have themselves been brainwashed by European education into devaluing their peoples' own culture. Ngugi wa Thiong'o from Kenya contrasts the Chinese or European schoolchild imbibing his or her own literature before attempting to take in other worlds. 'Not so in Africa,' he points out, 'and in the colonized world as a whole', where English or French or Spanish or Portuguese is the language at school. He tells how he found his son trying to memorize Wordsworth's 'Daffodils', which the child supposed were little fishes in a lake.[7]

Cultural hegemony is almost certainly as powerful a force working on human behaviour as political or economic hegemony. But it should not, therefore, be assumed that it is all-powerful.[8] Criticism in UNESCO publications of 'cultural imperialism', when this UN agency was led by an African director-general, resulted in the withdrawal of the financial contributions of the US and UK governments. But the criticism was a nuanced one, targeting both metropolitan powers and local élites and envisaging a dialectic from which new truths could emerge. Here is an example, in a reference to the transition of the formal educational system from the colonial to the post-colonial period:

The schools are an extension of the metropolitan structure, just as are the economy, polity and social structure. As long as the national bourgeoisie in its colonial role dominates the domestic pyramidal structure, we can expect that the school will prevent liberation on two levels: liberation from the definition of culture and development by the high-income imperial nations, and liberation from the domestic pyramidal structure ... Schools are organized to fit children into predetermined roles in the pyramidal structure, but education is also committed to teach children to question. When the questioning cannot be controlled, the pyramidal structure and the international system come under scrutiny too. Colonial institutions may raise consciousness in spite of themselves and those whose consciousness is raised require increased rewards to stay in the roles assigned to them. When the system cannot bribe them sufficiently, they begin to attack it. Increased marginality in the peripheral structure can pose an important threat to the post-colonial structure.[9]

It was many years before the threat became imminent, but, as the source of the bribes dwindles, the attack appears today to have attained critical proportions. And it is paradoxically the World Bank, which set out to reincorporate the African economies into the global system, that has done most to marginalize the continent and at the same time to rekindle the slow-burning threat from within to the whole post-colonial structure.

Some will doubt that there is any real 'threat from within' but only an old agrarian society dying and a new industrial society waiting to be born. The evident resilience of grass roots organizations in rural areas, in spite of drought and migration to the towns, combined with the massive burgeoning of the urban informal economy, suggests something different. It is the profound conviction of African thinkers and writers that there is an African road to development that cannot be the European road. In the words of the Senegalese economist, E.S. Ndione, 'One must not impose the norms of a system on persons who function according to the norms of another system.'[10] Technology has to be cleared through cultural customs, as Karl Polanyi would insist, and African culture is not European culture and cannot simply be transplanted. Writers as different as Claude Aké and Chinua Achebe of Nigeria, George Ayittey of Ghana and Hassan Zaoual of Morocco, whose works we shall be studying, agree on one basic proposition: the African way, while not communistic, is communitarian. Despite the monstrous dictators at the top, African society is profoundly democratic. Collective duty and social relations come before individual economic interest.[11] According to Zaoual, 'The African model exists and is alive but it is not a model of economic rationality.'[12] We shall try to discover in this book what that means.

The IMF and the World Bank's Prescriptions

The second influence on my thinking came from my studies of Africa's foreign trade. While learning from Davidson's *Black Man's Burden* and from the controversies inside UNESCO about the dilemmas of Africa's inheritance from Europe of its culture and of the nation-states as the framework for political economy, I had come to see the need to understand more exactly the results of World Bank and IMF policies in Africa. Were they, as some claimed, enabling the 'release of the people's organizational genius at solving community problems'[13] or were they reimposing an alien structure that was disintegrating? I had been commissioned by the Transnational Institute of Amsterdam to write about the World Bank's policies for African trade under the working title of 'What Hope for Africa's Trade after the World Bank?'.[14] My brief was to examine the actual viability, in the current world economy, of the Bank's structural adjustment strategies for Africa, all of which were designed to encourage export-led growth. Could they be made to work even on the Bank's own terms?

As I looked at one African export commodity after another, it became absolutely clear that they could not work. The adjustment was needed more in the Bank's policies than in those of the African governments. For the Bank was encouraging an expansion of primary commodity exports not only from Africa, but also from all over the Third World – and this in a period of world economic recession. The rationale for these expanded exports was the need to pay off Africa's foreign debts. The result had been gross over-production and growing stocks of commodities, which had led to sharply falling world prices of primary products and thus to a collapse in the earnings of African countries, whose national incomes are heavily dependent on primary commodity exports. We in the North may not have noticed that our coffee or chocolate was any cheaper, but the giant transnational companies which trade with Africa were benefiting from cheaper inputs. Meanwhile, the peoples of Africa were suffering desperately from a mounting burden of foreign debt as they sought to export more and more to compensate for lower and lower prices.

It was clear enough what was happening in Africa's external relations, but what was happening inside the fifty-six nation-states? The structural adjustment programmes (SAPs) of the World Bank were evidently failing. Living standards in Africa were everywhere declining. Summarizing the experience of a decade of these programmes in Africa, a UNICEF report in 1992 declared:

Poor compliance cannot . . . be considered a main cause of the poor performance of the 1980s. Exogenous factors certainly exerted a negative influence on
the poor performance of adjustment programmes. However, over the long
term several of the external influences (such as terms of trade losses and
agricultural losses due to droughts) cannot be seen as exogenous but are the
result of policy failures.[15]

From all the evidence to hand, it appeared that the foreign experts
from the IMF and the World Bank had been persuading African
governments to adopt policies that were actually causing overproduction
and worsening terms of trade, land degradation and drought, which
were destroying what was left of the strengths of African societies –
skilful small-scale farming, the central role of women in the village
economy, mixed cropping, urban crafts, a balance between urban and
rural life and fruitful exchanges between agriculturalists and pastoralists.
All these strengths had been undermined by large-scale mechanized
farm projects and stock ranching, by gigantic and ecologically unsound
hydro-electric and irrigation projects, by deforestation, by waged work
for men and the marginalization of women, by new industries dependent
on imported machines and spare parts and raw-material inputs and by
prestige projects in the big cities. On this reckoning, the outbreaks of
civil violence and internecine wars in Africa seemed to be more the
result of the impasse of accumulating debt and the destruction of old
forms of community action than of any irreconcilable differences between ethnic groups.

The World Bank's adjustment programmes had been preceded by
plans for industrialization and for economic take-off and then for
targeting poverty, and the adjustment programmes were followed by
crisis management. All these were prescriptions proposed from *outside*
Africa as solutions for the *outsiders'* perceptions of what were Africa's
problems. Each new prescription only aggravated the illness that was
supposedly being treated. All the proposed cures had two elements in
common: first, they were thought up outside Africa and applied without
consultation with Africans at any level below a narrow élite of ministers
and officials, and not always at that level; second, they had done
nothing to correct the colonial inheritance of a continent divided into
fifty-six artificially created states, each supplying just two or three
specific commodities to one or other of the industrialized powers or their
giant companies.

What Africans are Seeking

From their side, Africans were asking us in the North to recognize their capacities. Even the World Bank had begun by the late 1980s to speak of 'the importance of respecting Africa's indigenous roots in attempting to build its future'.[16] African writers – economists, philosophers, scientists, poets – had gone further in arguing that Africa's future development must in fact be founded upon these roots wherever they were still alive.[17] And many political leaders had taken up the cry. In 1989 the UN Economic Commission for Africa was claiming that not markets, nor states, nor parastatal institutions, but human beings in their own households and community associations must be the 'fulcrum of development',[18] the point at which all the levers of change should be brought to bear. But a question remained whether these kinship and community structures still had the strength to take such pressures. Could they be linked to wider local, national and regional structures which would supply a new framework for major development? What support could they get from outside Africa – for reducing the burden of debt and establishing new and more equal trading relations?

Africans' own choices begin with concern for food security but go on to look to intra-African cooperation in developing exchanges of a diversified range of products, drawing upon Africa's rich natural resources for their own and not others' development. This is not envisaged as a move towards autarky; most Africans reject isolationism. The theoretical arguments between those who believe in 'delinking' leading to total self-reliance and those who see international trade as an important element in economic development take place in the Common Rooms of European and North American academies, and even in those of some African universities.[19] In the event, however, the balance between production for home consumption and production for export is generally decided by ordinary Africans on quite pragmatic grounds. They say – and it is the women who say it:

I have to feed my family, but I must have the tools that aren't yet made in my country to do the job. My mother's digging stick and water jug are not enough to provide food and water for so many who now live on our land. We should begin to make our own tools, but that is not what the industries which we have here seem to be doing.[20]

Africans want new and different industries of their own to meet these needs but they will need to have help from outside Africa in establishing them.

Aid and Development

The difficulty for Europeans and North Americans, who truly wish to help from their position of wealth and privilege, is that as a starting point they have to recognize not only differences in cultural history but the equality of cultures and the commonality of the human struggle for survival.[21]

'If you have come to help me, you can go home again. But if you see my struggle as a part of your survival, then perhaps we can work together.'[22] It was an Australian Aboriginal woman who said this, but it could well have been an African. Only if we recognize this equality will we have something useful to say, and the main thing to be said is that the structural adjustments have to take place at home in our economic structures in the North – and it should help that ordinary people in the North suffer from these too. If the people of the South are poor, then they cannot buy the goods which we make in the North; if their poverty leads to violence and war, the cost and the terror reach us; if Northern traders pay a higher price for coca than for cocoa from the South, it is our young people who pay the price as junkies; if the people of the South cut down their forests in the South to pay their debts to Northern banks, the whole eco-balance of the planet is disturbed.[23]

The first adjustment to be made in the North is to cancel the debts owed to the Northern banks, at least those owed by the poorest countries in the South, most of which are in Africa – and there should be no conditions attached, except the requirement of cooperation on equal terms in ecological and conservation measures. The second adjustment is for the North to remove the protective barriers which now keep African products out of the markets of Europe and North America. This protectionism harms us too, for it deprives us of these products and reduces the ability of Africans to purchase what we produce. There are barriers not only to competing foods like cane sugar and beet sugar, palm oil and rape seed oil, but also to products where each stage of processing meets higher and higher tariffs – cotton to clothing and textiles, leather to shoes, palm oil to margarine, cocoa butter to chocolate, green coffee beans to soluble coffee preparations. These tariffs are imposed to protect employment in the processing plants in the North, but this only means that other jobs are lost in the North from the poorer markets in the South. The third adjustment is to end the concealment of transactions by Northern-based transnational companies, which abuse their internal transfer pricing to deprive African producers of the true value of their produce.[24] These abuses impoverish the South, while only benefiting the profits of the companies, who need not pass on any of the benefit to people in the North.

Such adjustments in the North will, of course, in their turn require governmental and inter-governmental action in Africa, but such a change of policies in the North will demand a new consumer movement here, which looks for a guarantee that the goods in the shops are both produced without harm to the natural environment and without harm to the human producers. That is the basis of the Fair Trade movement which now runs parallel to the Green movement.[25]

If a beginning were made with these adjustments in the North, many of the necessary adjustments could be made by Africans, since they do not dispute that adjustments have to be made in their economic and political structures, only that the ones required of them by the World Bank have been appropriate to their condition.[26] Without the structural adjustment in the economic relations of the North, it is probable that Africans will in the end make their own adjustments; but the process will be more difficult and more prolonged. The choice facing the peoples of the North lies between, on the one hand, forms of development of their own economies that offer them short-term advantages at the expense of a marginalized South and, on the other, the recognition that we all share one world, in which the 'free development of each is the condition for the free development of all'.[27] The problem for Africa is that it is the most easily marginalized of all the regions of the South, because its trade is still confined to imports of manufactured goods and to the export of a number of primary products of which the continent is not the sole supplier in the world.[28]

None of the steps required to make adjustments in the North to the needs of the South should be confined to relations with Africa. In this book the African example is taken but, despite the specific differences of each region, much that is said here could be applied equally to other regions. Africa is only a special case in that so many of the poorest countries are found in Africa and Africa, more than any other continent in what we call the 'Third World', was subjected at a crucial moment of its history to that particular form of colonial dependence which consisted of the export first of bonded labour and then of primary produce from the South to serve the industrial development of the North. The conclusion, I have already suggested, is not that all ties between the North and the South should be cut but that a new framework of fair trade for balanced and sustainable development be established. This will not happen as a result of some ukase from above but from the efforts of groups of producers and consumers in the South and the North working together from the grass roots of their several societies to build new economic relations.

PART I

WHAT WAS PROPOSED FROM OUTSIDE

'When the axe of the wood cutter is heard in the forest, the trees that are standing whisper to each other: Remember that the handle of the axe is made of wood!'

African saying, quoted by Basil Davidson in *The Africans*

CHAPTER I

How Old is Africa's Crisis?

Why does Swissair fly to as many as 17 African cities? – Because you can
find there: oil, gold, diamonds, copper, iron, platinum, wood, cocoa,
nuts, rubber, tobacco, spices, fruit, coffee, cotton, rare animals,
magnificent sandy beaches.

> Advertisement in *Der Spiegel*, October 1972, to which *Terre Entière*,
> September/December 1972, responded:

Imagine the surprise of the Swissair passengers, when they disembark, on
discovering that there are also *people* in Africa . . .[1]

There are nearly 600 million people in Africa, of whom 450 million live
in sub-Saharan Africa, which will be the main concern of this book.
That is about one in ten of the whole world population, and numbers in
Africa are growing faster than on any other continent.

No one doubts that Africa is in crisis. Living standards are falling.
The people are not being fed. Township violence is endemic. Civil wars
are spreading. According to the statistics, national income overall failed
to grow as fast as population in the 1970s and 1980s, and that included
food production, which in many countries actually declined.[2] Even if
you don't believe the statistics – and there can be few who would swear
by them[3] – there are pictures of starving children and widespread
reports of famine conditions, of wars and violence, enough to support
the general supposition of a deep-rooted crisis.

Causes of Africa's Crisis

Famine and wars are blamed upon a series of exceptional periods of drought – in 1973–5, 1983–5 and again in 1990–91.[4] The Sahara is said to be moving southwards, but some say that it has been moving southwards for centuries. Hunger is only too frequent in the Sahel and can be borne, but famine is the result, they say, of bad land use and over-population.[5] Misuse of the land is attributed to the increase in cash cropping, especially for export, at the expense of staple food production. The facts, however, do not entirely bear this out. While the area devoted to export crops was increased between 1960 and 1989, the area devoted to food crops was increased much more, so that export crops took up only 14 per cent of total cultivated land in 1989 instead of 18 per cent of the total in 1960.[6] Export crops have certainly benefited most in the last two decades from increased use of fertilizer and the extension of irrigation, and land has suffered from degradation due to misuse and the destruction of tree cover.

A quite different argument would be put forward by the World Bank and the IMF and their associated advisers. This would be that excessive state regulation, and in particular the levies imposed on farmers by agricultural marketing boards, have acted as a disincentive to agricultural production. And this has been compounded by wasteful state expenditure from these levies and by the protection of inefficient industries seeking to produce substitutes for imported goods.[7] The answer to all Africa's problems is, they say, to open up national markets to world competition and free trade. Unfortunately for this argument, while the IMF and the World Bank have together persuaded more than thirty African governments to follow their advice, the result has been even worse economic decline in these countries than in those which did not adopt the Bank's structural adjustment programmes.[8]

To find the explanation for Africa's food crisis today, it is necessary to go back much further than two decades and to look into Africa's colonial and pre-colonial heritage. Many readers will assume at this point that I shall either repeat the tired complaints of expatriate 'old Africa hands' that Africans have never emerged very far from their primitive, warring tribal societies and are not yet ready to cope with modern political and economic structures, or else that I shall blame everything on colonial rule in Africa and subsequent neo-colonialism.[9] This means that authoritarian, even piratical, rule by African leaders like Mobutu in Zaire has been held in place by the United States and by the one-time colonial powers. There is a certain truth in the last proposition, but none at all in the accusation of primitive tribalism, any more in Africa than in Northern Ireland or in Bosnia.

Africa's Pre-colonial Heritage

Nobody, perhaps, today would be prepared to subscribe to the 1920s' Oxford professor's description of pre-colonial Africa as 'blank, uninteresting, brutal barbarism',[10] although one of his successors as Regius Professor of History at Oxford was still talking in 1963 of African history as 'no more than barbarous tribal gyrations'.[11] Nobody now questions that the great walls of Zimbabwe were built by Africans and that the Chinese Ming pottery found on the shores of Lake Nyasa was used by Africans, and not by some long-lost white tribe, descendants of the Queen of Sheba or of some Phoenician traders.[12] Martin Bernal has demonstrated that Greek civilization had African origins and we all know that Hannibal, who nearly conquered Rome from his base in Carthage, was an African and that the great Moorish civilization in Spain was African in origin. What is perhaps less well known is that Francis Bacon, the founder of modern European science, had to go to Morocco to learn mathematics[13] or that the gold which circulated as coinage throughout medieval Europe was mined and refined in West Africa.[14] Why else would the standard British gold coin be called the golden guinea?

Historians of Africa have concluded from evidence on the ground that, following upon the great Bronze Age civilizations of the Nile valley, Iron Age societies spread throughout Africa at about the same time as they did in Europe. They tamed a hard and inhospitable continent, and many of the methods of cultivation they discovered are only now being recognized by European agronomists as more appropriate to African conditions than those that were imported later from Europe.[15] Far from performing 'barbarous tribal gyrations', African societies developed strong and continuing institutions. These took the form of kingdoms covering more than one ethnic group, not unlike those of medieval Europe. Kingdoms rose and fell, and ambitious kings of warrior peoples absorbed new territories, as the Normans did in Europe. Settlements grew, more land was cleared and subject peoples were enslaved, but not as chattels and not without the possibility of manumission.[16]

The essential characteristic of the exercise of power in African society was an 'acknowledged recognition of ties of mutual obligation and respect'.[17] This is Basil Davidson's conclusion from his studies; and a modern Malawi poet, Jack Mapanje, comments: 'Pre-colonial chiefs and kings tolerated court singers and praise poets who had a double role: to celebrate the chief's war victories and also point out his failings.'[18] Mapanje was not so lucky in his celebrations of the failings of Dr Hastings Banda, who confined him to jail for two and a half years for his poems.

In pre-colonial Africa, the unity and stability which government bestowed had to be balanced by accountability. 'In "traditional" Africa,' Davidson insists, 'this concept of an indispensable partnership formed the hearthstone of statesmanship.'[19] He gives striking examples from one of the greatest and latest of the African kingdoms, that of the Asante, and quotes from a British observer in 1886, the year when the British colony of the Gold Coast was established in Asante lands:

The Asantemanhyiamu was a kind of Parliament, at which all matters of political and judicial administration are discussed by the king and chiefs in council, and when the latter answer all questions relating to their respective provinces, and are subject to the consequences of appeals, from their local Judicial Courts, to the Supreme Court of the King in Council.[20]

The Atlantic Slave Trade

Until the Atlantic slave trade began, trade between Europeans and Africans was a trade between equals, first by camel caravan across the Sahara, carrying salt and fine tools and swords from the north in exchange for gold and silver, nuts and ivory from the south; later, the trade was continued down the Atlantic coast from Portugal. Slaves, as household servants, had always entered into this trade, but not until 1510 – eighteen years after Columbus's landfall in the Americas – were slaves exported from Africa as chattels for sale.[21] On the orders of the Spanish king they were sent across the Atlantic to the West Indies to make good the decimation of local labour among the Indians in America. The cargoes of British slavers were soon to follow.

The results were world-shaking. The total loss to Africa over the three hundred years of the Atlantic slave trade is beyond computation. It comprised not only the loss of numbers of mainly young men, but also the lost skills. Miners from Africa were particularly sought after to work the mines in the Americas.[22] Perhaps 23 million men and women in the prime of life were exported, about half of them crossing the Atlantic. An equal number are thought to have died *en route* or in the accompanying slave wars in Africa. In 1850, when the trade had largely ceased, the whole population of Africa was estimated at only 54 million.[23]

The loss of population was not more serious for Africans than the loss of confidence in their historic evolution. White people came to justify slavery by an assumed racial superiority. Black people were treated as inferior, their achievements scorned, their history buried, their resources plundered. Their supposed inferiority became the excuse for colonial rule by the European powers.

Africans themselves had always been involved in the Atlantic trade, as chiefs importing guns from Britain in exchange for slaves and as traders rounding up the human commodities for sale. One strange story from the last days of the Atlantic trade bears on the nature of Africa's crisis. Basil Davidson has revealed for us the origins of the Creole traders on the West African coast, whose settlements were by the middle of the nineteenth century supplying a major market for British textiles and even doctors from their college at Fourah Bay for the British army medical service (James Africanus Horton reached the rank of Lieutenant-Colonel). These people had been slaves destined for the West Indies, but recaptured on the high seas by British gunboats patrolling the West African coast to stop the trade after Britain had banned it in 1807. The places where they were landed were not at all the parts of Africa where they had come from, but they were appropriately honoured by being named Freetown in the British colony of Sierra Leone and Monrovia (after United States President Monroe) in the United States colony of Liberia. These so-called 'recaptives' did not know the languages of the peoples among whom they were settled, nor were they at all welcome, but they developed their own language, a kind of Pidgin English, which they called *krio* (creole), and they prospered and attracted others from the Caribbean to join them.[24]

The importance of this story is not just that these people and their descendants traded successfully all down the West African coast and established their own schools with missionary assistance – forty-two primary schools in Sierra Leone alone – or that they formed learned societies and ran several newspapers – several dozen throughout West Africa. What mattered was that they became ardent Christians and champions of the emancipating and civilizing mission of the British empire. By following the British example they believed that Africans could come to rule in their countries just as well as any white man.

They despised the traditional ruling chiefs of African society and
became a *petit bourgeois* class which could afford in time to send their
sons to study law and medicine in England. By the middle of the
nineteenth century it is recorded that in the West African colonies,
'almost every senior official post including governor and chief justice
was held by a man of part-African (most of them of Caribbean)
descent'.[25]

Colonial Rule in Africa

This process of 'Africanization' of the British colonies was not to last
after the 1860s. In the 'scramble for Africa', European opinion changed.
Land was annexed inland from the trading posts on the coast and by
1880 frontiers were being drawn by the European powers marking off
their colonies and their protectorates. Their soldiers advanced in the
footsteps of the discoverers and the missionaries. Archbishop Tutu,
receiving the Nobel prize for peace in 1984, told how it was said long
ago: 'When the missionaries came, they had the bible and we had the
land. They said, "Let us pray!" They taught us to close our eyes to pray
and when we opened them again, we had the bible and they had the
land.'[26]

In fact, fierce resistance was encountered from the inhabitants. In
Professor Terry Ranger's words, 'virtually every sort of African society
resisted and there was resistance in virtually every region of European
advance'.[27] Conquering armies carried racism everywhere. Ethnic
groups were divided between separate administrations. The Europeans
believed that all Africans belonged to tribes, and in pursuit of the policy
of divide and rule cheerfully made and unmade tribes for administrative
convenience. Chiefs and even kings were enthroned and if they got
above themselves just as expeditiously dethroned.[28] Africa was partitioned into over fifty separate territories.

There was no place for educated Africans like Lt.-Col. Africanus
Horton, RAMC. 'They formed learned societies. They presided over
racecourses. They founded musical circles, debating clubs, charitable
exercises. Above all they started newspapers – several dozen in British
West Africa alone,' as Basil Davidson records, but he adds, 'it did them
no good, the more they proved they knew, and the more artfully they
argued their case for admission to equality of status, the less they were
listened to.'[29] Merchants were brought in from the Levant to manage
the export trade. Educated Africans were told that they could return to

the 'savage backwoods' from which they had sought to emerge and distinguish themselves.[30] But that Africans would one day rule themselves, they did not doubt, and they fashioned all kinds of constitutions and federal projects for the time when it should come. At the centre of all these was the concept of nation building, which they had learned from British history. They called themselves nationalists and their resistance to colonial rule the 'national liberation struggle'.

These 'Europeanized negroes' were given short shrift by the European rulers and dubbed as 'useless visionaries, contemptible clerks'.[31] But nothing would shake their belief that, once colonial rule was overthrown, their heritage would be their own nation-state. The institutions of government, from governor down through the generals, the judges and secretaries of state, parliament and Mr Speaker, complete with wig and mace, to the civil servants, the armed forces and the police – all would be theirs. Nothing less and no other model than the European model was thinkable.

The Colonial State

It was to be a terrible combination, the process of nation building in over fifty artificially created states, involving a 'more or less complete flattening of the ethnic landscape', as Basil Davidson has put it.[32] The commitment was total. The nationalists saw Africa's history as largely irrelevant except in the classical periods of Greece and Egypt, Rome and Carthage. They rejected the 'inherited privileges of chieftaincy', which the Europeans had encouraged, in favour of the 'acquired privileges of education',[33] meaning Western education. This the Europeans refused to acknowledge. But the Europeanized Africans had cut themselves off from their own people. E.A. Ayandele in his book *The Educational Elite in the Nigerian Society* speaks of the 'total and irrevocable rejection' of the Creoles by 'indigenous society' in Nigeria.[34]

In Sierra Leone the uprisings of the Temne and Mende peoples of the interior, which led to the massacre by the colonial rulers of missionaries and native officials,[35] became the pretext, in the view of some historians, for the execution by the English of their main Creole trading rivals.[36] However that may be, the Creole merchants had disappeared by the end of the nineteenth century.

Basil Davidson has asked us to imagine

what would have happened in and to Japan, if the western world had made

Japan a target for colonial enclosure and dispossession in the second half of the nineteenth century? Precisely at the time, that is, when Japan was entering a period of radical and internally directed reforms of structures and commercial habits?[37]

Perhaps because of the homogeneity of the Japanese people and the ease of communication between their islands, perhaps because of the structure of Japanese feudalism, Japan's rulers successfully held the Europeans at bay and copied only what they had to.[38] Whatever the reason – and it cannot be the lower level of social development in Africa than in Japan by the end of the eighteenth century – it is enough to imagine the difference to doubt whether Japanese history in the twentieth century would have been other than that of Africa.

Sierra Leone, which little over a hundred years ago was a country of a rich merchant class with three newspapers and fifty schools and colleges, has today, according to the UN Development Programme, 'the worst standard of living in the world. Seventy per cent of its people live in absolute poverty and, at 42 years, average life expectancy is lower than that of any other country.'[39] What was the purpose, then, of the colonial state? It cannot just have been to decimate and impoverish the population if trade was the aim of European rule. The answer lies in the list of the products to be found in Africa in the Swissair advertisement at the head of this chapter, without mention of the people. Africa was found to be rich in natural resources, which the Europeans needed for their industrialization. Colonial territories were each formed around the extraction of two or three primary products, either agricultural or mineral.[40] The colonial state was there to protect the Europeans' investment.

The result was a patchwork of colonial possessions – British, French, Belgian, Spanish, Portuguese, German, Italian – each with its own frontiers and frontier controls. Inside each, quite separate development took place: different European languages became the common tongue, different legal systems were introduced from the European states, different trading companies took over the export business, different mining and plantation companies owned and controlled the means of production for export. Where conditions were tolerable for white men to survive, along the Mediterranean coast, in the Kenyan highlands and in Rhodesia and South Africa, settlements were established – colonies in the original sense of the word – and the colonists became the most insistent advocates of the white man's superiority. In many cases the settlers pulled the home country's governments into actions that they would not have embarked upon without such local pressures.[41]

The Exploitation of Africa's Resources

The *raison d'être* for establishing colonies was that they should be developed as suppliers of primary produce; the later stages of production – refining, processing and manufacture – were to be carried out in the homelands of the colonial powers. African historians have distinguished three broad colonial zones, not by the European powers occupying them, but by the economic functions they were designed to serve.[42]

The first was the earliest – the colonial trade of the Atlantic coast and North Africa. This was almost exclusively based on the extraction of cash crops from peasant farmers through marketing boards of the colonial power which monopolized the trade – in coffee, cocoa, tea, cotton, et cetera. Peasant farmers were forced to grow such crops by the simple device of a poll tax that could only be paid by earning cash from the sale of crops for export. The second was the zone of the concession-owning European companies, especially in the Congo basin, but distributed also throughout Africa. These companies, like the United Africa Company (Unilever), the Royal Niger Company and the Belgian Royal Company, directly employed labour on the plantations, even, as in the Belgian Congo, using forced labour in the collection and processing of rubber. During the twenty years of King Leopold's personal holding of the Belgian Congo the conditions of labour were such that the population was officially estimated to have been halved.[43]

The third form of labour exploitation consisted of labour reserves for the mines of South Africa and Rhodesia drawn from as far afield as Kenya and Uganda, as well as from all the neighbouring territories. These reserves were drawn upon by the imposition of the poll tax, by acts of enclosure or by curbs on petty commodity production. Through the forests and savannahs of southern Africa there were tracks which the young men followed on the road to 'Goli' as migrant workers, whose status was in effect semi-permanent employment, with occasional visits home. They lived in company barracks near the mines and were fed from company stores, until mining accidents overtook them or their health broke down and they were replaced with new recruits. Racism was thus institutionalized and such reserves of labour were also drawn upon for the white settlers' farms in South Africa and the Rhodesias (now Zambia and Zimbabwe) and also in Kenya and the Portuguese colonies, where contract workers on sugar and cocoa plantations in São Tomé and cotton plantations in Angola were treated as virtual slaves right down to the 1970s.[44]

Each territory was developed for just two or three primary products – both crops and minerals. Ports were developed and roads and railway lines constructed from the coast to the mines and plantations inland. When a mine was worked out nothing was left but a hole in the ground, a disused track and rusting cranes on a quayside. No road or rail communication connected the separate territories in the interior. The inheritance of this system remains today. More than thirty African states came to depend upon primary products for over 75 per cent of their export earnings. A dozen still depend upon just one product for their exports (see Table 1.1). And such earnings make up for these countries more than a quarter of all their incomes.

Northern Rhodesia, which was to become Zambia, may be taken as an example. By the time of independence, the economy had become totally dependent upon the copper industry. This supplied 40 per cent of national income, between 50 and 70 per cent of government revenue (depending upon the price of copper in world markets), and about 90 per cent of the country's exports (again depending on the copper price).[45]

In economic theory such concentrations of production on a few crops or minerals in any single country or region have always been justified by reference to Ricardo's Law of Comparative Advantage: each country and region should concentrate on producing what it is best at, export these and meet their other needs from imports. Then all will benefit; but the law does not say that all will benefit equally.

For such producers, having only one product to offer on the world market creates a weak bargaining position; and there are other reasons why producers of primary products are in a weaker bargaining position than those producing manufactured goods: many primary products are perishable and cannot be held off the market until the price improves; increases in productivity of manufactured goods have for long moved ahead of such increases in primary production; most disabling of all, there are millions of small primary producers in the world all facing a few large buyers and large producers of the machines which the primary producers need if they are to advance their own productiveness. The breaking up of Africa into competing producers of a range of primary products replicated on a continental scale what was a worldwide phenomenon.[46]

The African Nation-states

The territories which achieved independence when colonial rule in Africa ended rarely had the logic of any national homogeneity. Ethnic groups with traditional rivalries like the Asante and Fanti in the Gold Coast, the Yoruba and Hausa in Nigeria, the Ndebele and Shona in Southern Rhodesia, were included within single state boundaries. Other ethnic groups were divided up between two or more states, as the Ewe between the Gold Coast and Togoland, the Ibo between Nigeria and Cameroon, the Somali between Ethiopia, Somalia and Kenya.[47] The hinterlands that had been attached by the colonial powers to their trading posts on the coast had often much more in common with each other, including close trading relations, than they had with the original colony.

Many of the colonies were exceedingly small, not only the islands like Cape Verde, the Seychelles and São Tomé, but also a dozen territories in all with a population of less than a million each and twenty-five with less than seven million each. Only fifteen had populations of over 10 million, but one single state, Nigeria, by contrast, had a population drawn from many ethnic groups which together comprised more than one-fifth of the total of the other fifty in all of sub-Saharan Africa. Sixteen states were landlocked, some, like Chad and Zaire, with vast territories. The official language of each state was that of the colonial power.[48]

It seemed an unpromising inheritance for any nationalist leader. But the appeal of 'having your own state' was overwhelming, given the longing for independence, for an end to the insults and imprisonments endured by the nationalists. No longer would they have to take their shoes off in the presence of a District Officer. No longer would all but the lowest ranks in the armed and police forces, all but the most menial tasks in government and commerce, be reserved for white men. No longer would they serve long prison sentences for 'trouble-making', calling political meetings or staging demonstrations.

As the inevitable day of independence drew near, it seemed that the colonial powers were even seeking to tighten their hold. More colonial officers were recruited from the home country. Little or nothing was done to train Africans for the transfer of power. White men were to stay on in key positions as judges and generals. The great imperial companies were to remain in place. There was a sense almost that the end of the white man's rule could never come. It was all the more to be desired and on any terms, even within the narrow confines of a mini nation-state.[49]

In Europe nationalism had been developed over many years with the nation-state as its handmaiden, to win hearts and minds for a common purpose that would override class conflict. The nation was offered to the exploited wage-earner as an extended community with which he or she could identify through shared language, customs and history.[50] At the same time, control of the European state machine gave access not only to political power and legitimacy but also to economic power. What was learned by the African nationalists in their European studies was not so easily applied to African conditions. National liberation struggle was evidently a struggle for state power, but nationalism in the Marxist canon, which many of the nationalists followed, was seen as a false consciousness. So, in fighting an external oppressor's control over the state, national liberation had to be said to be 'at root' a class struggle.[51]

What, then, was the nation in Africa? It was those ethnic groups which happened to fall within a particular territory that the colonial power had carved out. Some, like the Asante, had long histories of unified clans, of empire building over other groups, of democratic institutions and of the rise of a bourgeois class among them. But the British colonial territory of the Gold Coast did not correspond with the lands of the Asante, the modernizing nationalists rejected the traditionalism of the Asante chiefs, and their king was not present at the celebrations of Ghana's independence.[52] In post-colonial Africa, nations had to be built so as to fit the inherited state. This was a complex operation, cutting across both ethnic groups and emergent economic classes, but any questioning of the nation or of the national frontiers was taken as a betrayal of the cause of popular liberation.

Tribes, Classes, Kinship Groups and Elites

What we have called ethnic groups, and the colonial rulers called tribes, were in effect kinship associations. We might think of them like Scottish clans with shifting wider loyalties, which the rulers could take advantage of.[53] Their special importance in Africa is believed by African scholars to derive from the time of the Atlantic slave trade. When African kingdoms failed to protect their peoples from enslavement, and their chiefs even took an active part in establishing what were in effect slave states, 'the state grew apart from society' and the people had to seek other forms of defence.

'The response to the violation of the citizenry by the state in its sponsorship of the slave trade was,' Peter Ekeh writes, 'the entrenchment of kinship corporations.'[54] Far from dying under the colonial state, these associations based on kinship survived and drew strength from the common need to resist an alien predator. They were to live on and take new forms when colonial rule ended.

Trouble from these kinship associations arose soon after control of the state was achieved by the nationalists. The interests of the leaders and the led, which had been consonant during the struggle for liberation, began to diverge. The new rulers were an élite of intellectuals who made up the core of the nationalist movements. Only rarely, as in Zambia, was there an organized working class with which the nationalists were associated.[55] While Africa was incorporated within the world capitalist system, there were few if any indigenous owners of capital. The development of capitalism in Africa had been foreclosed by European conquest. Alongside the European colonial rulers and European merchants, there were some local merchants and other middlemen, sometimes African but more usually of Asian or Levantine origin, who were the local agents of foreign companies.

It was in these circumstances that the nationalist leaders took over state power from the departing colonial administrations, and had at the same time to take responsibility for the economic life of their countries. They had at once to make accommodations with foreign capital in the form of the mining and trading companies, unless they were to assume control over their activities by nationalization, which they were in most cases in no position to do. Their establishment of joint ventures, marketing boards and other parastatal organizations put them in the position of agents of capital and indeed of foreign capital.[56] They had rejected traditional African society in the rural areas, they became distanced from the small working class of the mines and plantations. Where were they to look for support? The answer was in kinship associations.

Political leaders in Africa, by their access to state resources, were able to build up and retain a clientele of followers at national and local level. For reasons that go back to the founding of African colonies around a trading port and fort, which then became the state capital, the group or groups most likely to be dominant were the ones that occupied that area and its immediate surroundings.[57] Where in some of the new states, and especially in Nigeria, there was more than one such centre, rival groups claimed power and faction fighting broke out. This is what the outside world refers to as tribalism, but, in the historians' view, is better described as clientelism.[58]

Colonial rule had been by its nature highly centralized. Power rested in the colonial offices of governments in Europe, whether in London, Brussels, Lisbon, Rome, Madrid or Berlin. This power was delegated to a governor and to his officials at the capital city and in the districts. Where authority was granted to local chiefs, it was not on account of their representative capacity but as the appointed agents of the governor. Not only was there no institutionalizing of the existing organizations of the people – communal associations, peasant cooperatives, literary circles, religious societies – but these were simply 'left out of the mainstream of government'.[59]

Law and order in the colonies were imposed according to European principles and with European judges and magistrates and European law enforcement officers, and the courts as well as the government offices were in the capital city. In social and economic affairs the centralization was equally evident. The main schools and hospitals were in the capital, as were the post office, hotels and larger shops and the local offices of the European companies operating in the colony. Central state marketing boards were established for collecting and storing the cash crops of the territory and state monopolies for exporting them. Africans living in the capital had far greater opportunities for advancement than those outside; and from their ranks, the descendants of the recaptives and their associated ethnic groups, were drawn the nationalist leaders and their clients.[60]

The colonies existed for the colonial trade; and it was in the very nature of the colonial trade that not only was wealth drawn from African produce to be spent in Europe and not in Africa, but also that most even of the consumer goods in the African cities had to be imported from Europe.[61] Exports were of primary products with little or no local processing, refining or manufacture. While some food was drawn into the cities from the surrounding countryside, thus spreading the city's wealth outwards, the growth of the cities failed to encourage a much wider circle of activity as it had done in London, Amsterdam or Paris in the seventeenth and eighteenth centuries.[62] African cities engendered a local *petite bourgeoisie* that was dependent and parasitic on the European connection. It was this that Frantz Fanon railed against in his study of the French colonial influence upon the poor people of Africa, in his book *The Wretched of the Earth*.[63]

Africa's crisis is not, therefore, so much a manifestation of new circumstances but the latest episode in an old story. The Atlantic slave trade followed by European colonial rule distorted and then assaulted the established strengths of traditional African society. More than this, there was thus created a successor ruling élite that took power while itself equally rejecting African tradition. The whole pattern of African development after independence was moulded and reinforced by the kinship–client collusion in corruption of the urban masses and their leaders. The rural areas were regarded as fair game for plunder.[64] But the countryside had not been enriched. It was as if the *plebs urbana* of Rome had made their claim upon the public purse before and not after the booty of empire had made the country rich.

TABLE 1.1 African Exports Concentration Ratios, 1982–6
Countries where 1, 2, 3 or 4 primary products account for over 75 per cent of export earnings

One Product

Algeria: oil and gas
Angola: oil
Botswana: diamonds
Burundi: coffee
Congo: oil
Gabon: oil
Guinea: bauxite
Libya: oil

Niger: uranium
Nigeria: oil
Rwanda: coffee
São Tomé: cocoa
Somalia: livestock
Uganda: coffee
Zambia: copper

Two Products

Cape Verde: fish, fruit
Chad: cotton, livestock
Comoros: vanilla, cloves
Egypt: oil, cotton
Equ. Guinea: cocoa, timber
Ethiopia: coffee, hides
Ghana: cocoa, bauxite

Liberia: iron ore, rubber
Malawi: tobacco, tea
Mali: livestock, cotton
Mauritania: iron ore, fish
Réunion: sugar, fish
Seychelles: oil, fish
Zaire: copper, coffee

Three Products

Benin: oil, coffee, cocoa
Burkina Faso: cotton, veg. oil, livestock
Cameroon: oil, coffee, cocoa
CAR: coffee, diamonds, timber

Guinea Bissau: cashews, groundnuts, palm oil
Kenya: coffee, oil,*tea
Senegal: fish, groundnuts, phosphates
Sudan: cotton, veg. oil, livestock

Four Products

Côte d'Ivoire: cocoa, coffee, oil,* timber
Madagascar: coffee, cotton, cloves, fish
Sierra Leone: diamonds, cocoa, coffee, bauxite
Togo: phosphates, cocoa, cotton, coffee

Others With Less Concentration

Djibouti, Gambia, Lesotho, Mauritius, Morocco, Mozambique, Swaziland, Tanzania, Tunisia, Zimbabwe

*Note: petroleum products from refineries only.
Source: M. Barratt Brown and Pauline Tiffen, *Short Changed: Africa in World Trade*, Pluto Press, 1992, pp. 165–9, derived from United Nations Expert Group, *Africa's Commodity Problems: Towards a Solution*, United Nations, 1990, Table 2, pp. 103–13.

CHAPTER 2

Alternative Growth Models in the Post-colonial State

Modernizing élites tend to perceive a socialist order with its promise of radical change, coordinated planning and élite leadership as offering a more realistic and short-cut strategy for their countries' transformation.

Dele Olowu, 'Centralization, Self-Governance and Development in Nigeria' (paper dated 1985) in Dele Olowu and James S. Wunsch (eds), *The Failure of the Centralized State: Institutions and Self-Governance in Africa*, Westview Press, 1990, p. 205.

In the more general case, the take-off awaited not only the build-up of social overhead capital and a surge of technological development in industry and agriculture, but also the emergence to political power of a group prepared to regard the modernization of the economy as a serious high-order political business.

W.W. Rostow, *The Stages of Economic Growth: A Non-Communist Manifesto*, Cambridge, 1960, p. 8.

'Seek ye first the political kingdom,' the Ghanaian Kwame Nkrumah counselled his fellow nationalists in the 1960s, 'and the rest will be added unto you.'[1] The political kingdom they sought was the ex-colonial territory. Such was their commitment to the inheritance of the colonial state that for more than forty years the fifty or more states created in Africa on successive independence days, from Guinea in 1950 onwards, have remained almost unchanged within the same frontiers. With the exception of Tanzania, the post-independence leaders in African nation-states have resisted all attempts at federation or other forms of unity across the borders established by the colonial powers. (Nigeria was already a federation under British rule.)

Inside their inherited territories, these new states, at the same time, strengthened the centralized state structure. Far from seeking to destroy the colonial state machine and replace it with older pre-colonial popular

structures, they set about destroying much that was left of local democracy. Federal clauses were quickly removed from constitutions in
Cameroon, Ghana, Kenya and Uganda. Nigeria was far too big to remain
as a unitary state, but in spite of a federal constitution, twenty years
of military rule (out of thirty since independence) have continuously
strengthened power at the centre.[2]

Command Economies

The state had been the source of the white man's power. Put black men
(sic) at the centre and the condition of the people could be ameliorated.
At the very least, access to the spoils of the state would make provision
for the clienteles that surrounded the nationalist leaders. The departing
colonial powers had generally acted to encourage a certain continuity
in the leading groups of nationalists by the way that power was
transferred, even where the transfer followed a war of liberation as in
Zimbabwe.[3] For many African national leaders, however, the centralized power of the state was seen as the essential lever for economic
development. Lenin's *The State and Revolution*, with its lesson that the
capitalist state must be destroyed, was not what attracted them to
socialism. It was Stalin's success in developing Soviet industry through
centralized state planning.

The model of the Soviet Union seemed then to shine like a star in the
east. Had 'socialist' planning not changed an agrarian into an industrial
economy in twenty years, resisted invasion from the massed armies of
fascism, rebuilt a war-torn land, launched the first astronaut into orbit
and become within fifty years of 1917 one of the world's two super-
powers? And who but the Soviet Union and its Eastern European allies
would supply the arms for African peoples engaged in the struggle for
national liberation and then maintain in power those regimes that
joined the 'socialist' camp?

Before they achieved power, most African nationalists committed
themselves to Marxism as their philosophy, but they split between those
who espoused the 'African way' to socialism without class struggle and a
more orthodox 'Afro-communism'.[4] Either way they embarked upon
what they called 'socialist construction'. This was just as true in Gambia,
Ghana, Côte d'Ivoire, Kenya, Morocco, Senegal, Sudan and Tunisia,
with what might be regarded as conservative or 'reformist socialist'
governments, as in Benin, Burkina Faso, the Congo, Guinea, Madagascar, Mali and later in Ethiopia, Mozambique and Zimbabwe, where

governments for long claimed the mantle of Marxist-Leninism. The object everywhere was not so much ideological as practical – to move as soon as possible from an agrarian economy towards an industrial economy capable of rapid economic growth.[5]

The case for centralized state economic planning was widely accepted in Africa in the 1950s and 1960s. The Nigerian political scientist, Dele Olowu, writing in the 1980s about 'African Economic Performance', was able to quote an American authority from the 1960s arguing that, where both local capital and entrepreneurial spirit were lacking:

The state must assume the role normally allocated to private enterprise in Western economies, such as the United States, the British Commonwealth or the advanced countries of the Common Market. Two functions must be undertaken: the direction of new enterprise and the active support of most new projects. This latter would mean government ownership and operation, perhaps utilizing hired foreign technicians to fill the skill gaps.[6]

Olowu's essay appeared in his joint study with James S. Wunsch of the *Failure of the Centralized State* in Africa, where they outlined the core assumptions of central state economic planning, which, they say, were accepted by most African nationalist leaders:

1. a one (or no) party system, 'ostensibly dedicated to national unity';
2. unified bureaucratic structures of central government to define, organize and manage the production of public goods and services '*at all levels* by a national plan';
3. no significant role for local government, either for traditional ethnically related groups or for modern institutions;
4. executive authority maximized at the expense of the legislature, judiciary, regional government and press and private organizations;
5. a national budget as the primary source of funding for development, raised from the largest economic sectors, either agricultural marketing and/or mineral extraction.[7]

The implications of such a combination of strategies were clear: small-scale farming would give way to large-scale plantations, prices would be fixed for agricultural products, both for export and food crops, state-owned or joint ventures would be established in mineral extraction, exchange-rate policies would encourage import-substituting industries. The hand of the state was to be everywhere – pushing, pulling, planning, managing, evaluating, directing and controlling.[8]

Such massive involvement of the state in micro-level economic responsibilities as well as in macro-strategy would have put severe strains upon a large and experienced corps of civil servants. In none of the new nation-states of Africa did such a body exist. None had even a tithe of the small but brilliant élites of Moscow and Leningrad and Kiev, with long traditions of intellectual activity and bureaucratic expertise. Moreover, none had the vast resources of Russia or of the Ukraine and none enjoyed the Soviet Union's slow growth of population to sustain per capita growth rates.

The new African states had to rely on exporting a narrow range of primary products and reach accommodations with the big foreign companies which controlled their trade. Statist policies in Africa were always a witches' brew of top-downwards commands inside the country and domination and corruption at the top. The democratic element in socialism was hardly to be seen. In countries whose leaders made no claim to socialism, and even in some where they did, the leading Party soon became the substitute for mass participation and in the end personal dictatorship the substitute for both.[9]

Economic Growth and Increasing Inequality

The aim of centralized national economic planning in each of Africa's nation-states was to achieve a rapid rate of economic growth based upon increasing industrialization of what had been almost entirely agrarian economies. Growth there was in the 1960s in sub-Saharan Africa, but below the rates in other developing countries and in Eastern Europe, especially when population increases are taken into account in calculating per capita growth (see Table 2.1). An increased share of industry and of manufacturing in the national product was also achieved, but these increases did not nearly bring the industrial share of African economies, still less the manufacturing share, up to the level of those in developing countries as a whole (see Table 2.2). The share of agriculture in African national production was more than proportionately cut back. This was partly the result of the slow growth in agriculture – typical of all developing countries – but also because of the rapid growth of the service sector up to 1970.

This relative decline of agriculture is not a peculiarly African phenomenon but, given the high proportion of national production taken by agricultural exports in sub-Saharan Africa to pay for high levels of imports compared with other developing countries, it meant a skewing of the rural economy towards foreign trade. This might have been generally advantageous, but the fact was that rural producers for export markets were being heavily taxed to finance largely urban development and a largely urban bureaucracy. The gap between urban and rural incomes widened to such an extent that by 1970, in Monrovia, average income was eight times the average in Liberia as a whole and, in Lagos, six times that in northern and eastern Nigeria.[10] Michael Lipton, asking in the 1970s *Why Poor People Stay Poor*, believed that the answer lay in the political dominance of urban élites.[11]

Olowu has given figures to show how the impact of the centralized state upon the whole structure of African economies made for even wider urban–rural differentials in Africa than in other developing countries:

* Africa had by the early 1970s the highest average of non-agricultural employment in the public sector, as compared with the private sector;
* Africa had the highest concentration of non-agricultural public sector employment at the central government level, as compared with lower levels;
* African government officials had the highest differentials in pay, as compared with national average earnings;
* in Africa the concentration of these officials living in the capital city rather than in the rest of the country was higher;[12]

and one might add that the largest accumulations of wealth have been made by African political and military leaders.

The Case of Nigeria

Nigeria provided in the 1960s and 1970s the most extreme case of large industrial and agricultural investment, with what an ILO report described as 'relatively little impact on the conditions of the majority of the population'. The report noted 'heavy incidence of diseases and poverty, widening inequalities, regional imbalance, inadequate urban facilities and continued dependence on oil accompanied by the decline of other economic sectors, notably agriculture'.[13] The Biafran war between 1967 and 1970 must account for some of the lost agricultural production, but the absence of any increase in agricultural production *per head* in the 1960s – and production actually fell in the 1970s – represented a disastrous failure of development. Even before oil replaced agriculture in the mid 1970s as the largest contributor to the national income, the share of agriculture in GNP fell from 64 to 36 per cent (see Table 2.2).

Nigerian investment and public expenditure became increasingly concentrated upon a quite narrow section of the population. Federal government spending replaced local expenditure and crowded out private investment. Small- and medium-scale producers were driven out of business, in industry by the local investment of foreign companies, in agriculture by loans from the World Bank and other foreign sources for large-scale irrigation projects and farm mechanization. Production increasingly depended on inputs from abroad – not only of machines but also of semi-processed materials, fertilizers, etcetera – imported by foreign companies for their operations, and on fuel oil which the poorer farmers could not afford.[14]

Such processes of modernization of the economy might have been expected to lead to some general economic development but for the ever increasing share of the national product taken by the administration of the burgeoning state companies and parastatals, totalling over 300 in number by 1980. The civil service grew from a staff of 200,000 in 1960 to 3.2 million in 1983, 40 per cent of these in Lagos state.[15] Associated with this centralization of power and wealth was widespread corruption of public life spreading from the top downwards.

'The private sector in the Nigerian economy is a myth,' declared one group of Nigerian academics. 'There is actually only a single private sector, organized by those in control of government for private accumulation and the multi-national corporations.'[16] The same group of academics, from Ahmadu Bello University (Zaria, Nigeria), in their study of Nigeria's economic crisis, went on to list the names of twenty top Nigerian public servants who had 'retired' in the late 1960s and early 1970s to directorships on the Nigerian subsidiaries of giant transnational foreign-based companies.[17]

The Capitalist Way: Rostow's 'Stages of Growth'

Corrupt centralized power harnessed the kinship relations of African society and drove underground into informal and illicit operations those – the vast majority – who were excluded from the groups surrounding the ruling élite. Traditions of democratic practice and popular accountability were buried. The excessive centralization of economic power was to become the chief target of criticism aimed at African governments by the World Bank in the 1980s, because in the end it also drove out international capital. There had always been an alternative to socialist construction and centralized state planning offered from outside to the new leaders of nascent African states. This was the capitalist way. The most widely influential of its exponents was W.W. Rostow, whose *Stages of Economic Growth* was published in 1960, the year of Nigeria's independence.

Rostow, an American economic historian, had been a US presidential adviser and was the brother of a director of the Central Intelligence Agency. It was not for nothing that he subtitled his book *A Non-Communist Manifesto*. He denied that his stages of growth were more than an 'arbitrary and limited way of looking at the sequence of modern history'. But he did claim that his system can 'challenge and supplant Marxism as a way of looking at modern history'.[18] At the heart of the book was the assumption that recognition of the five stages of economic growth, if not a theory of growth, provided the key to understanding the evolution of modern society. These stages were categorized by Rostow as: the traditional society, the preconditions for take-off, the take-off, the drive to maturity, and the age of high mass-consumption.

It was important for the argument that such societies had evolved without revolutionary breaks. Britain was the first exemplar, but what had happened subsequently in Western Europe and in North America could happen elsewhere if a similar course were followed. The name given to this happening was 'development', which had received a new and particular meaning in President Truman's 1949 inauguration speech, when he referred to the southern hemisphere as 'underdeveloped regions'. From that moment peoples in the North and the South perceived themselves as respectively developed and developing, and the highest aspiration of those in the South was to develop like the North.[19] Rostow's book was designed simply to map out the way.

In the first stage, according to Rostow, there are everywhere to be found 'traditional societies', not too dissimilar from those which preceded 'development' in Europe and North America. The essence of this stage is that there is no growth, 'a ceiling exists on the level of attainable output per head',[20] nothing changes, men and women go about their daily business as they have done since time immemorial. This was, of course, a challenge not only to the Communist Manifesto, with its distinction of the social formations of earlier epochs of history – communal, slave, feudal or Asiatic – based upon earlier levels of technology prior to the industrial revolution and modern bourgeois society;[21] it also challenged the concept of the successive intellectual ages of man in Hegel's thought, not to mention the only too visible differences in that great range of societies that were lumped together as 'underdeveloped regions'. In a brilliant and scathing critique of Rostow, written in the early 1970s, when copies of *Stages of Economic Growth* were on every college reading list from California to Tanzania, Basil Davidson pinned down Rostow's error: it was to perpetuate the colonial rulers' myth, that Africa, along with other one-time colonies, had no history.[22]

This alleged absence of any important differences to be taken into account at the starting point of the development process in different regions allowed Rostow to impose his own prescription for the necessary preconditions for development from the first stage. In looking at the history of Europe and of the lands of European settlement, he was at pains to distinguish the special technological and socio-political conditions of economic growth, not normally taken into account by economists, that had made possible the first step from 'traditional' to 'transitional'. Elsewhere, he believed, the necessary conditions had been largely brought about by European intrusions. Although Rostow recognized that 'the imperial powers usually set up administrations and pursued policies which did not optimize the creation of the preconditions for take-off' (this must be one of the understatements of the century and could equally be applied to United States policies), he went on to say that 'they could not avoid bringing about transformations in thought, knowledge and institutions – as well as in trade and in the supply of social overhead capital – which moved the colonial society along the path towards take-off'. [23]

For the study of African development, it is of particular interest that Rostow singled out as crucial the emergence of a 'concept of nationalism, transcending the old ties to clan or region'. As a result, it was his view that most of the societies in the 'underdeveloped regions' had, at the time when he was writing, reached the second stage, the so-called 'transitional' stage in preparation for what, following the early spacecraft launchings of his day, he described as 'take-off' into modern society. This was the long-awaited moment, when, in the jargon of the time, 'all systems stood at "go!"'.[24]

The Conditions for Take-off

Rostow defined his concept of 'take-off as requiring all three of the following related conditions:

1. a rise in the rate of productive investment from, say, 5 per cent or less to over 10 per cent of national income;
2. the development of one or more substantial manufacturing sectors,

with a high rate of growth (these are taken to include the processing of agricultural products or raw materials by modern methods);
3. the existence or quick emergence of a political, social and institutional framework which exploits the impulses to expansion in the modern sector and the potential external economic effects of the take-off and gives to growth an on-going character.'[25].

When Rostow was writing in 1960 he only felt able to include three African countries as possible candidates for take-off. These were what he called 'enclave economies', with the necessary savings and investment levels in industry, but which were held back in a transitional stage, either because domestic conditions – condition 2 above – had not been achieved – the case of the Belgian Congo (Zaire) and Southern Rhodesia (Zimbabwe) – or because net capital exports were large – the case of Nigeria.[26]

By the late 1960s, when most African countries had achieved independence, several others could have been added to the list of those with an increase of domestic savings, substantial investment in industry and growth in manufacturing production – certainly Côte d'Ivoire, Zambia, Liberia, Kenya, Tanzania and Ethiopia (see Table 2.3). For Rostow's hopefuls, the outcome was disappointing. Zaire was engulfed in civil war and then locked into the grip of the transnational copper companies through the agency of a monster who tyrannized the country, while lining his own pockets, and continued to do so from 1965 up to this day.[27] Southern Rhodesia (Zimbabwe) found the political and institutional framework for expanding the modern sector of industry during the 1960s through the exigencies of UDI and with the support of South Africa. But in this case a social framework which excluded the majority black population could not last and was overthrown in guerrilla warfare. Despite abiding weaknesses in agricultural production resulting from the absence of any major land reform, Zimbabwe could still be said to have taken off in Rostow's terms. Nigeria, as we have already seen, continued throughout the thirty years after Rostow wrote to suffer from over-large net exports of capital and, while manufacturing industry grew rapidly with the oil boom in the 1970s, it collapsed in the 1980s.[28]

In looking at the list of hopefuls in the African growth stakes way back in the 1960s, it is still relevant to apply Rostow's criteria and particularly his emphasis on the social framework for encouraging growth as a necessary precondition and on the drain of capital exports as a major deterrent. It was Rostow's insistence on what he saw as the absolutely crucial, necessary condition for take-off which so enraptured the leaders of the new nation-states of Africa and other 'underdeveloped regions'. This was the social requirement that there should emerge 'a new élite, a new leadership', believing in what he called 'an appropriate value system' which regarded the 'modernization of the economy as a serious high order political business'.[29]

There was no doubt in Rostow's mind or in those of most of his readers that this necessary system was the capitalist system, but take-off was possible under very different political regimes. Britain, according to Rostow, had taken off under an hereditary oligarchy in the last quarter of the eighteenth century, the United States under a 'whites only' democracy in the middle of the nineteenth century and Russia under the *nomenklatura* of Stalinist dictatorship in the 1930s. Clothed in the uncontroversial sobriquet of 'modernism', Rostow's thesis appealed at once directly to the hearts and minds of many of the new African élites. Some of them might mouth the rhetoric of socialism, but the reality was the modernization of the economy by developing industries.

Traditionalism versus Modernism: in Tanzania

Colonial rule had left behind two sectors, the 'modern' and the 'traditional'. The two contrasting ideologies have been well described by Issa Shivji in recounting the debates over Rostow's thesis which opened up in Tanzania at the University of Dar es Salaam in the mid 1960s:

the traditional sector epitomized poverty and backwardness. Its ideology was parochial tribalism while its members related to each other in terms of kinship governed by status. The opposite was the so-called modern sector. Dominated by values of individualism, bound together by contract and producing for the market, it was forward and outward looking and therefore the image of the future, of economic progress and national polity.[30]

Shivji's story of the debates in the University of Dar es Salaam in the 1960s is highly instructive. Many of the so-called 'modernizers' wished truly to modernize on the basis of historic African democratic initiatives. The University of Dar es Salaam 'school of history' was a particularly distinguished example. On the other side, many academic socialists were seen as covering up political inactivity with rhetorical denunciations of foreign imperialism and its Tanzanian 'lackeys'. Even the 300 students who were expelled from the university in 1967 for demonstrating against conscription were protesting not so much from pacifist or anti-imperialist conviction as from a more selfish desire to protect their privileged élite position which carried exemption from call-up.[31] They were looking to join the burgeoning bureaucracy, which saw the institutions of the state as their base for accumulating power and wealth.[32]

In the 1960s and 1970s, Tanzania was one of those African countries where savings and investment had broken well over the base line of 10 per cent of national income, while manufacturing output was growing at over 5 per cent a year to a level approaching 10 per cent of GDP (see Table 2.3). Tanzania was, moreover, the one African state which had been formed by successfully merging previously separate territories. Tanganyika had been a German colony (together with Burundi and Rwanda) which had been mandated to Britain in 1919 (the other two territories went to Belgium). Zanzibar, with other off-shore islands, was a British protectorate. The two merged in 1964 to make a republic of some 20 million people, Zanzibar retaining a considerable degree of autonomy. Tanzania could be said to provide a model of social and political stability – indeed, it remained for nearly thirty years under the rule of a single party and the presidency of Julius Nyerere.

The country has little in the way of mineral resources. Agriculture remained the major sector of the economy (see Table 2.2). Most Tanzanians are peasant farmers living in rural villages and growing food for themselves and for sale in the towns, but cash crops – coffee, cotton, tea, sisal, pyrethrum and cashew nuts, together with cloves from Zanzibar – were and remained important income earners in home and export markets.[33]

What chance was there here for Rostow's stages of economic growth? Immediately after independence Tanganyika remained, with Kenya and Uganda, within a loose economic grouping which included a common external tariff. Most of the foreign capital investments continued to flow into Kenya, where there were British settlers who 'exercised a well established pressure group in London'.[34] After proposals for federation collapsed, even the loose Community broke up in inter-state disputes exacerbated by Idi Amin's seizure of power in Uganda. It was clear that for take-off to take place outside investment was required to increase the value added to Tanzania's primary products like coffee and cotton by processing and manufacture and to substitute local production for imports in the case of such products as beer, cement, cigarettes and soap. With such a limited resource base, this was a major challenge to Tanzania's modernizers.

The fact was that the new leadership in Tanzania 'with an appropriate value system' was not capitalist. Tanzania lacked anything like an indigenous capitalist class. Nyerere himself and many in his party were committed socialists. Most of the civil servants and many Party members, however, could see that industrialization through parastatal companies was the way to establish an economic base – primarily for themselves.[35] The speeches and even more the actions of the ruling party of Tanzania, the Tanganyika African National Union (TANU), revealed more openly than most others in Africa the contradiction between a commitment to an African socialism and the pursuit of economic growth based on institutions of the state.

In 1967 President Nyerere declared that development in Tanzania up to that time had resulted in

an increase in the amount of economic inequality between citizens, and this was leading towards attitudes of social inequality ... The country was beginning to develop an economic and social *élite* whose prime concern was profit for themselves and their families, and not the needs of the majority for better living standards.[36]

Nyerere decided to move towards a form of socialism (*ujamaa*) as a state policy through decentralization in agriculture and through extensive nationalizations of manufacturing industry. This was the import of the Arusha Declaration of February 1967. The decentralization in the event simply spread the bureaucracy still wider. The effect was neither to step up agricultural production nor to reduce the role of foreign capital. Output of both food and cash crops declined, so that by 1975 food aid was required and shortage of agricultural materials was reducing industrial output.[37] Foreign trade stagnated after the boom of the early 1970s and the nationalizations of private and foreign companies led to the rapid expansion of parastatal employment, which became the economic base for the new bureaucratic élite. Employment in manufacturing parastatals increased but the value added did not rise in line with the jobs created.[38]

Ujamaa failed tragically. It failed to strengthen the power or to enrich the lives of Tanzania's villagers, many of whom were uprooted from their ancestral homes and herded into artificial communities where local self-government was replaced by party bureaucracy. State Marketing Boards siphoned off profits from export crop earnings supposedly for rural development programmes but frequently for increasing the number and remuneration of those who managed them. The consequent low prices paid to the producers discouraged production.[39] The much hoped-for growth became an actual per capita decline in the 1970s (see Table 2.1).

Looking back over twenty years in power, Julius Nyerere in 1984 confessed:

There are certain things I would not do if I were to start again. One of them is the abolition of local government and the other is the disbanding of the cooperatives. We were impatient and ignorant . . . The real price we paid was in the acquisition of a top-heavy bureaucracy. We replaced local governments and cooperatives by parastatal organizations. We thought these organizations run by the state would contribute to progress because they would be under parliamentary control. We ended up with a huge machine which we cannot operate efficiently.[40]

Would it have been different if local private capital had been encouraged according to the capitalist way? This is a question which is hard to answer.

The Obstacles to Take-off

In Rostow's catalogue of stages, take-off was to be followed by regular growth as increasing proportions of the national product were invested in new means of production. First in agriculture and mining and then in manufacturing industry, sector by sector, modern methods of production would take the place of the old. It was not described as an industrial revolution, perhaps because the second half of the term had subversive implications and this was, after all, a non-Communist manifesto. But such a change from an agrarian to an industrial society as had taken place in Western Europe and North America had in fact involved a political revolution, and without it the new structures of laws and government, the extended systems of transport and communications and the financial institutions with effective systems of contract, credit and money markets, the municipal services for providing public education, health and sanitation, the research institutions for the discovery and adaptation of new ideas – these and other prerequisites for all-round industrialization could not have emerged. For African countries to borrow all these from outside was not only to continue the economic dependence from which they had only recently hoped to extricate themselves but also to engage in reality with a singularly tenuous and unreliable connection.[41]

The colonies of Africa had been created by the European powers with the aim of supplying raw materials for processing in European and, to a lesser extent, North American industries. Escalating tariffs had been imposed on imports from Africa, increasing in rate at each higher stage of processing. Breaking out from this artificial division of labour implied not only simply political independence, but also changing the whole nature of the trade exchanges between Africa and the North. Infant industries in Africa would need to be protected against manufactured imports from the North, while machinery from the North would have to be obtained both for modernizing agricultural production and for industrialization. Such imports would then have to be paid for with traditional exports of unprocessed crops and minerals, although some part of these primary products would be needed to provide the raw material for local industry. Without access to European and North American markets for the first products of new industries in Africa, the question was how the scale of production required by modern industry could be achieved.[42]

There was a particular problem of market scale. Most African nation-states were extremely small and the larger ones, like Nigeria, suffered from very poor internal communications. Nationalism, the concentration of power in the capital cities, the ruling élite's monopoly of the winnings to be had from their parastatals, combined with their lack of interest in the hinterland, prejudiced the establishment of wider regional federations. The Organization of African Unity, established in 1963, had accepted the colonial borders as the natural boundaries of the newly independent states. Subsequent attempts to create a union between Ghana and Guinea and an East African Community and common market between Kenya, Tanzania and Uganda collapsed.[43]

What Finally Destroyed Africa's Take-off?

The destructive results for economic development from continued dependence of African economies on traditional colonial exports were mitigated by the boom in nearly all primary product prices in the mid 1970s. It was not only the price of oil that shot up following the decision of OPEC in 1974 to restrict output, but prices of other minerals and raw materials rose sharply at the same time. The boom which was the result of the rapid growth of economic activity in the industrialized countries turned to slump as demand faltered. Commodity prices peaked in 1977 and then fell steadily away, apart from a brief blip in 1984-5, while those of manufactured goods in world trade continued to rise. African countries whose entire economies were dependent on importing manufactures and exporting primary products were caught in the scissors of uneven development. Many of those in the process of industrialization had contracted to buy large quantities not only of machinery but also of semi-processed raw material inputs for their new manufacturing plants.

Not all African countries suffered equally from the movements in world prices. Those countries which had oil reserves were not hit so hard, but those which depended on fuel imports faced disaster. They were only able to survive by borrowing to pay their bills. The oil price hike had put huge sums into the balances of the oil-producing countries, especially the major producers in the Middle East, and, as these were banked in North America and Western Europe, they became available for the oil-dependent countries to borrow from.[44] And the banks, in pressing their lending facilities, established a large requirement of debt servicing in the balance of payments of most African countries.

The foreign debts incurred at this time were to drag down development in the 1980s throughout the developing world. The growth anticipated in the Rostow thesis had been realized only in a few special cases, and particularly in East Asia. It had hardly occurred in Africa at all. Growth of GDP in the decade of the 1970s had fallen behind that in the 1960s everywhere, but particularly badly in Africa and worst of all in sub-Saharan Africa. With rising populations, growth per head in the 1970s had fallen on average to less than a half of one per cent. What was most serious, growth per capita in agricultural production, both of food and non-food products, actually declined on average in the 1970s by nearly 2 per cent a year.[45]

The share of agriculture in the national income of African countries had fallen by the end of the 1970s to one-quarter compared with nearly one-half at the start of the 1960s. The share of industry had risen to over one-quarter, twice the proportion in 1960, but this was accounted for by the decline in agricultural prices and by increased mineral extraction and first-stage mineral processing. The share of manufacturing in the national product actually fell back throughout Africa in the 1970s, to only 7.5 per cent in sub-Saharan Africa, while in South and South-East Asia it had risen to 20 per cent. African countries had kept up with their Asian counterparts only in the share of their output going into exports. This had everywhere risen to around a third of national income by 1970, but African exports of manufactured goods had failed to keep up. Such exports had risen to over a half of the total in Asia, while they still made up less than 5 per cent of the total in Africa (see Tables 2.1 and 2.2). Why did Africa fall behind?

The Contrast with Asia

There are many criticisms that may be made of African governments. Dr Martyn Ngwenya of the Economic Commission for Africa has summarized some of them: 'excessive reliance on external financing ... undue expansion of public expenditures, distortions in fiscal and monetary policies, general economic mismanagement and massive corruption in a few but increasing number of countries'.[46] But the whole structure of Africa's trade told against African economic development. Very little of the value which is ultimately received for Africa's produce actually stays in Africa, and practically nothing with the original producer. Examples, which we found in the studies for the book on *Africa in World Trade*,[47] showed the growers' share in the 1980s of the value of the final product ranging from 3 or 4 per cent for coffee, cocoa and cotton goods, through 6 per cent for tobacco and bananas to 15 and 20 per cent for tea.

In all these cases, except that of tea, practically none of the processing or manufacturing was done in Africa. The proportion of the final value that stayed in Africa was generally about 25 per cent, including state taxes. As the price of tropical products fell at the end of the 1980s, the proportion remaining with the producer was reduced still further – in the case of coffee to no more than 1 per cent, a penny for the coffee cherries which went into making one pound's worth of soluble coffee. This was not enough to cover the growers' labour, but coffee still had to be produced each season by the families in coffee-growing areas to find the cash expenses for daily living.[48]

When African governments attempted to increase the proportion of the value added remaining in the country of origin by the operations of local marketing boards, there is much evidence that the result was that the actual growers – in Africa, almost entirely small-scale peasant farmers – got less, and the proportion of the value kept in the country remained the same.[49] With escalating tariffs on goods entering Europe, North America and Japan, which can start at nil or 2 or 3 per cent on the raw material and rise to 25 per cent for the finished product (margarine, fruit juice, coffee bags) and even 60 to 70 per cent (cigarettes), and with limiting quotas on imports of clothing, it has proved extremely difficult for African firms processing their own materials to get into the rich markets of the industrialized countries.[50] They need, moreover, to establish their own shipping, insurance, storage and marketing services and their own information networks to compete with the giants who already occupy the markets.

Why were Asian countries able to enter these markets when Africans failed? One answer, which is regularly given by the World Bank, is the preparedness of Asian countries to open up their lands more freely to transnational companies' investment, in free enterprise zones, for example. In fact, a number of African countries have set up such export processing zones, to offer special concessions to transnational companies to persuade them to base some of the assembling and finishing processes of their production synergy outside their own industrial homelands. These zones offer cheap labour for those processes that are not yet automated and such tax concessions and trade facilities as those which are available in Hong Kong, Singapore, Greater Colombo, Manila or the *maquiladores* on the Mexico–US border. The only African zone that proved successful was in Mauritius, but there were special circumstances on this sugar island, including a Chinese *émigré* colony having links with large Hong Kong textile companies, which were interested in by-passing the quota limits on imports into Northern markets from Hong Kong. Such successes almost perfectly illustrate the model of dependent development, subject at any time to switches of location by giant transnational companies.[51]

The explanation for the success of Asian countries like South Korea and Taiwan is quite different. Japanese trade policy has always differed from that in Europe and North America in one crucial respect. Japan has consistently handed down to its neighbours, even as colonies, the necessary technology and overseas markets for them to manufacture and export goods at a level of technology which Japan had moved out of. As a result, whereas Europe and North America have tried to hold on to their first stage labour-intensive production industries – in clothing and footwear, for example – and their intermediate stage processing industries – like iron and steel and aluminium – by retaining high protective tariffs, Japan has largely moved out of these industries into high technology. Government departments in South Korea and Taiwan have worked closely with their Japanese mentors to step up the technology of their industrial companies, stage by stage with Japanese technical and financial support, and to move into markets for products which the Japanese were prepared to relinquish. The same handing-down of techniques and markets is now being applied by South Korea and Taiwan to Indonesia and Malaysia.[52]

It has been very different in Africa, where the traditional, colonial division of labour between primary production in the South and manufacturing in the North has been preserved and even today reinforced by the transnational companies of European and North American industry.

African development was held back by European invasion just when many African peoples were ready for fundamental economic change. Japan escaped this fate, but also learnt in the process that its own prosperity depended upon the development of its colonies. The same lesson was applied by Britain to her overseas dominions, which became important markets for British goods as well as suppliers of raw materials.[53] It was never applied by Britain to her African colonies. Both parties have been the losers ever since as a result.

TABLE 2.1 African and Developing Countries' Growth Rates, 1960–80

| Region | Growth of GDP (% p.a.) | | | | Growth of Agricultural Output (% p.a.) | | | |
| | Total | | per capita | | Total | | per capita | |
	1960–70	1970–80	1960–70	1970–80	1960–70	1970–80	1960–70	1970–80
All Africa	5.4	4.3	2.6	1.4	2.8	1.4	0.2	−1.4
Sub-Saharan	4.4	3.4	1.7	0.4	2.8	1.1	0.1	−1.7
Nigeria	4.4	4.7	1.4	1.3	2.9	1.4	0.0	−1.9
Kenya	8.5	5.2	4.8	1.4	3.7	3.2	0.4	−0.6
Tanzania	7.8	3.2	4.8	−0.3	3.1	3.9	0.0	0.5
Zimbabwe	4.6	1.4	1.3	−1.7	3.7	2.3	0.3	−0.7
All Developing	5.8	5.6	3.2	3.1	2.8	2.8	0.2	0.4
East Europe	6.1	5.5	5.6	4.4	3.6	1.5	2.6	0.6
S. and E. Asia	5.1	6.0	2.6	3.6	2.6	3.1	0.1	0.8

TABLE 2.2 African and Developing Countries' Economic Structure, 1960–80 (Shares % in GNP)

Region	Industry			Manufactures			Agriculture			Services			Exports		
	1960	'70	'80	1960	'70	'80	1960	'70	'80	1960	'70	'80	1960	'70	'80
All Africa	14	22	34	9	10	8	40	22	19	40	46	40	21	24	33
Sub-Saharan	12	17	28	6	9	7	46	33	25	37	44	40	22	24	29
Nigeria	7	12	37	5	4	5	64	36	21	26	43	35	15	16	31
Kenya	–	12	13	–	9	11	–	33	28	–	49	53	–	28	29
Tanzania	–	14	12	–	10	10	–	34	39	–	47	45	–	23	11
Zimbabwe	–	29	34	–	19	23	–	14	13	–	52	50	–	26	30
All Developing	21	24	33	16	18	18	32	22	15	43	48	46	16	16	16
S. and E. Asia	16	18	26	14	16	20	44	36	20	36	42	44	13	14	30

Notes: All Africa excludes South Africa. Industry includes mining.

Sources: UNCTAD *Handbook of International Trade and Development Statistics, 1991*, New York, Tables 6.2, 6.3, 6.4 and 6.5 and for 1960 Nigeria: Dele Olowu, 'Centralization, Self-government and Development in Nigeria' in James S. Wunsch and Dele Olowu, *The Failure of the Centralized State, Institutions and Self-governance in Africa*, Westview Press, 1990, p. 213.

TABLE 2.3 African Countries Fulfilling Rostow's Criteria, 1965–80

Country (in order of savings proportion)	Savings 1965	Investment (as % of GDP)		Transfers Net ($m) 1970	Debt (%) 1975	Shares of GDP (%)		Growth of Mf'ing (% per annum)	
		1965	1980			Industry 1965	Mf'ing 1965	1965–80	1980–89
Zambia	40	25	23	−65	13	54	6	5.3	2.5
Côte d'Ivoire	29	22	27	+33	9	19	11	9.1	8.2
Mauritania	28	14	27	−8	22	36	4	–	–
Liberia	27	17	18	+19	8	40	3	10	–
Zaire	26	11	25	+44	18	32	–	2.0	–
Zimbabwe	23	15	19	+9	1	21	20	–	2.6
Togo	23	22	36	+4	12	14	10	–	0.2
Tanzania	16	15	23	+44	8	18	8	5.6	−1.6
Kenya	15	14	30	−2	9	13	11	10.5	4.8
Nigeria	12	13	24	−207	4	13	6	14.6	0.8
Uganda	12	11	3	+11	8	13	8	−3.7	4.2
Ethiopia	12	13	10	+10	9	14	7	5.1	−1.6

Notes: Debt (%) = Debt servicing ratio to exports; – = figure not available.

Sources: UNCTAD, *Handbook of International Trade and Development Statistics, 1991*, Tables 5.5 and 5.14; World Bank, *World Development Report, 1991*, Tables 2, 3, 9 and 23.

CHAPTER 3

Redistribution and Basic Needs

And in *this* new world, the needs discourse becomes the pre-eminent
device for reducing people to individual units with input *requirements*
(emphasis added).

> Ivan Illich, 'Needs' in Wolfgang Sachs (ed.), *The Development Dictionary*,
> Zed Books, 1992, p. 98.

It had been a central assumption of the Rostow growth model that
economic growth, the increase in output per person in an economy,
brought benefits for all. It was said that the rising tide lifts all boats. By
the 1970s it was clear that it did not; some were holed and some could
not carry the load of passengers packing into them. When the tide
turned in the 1980s, the ebb revealed many sunken wrecks; other
craft were beached and beyond repair. While a few in ail parts of Africa
had done well, and average living standards had improved, poverty
remained widespread, seemingly unaffected or even in some places
deepened. It was not long before the aid agencies were reporting famine
in Africa. The great Sahelian drought lasted from 1968 to 1973. The
drought of 1983–5 was worse, in spite of a $10 billion international
programme for rehabilitating the stricken lands after 1973.[1] Even where
there was no drought, food production was failing to keep up with
population growth. This was true of every single region in Africa except
for French-speaking West Africa, and there it was failing in Senegal and
Mauritania.[2] By 1984 twenty African countries required emergency
food aid.

Africa, even sub-Saharan Africa, still showed some economic growth
for most of the 1980s, not as fast as in the 1970s, but still growth.
Unfortunately, populations were growing as fast, so that there was no
growth per capita and even on average a decline; and the continent
could not feed itself (see Table 3.1). The rich were growing richer, but

the poor were growing poorer – especially the women, and this at the end of the UN's Decade for Women![3] Something was evidently going wrong with the growth models. As the towns grew – the urban population doubled between the mid 1960s and mid 1980s to 28 per cent of the total in sub-Saharan Africa[4] – unemployment grew, and in the countryside it was the small farmers who were suffering. The big aid projects for dams and irrigation schemes and electrification were not benefiting them.

Medical facilities – often high-technology provision – and schools and colleges were concentrated in the cities and towns.[5] But public sanitation and housing conditions worsened not only in the shanty towns around the cities, but also in the cities themselves. There were food riots and strikes and demonstrations, in which doctors and nurses joined with students and workers.[6] At the heart of the development establishment, along the corridors of the World Bank under Robert McNamara's presidency, it began to be recognized that something was wrong and some change was needed in the formula for growth. The new slogan was 'redistribution through growth'[7] and the 'Basic Needs Approach' became the latest fashion in prescriptions for poor Africa.

'Redistribution through Growth'

Economists at the International Labour Office (ILO) had already in the 1960s identified the problems of applying modern technology, imported from the industrialized countries, with the aim of introducing a modern sector into the economies of developing countries. This is what they said:

One, modern technology has high labour productivity as compared with techniques in use in the traditional sector, and uses relatively more investment- and skill-intensive techniques as compared with traditional techniques;

two, the modern sector employs only a small proportion of the work force of the country – generally under one-fifth;

three, incomes generated in the sector – wages and salaries – are substantially higher than incomes elsewhere in the economy;

finally, for most countries the modern sector will not absorb additions to the labour force for many years and cannot begin to absorb any underemployed from those already in the traditional sector.[8]

This conclusion quite contradicted the generally accepted neo-classical economic theory concerning economic growth. This had been based on three assumptions which, when applied to new countries in the process of development, proved in most cases to be quite false. First, it was assumed that the profits and higher wages earned in the modern sector would be available as savings for reinvestment in the rest of the economy; second, that demand for inputs into the modern sector would generate increasing employment in the traditional sector; and third, that there would exist a wide-ranging mixture of labour- and capital-intensive processes available to countries in the process of development, from which entrepreneurs could choose according to their circumstances.

In fact, in most developing countries the profits from the modern sector were remitted to investors in the industrialized countries and the higher incomes of local employees were spent on imported goods; the modern sector drew most of its inputs from the industrialized countries, only generating very limited local incomes, mainly in the informal sector; and it was the most advanced technology designed for a modern sector which was made available to developing countries from outside.

What was therefore proposed by the ILO was a combination of policies: restructuring the traditional sector, particularly in agriculture, by land reforms and small-scale technical improvements; redistributing incomes, so that more of the new wealth created in the modern sector stayed in the country; and introducing forms of intermediate technology to strengthen the so-called informal sector. The most explicit and extended exposition of this thesis came in the report of the ILO mission to Kenya, published in 1972 as part of the ILO's World Employment Programme, launched in 1969.[9] Kenya's first post-liberation decade had been widely regarded as a great success story, with real growth in GDP during the 1960s of over 8 per cent per annum, nearly 5 per cent per capita, continuing into the 1970s, and the share of manufacturing in GDP at over 10 per cent and rising.[10]

The Case of Kenya and the ILO Report

There were special reasons for Kenya's rapid growth immediately after independence during the 1960s. Kenya is one of Africa's larger states, having a population then of about 12 million, which has been growing fast even by African standards, doubling in less than twenty years. Its territory is large and varied. While the north is arid, semi-desert, a part of the Sahel that stretches right across Africa south of the Sahara, and there is semi-arid savannah in the south-east, except for the coastal strip facing the Indian ocean, most of the population is concentrated in the south-west. This includes the low-lying lands along Lake Victoria and the 'White Highlands' around Mount Kenya, a snow-capped mountain on the equator. Kenya shares with Rhodesia the distinction of being one of the two parts of tropical Africa in which Europeans could survive. At the end of the nineteenth century it became a British colony, in the proper sense of a colonial settlement. A railway was built from Mombasa, on the Indian Ocean, inland to Lake Victoria and Uganda. The settlers prospered, growing coffee in the Highlands and growing wheat and grazing sheep along the Rift Valley, on fertile lands which they appropriated from the local people. An Asian population, some of whom had been brought in to build the railway, established a thriving commercial community.[11]

The peoples of Kenya comprise several linguistic and ethnic groups. Swahili is the official language, but the Kikuyu with 20 per cent and the Luo with 13 per cent of the population form the dominant groups. It was among the Kikuyu whose lands had been expropriated by the British settlers that initial protests against colonial rule began. Jomo Kenyatta, who became Kenya's first president after independence, lived in England in the 1930s and became well known as a champion of African rights. The Second World War greatly advanced the demands of Africans for independence, but most particularly in West and East Africa. The British raised three divisions of East African soldiers (the first, second – later twelfth – and eleventh), which saw service both in Africa and in Burma and suffered some heavy losses. Those who came back were no longer content to remain colonial servants. Basil Davidson quotes from a West African private in Burma: 'We all overseas soldiers are coming back with new ideas ... We have been told what we fought for ... That is "freedom". We want freedom, nothing but freedom.'[12]

In 1944 a group of African intellectuals from several ethnic groups formed the Kenya African Union to press for political reforms and to oppose the granting of self-government to Kenya, i.e. to the white settlers. They were ignored and in 1947 a guerrilla movement known outside Kenya as the Mau Mau began to fight for the expulsion of the settlers and the restoration of the expropriated lands. By 1952 local resistance had become a large-scale insurrection. Kenyatta returned to Kenya in 1946 and became president of the Kenya African Union. He

was arrested and imprisoned. But the British conceded African representatives in the legislature and KANU (the Kenya African National
Union), which had been formed to fight the election, won overwhelmingly. Kenyatta was released and KANU formed a government together
with a minority party, KADU (Kenya African Democratic Union).
This last party represented minority ethnic groups on the coast and dry
lands, resented Kikuyu and Luo domination and wished for the establishment of a federal state. In the event it was absorbed into KANU.
Kenya was founded at the end of 1963 as a unitary state and in 1964
KANU became the only political party.[13]

Between 1964 and 1966, the estates of the white settlers were taken
over and some land was given to peasant farmers which became the
basis for Kenya's early economic growth. Still more land was bought by
Kenyans employed in government or in business or in both, who were
leading figures in KANU and associates of Kenyatta. This small élite –
so graphically portrayed by the Kenyan writer Ngugi wa Thiong'o in
his novel *Petals of Blood* – benefited also from the restrictions imposed on
Asians in the 1970s. It received a special boost from the short-lived East
African Community, which gave to Kenya as the most industrially
advanced member a much wider market for the local production of a
wide range of consumer goods. A local capitalist class had already
emerged in the 1930s, often in conflict with the white settlers but with
links to British companies, both in trading and manufacturing.

After independence, this class established itself in close integration
with the ruling élite.[14] Mobilizing state support for industry and greatly
strengthening its links with international capital, this élite of businessmen and politicians developed Kenya in the 1970s as a strong candidate
for full Rostowian take-off into cumulative growth. The rich resources of
the land, the high world prices of cash crops, especially of coffee and
tea, in the late 1960s and early 70s,[15] the inflow of investment by
transnational companies following the settlement with the white farmers
and the passing of the Foreign Investments Protection Act in 1964,[16] all
appeared to guarantee Kenya's economic future.

What the ILO mission found on the ground in 1971, however, led
them to see Kenya's economic growth record as quite unsustainable.

At the end of the 1960s the top 12 per cent of Kenyans accounted for 57 per
cent of the country's annual income, while the bottom 12 per cent received
only 2 per cent ... One-third of Kenyan households were still unable to buy
the food necessary for a minimum level of nutrition and were thus defined as
'absolutely poor'.[17]

Both the large-scale farms and the modern sector of manufacturing industry were highly protected behind monopoly positions.[18] Small-scale farmers were generally neglected or, in the case of the sugar-factory contract farmers and those farming irrigated rice lands, forced to grow the food they needed, apart from sugar or rice, on marginal lands. The incomes from their cash crops were not enough to meet their needs. The women suffered particularly in these cases because they did not receive the cash but had to feed their families. The result was that, to the consternation of the researchers, nutritional levels of children in sugar- and rice-growing areas, which had the richest lands, were found to be actually lower than elsewhere.[19] With such poverty in the rural areas the market was too narrow to allow for efficient production of the sophisticated goods and services by protected capital-intensive companies in the cities using advanced foreign-owned technology and imported inputs. This created a vicious circle of inequality and the consequent further stagnation of the domestic rural and informal sectors.[20]

The ILO mission in their report summed up the situation as follows:

Since independence, economic growth has largely continued on the lines set by the earlier colonial structure. Kenyanization has radically changed the racial composition of the group of people in the centre of power and many of its policies, but has had only a limited effect on the mechanisms which maintain its dominance – the pattern of government income and expenditure, the freedom of foreign firms to locate their offices and plants in Nairobi, and the narrow stratum of expenditure by a high-income élite superimposed on a base of limited mass consumption.

Indeed, the power of the centre over the periphery may well be greater today than it was before, since there is now a closer correlation of interests between the urban élite, the owners of large farms and the larger foreign-owned companies.[21]

In a later passage, the authors of the report expressed their belief that such inequalities would tend to be perpetuated and intensified in the Kenyan social and economic system:

Unless there is a change in development strategy and policies, and in the absence of effective and powerful redistributive mechanisms, the heavy concentration of income is likely to continue and may be further intensified in the future. A high degree of inequality is a characteristic feature of private enterprise economies in an early stage of development. Further, these inequalities tend to be intensified with the growth of the economy over long periods of time.[22]

The main recommendations of the mission all centred around what was called 'redistribution through growth' – redistribution of incomes to the 'working poor' and the mobilization of resources for employment-creating development projects.[23] To these ends, improved tax collection and a progressive tax structure plus an income freeze for five years would be imposed upon the one per cent top income earners in the population. Only small increases would be allowed to these top earners for the next seven years, so that by 1985 the legal minimum wage adopted for Nairobi in 1966 could be made universal and funds could be channelled into investment to raise rural incomes and foster the informal sector. At the same time, the large farms taken over from white settlers by rich Kenyans would be redistributed into smallholdings, with credit and services supplied under a Rural Development Programme. To top this draconian plan, stricter terms would be imposed on foreign investors and existing protection of monopolies would be revised and measures of company taxation tightened up.[24]

As Colin Leys, reviewing these recommendations in 1975, wrote:

To put it in a nutshell, the people who had fought their way to positions of power and wealth in the Kenyatta regime – ministers, MPs, councillors, KANU office-holders and their various clienteles – were to agree to surrender a significant part of the advantage they had gained for themselves and their families ... Those with large farms who were seriously in arrears with payments ... would have their farms taken away ... In the longer run, landowners would have to agree to a land tax ... The better-off smallholders, teachers, traders and the like who had obtained the larger low-density plots ... would be put under similar pressures to ... sell off ... Those traders, distributors, transporters, owners of service enterprises, in fact all African businessmen who had succeeded in breaking into some more or less protected area of activity, where a more substantial and secure profit could be made, would have to give up their new-found protection so as to give encouragement to the unregulated and competitive (in the mission's terms, 'informal') sectors ... Higher civil servants and company executives would accept a five-year freeze of salary scales (though the mission thought that their annual increments might keep their real earnings level with inflation) ... The areas of the country best provided with services ... were to give up their lead so that services elsewhere could be brought up to a comparable level. Last but not least, foreign enterprises would pay higher corporate taxation, drastically reduce their profit remittances, and shift away from the capital-intensive technology and imported inputs usually supplied by their parent companies without a significant loss of enthusiasm for investment in Kenya.[25]

'The obvious puzzle,' Colin Leys concluded, 'presented by these proposals is what incentive the mission thought all these groups – the heart and soul of the alliance of domestic and foreign capital – might possibly have for making such sacrifices.'[26] The only incentive that the mission offered in its report is summarized in a section headed 'The Cost of Inaction'. It comes down to an appeal to fear that 'The frustration of younger people in search of opportunities – frustration instilled by their present preparation for life – may lead to alienation and intolerable tensions . . . the problem may become insoluble in future, whereas it can still be avoided by timely action.'[27] The leading groups in Kenyan society were not perturbed.

The Informal Sector

The response of the Kenyan government to the ILO's recommendations was bland: 'in most cases, proposals in the report reflect, or are consistent with, current government policies.'[28] This was certainly true of the government's populist rhetoric, but those radicals who sought to realize these policies had already been driven into opposition, like Oginga Odinga, or murdered, like J.M. Kariuki. The government was not too worried by the fear of 'intolerable tensions'. The ruling party felt able even after Kenyatta's death to combine social control, based on clientelism, with 'a restrained but effective system of repression, in which organized opposition was outlawed'.[29] The government responded particularly warmly to the report's recommendations concerning the informal sector, describing these as 'refreshingly innovative'.[30]

There is a certain ambivalence in African views about the so-called informal sector, which we shall explore in greater depth in the second half of this book. The sector ranges from the black market, smuggling goods across the arbitrary frontiers of African states and other highly profitable, but illegal, activities of petty trading, on the one hand, to the most intense exploitation of labour on the other in small workshops, where men and women work long hours in sickening conditions for very low wages. In between there are what the ILO report believed to be 'the bulk of employment in the informal sector . . . economically efficient and profitable, though small in scale and limited by simple technologies, little capital and lack of links with the other ("formal") sector'. The report instances 'a variety of carpenters, masons, tailors and other tradesmen, as well as cooks and taxi drivers, offering virtually the full range of skills needed to provide goods and services for a large though often poor section of the population'.[31]

The economic activities of this sector, to be found in both urban and rural areas, and including the production of many agricultural smallholdings, were characterized, according to the report, by ease of entry, family ownership, reliance on indigenous resources, smallness of scale, labour-intensiveness and 'adapted technology', skills acquired outside the formal school system, and by unregulated and competitive markets.[32]

It was the view of the mission that the informal sector was a dynamic sector, which needed encouragement and support from the government in place of the harassment which was its normal usage. The very low wages in the sector were seen to be due to lack of skills training, to the low incomes of those whom it served and to its lack of demand from the formal sector. Many of these lacks could be remedied by positive government action. But, as Colin Leys pointed out, the informal sector was not at all characterized by lack of links with the formal sector; it was absolutely essential to the formal sector. How else could the protected formal sector, including the foreign-based companies operating in Kenya, hope to remain so profitable if it could not rely upon cheap labour, which in its turn depended on the produce from even cheaper labour production in the informal sector?[33]

The mission was evidently anxious that more of the inputs of the modern sector in Kenya should be obtained from indigenous sources and more of the spending of incomes from the modern sector should be on Kenyan products. In their report, however, the mission failed to recognize adequately the problem that, apart from craft products catering for the tourist markets, the effect of widespread advertising, especially by television, created a strong preference for imported goods among those members of the Kenyan public with more than minimal incomes. Leys makes much of this fact, but others argued that he too easily dismissed the possibility that the more intensive use of labour by small African firms would do something to relieve the problem of unemployment. Any shift from imported goods to local production would be bound to help Kenya's development to some extent. He was probably nearer the mark, according to his critics, in doubting whether the mission's hoped for 'increased trade union activities . . . [would] protect the interests of small farmers, casual workers and landless labour' as well as full-time urban workers.[34]

Basic Human Needs: 'Strong' and 'Weak' Versions

If political and economic structures in Africa made it difficult, if not impossible, for redistribution of income and power to be effected by government measures proceeding from the top, then perhaps it had to be recognized that it would be better to start from the bottom, by involving the people themselves in determining their own needs and participating in the political process of achieving them. There was no doubt about their needs. The outstanding facts about Africa's condition in the 1970s were revealed in a series of UNICEF reports published in 1980. They are summarized in Table 3.1. Life expectancy at birth was still less than 50 years in Africa compared with 72 in the developed countries, infantile mortality was still 140 per thousand compared with 20 per thousand, the adult literacy rate was only 24 per cent compared with 97 per cent and school attendance at age 6–11 was 51 per cent compared with 94 per cent, at age 12–17 it was 32 per cent compared with 85 per cent. Moreover, the gap between the percentage of girls attending school and the percentage of boys so doing was very wide. Yet in some of the poorest parts of Kenya, for example, as many as 30 per cent of households were headed by women.[35]

Such indicators truly represent basic human needs, and the notion spread among concerned people in the industrialized countries that, by defining and targeting needs, more progress would be made in supporting the increasingly radical demands of the poor than by providing aid to governments, even with the aim of reducing inequalities by 'redistribution through growth'. Table 3.1 shows their extent.[36] Thus it was that when the ILO convened its World Conference on Employment in 1976 it marshalled all the critics of economic growth orthodoxy and announced a Programme of Action which began with the following statement:

1. Strategies and national development plans and policies should include explicitly as a priority objective the promotion of employment and the satisfaction of the basic needs of each country's population.

2. Basic needs, as understood in this Programme of Action, include two elements. First, they include certain minimum requirements of a family for private consumption: adequate food, shelter and clothing as well as certain household equipment and furniture. Second, they include essential services provided by and for the community at large, such as safe drinking water, sanitation, public transport and health, educational and cultural facilities.

3. A basic-needs-oriented policy implies the participation of the people in making the decisions which affect them through organizations of their own choice.

4. In all countries freely chosen employment enters into a basic-needs policy both as a means and as an end. Employment yields an output. It provides an income to the employed and gives the individual a feeling of self-respect, dignity and of being a worthy member of society.[37]

Ben Wisner, who has worked with grass roots groups in several parts of Africa over a twenty-year period, has learnt to make a distinction between 'strong' and 'weak' versions of the 'Basic Needs Approach', the difference depending upon the extent of what the ILO, in its follow-up of the World Employment Conference, called 'effective mass participation of the rural population in the political process in order to safeguard their interests'.[38] Wisner concluded from direct personal studies, mainly in Kenya, that it was the weak version of the Basic Needs Approach that had generally been applied in Africa, and his studies are confirmed by many others.[39] Typical of this version is the belief in a 'quick fix'. A technical package of inputs is simply delivered, usually by an aid organization, voluntary or official, from the North. This 'fix' can be applied equally to primary health care, to clean water supply, to improved food production with new seeds and fertilizer, to modern building materials for housing, food storage and sanitation systems, to mechanical road transport and to imported packs for basic education and business organization.[40]

When the package failed to improve things, a new, better, improved package was offered, perhaps incorporating some of the results of the new bio-technological revolution, 'with or without a garnish of "farm systems research" and "applied anthropology"', as Wisner snidely described the presentation of the African green revolution.[41] He added that no confession of failure was provided by those who had offered the advice that had failed and were now presenting a new package. 'Harvard advisers probably outnumber rhinos in Kenya and are definitely *not* an endangered species,' he comments.[42]

It was a further complaint of some Africans about basic-needs packages that foreign aid workers, including those from non-governmental organization (NGOs) in the North, frequently worked out their programmes of delivery with local government officials and village headmen and also themselves stayed on in the country in key positions of responsibility. The people at the grass roots were not involved. There was a confusion of participation with decentralization. Particular groups that were selected for aid by foreign NGOs on local advice became isolated islands of privilege which failed to raise the general condition of the people.[43]

It was not only in relation to food production that faith in technological miracles spread among the administrators of aid programmes. UNICEF, in its 1982–3 report on *The State of the World's Children*, announced its Child Survival Revolution. This was to consist of four simple actions to be taken to improve children's health in developing countries. It was called the GOBI programme from the acronym of the four actions. They were Growth monitoring, Oral rehydration therapy (with sachets of imported salts), Breast feeding (as opposed to early weaning and/or bottle feeding) and Immunization.[44] GOBI was, in effect, to replace the general strategy of social programmes of health and education, which the WHO and UNICEF had been advocating as prerequisites of improved child health.[45]

These two UN institutions had been at pains to dispel suspicions that 'basic needs' was being introduced deviously, as the developing nations were claiming in international meetings, as a 'substitute for the urgent need to rewrite, in the light of current world realities, the rules and principles governing world trade'.[46] When first introduced, GOBI was presented as one element only in an overall development strategy encouraging self-reliance and control by people and especially by women over their own lives. An important conclusion had been reached. 'If popular participation is to be limited solely to the execution of tasks, it will have little chance of obtaining real and lasting support.'[47] But the conclusion was not acted upon.

'Poverty is Natural'

The year 1984 appears as a turning point in the approach of the official international institutions to human needs. Worldwide economic recession and monetarist economics were discouraging all talk of income redistribution or of a new international economic order. Starting with the FAO World Conference on Reform and Rural Development in 1979, questions were raised about the 'carrying capacity of African land'.[48] The World Bank's *World Development Report* for 1984 blamed poverty on population growth.[49] UNICEF seemed to have come to accept, along with the WHO, that poverty was somehow a natural and inescapable fact of life, and that technological innovation, and not parental empowerment through social change, was the only hope for improved health care. Another acronym, FFF, was added to GOBI – Food supplements, Family spacing and Female education. As malaria returned to lands freed from it and as acute respiratory infections spread, new technologies were added for home treatment. All the emphasis on community action, mutual support and the training of village health workers disappeared. The health packages were to be delivered direct to individuals along with solar cookers and wood-burning stoves.[50]

But what could direct delivery mean? The question was rarely asked who the aid was to be delivered to or how those 'aided' were expected to participate in using the package(s).[51] The result was continuing failure: women wouldn't take the pill or use the wood-burning stoves; the men couldn't work the solar heaters. There was a universal complaint that 'Africans are hopeless and helpless; it's no good giving them the tools for self-advancement, they only mess them up.' It would, of course, have been better to ask their opinion in the first place. That would have been the 'strong' Basic Needs Approach. Of course, there were some who could and did use the packages, but they were not the poor in the villages; it was better-off sisters in the towns who bought them when the imported goods arrived in the markets.

Participation, as indicated in the third and fourth clauses of the ILO programme quoted above, is the essence of the 'strong' approach. We have noted earlier how experts with long experience in Africa have come to recognize the deep understanding and the expert skills which Africans have displayed throughout their history in feeding a steadily increasing population from production on the fragile soils of their continent. That these skills are not wholly forgotten or totally destroyed today may be learnt from the tribute of the Executive Coordinator of the UN Office of Emergency Operations in Africa spoken on the eve of the UN Special Session on Africa in 1986:

African farmers are among the best farmers in the world, you know. They are mostly women – something like 80 per cent of farmers are women – so when you say the farmers you should say 'she', not 'he'. I'm a farmer myself and I'll tell you, under the conditions that they work, they are tremendous farmers. All they need is a little support and they'll be able to feed themselves. Africa *can* feed itself – it used to do so.[52]

Of course, the secret of good farming in Africa, as elsewhere, was knowledge of local soils and climates. This explains the wide range of different farming techniques practised in different parts of the continent – hunting, gathering, shifting, bush fallowing and other rotations, intercropping, ridging, terracing as well as irrigation and field cultivation.[53] Much of Africa's failure to feed itself can be traced back to the refusal of experts from outside to involve the local farmers, and particularly the women, in attempts to raise the productivity of land and labour. Popular participation was not, however, what the international authorities had in mind for Africa in the 1980s. African governments were to be required to reduce their involvement in their economies and open them up more actively to outside influences through measures of structural adjustment.

TABLE 3.1 Basic Needs Indicators, 1970s

Basic Need Indicator	Kenya	East Africa	Africa	Less Developed Countries	More Developed Countries
	(Figures given for males and females)				
Life Expectancy at birth (years)	54/58	46/49	47/50	54/56	68/76
Infant Mortality (1970s) (deaths/year/ 1000 live births of those aged under one year)	90/76	142/121	151/129	116/104	24/18
% in school of population aged 6–11 (1975)	98/91	52/41	59/43	70/53	94/94
% in school of population aged 12–17 (1975)	59/40	33/20	39/24	42/28	84/85
% of adult population literate	30/10	29/14	33/15	52/32	98/97

Source: Haub *et al.*, 1980 quoted in Ben Wisner, *Power and Need in Africa*, Earthscan, 1988, p. 23.

CHAPTER 4

Structural Adjustment – by the World Bank

Nobody knows what an effective structural adjustment programme looks like. We cannot anticipate the adverse effects of structural adjustment policies.

Edward (Kim) Jaycox, Head of the Africa Bureau, World Bank, 1990.[1]

Structural adjustment in the 1980s was the latest panacea offered to Africa from the outside world. It was the Berg Report, the World Bank report of 1981 on *Accelerated Development in Sub-Saharan Africa*, so-called after Elliot Berg, the chief author, which began the argument for structural adjustment in Africa. The report was a response to the deteriorating situation in Africa in the 1970s, which showed practically no growth in average incomes over the decade and an actual decline in per capita food production. It was also a counterblast to the African governments' own Lagos Plan of Action, which sought help for a combined African recovery programme.

The World Bank's Berg Report offered help, but only to individual African governments which were prepared to adjust to the requirements of the international financial institutions. The rising tide of debt following the second oil price shock led to a whole change of mood in the World Bank. This was personified in the accession of the conservative Clausen to the presidency of the Bank in place of the liberal McNamara; and this itself reflected changing world financial opinion as the new conservative governments in the North embarked on monetarist policies which involved 'strong deflationary measures'.[2]

The change in World Bank policies for Africa took place without any self-criticism in the Berg Report concerning the failure of previous policies for which the Bank had been responsible. Although the authors of the Bank's technical reports and staff working papers were self-critical, as is often the case, this was not reflected in the final official report. This was particularly unfortunate, because the author of a staff working paper, also published in 1981, had put his finger on two important elements in previous failures – the neglect of small-scale producers and the emphasis on large-scale irrigation projects connected especially with raw material extraction for European and North American markets.[3] The first, the neglect of the peasants, was recognized by Berg, but the second, the need to correct the emphasis on export-led agriculture, was not heeded. African experts at the time were making the point even more strongly than the World Bank's experts. Samir Amin, criticizing the Berg Report, wrote that 'more than half of the $5 trillion in aid money spent in Africa between 1973 and 1980 came from the Bank. Most of the money went into "green revolution" experiments, which failed miserably, while the small peasants were left to fend for themselves'.[4]

What were African Governments Doing Wrong?

The Berg Report laid the blame squarely, if not fairly, on the governments of the African states, accusing them of gross mismanagement, faulty exchange rate policies, excessive state intervention and particularly of the protection of inefficient producers, unnecessary subsidies of urban consumers, extraction of high rents from rural producers and general corruption.[5] Few of the criticisms can be denied, and few Africans outside government circles themselves would essay denials. But the 'naivety of political analysis is startling,' as Paul Mosley put it in his major study of 'The World Bank and Policy-Based Lending'.[6] The accusations, however justified, miss the main target: the question for African governments to answer is not how much intervention, but intervention in whose interests? And the overwhelming answer must be that they intervened not only in their own interests, but as much in the interest of the export sector and the transnational companies with which they were inextricably connected.[7] So the essence of the Bank's message was: improve the export sector; it's not working properly for the transnationals.

The answer from inside Africa was not only to challenge the policies of the transnationals and their local agents in government but also to prescribe a combination of social transformation and inter-state cooperation, which we shall consider in the second part of this book. Another answer carried criticism of African governments much further. It came mainly from outside Africa, but had some support inside African intellectual circles. This was the argument that the only way to challenge the transnationals was to break with them, for Africa to delink from the North and pursue policies of self-reliance. The argument was given a very persuasive twist: put 'food first' before cash crops.[8] African people were starving and, even where they were not, more and more countries were importing food and in ever larger quantities. Between 1969 and 1981 imports of food into Africa rose tenfold in value, that is about threefold in volume, since grain prices roughly trebled during that period.[9]

The increase in food imports did not occur in all or most African countries but, in some of the larger countries, the share of food in total imports doubled. This was true of Ethiopia, Kenya, Nigeria and Tanzania. In some others total imports were cut back to allow for increased food purchases. The question was posed whether it was surely not obvious that growing cash crops for export was taking the place of food for the local population. It was also leading to the denuding of the land, destruction of the forests and with them the availability of fuel wood supplies, desertification and the break-up of the basic agricultural subsistence system. Governments, it was argued, should put food first.[10]

It was not as simple as that. In the first place, it was not true that, in general, land was being switched from food production to cash crops for export. Secondly, most African food producers were also producers of cash crops, on which they relied for money incomes. According to the FAO's statistics, the area of cultivated land devoted to cash crops in sub-Saharan Africa was increased from 15 million ha to 18 million ha between the 1960s and the 1980s. Over the same period, the area under food production was increased from 70 million ha to 113 million ha, the increase being at the expense of forest and woodland.[11] There were, of course, wide variations between different countries. In general, the growth in output of cash crops for export, which was much greater than the land-use figures would indicate, came mainly from the additional use of fertilizer, but agricultural output depends everywhere also on the weather.

Immediately following the drought of 1983-4 remarkable crop increases were recorded in 1985 in many African countries, including those of the Sahel, both in food production and non-food agricultural production.[12] This seems to demonstrate not only an extraordinary capacity for survival among Africa's farmers but also no obvious shortage of land-for growing food on. The conclusion of Professor Shanmugaratnam, a distinguished agriculturalist from the South, after reviewing the viability of sustainable food production systems in the Sahel, is relevant:

It does not make sense to write off cash crops altogether because of past experience in production for export. A more balanced analysis is needed. It can be argued that it was not the production of cash crops *per se* but the social relations that governed their production and exchange that led to over-exploitation and environmental degradation. Practising monoculture in the way that it was done violated the basic requirements of economic, as well as agro-ecological, sustainability.[13]

If the governments of African states were already, apparently, encouraging their export sector, what was the main charge against them? There is almost unanimous expert agreement that they were giving inadequate support, even to the extent of providing actual disincentives, to the African peasantry, the small-scale farmers, mainly women, who comprise by far the greater part of Africa's rural population. At the same time, they gave too much support, both to large-scale mechanized and irrigated agriculture and, through food subsidies and clientele benefits, to the urban population. Even in the early 1980s the population of towns and cities amounted on average to less than a quarter of the total.[14]

The fact, moreover, was that in sub-Saharan Africa large-scale production on plantations or estates remained the exception; it was the small farmer who was the main producer not only of her family's subsistence but also of food for the towns and cash crops for export. She was indeed, as African women writers have begun to tell us, 'the invisible woman', who did not appear in the reports of the financial institutions or even of the agricultural advisory services.[15] We shall see in the second part of this book what it is that she has had to say. It was not, however, a structural adjustment of gender relations that the World Bank had in mind. It was something very different.

The IMF and World Bank Policy Conditions

The central argument of the Berg Report was that the state should withdraw from intervention in the economic life of African countries and open up all economic activity – especially in agriculture – to market forces; and this opening-up should be extended to the freeing of foreign trade and exchanges from controls, whether in the form of artificial exchange rates, subsidies, tariffs, export taxes or whatever. This in effect meant cutting back government expenditure, much of which was spent on subsidizing imports and was derived from taxes and other imposts on the countries' chief exports. By thus liberalizing foreign trade, it was supposed that imports would be reduced and exports increased, so that the deficit on the foreign balance of payments could be cut back and some of the outstanding debts repaid. Taking steps in this direction was, therefore, made a condition of what were called structural adjustment loans and later of sectoral adjustment loans which were provided from the Bank to 'assist countries ... prepared to undertake a program of adjustment to meet or to avoid an impending balance of payments crisis'.[16]

Such requirements had always been an absolute condition of the receipt of funds from the IMF. Under the Bretton Woods Agreement of 1944 the two international financial institutions, the Fund and the Bank, had been given separate functions, depending primarily on the length of the period for which financial support was required. The Fund was to meet short-term payments difficulties and the Bank long-term structural problems. This was clarified in the 1960s by distinguishing the stabilization programmes of the Fund from the development projects of the Bank. By entering the field of balance of payments correction from the early 1980s onwards, the Bank was entering IMF territory. At the same time, the IMF had from 1974 been allowing its short-term loans to developing countries to stretch out into the middle-term through its Extended Fund Facility (EFF). The Bank insisted that it was able to take a long-term view, but it preferred making loans to countries where the IMF already had a stabilization agreement. Both institutions set conditions, but the IMF conditions were quantified, precise and non-negotiable in terms of reducing the country's payments deficit. The Bank's terms were qualitative, general and negotiable.[17]

It is not surprising that the governments of borrowing countries sometimes confused the loan conditions of the two institutions, but it was clear to all that the Bank's new conditionality clauses were there to provide a lever to bring recalcitrant debtors to heel, insisting that they expand their exports to pay their debts and open their markets to foreign investors. These would then provide private funds, either by debt for equity swaps or in other ways, to improve the quality and marketing of Africa's exports. To take but one example, one of the objectives of the structural adjustment programme for Nigeria is stated as follows (page 4):

The essence of this strategy [of structural adjustment] is the restoration in the medium term of a healthier path of national economic development as a component of an integrated world economy ... All external support is welcomed and solicited actively.

In quoting from this report, the Nigerian economist, Bade Onimode, gives special emphasis to the last two lines and comments ironically that this was in a country which was supposed to be pursuing a policy of national self-reliance.[18]

Ghana's Economic Recovery Programme: A Case Study

It should not be imagined that African governments were entirely undisposed to accepting the conditions imposed upon their borrowings from the Fund and the Bank, and not just because debt relief was tied to acceptance of these conditions.[19] The Ghanaian military government that followed upon the coup which unseated Nkrumah had accepted conditional IMF loans after 1966. The case of Ghana is thus particularly instructive for two reasons: first, because the Rawlings government in 1982 formulated an Economic Recovery Programme and then went to the IMF to finance it and, secondly, because the World Bank's policy reform loans were only a smallish part (some 15 per cent) of the whole programme.[20]

Ghana is also a good case to take in assessing the effect of structural adjustment loans because of the desperate condition of the country in 1982 and because Ghana's subsequent progress is claimed as an important success story for IMF/Bank policies.[21] Dr J.L.S. Abbey, the Ghanaian Commissioner for Finance and Economic Planning in the 1980s, who was the principal architect of Ghana's Economic Recovery Programme, has described how, 'at independence, there was the general feeling that Ghana had the basis for rapid development . . . producing about a third of the world output of cocoa, and backed by considerable natural resources . . . large foreign exchange reserves and a core of trained people to guide economic growth . . . a fee-free education system soon to be put in place . . . to . . . supply . . . trained manpower . . . completion of . . . the Akosombo hydro-electric dam . . . to provide a further boost to . . . industrialization'.[22] But what in the event followed he categorizes as a 'decade of development without growth', followed by 'three years of growth without development' and then disaster, so that 'by the end of 1983 Ghana had experienced two decades of almost uninterrupted decline'.

New cocoa-tree planting effectively ceased in 1960, the foreign exchange reserve disappeared, income per head fell at an average rate of 2 per cent a year for two decades, food production per head was falling by an annual rate of 6 per cent in the 1970s, industrial output by 7 per cent, transport and distribution were 'in sad shape'. Thus it transpired that real consumption per head had reached its peak in 1960 and by 1982 it had fallen by more than one-third from that level.[23]

What had happened? The economic answer is given by John Toye, director of the Institute of Development Studies at the University of Sussex, as 'the failure to provide adequate incentives for producers in the primary product sector which generates the bulk of the country's foreign exchange via exports. In Ghana's case this was, and still is, the cocoa sector.'[24] This view is confirmed by the most detailed economic analysis of the Ghanaian cocoa industry by Dr Frimpong-Ansah, who had been deputy governor of the Bank of Ghana under Nkrumah and governor under his successor. Dr Ansah concluded his studies as follows:

Throughout the history of the industry a sustained optimum incentive has been available only for two periods: from the initial phase to about 1917, and from 1947 to 1960. The development of the entire tree stock has been the result of these two maximum incentive phases alone ... Real producer prices [i.e. what the cocoa farmers could buy from their sales of cocoa] began to fall in 1955 ... accelerated decline began in 1974 ... the 1980s may have wiped out approximately 34 per cent of the tree stock ... Sustained higher prices are required for the very long-run rebuilding of the tree stock ... Tax policy had squeezed the farmers' incomes excessively to fund failed development and other uneconomic state expenditures.[25]

The views of Dr Ansah and Dr Abbey have to be seen in context. Both support structural adjustment but find different explanations for Ghana's economic decline. Dr Ansah was not only on the governing body of the Bank of Ghana under Nkrumah and his successor, but more recently a senior consultant at the London-based Standard Chartered Bank.[26] Dr Abbey, a member of the Rawlings government and the architect of Ghana's Economic Recovery Programme, was earlier responsible for economic planning under previous governments. He blamed exogenous factors, emphasizing the deterioration in the terms of trade for Ghana's exports and the consequent dwindling government revenues from exports. This in turn led to controls being imposed on exchange rates, prices and distribution, then to monetary expansion, inflation, currency overvaluation and the erosion of incentives to producers and finally to the collapse of formal markets. These were replaced on the one hand by state hand-outs and on the other by the emergence of parallel markets (i.e. grey or black markets). The turnover in such informal markets rose to a figure which was estimated in 1982 to be equal to about a third of the whole national GDP.[27]

To follow Dr Ansah's argument, no one will doubt him when he says that, in his own words, 'the [cocoa] industry was at the core of [Ghana's] political and economic decline'.[28] The industry had been responsible in 1955 for 70 per cent of the country's exports and 19 per cent of GDP. By 1982 the proportions were respectively 50 per cent and 1 per cent. But it was not just a matter of the falling world price of cocoa. World market prices for cocoa during this period had risen and fallen again. After the mid 1980s, however, they fell back steadily for a decade to only half the 1960 level.[29] These were the years of real disaster. The first two decades of Ghana's decline after independence cannot, however, just be explained by the falling world prices of cocoa. What was much more serious was that cocoa production itself fell year by year after 1973 from an annual average of around 400,000 tonnes between 1963 and 1973 to less than 200,000 tonnes in 1982, as the price paid by government to the producer in real terms fell to a third of what it had been.[30]

A full explanation of the decline of Ghana's major source of income must take into account the reasons for the neglect of the rural sector and particularly for the position of the cocoa farmers. Under British rule, colonial policy was to encourage cocoa production by peasant farmers together with certain mineral industries; a railway system was built largely to facilitate the export of minerals. Urban trading and administrative centres developed, but the rural sector as a whole was neglected. Even the cocoa beans had to be carried on head-loads to the nearest railway line. Rural roads barely existed. As Dr Ansah sums up what he calls the 'colonial predatory state', it was a 'dual society with a prosperous export sector superimposed on an impoverished peasant economy'.[31]

Land in Ghana was owned in common for the most part, but there were wealthy indigenous cocoa farmers and it was on their investment in trees that the industry depended, with credit supplied by the local purchasing agents. When the Cocoa Marketing Board was established, it was more to bring the industry under the control of the colonial state, and to marshal convertible currency reserves for the sterling area, than to do anything effective to protect the producer.[32] As independence approached, these reserves and the Marketing Board's income became the obvious targets for taxation by the new nation-state to finance the economic development which African nationalists dreamed of.

To use these funds for development rather than to lose them as colonial tribute was a very proper aim; but to develop what? The nationalists, and particularly those like President Kwame Nkrumah who were socialists, saw the future in terms of industrialization. 'It was,' he said, 'when they [the colonial government] had gone that we were faced with the stark realities ... there were slums and squalor in our towns ... there was much ignorance and few skills ... of industry we had none ... we made not a pin, not a handkerchief, not a match.'[33]

One of the advisers, first to the British Colonial Office and then to Nkrumah, was the Jamaican-born economist, Arthur Lewis. His advice was unqualified: 'In any programme of colonial development agriculture must come first ... Agricultural productivity must keep ahead of manufacturing and urbanization.'[34] 'The secret of industrialization is a rapidly progressing agriculture, and more particularly ... measures to increase food production per head.'[35]

Nkrumah seemed to have taken the message, at least in part, as he described the new government's position in 1957:

Cocoa was the mainstay of the economy, accounting for 68 per cent of exports in 1955. It belonged to the country and affected everyone, and so 'we had to think of the general public as well as of the cocoa farmer'. The reliance on the single crop of cocoa was disadvantageous to the stability of the economy. A tax on cocoa was therefore justified and 'the funds that accrued to the government would be used on expanding the economy of the country as a whole, *with special reference to agriculture*'. The maintenance of a high producer price would not only deprive the government of direct revenue for development but would also raise the cost of development.[36]

The words that reflect Lewis's view have been emphasized here, but the 'special reference to agriculture' turned out to be support for large-scale mechanized farming and the establishment of processing plants for beef, tomatoes, vegetable oils, jute, sugar and cocoa, without any attempt at transforming the peasant relations of production. The large-scale farms proved an almost total failure.[37] Nkrumah's support did not come from the rural areas and he did not attempt to build on the peasantry for what his Marxist advisers from Britain regarded as sound socialist reasons.[38] The 'initial coalition' that remained the base of most of the subsequent Ghanaian governments is categorized by Dr Ansah as consisting of 'nationalist politicians, indigenous businessmen – mostly small-scale traders – the mass of urban labour and a number of demobilized and dependent farmers'.[39] Nkrumah's arguments reproduced above were used to support the introduction of the Cocoa Duty and Development Funds (Amendment) Bill of 1954, which established the principle of a producer price ceiling for cocoa, the difference between that price and the world price going to the government and the marketing board. The price was then set at 72 shillings for a 60 lb. load, less than half the then current producer price. The Asante cocoa farmers were furious.[40]

The explanation for this manifestly draconian cut was as much political as economic. The funds were undoubtedly needed for development, but the fact was that most of the best cocoa growing land was in Asante territory, the heartland of the historic Asante kingdom. In claiming power as successors to the colonial government, the nationalists had challenged the power of the traditional rulers. The king of Asante had not attended the independence celebrations and the Asante demanded political autonomy. Nkrumah was able to exploit ancient divisions between the Asante and the neighbouring Brongs and Ahafos, who were also coffee producers, by promising a Brong–Ahafo region separate from Asante, and got his bill through parliament. But the result was to shatter the confidence of the farmers living in the more productive areas of Asante.[41]

At the same time, the government made several successive reorganizations in the management of the cocoa industry, which resulted in the creation of the United Ghanaian Farmers Council Cooperatives (UGFCC). This became the sole buying agency for cocoa and also the political arm in the cocoa industry of Nkrumah's party, the Convention Peoples Party (CPP). By 1964, when Ghana became a one-party state, the UGFCC, together with the other so-called 'wings of the Party' – the unions, the students, the young pioneers and the workers' brigades – were incorporated into the Party, and the secretary general of the UGFCC became the spokesman for farmers as a whole. It was the UGFCC which took the decision to accept lower producer prices for cocoa and to donate farmers' funds for development. It was the swelling ranks of the UGFCC bureaucracy and the associated Cocoa Marketing Board (COCOBOD) which took a large part of the funds supposedly allocated for 'development'. The situation did not change under Nkrumah's successors. Colonel Acheampong's government from 1972 to 1978 has been described as a 'rule of kleptocracy'.[42]

Critics of the successive governments of Flight Lieutenant Jerry Rawlings after 1978 are not inclined to believe that the 'vampire state', as Dr Ansah called it, had been cleaned up. Indeed, Dr Ansah spelled out how he saw the Rawlings clientele in 1990:

The band with which Rawlings II took the stage in 1981 consisted of the discontented urban masses, disaffected other ranks in the military, students, the urban unemployed, lower level trade unionists, a group of radical left-wing intellectuals and a sprinkling of disaffected politicians. All these were hard-core constituents of the urbanized vampire state.[43]

Even those who were members of the early Rawlings government – later to become disillusioned left-wing intellectuals – who had hoped for a revolution that would bring the people of Ghana back once more into the control of their destiny, failed to mobilize the farmers (some 70 per cent of the population) behind their revolutionary demands.[44] When Rawlings called for Peasant and Workers' Defence Committees to be formed to support his coup of 31 December 1981, the response in the rural areas was reported to have been 'slow, suspicious and cynical'.

There were at least two good reasons for continuing peasant discontent in Ghana in the early 1980s, apart from the low producer prices for cash crops for export: the first reason must be that the 'revolutionaries' made the Stalinist error of seeking to win over only the poor peasantry, assuming they could be divided from the richer peasants. Zaya Yeebo, an early Rawlings minister who later resigned in protest at the government's drift to the right, states that: 'Poor peasants and agricultural labourers, mainly from northern Ghana or migrants from Burkina Faso, Togo, Mali and Niger, remain the most important category of the peasantry. They produce primarily for subsistence and in some cases are indebted to rich farmers.'[45] Note that it is not even claimed that they were the largest category or showed any sign of being the most radical, and they must have included a large proportion of the Ghanaians forcibly repatriated from Uganda during the long terror of Idi Amin. The second reason followed from the first: over-zealous members of Workers' and Soldiers' Defence Committees were reported by Yeebo to have seized food products and even seed grain from peasants, believing them to be overcharging, and sold these at low prices in the cities.[46]

The Results of Structural Adjustment Policies

Thus it was that farmers, rich and poor, continued for long to be alienated under successive post-independence governments in Ghana. Their falling production in the 1970s, both in food for home consumption and in export crops, had been the main cause of the collapse of national income per head in that period, when agricultural output had fallen not only per capita but also absolutely. This decline was what the Economic Recovery Programme of the mid 1980s was designed to correct. There is no doubt that after the collapse of 1983 Ghana did enjoy five years of recovery in national income and in food production per head. Both were checked in 1988-9, when agricultural output fell by over 10 per cent.[47] The reasons for this check will be examined in a moment, but how far was the recovery from 1983 to 1988 ascribable to IMF prescriptions?

The policy conditions required by the IMF comprised: devaluation of the currency, increased prices for cocoa producers, higher interest rates, repayment of foreign debt (including by 1982 $580 million of arrears) and reductions in government expenditure and payrolls.[48] The devaluation in 1983 reduced the currency to a tenth of its previous value in relation to the US dollar and this was to be further reduced by inflation to as little as a hundredth. The price of imported goods became prohibitive, although fortunately the world price of oil fell back. Exporters of products for hard currency, such as cocoa, should have benefited. Certainly, by 1987 the real price to the producer of cocoa for export was trebled, and this brought the price back up to the 1972 level.[49] Farmers were persuaded that cocoa would once more become the most profitable crop.[50] Ansah's conclusion in 1990 still stands: 'average normal production (exclusive of weather factors) may not be more than 250,000 tonnes [the 1982 level not reached since] until a major sustained optimum producer policy has been enforced for at least ten years ... to reach the optimum production cycle of trees.'[51] Ghana's annual cocoa output was over 400,000 tonnes throughout the 1960s, but was still not more than half that amount in the early 1990s.

The government of Ghana did its best to fulfil the other IMF conditions. Interest rates were somewhat raised, debt payments were rescheduled by calling upon the World Bank for EFF and SAF and then ESAF loans, and a major cut was made in government expenditure and payrolls. The cuts in the Cocoa Marketing Board's payroll had to be made before the Export Rehabilitation Credit from the Bank could be received. By the end of 1985 retrenchment had reduced numbers by some 16,000. In 1987 10,000 'ghost workers' were removed from the payroll and a further 14,000 workers made redundant. By late 1988 the COCOBOD had just under 50,000 staff left, a little over half the original number. It was still, in the view of some observers, far too many, but the Board was by then financially autonomous.

The key change was that farmers were freed in 1991 to market their own cocoa, subject to state controls on quality and export. The subsidies on farm inputs, such as fertilizer and insecticide, were considerably reduced but by no means ended. The privatization programme moved forward slowly; in the cocoa industry, about a half of the state plantations were sold off and joint ventures established for the insecticide factory and cocoa processing plants.[52]

Other government spending cuts were supposed to include a reduction of 15,000 civil servants each year from 1987 to 1989. This was not achieved but it was made easier by the fact that the same number – 15,000 – were again found to be ghost workers, whose wages were received by others than the 'ghosts' shown on the payroll. The civil service was undoubtedly overblown and needed trimming, but the spending cuts fell particularly heavily on health and education. Poorer Ghanaians were unable to afford health treatment or school books and further education, all of which had been the pride of the Nkrumah years.

What then was the overall effect of these structural adjustments? Although support was given to the cocoa farmers both by the higher producer price and by the elimination of some of the parasites in COCOBOD, the result, in the absence of support for non-cocoa food production, was that a relative price disincentive to grow food was created. Given the reduction of farm input subsidies, the condition of food crop producers actually worsened, especially that of northern farmers and of women farmers in the south.[53] None the less, after 1983 food production per head did just rise – by an average of 1 per cent a year, which was very much better than the 3 per cent a year fall over the 1970s. Unfortunately, this improvement was not well distributed. Throughout the economy, the cuts in public spending meant not only higher unemployment but a considerable widening of inequalities. As well as the loss of free provision of health services and education, the poor lost most from the inflation since they had no assets to accrue.[54]

Some observers have not been impressed by any great improvement in methods of government management and a general view remained in the early 1990s that 'the roll-back of corruption still has a long way to go'.[55] The reasons given for this included the absence of political pluralism and of any forum for the discussion of policy options. The withdrawal of the opposition candidates in the first post-Rawlings elections of 1992 did not suggest much advance in making good such deficiencies, although the main opposition group sought to establish a dialogue with the party in power. It appears that Rawlings had shed the support of the groups on which he originally relied (students, urban workers, left-wing intellectuals) without having gone far in winning over the originally hostile urban middle class. He is reported to have had support in the election from among the farmers, especially the larger cocoa farmers. His original left-wing supporters see him as a Bonaparte who 'won his power only by flattering the basest of passions of human beings and can maintain it only by purchasing new accomplices day after day'.[56]

More pragmatic Ghanaians believe that after the 1992 elections, there is at length a changing governmental framework within which economic recovery and human rights can be maintained. The closing down of the marketing boards and other measures of privatization leave a space, which may be mainly occupied by foreign private companies and big local traders, but can also offer an opening, if they can develop the necessary expertise, for the producers' own organizations.[57]

This is an important opening which we shall examine later. How far the Ghanaian government is prepared to encourage independent local producers, both farmers and manufacturers, is, however, unclear.

Dr Kwesi Botchwey, who has been finance minister since the early 1980s, has based his strategy on attracting foreign direct investment. In 1993, he stated:

A number of multinationals who quit in the 1970s are coming back. They are looking at the comparative labour costs and are interested in producing on a large scale for export. There is tremendous scope for rapid expansion in agroprocessing industries and in wood processing.[58]

Dr Botchwey is supported in his views by the local representative of at least one multinational, Mr Ishmael Yamson, chairman of Unilever Ghana, who is quite sceptical of independent local business:

If we think that small manufacturers can suddenly become exporters, we are dreaming. We need to attract multinationals on the basis that they can come to exploit our cheap labour and natural resources.[59]

Leslie Crawford, reporting for the *Financial Times* in mid 1993, commented on Ghana's determination to press on with a programme of structural adjustment:

If Ghana's democratic transition requires a leap of faith, then greater faith still is needed to believe that after a decade of economic reforms, the country is ready to make the qualitative leap into accelerated export-led growth.[60]

The IMF and the World Bank had set their sights in the first instance on Ghana reducing its foreign debts by export-led growth. In the event Ghana's debt in relation to the national product rose from about 30 per cent at the beginning of the decade to 60 per cent by the end and the proportion of exports going to service debt from 7 per cent to over 50 per cent.[61] Exports were very rapidly stepped up in 1985 and 1986, to take up 10 per cent of GDP, compared with 6 per cent in 1983, but to no avail.[62] A large part of the increase in exports came from a threefold expansion in the volume of exports of timber in just three years, a development which must have serious ecological implications, given that the government appears to have no conservation plan for forest exploitation.[63] The failure of exports to grow after 1987 must be attributed mainly to the collapse of the world price of cocoa to a level in the early 1990s less than half that in the 1980s.[64] There was a slight recovery in 1993, but the World Bank's predictions of a steady price rise in the 1990s proved to be hopelessly wrong. Can it have been that the Bank did not take into account the effects on world prices of the increased output which it was encouraging Ghana to put on to the market?[65]

The Failure of Export-led Growth

Ghana's cocoa was not the only primary product where the Bank got its figures wrong. The prices of nearly all primary products took a sharp downward turn in 1989 after a brief recovery in 1986–7, to continue on their steady downward trend from the late 1970s. The cause must in part be the Bank's encouragement of all primary commodity producers to pay off their debts by increasing their exports. As stocks pile up, prices fall and if demand remains unresponsive to lower prices, a further fall in prices is inevitable. Given the desperate need of primary producers to pay off their debts, lower earnings, far from suggesting that they should withdraw from the market, only encourage them to produce still more.

The fact of the concentration of exports from each of the nation-states of Africa on two or three commodities has to be remembered, together with the fact of the very large number of primary commodity producers throughout the world, compared with the small number of giant transnational trading and manufacturing companies. This combination of facts has placed the primary producers in a very weak bargaining position, particularly where primary products are perishable and storage is expensive or virtually impossible. Only where there is a small number of producers, as in the case of the fuel-oil producing countries, has it been possible for producers to unite to protect the value of their natural resources. For nearly all non-fuel primary commodity producers, the situation has been made much worse in the last two or three decades, as a result of the increasing use of artificial substitutes for natural materials and because of developments in bio-technology.[66]

These tendencies have been part of a general trend in the industrialized countries to use less raw materials in producing goods and to devote a smaller proportion of personal income to spending on goods and more to services. In all these ways the demand for primary products has not grown in line with world demand as a whole. On top of all this, there has also been a major recession in economic activity in the developed industrialized world in the last decade, together with the total collapse of demand in Eastern Europe and what was the Soviet Union.[67] (The sharp rise in coffee prices as a result of frost in Brazil in the spring of 1994 is likely to prove to be only a brief blip on the downward trend.)

All these trends which have been working against primary producers have been aggravated for producers in the South by the fact that the North has begun itself to produce agricultural products like sugar and vegetable oil seeds and has protected this production with subsidies. These have cut prices so as to make it virtually impossible for producers in the South to compete. By the 1990s, the situation had reached crisis proportions for African countries on account of a spiralling vicious circle of economic decline leading to the breakdown of government and outbreaks of violence, which have themselves discouraged Northern companies from buying African products and investing in African production. The end result was still further decline. Buyers in Europe and North America of agricultural products available both from Africa and elsewhere were turning down the produce of the old trees and bushes of small-scale African farmers in favour of the high yields on large plantations in South-East Asia where new plants have been developed through bio-technology. The giant companies which have introduced these techniques in Asia have not been investing in Africa. Nor have the big mining companies been maintaining their investment in African mines; instead they have been turning to Latin America.[68]

When giant transnational companies switch the location of their investment, they in effect ruin the country which they are abandoning. This is because they not only temporarily increase productive capacity and thus force down world prices, but also they abuse their internal systems of transfer pricing. The profits of the subsidiary which they are abandoning are collected in a 'dummy' company registered in Switzerland or in the Cayman Islands, where taxes are not paid and disclosure of company accounts is not required. The producer countries simply do not know the final market value of their produce so as to obtain a proper share either by taxation or from joint ventures. Such secretly transferred profits are the normal practice of transnational companies, but the amounts are increased when a switch of investment location is taking place or is planned. Transfers from Africa of profits on mineral exploitation over the decade of the 1980s are estimated to have been large enough to pay off all the continent's accumulated debts.[69]

Although one of the main aims of World Bank finance has always been to encourage private direct foreign investment, in fact this has been thwarted. During the years of structural adjustment foreign investment in Africa has fallen, while it has risen elsewhere, so that by 1985 Africa's share of worldwide investment in developing countries had been halved - from 27 per cent of the total ten years earlier to just 14 per cent.[70] It was cut back even further thereafter. Ghana, for example, failed to attract investors in spite of structural adjustment programmes, while Zambia, which has been compared with Ghana as a country which had *not* carried out World Bank economic reforms, obtained increased foreign investment.[71] According to some calculations Zambia did better than Ghana in general economic growth. In the pairing studies of countries with similar previous growth records, economic structures, levels of industrialization, degrees of export concentration and trends in the terms of trade, a clear conclusion was reached:

Despite having a stronger growth record in the latter half of the 1970s, and despite receiving programme aid, the SAL (structural adjusting) group of countries have performed significantly worse than their non-SAL counterparts, in terms of the GDP growth rate criteria.[72]

This only confirmed the findings in 1989 of the Economic Commission for Africa. These had flatly contradicted the World Bank's report of that year on *Africa's Adjustment and Growth in the 1980s*, which purported to show that SAL countries had been performing better than others.[73]

The *Economist* quipped that only Africans would complain when someone said that things were going better for them. But the same paper rightly argued that much of the wasted aid to Africa - those grandiose prestige projects that have come to nothing - were in fact financed by the World Bank as its projects.[74] Africa's resources had been plundered for a hundred years, and what, asked many well-informed Africans, was there to show for the investment from abroad but a hole in the ground where there had been a mineral deposit and a desert where there had been cash crops?[75] After fifty years of pontificating to African farmers, even the most senior directors of the World Bank were beginning to be self-critical. As the Bank's Senior Vice-President, Ernest Stern, confessed:

We have not always designed our projects to fit the agro-climatic conditions of Africa and the social, cultural and political frameworks of African countries. This is evidenced by the percentage of poorly performing projects in the agricultural portfolio and by the fact that we, and everyone else, are still unclear about what can be done in agriculture in Africa.[76]

There will be many African farmers, as we shall see, among the 'everyone else' who would say, perhaps quite sharply, 'You can speak for yourself; we have never been given the chance to tell you what we need.' None the less, a little more of this humility and that shown by Kim Jaycox in the quotation that heads this chapter would certainly be helpful.

CHAPTER 5

Crisis Management: Commodity Exports and Debt

Some seventeen sub-Saharan African countries have been identified, in which the financial crisis is so deep, the debt burden so heavy that they will not make it.

Edward (Kim) Jaycox, Head of the Africa Bureau, World Bank, 1990.

Such was the anxiety expressed after the challenge made by the Economic Commission for Africa to the World Bank's self-congratulatory report in 1989,[1] both by African governments and by members of the Bank's staff in the field (see the quotation above), that an Expert Group was set up by the UN Secretary General to consider 'Africa's Commodity Problems' and find a 'solution'.[2] It was a most prestigious group under the chairmanship of Malcolm Fraser, one-time Conservative prime minister of Australia. But, before the group reported, two members resigned – the one-time foreign minister of France under President Mitterand, M. Cheysson, and the one-time president of Nigeria, General Olusegun Obasanjo; and the Egyptian member, while not resigning, described the report as 'an act of faith in the market forces'.[3] The message of the report when it appeared in 1990 was little different from that of the World Bank, whose Washington staff had assisted in its preparation, to wit, that African governments must cover their debts by increasing their commodity exports.[4]

The Fraser Report on Africa's Commodity Problems

The Expert Group, however, in deference to some of the Bank's critics, took up a somewhat ambiguous position on key issues:

During the course of economic development the relative importance of the commodities sector invariably declines over time. The speed with which it declines is a product of development itself. In the African context, the most obvious route to overall transformation is thus *paradoxically* to strengthen the commodities sector.[5]

'A paradox! A paradox! A most ingenious paradox!' as Gilbert and Sullivan would have chanted. But what were African countries to do in the face of massive over-production of commodities and falling prices everywhere?

The Expert Group was particularly anxious to encourage investors into Africa to develop and to diversify commodity exports. They recognized the obstacles in the way and appealed to the rich countries of the North. They argued:

Over thirty [African] countries are now embarked on [structural adjustment] programmes. Some countries have stuck to the programmes for five or six years and are determined to stick on the track. There is, however, a high probability that such programmes will fail unless the international community takes a wider view of its overall responsibilities.[6]

To this end, the Expert Group recommended that debts should be scaled down, especially those of the twenty-eight least developed countries in Africa, that aid from the rich industrialized countries should be increased and that access to markets in these countries should be opened up. Sub-Saharan African countries' debt was estimated at $150 billion in 1992, equivalent to about 90 per cent of their combined GNP and requiring about a fifth of all annual export earnings to service.[7] At least $100 billion had been remitted from these countries to the North between 1982 and 1990. The head of the World Bank Africa division drew the lesson that had to be learnt from his prognosis quoted at the head of this chapter:

For seventeen countries in Africa . . . the financial crisis is so deep, the debt burden so heavy that they will not make it . . . [Structural adjustment programmes] will not, in fact, work unless there is an increase in the flow of resources from outside.[8]

Even on conservative estimates of resource requirements and optimistic estimates of resource availability, Mr Jaycox was summarized as saying that a financing gap of at least one billion US dollars remained.[9] For the whole of sub-Saharan Africa gross disbursements of grants and loans from the North were in 1990 exactly offset by repayments and interest on past debt.[10]

The Expert Group made it clear that African countries needed aid, not only for remission of debt, but for development. The Group estimated a savings gap in sub-Saharan Africa of some $27 billion at 1987 prices.[11] The aid from Northern governments in the past, which took the form of loans and credits, makes up part of the debt. Two-thirds of African debt is owed to such government creditors, so that the appeal of the UN Secretary General in 1991 for the cancellation of all such official bilateral debt and export credit, as well as for the reduction of multilateral debt, could have been achieved by the action of industrial countries' governments.[12] Instead, rescheduling and refinancing continued, which leaves the total debt to be paid further increased by accumulated interest. World Bank loans were disbursed under one facility after another – the Structural Adjustment Facility, followed by the Enhanced Structural Adjustment Facility, supported by the Compensatory Fund Facility to include cereal imports and IMF contingencies, then the Special African Facility and the eighth replenishment of the IDA soft loans. Added to these were concessions of longer grace and maturity periods for debts negotiated with the creditor countries at what is called the Paris Club.[13]

All these facilities have been made available to fill the payments gap, under new and more demanding conditions. The latest condition from the Expert Group is that military spending is to be cut – an admirable sentiment but one that comes ill from the state arms traders in the North, of both the East and the West, who press their wares upon African governments with ever greater inducements. Other conditions are being slowly complied with. Free elections are being called to challenge dictators who for years have been held in place by their North American or European masters. Human rights are to be respected, but this is almost impossible to ensure in situations where law and order are breaking down as inflation soars and economies collapse.[14] And in these circumstances, private investment was not likely to be attracted.

This is why it is said that Africa is becoming marginalized. The UN Centre on Transnational Companies in its *World Investment Report for 1991* declared:

The marginalization of the least developed countries, most of which are located in Africa, is likely to continue since flows to developing countries are highly concentrated in newly industrializing and resource-rich countries.[15]

The hoped-for increase in foreign private direct investment which was to follow structural adjustment has not been realized and a major reason is apparently that investors are actually deterred by elements in the structural adjustment programmes. Liberalization means that the local market is not any longer a protected one. Prices of imported inputs *are* increased by depreciated local currency and by tariffs and other restrictions on imports. Higher local interest rates and increased energy prices are further deterrents, but the most serious are the required cuts in state expenditures, which have undermined many of the services upon which foreign companies rely, such as communications, transport, water supply, sewerage and education.[16]

One of the strongest recommendations of the Fraser Report was that markets in the North should be opened to African products in more highly processed forms than the primary produce. The authors were evidently aware that, in contrast with Japan's treatment of its Southern neighbours' economic development, the practice of the European and North American powers has been to concentrate on extracting primary products from the countries of the South and to reserve to themselves the more advanced stages of processing and manufacture. This was particularly the case with the countries of Africa, most of which were one-time European colonies. Thus the Expert Group stated their belief that the main reason for the decline of foreign investment in Africa was that:

many multinationals believe that, despite a reduction in the overall level of formal protective measures imposed by developed countries . . . [such measures] are being used more readily and with greater arbitrariness, particularly by the United States and the European Community. Against that background, international business will not provide considerable sums for export-oriented investments in Africa if they believe that market access to industrial countries might be shut off. A doubt is sufficient to prevent the investment.[17]

The Expert Group felt bound, evidently, to express itself strongly about the locus of responsibility for this situation:

Given their overall persuasive power . . . [the Fund and the Bank] have not taken sufficient steps to make sure that countries [subject to conditionality] embarking upon a diversified and expanded production base will gain adequate access to markets in industrial countries.[18]

After that, there is really not much left to say of the whole exercise in economic reform which the Fund and the Bank imposed upon the continent of Africa in the 1980s.

Debt Reduction, Diversification and Regionalization

The World Bank was not apparently discomforted. In the Bank's *World Development Report, 1991*, subtitled 'The Challenge of Development', the authors felt able to conclude a major section on 'Trade Routes to Growth' with the following ringing sentences:

The industrial countries of today grew prosperous through trade. No effort should be spared to ensure that the developing countries can follow the same path to progress.[19]

A year later the tone of the Bank's report was more restrained:

Despite good progress over the past generation, more than one billion people still live in acute poverty and suffer grossly inadequate access to the resources – education, health services, infrastructure, land and credit – required to give them a chance for a better life.[20]

'Good progress over the past generation' could be recorded because of the considerable success of a number of developing countries, particularly those in East Asia, in stepping up the share of manufactured goods in their total exports. As a result, it appears that for all developing countries manufactured goods amounted by 1987 to 60 per cent of their non-fuel exports, compared with 15 per cent in the 1960s. The fact was that these manufactured goods exports from developing countries still contributed only 14 per cent to the world total (11 per cent in the 1960s), and half of this was accounted for by just four countries – the 'little dragons': Hong Kong, South Korea, Singapore and Taiwan. Africa contributed no more than three-quarters of 1 per cent, an actual reduction from 2.5 per cent in the 1960s.[21] Most African countries fell into the category of the one billion people still living in acute poverty.

The UNCTAD secretariat, in submitting their *Analytical Report* to the eighth UNCTAD conference in 1992, were led to conclude a section on 'Commodity Export Dependence and Economic Growth' as follows:

In a number of countries manufactured exports have surpassed or attained the level of commodity exports and have become the most dynamic sector in their economies. Nevertheless, for the majority of developing countries, commodities will have to continue to form the engine of growth, in particular for those which have little opportunity to diversify out of commodities.[22]

Undismayed, the authors of the World Bank's *World Development Report* for 1991, which we quoted from above, insisted that the evidence showed that 'primary-product exporters also stand to gain from rising exports'.[23] The evidence supplied was a graph showing that, while the prices of primary-product exports had been falling sharply after the mid 1970s relative to prices of manufactured goods exports, the *volume* of primary-product exports had been rising. Therefore 'export earnings from commodities had remained relatively constant in relation to those from manufactures'.[24] To put the matter rather more simply, the primary-product exporters had to run faster and faster to stay in the same place, i.e. to produce more and more to pay off their debts. And it can hardly have escaped the notice of the experts from the World Bank that, by encouraging all commodity exporters to increase their exports of the same range of products, stocks pile up and prices collapse still further.

To answer the many critics of the Fraser Report, it was announced that a new Expert Group had been appointed by the UN Secretary General in 1992, to look at 'Debt Relief, Diversification and Regionalization'. The concept of this title appeared to follow from the World Bank's conclusion for the 1990s that exports from primary producers could not be expanded any further in the markets of the industrialized countries and that most of the poorer developing countries could not move into producing manufactured goods for these markets. The answer was diversification within regional markets inside the developing countries themselves. Only a quarter of all developing countries' exports went to other developing countries at the end of the 1980s, only 15 per cent of Africa's exports (although this figure would possibly be doubled if smuggling within Africa was included).[25]

The proportions for intra-trade in total trade among all developing countries had in fact been declining since the 1960s, in spite of the fact that their expansion had been widely advocated. There were two main reasons for this failure on the part of African countries, in both cases implicating World Bank policies. The first was that the Bank had always treated African states individually and never given support to regional groupings and potential fields of specialization. The second was that the pressure upon African governments to repay their foreign debts meant that they had to earn hard currency, which could only be done by exporting to the industrialized countries.

By the end of 1994 there was in fact no sign of a second UN Expert Group report on Africa, but the World Bank had published a Policy Research Report on *Adjustment in Africa*. This report firmly defends the absolute necessity for the adjustment reform programmes, because of African countries' failing growth and rising trade deficits. The reforms especially had to reduce the state's role in production and in regulating private economic activity and to give more emphasis to exports and to reducing overvalued exchange rates. Insofar as these reforms have been implemented, the authors of the report believe that improvements in economic stability and international competitiveness have followed. Areas where there has been least success are said to have been in the reform of public enterprises and financial sectors. It is recognized that: 'Achieving long-term, equitable growth also requires more investment in human capital and infrastructure, greater expansion of institutional capacity, and better governance' – all of which one would suppose would be matters of state regulation, if not of state management.

The report's concluding explanation, however, of

Africa's disappointing aggregate growth is the lack of sustained reform, not a failure of the reforms themselves. The challenge for the future is to pursue policy reforms with stronger commitment and with a rethinking of the adjustment strategy in the areas that have met with least success.

While the burden of Africa's external debt is acknowledged, it is insisted that debt reduction 'alone will not restore private investment and commercial lending' and must 'be linked to comprehensive reform programs'. There is no suggestion in the report that the Bank might lead the way, bearing in mind that one third of Africa's foreign debt is owed to the IMF and the Bank itself.[26]

Africa's debts as a proportion of total world debt are not large, and have therefore not engaged the Northern bankers in the same way as the enormous Latin American debts. But in proportion to national incomes and export earnings, the debts of many African countries, and particularly of the poorest, are overwhelming. In 1990 the external debt of the sub-Saharan African countries was equivalent to nearly the whole of their combined national incomes. At the beginning of the 1980s the proportion of debt to national income had only been half that, and debt service payments had only taken up a tenth instead of a fifth of export earnings.[27] Most of these debts were owed to official creditors, both bilateral and multilateral, i.e. on loans from industrialized countries' governments and from the IMF and the World Bank.

As the decade ended, payments, delayed and rescheduled, had made the total of sub-Saharan Africa's debt, by 1992, something over $150 billion. With the IMF, repayments plus interest rose to a figure double that of receipts. With the World Bank, repayments came to equal half of what was being disbursed. An actual reverse flow of funds out of Africa and into the industrialized countries was established. 'After eight years of "crisis management",' concluded Percy Mistry, a former World Bank senior manager, speaking at an IMF seminar, 'that is indefensible in a continent where per capita incomes are still declining from levels that are already abysmally low.'[28]

The authors of the World Bank 1991 Report allocate responsibility for this crisis with an even hand: 'Contributing to the crisis was a complex brew of policy error (large fiscal deficits, over-valuation and a bias against exports), external shocks (rapid increases in world interest rates, falling commodity prices, and world recession), and the overly expansionary lending policies of 1979–81.'[29]

The World Bank's Performance Assessed

The World Bank could not be blamed for the world recession, but could not escape its share of responsibility for all the other elements in this 'complex brew'. The IMF and Bank conditions for structural adjustment loans were supposed to deal with the policy errors, but in fact they only made them worse: currency revaluation increased import prices, high interest rates followed directly from liberalization, falling commodity prices fell further from over-encouragement of exports, while much of the over-expansionary lending was quite directly the result of World Bank policies. This is not just a wild accusation from outside, but the sober conclusion of the Bank's own Portfolio Management Task Force, led by Willi Wapenhans and set up by the Bank's president in February 1992.[30] The Bank's managers have always to remember that the Bank is a bank, which raises its funds in the financial markets to invest in projects and has to maintain a portfolio of investments that provides a return to the investors as good as they could hope to get elsewhere at the time.

The conclusions of the Task Force Report make for compulsive reading:

The share of projects with 'major problems' rose from 11% in 1981 to 20% in

1991, 30% of those in their fourth or fifth year, 42% in agriculture and 43% in water supply and sanitation.

New areas of lending are also encountering major problems: poverty (28%), environment (30%), and private and public sector reform (23%).

Performance problems were most severe in Africa.

World-wide, 39% of the borrowing countries had more than 25% problem projects ... The number of projects judged unsatisfactory at completion increased from 15% of the cohort reviewed in 1981 to ..., 37.5% of the cohort reviewed in 1991.

Cancellations have increased by some 50% in the past three years ... The actual time required for project completion (nearly seven years) exceeded the time estimated at appraisal by an average of more than two years.

Deterioration has accelerated in the last three years ... The portfolio is under pressure. This pressure is not temporary: it is attributable to deep-rooted problems which must be diagnosed and resolved. (pp. 3–4)

In examining the reasons for the declining success rate, the most indicative finding of the Task Force was the following:

Satisfactory projects are those prepared by Borrowers rather than by the Bank; and if elapsed time for effectiveness (combined with less Bank input for preparation) is taken as a proxy for Borrower commitment (usually flowing from prior participation), the most satisfactory projects are those in which there has been most Borrower participation. (p. 8)

The report quotes 'the frequent absence of explicit consideration of alternative technical solutions and options ... and (not infrequently yet critically) *failure to accurately gauge country commitment and local support* ... Borrowers report an increasingly prominent role of Bank staff in project preparation, one that can prejudice its objectivity at appraisal' (p. 12) (emphasis added).

The more satisfactory nature of projects which had the 'most Borrower participation' is perhaps not surprising when we learn that:

Work done at Headquarters accounted for about 70% of time spent on portfolio management, field work for only 30% (p. 17) [and that:] Task managers are not only overworked, but are also overwhelmed by responsibilities for which they have little or no pre-Bank experience or in-Bank training (p. 17). ... Only six large Resident Missions (two in Africa – Nigeria and Kenya) have *full* responsibility – and then only in specific sectors – for project supervision (p. 19).

The recommendations of the Bank's Task Force included improving the quality of projects entering the portfolio, defining the Bank's role in project performance management and improving its practices, but it emphasized particularly the need to introduce the concept of country performance project management and country portfolio restructuring in structural adjusting countries. After all that there is nothing about reducing what was called the 'pervasive preoccupation with new lending'. Sub-Saharan Africa would continue to receive more than a quarter of all international finance for developing countries, about a half of this from the IMF, World Bank and IDA.[31] There was to be rather closer supervision, but could there be any improvement in performance without major measures of debt reduction?

If projects in future were to emphasize diversification and regionalization, external debt would have to be reduced. Bilateral official creditors have been rescheduling debt under 'the progressive softening of the [industrialized countries'] Paris Club rescheduling terms with the Venice Agreement in 1988, the Toronto terms in 1989, and the wider application of Trinidad' (or even better the Dutch Minister Pronk's terms in 1991). They were congratulated in 1992 for their 'Herculean efforts' by Percy Mistry, but he added that:

what has been achieved still amounts to marginal trimming of the remote branches of the problem and not hacking away at its roots. Debt relief is still being provided to Africa on a 'too little, too late basis'.[32]

The Case of Malawi

Malawi is a land-locked East African state of 7 million people, with a per capita income of just under $200 in 1989, one of the lowest in Africa. It was ruled since independence in 1964 by a single-party system under the personal dictatorship of its Life President Dr Hastings Banda, until its first multiparty elections, forced upon it by its external creditors, in 1994. It is of special interest as a test case of World Bank policies because it is one of the few African states which has received, first, IMF assistance and then, three successive World Bank structural adjustment loans after 1980 and finally, from 1988, a series of Bank sectoral adjustment loans.[33] Despite all this aid, income per capita, low as it was, actually declined by 0.7 per cent per year on average in the years from 1980 to 1990, while the debt burden rose from 45 per cent of the national product to over 100 per cent and debt servicing from 21 per cent to 37 per cent of the value of exports.[34]

In a country where the rural population makes up nearly 90 per cent of the total, Malawi produces tobacco, tea, sugar and cotton for export and has also in some years had a surplus of maize for export. The country inherited from colonial rule a tri-modal system of agriculture, made up of large estates producing crops for export (mainly tea and tobacco), a smallholder sector supplying a marketed food surplus, and also about a half of the export crops, and a labour reserve sector, including poor subsistence farmers providing estate labour and migrant labour to surrounding countries.[35]

Dr Banda made no attempt to change this system fundamentally, but turned it to his own advantage by using parastatals and large holding companies in his own ownership and that of his entourage of politicians and bureaucrats to promote estate agriculture. This was financed by the state Marketing Corporation (ADMARC), which purchased export crops from the smallholders at well below world market prices, a practice made easier by the deliberate exclusion of smallholders from growing the higher-value exportable crops like burley tobacco. The richer smallholders, the Achikumbe, a sort of kulak peasant class with land enough to produce a surplus even, in some years, for export, were induced to grow maize, but the majority of smallholders were increasingly driven into poverty and the labour reserve.

Malawi's economy grew during the 1960s and early 1970s, but it was then hit by a succession of external shocks – collapse of the tobacco price, the oil price hike, which raised also the cost of estate inputs of fertilizer, et cetera, rising interest rates on external debt and the cutting-off by rebel military activity of the railway line through Mozambique to the coast.[36] The government and parastatals maintained their own spending and ran into inflationary deficits, while funds which had been borrowed from outside for estate development and for prestige projects in building a new capital city became increasingly difficult to service. When the level of outstanding external debt trebled between 1975 and 1980,[37] Banda called in first the IMF and then the World Bank.

The IMF set credit ceilings and government expenditure cuts as conditions for stand-by and compensatory finance. The Bank sought to correct what it saw as structural weaknesses. These included: slow growth of smallholder exports, narrowness of the export base, in particular excessive reliance on tobacco (as much as 60 per cent of export earnings in the 1980s), dependence on imported fuel as fuel-wood sources declined, rapid deterioration of parastatal company finances and rising state budget deficits. The Bank's prescriptions followed the usual pattern: liberalization of markets, higher prices for producers, removal of subsidies, devaluation of the currency and privatization of parastatal and government enterprises. In most respects the Banda government was a model pupil, although it may not be that privatization of parastatals into a trust controlled by Dr Banda was just what the Bank had in mind. 'Malawi does not even have autonomous capitalist interests which can assert themselves independently of Dr Banda,' was the comment of one observer, and a USAID official quipped that: 'Malawi's private sector was alive and doing well, and owned by the government.'[38]

In attempting to comply with the Bank's prescriptions in the most important sector of Malawi's economy, that of agriculture, the Banda government proceeded to undo the whole structure inherited from colonial times, upon which it had depended, without proposing anything to take its place. It was certainly the case that the 'previous estate-led, export-orientated development strategy was no longer viable'.[39] But the Bank's single-minded commitment to export promotion, combined with crop diversification and marketable food production, led its staff to overlook both the inefficiencies of the estates and the needs of the subsistence farmers who remained a majority of the rural population. Although several tobacco estates were facing bankruptcy, the Bank's 1980 Malawi report had summarized the performance of estate agriculture as 'very efficient'. The low level of rents and land taxes made for inefficient land use and the fact was that the estates did not have the finance to make better use of the land or to attract the labour necessary for expansion or for diversification. At the same time, the larger smallholders, upon whom the Bank concentrated its attention, were expected to respond to the incentive of higher producer prices in a free market, while their subsidies on fertilizer were removed or reduced.[40]

The Banda government desperately held on to the subsidies on food, which were a necessary popular offset to the oligopoly pricing policies of the parastatal purchasing bodies. It was clear that the whole foundation of Banda's populism would be undermined if he could no longer exploit the smallholders to develop the estates and to finance his government's hand-outs. The increasingly impoverished poorer smallholders were simply unable to respond to the demand for a marketable food surplus; and the export earnings from the estates were not enough to pay for imported maize.

There was an alternative, as so often elsewhere in sub-Saharan Africa. That was to give positive support to subsistence farming and to allow the smallholders to compete on equal terms in the market. But this would have involved a major restructuring of land ownership. In the Bank's thinking, the smallholders should be given parity with the estates but only in the prices they received for producing for export. Prices in the home market could be left to work themselves out. With no help for investment to raise their productivity, the poorer smallholders were simply uncompetitive – with the larger producers and with foreign grain imports. Many abandoned the land and sought their fortune in the towns. The Bank's insistence on cuts in government expenditure hit hardest at capital investment, particularly in agriculture. Total investment fell to 10 per cent of GDP in 1986 in place of 25 per cent in 1980,[41] so that the funds available in the National Rural Development Plan for supporting subsistence farmers were negligible. The Bank, moreover, gave no help to medium-scale agro-industrial businesses processing Malawi's primary products, which would have made a real contribution to diversification of the narrow export base.[42]

The Bank's programme of sectoral loans which replaced the fourth SAL programme in 1987 did, belatedly, attempt to rectify the lack of financial and other support for the smaller farmers. But to pursue fundamental structural reform would have been bound to encounter strong political opposition. The long delay in tackling the basic problem of an exploitative colonial economic structure perpetuated by the Banda government only meant that, as living standards continued to deteriorate, the resulting explosion would be violent. In 1991 the IMF approved a loan of US$15 million under a fourth year enhanced structural adjustment facility (ESAF), but the scale of the debt remained unchanged.[43] Malawi's agricultural production began to grow again in 1991 and, with it, income per head, but within this growth the inequalities between rich and poor were greater than ever, since more and more poor families, and especially women, lost their use of the land as the source of their livelihood.

Changing Food 'Entitlement'

The effects of structural adjustment policies on African agriculture in encouraging both increased production for export and more mechanization of farming, by means of the privatization of land holding and technical support for modern farming methods, have been subjected to some careful appraisal. The facts of worsening food insecurity were clear for all to see. Imports of food were growing even in food-exporting countries.[44] Famine, even after the ending of the drought years of 1984–6, had become endemic in some areas. The concept of food security itself reflected the need to think in a new way about hunger and malnutrition, focusing on food entitlement rather than food availability. In this sense 'entitlement' comprises the whole range of rights of ownership and access to use of land and to the means of production for both men and women.[45]

What has been happening to African agriculture, it is argued, is the result of three parallel and connected developments: first, the increase in cash cropping for export; second, the spread of mechanized farming methods; and third, the rapid growth of populations. The drought in the Sahel and in southern Africa, deliberate denial of food to hostile groups in conflict situations and the movements of refugees from war-torn areas have all compounded the problem, but they are not the basic cause. According to the Ethiopian Relief and Rehabilitation Commission, reporting on the 1984–5 famine after the fall of the Mengistu regime:

The primary cause of the famine was not a drought of unprecented severity, but a combination of long-continued bad land-use and steadily increased human and stock populations over decades, rendering a greater number of people vulnerable when drought struck.[46]

The change in entitlement can most easily be seen in the extremely rapid growth of urban populations as people in rural areas have lost their capacity to sustain a livelihood. This migration from the countryside to the cities, and especially to the big cities, came about directly through loss of local rights and actual displacement, to make way for irrigation schemes and large estates, but also indirectly through failing competitiveness, especially with imported foods, and through such lesser changes as the diversion of young workers and also of water supplies to large-scale agricultural operations.

While the overall growth rate of the population in sub-Saharan Africa has been averaging about 3 per cent a year, the urban population has been growing at 6 per cent a year, in Tanzania and Mozambique by over 10 per cent, and in the thirty-five major cities at an annual rate of 8.5 per cent, which means that they are approximately doubling in size every eight years. The populations of cities with an estimated million or more inhabitants had risen by 1990 to over 10 per cent of the sub-Saharan total, with such cities (the capital city in each case) in Angola, Central African Republic, Congo, Côte d'Ivoire, Guinea, Liberia, Mauritania, Senegal and Sierra Leone accounting for around 20 per cent of their total populations.[47] Even as early as 1970 between 50 per cent and 90 per cent of these city populations were living in slums or uncontrolled settlements. 'Entitlement' to a livelihood in these circumstances is obtained whether legally or illegally through the informal economy. A growing 'under-class' has emerged in the cities as the casualties of war and economic or environmental crises spread.[48]

The main impact of changing 'entitlement' remains in the rural areas, where 70 per cent of sub-Saharan African populations still seek to find a livelihood. Most of these populations have been engaged in the past either in subsistence agriculture or in pastoralism, but to say this is to pass over the importance of the enormous range of traditional practices appropriate to widely differing soils and climates, hunting, gathering, shifting cultivation, bush–fallow rotation, inter-cropping, permanent cultivation and pastoralism, both transhumant and nomadic.[49] Migration for waged work has also been widespread, including not only long-term emigration to the mines, especially in South Africa, but short-term and seasonal movements at harvest times and as a result of uneven development between neighbouring states. To these have now been added the attraction of waged work on large-scale, mechanized agricultural projects.

Many households and villages in sub-Saharan Africa, while practising mainly subsistence farming, have for long produced a cash crop as a money-earning supplement. The pressure from the World Bank and from the need for debt repayment has greatly increased the number of such *semi*-subsistence farmers. Market relations have become more general, not only in respect of traditional cash crops, but also of food crops as well. Small-scale farmers find themselves in competition with large-scale commercial estates and are forced to adopt more productive techniques. In agriculture these often mean the application of artificial fertilizers, more use of water, less care for inter-cropping, crop rotation and terracing; in stock herding, they imply the carrying of larger stocks and again more demand for water and for food grains in the dry season. Moreover, the national policies pursued by many of the African nation-states since they achieved independence, have had the effect of narrowing the markets both for labour and for produce and reducing the inter-state migration of herds.[50]

The result of all these changes has been to break up what has historically been the basic farming unit in many parts of Africa – the extended peasant family or household. Young men have gone to work on the new estates or have taken over individual parcels of land for more intensive farming of cash crops and of food for the market. The women and the old men are left to work the common land, which cannot be effectively done without the complete household. 'Modern' farming methods and deforestation for log sales and for what is a kind of 'agricultural strip mining' have, moreover, been degrading the fragile African soils and removing the women's source of firewood for cooking.[51] The spread of HIV/AIDS among the young men and women implies even more disastrous losses in Africa's effective rural labour force.[52] In the meantime, food insecurity becomes an ever more pressing problem.

The aid agencies from the industrialized countries, which have been increasingly called upon to respond to hunger in Africa, have had to recognize these fundamental changes in Africa's agriculture. Crisis management can no longer be limited to the delivery of food and blankets to starving refugees. Preventive action needs to be taken. Multilateral aid to sub-Saharan Africa rose by 1987 to 36 per cent of all such aid granted worldwide, although the combined population of these countries is only 10 per cent of the world total. While the IMF and the World Bank have been pressing forward with their structural adjustment policies, as a condition of this aid, involving ever greater cash crop production for export, the wider spread of market relations and more cuts in public spending, a safety net has had to be constructed to catch those who suffer in the process. The non-governmental organizations from the industrialized lands have been providing that net, in what has become a two-tier welfare system – of failing government provision and the ever growing unofficial aid from abroad.[53]

The chancellor of the University of Ghana has described this two-tier welfare system, perhaps rather optimistically, as 'adjustment "with a human face"' and attributes much of the credit to the UN Children's Emergency Fund (UNICEF). In writing on the human dimension of structural adjustment programmes, he quotes a 1987 UNICEF study on Africa, which concluded: 'No adjustment policy is acceptable which allows children to be sacrificed for the sake of financial stability. Yet it has happened and it need not happen.'[54] By 1989 UNICEF was able to report that the managing director of the IMF himself felt compelled to concede that: 'In most countries the real costs of such cuts [in food and agricultural subsidies] are being paid, disproportionately, by the poor and their children.'[55]

Thus, the non-governmental agencies providing aid from the industrialized countries have in effect been picking up some of the bill and providing many of the aid workers, doctors and nurses in the field. 'In a two-tier welfare system,' a British Oxfam worker commented in 1990, 'safety nets are based upon targeting assistance.' Oxfam and other agencies have attempted to rely in some way on 'communal forms of redistribuition or to support the semi-subsistence economy involved'. But he had to recognize that 'this donor/NGO system exists in a relation of contradiction and even antagonism to African governments'. It may even involve being drawn into apparently taking sides in civil wars, for example by sending supplies to Eritrea during its war with Ethiopia and into the south of Sudan, when the nominal governments of these territories were strongly opposed to such provision.[56]

This is a sad reminder that there are major and minor wars and outbreaks of violence taking place in almost every part of a sorely troubled continent. Crisis management by the World Bank or the IMF cannot raise peoples' living standards, cannot even provide daily bread, when a third of their limited incomes is mortgaged to debt repayment and when cuts in government spending create mass unemployment in the urban areas and begin to dissolve the very fabric of whole societies. The voluntary agencies cannot fill a gap of such proportions. The breakdown of law and order and the eruption of inter-ethnic fighting seems to follow as an inevitable result of debt and associated inflation and/or unemployment, whether the location is Northern Ireland, former Yugoslavia or the continent of Africa. This is such an important finding that it needs to be tested further.

CHAPTER 6

The Four Horsemen of the Apocalypse

'The new job [for] the post-Cold War world [is] to help build and
sustain a world order stable enough to allow the advanced economies of
the world to function without constant interruption and threat from the
Third World,' a task that will require 'instant intervention from the
advanced nations' and perhaps even 'pre-emptive action'.

> Peregrine Worsthorne, *Sunday Telegraph*, 16 September 1990.[1]

The association of debt with civil violence and actual civil war has been
convincingly established by a number of authorities.[2] In the Transnational Institute study, *The Debt Boomerang*, Dan Smith sums up his own
findings: 'Of the 25 third world states with the biggest debts, 12 were at
war in 1990 or early 1991. Of states with the highest debt service [to
exports] ratios, 12 of the top 27 were involved in war, and four of the
top five.' Looked at from the other side: 'Of the 41 states involved in
war in 1990 or 1991, data on debt are available for 38, of which 25 –
about two-thirds of the total – have heavy debt burdens. Long wars are
even more closely associated with debt; of 27 states involved in war for
more than a decade, data on debt are available for 24, of which 18 –
exactly three-quarters – have heavy debt burdens.' There were, in
addition, '15 third world countries in which, during the late 1980s and
the very early 1990s, there was major violence which did not amount to
war'.[3]

A question must remain about the sequence of causation. Wars have
undoubtedly resulted in states incurring debts. According to one estimate, 'between 1960 and 1987 third world governments borrowed close
to $400 billion to fund arms imports from advanced industrial states'.[4]
At the same time, heavy indebtedness and the measures taken by
governments to extricate themselves from debt can easily lead to violence
and civil conflict. The best-known examples are those of Romania,

where the Ceauşescu regime sought to wipe out its debts by draconian cuts in the living standards of the people, and of Yugoslavia, where the debt burden was a major factor in the breakup of the federal state and subsequent civil war.[5]

War does not only bring with it the death and maiming of the fighting forces. More than ever, today it involves mass casualties among civilians and great numbers of refugees from the sites of battle and from deliberate ethnic violence. The land is ravaged, fields are not sown and crops remain unharvested. Refugees move to find food as well as to escape involvement in the fighting and, where food is scarce, this is a further cause of conflict. Again, the causal links are uncertain. Wars create famine; famine generates conflict. What cannot be doubted is that where economic conditions are stable, and there is food security and hope of improvement, there is peace. When economic stability breaks down, conflict and violence reappear and the worse the breakdown, the worse the savagery. It cannot be by chance that Yugoslavia had the highest ratio of debt to national income in Europe, Somalia likewise in Africa, and Peru in Latin America.

Debt and Violence in Africa

Fairly reliable statistics are available of African countries' foreign debt and its relation to their national product and to their foreign earnings from export of goods and services. In 1988–91 out of fifty-two African countries (plus Réunion) for which there were figures, there were thirty-three which were heavily in debt. Details are given in Table 6.1 for 1988–91 and also for 1980 for these countries. Twenty-six of them had debt service/export ratios above the average for their part of Africa and another seven had outstanding debts in excess of their national income in the same period. That leaves a further twenty for which figures are available where debts were relatively low. Of the thirty-three heavily indebted countries only four, Niger, São Tomé, Senegal and Tanzania, can be said to have been spared conflict, ranging from strikes, riots and coups to outright civil war and genocide. Uganda can claim to have had relative peace for the last eight years, after a decade of frightfulness. Eight countries which enjoyed lighter debt burdens had also suffered from conflict and violence. Of these, Angola and Namibia are special cases, along with Mozambique, because of the involvement of South Africa in their wars; and of the others only Chad saw heavy fighting in this period. Finally, twelve countries where foreign debt was not overwhelming enjoyed relative peace.

The correlation between the heaviest debtors and the worst experience of violence and civil war has to be recognized as a fact. This is not to say that the debt caused the conflicts. In each case, there were serious ethnic and political differences, as there were, for example, in Yugoslavia. But there is an implication that the debt and the subsequent economic troubles stirred up old differences. Of course, the direction of causality might be the other way, and it was the wars that caused the debt. That might seem to have been the case with Sudan and Ethiopia and with Mozambique, but, after the West persuaded that unhappy country to join the IMF in 1986, its debt soared. The most important evidence in Table 6.1 is to be found in the great leap in indebtedness between 1980 and 1988–91 for just those countries with the worst experience of conflict – Uganda, Burundi, Ethiopia, Nigeria, Djibouti, Rwanda and Mali.

A key question concerns the connection between structural adjustment designed to pay off debts and its effect on local conflict. There are two possibilities: the first is that the requirement of the IMF and then of the World Bank that governments should cut food subsidies and other public spending was likely to cause social unrest. The argument goes that poverty leads to violence and the IMF and World Bank cuts in government spending led to poverty. (So-called 'IMF riots' in Nigeria and Zambia had long preceded the World Bank's deflationary conditions for granting loans.)[6] The second possibility is that the Bank's requirement after 1989 of 'good governance' triggered a long-pent-up movement of protest against arbitrary single-party rule. But the protest was not always violent. The fact remains – and it is a fact of the very greatest importance – that in the countries where the debt was not overwhelming the maintenance of multiparty rule or the transition to it has been effected without excessive violence.

Civil war in Africa has not only led to millions of deaths but has created an even greater number of refugees. However, it must be said that the refugee problem has not necessarily been connected with debt-fed social conflict, although in Sudan, Uganda and Somalia it certainly was. The popular view is that the basic cause of most deaths and migrations in Africa has been the succession of droughts. Aside from the conflicts involving South Africa and the Rwanda-Burundi tragedy, the worst outbreaks of violence and civil war have been in the Sahel. Here the drought has driven whole populations to fight each other for survival and to flee from their homes. The Sahel is the belt of savannah that runs from the west to the east right across the African continent south of the Sahara and north of the wooded grasslands of central

Africa. This narrow strip includes most of Mauritania, Mali, Niger, Chad, northern Sudan and northern Ethiopia (Tigray), Somalia and parts of Senegal, Burkina Faso, Kenya and northern Nigeria. The argument is that the Sahara has been moving southward into the grasslands, and this has resulted in the spread of desertification and with it recurrent famine, creating the appalling death toll in Chad, Sudan, Ethiopia and Somalia and the huge number of refugees both inside and outside these countries.

It is undoubtedly true that rainfall in the Sahel during the 1970s and 1980s was well below the average for the first half of the century. There were serious drought conditions from 1968 to 1973, but it was the drought of 1984–5 that hit the world's headlines. The water level in great rivers like the Nile and the Niger dropped to the lowest ever recorded and Lake Chad was reduced to half its normal size. Eighty per cent of Africa's dry lands, with a population of nearly 100 million, were categorized as 'moderately desertified'. Millions of people were forced to leave their homes in search of food, and nomadic populations almost ceased to exist.[7]

There have, however, been droughts before in African history – as recently as 1910–20 – without resulting in large-scale famine.[8] What is different with the last quarter of this century is partly that populations have increased, partly that the land is being misused, partly that subsistence farming is being replaced by food production for the market. There is, moreover, a fundamental difficulty in determining whether local wars have been another part of the explanation for famine conditions or whether the drought was part cause of the wars. 'Tribalism' is blamed for internecine fighting in Africa, as in Yugoslavia. But the 'tribes' have lived in relative peace over hundreds of years. Why, then, the eruption of civil war on such a vast scale? Is it just by chance that Somalia had in 1990 the highest ratio of debt service to exports of all African countries and Sudan and Ethiopia had well above average debts in this most heavily indebted continent?

The Case of Sudan – Misuse of the Land

We may take Sudan as an example. The population has been growing since the 1960s at about 3 per cent per year to reach a figure of 25 million in 1990. In the same period arable land has hardly been increased; what had been taken for cultivation by forest clearance in the last decade has been lost to urban growth. The ring of deforestation surrounding Khartoum has meant that the city's charcoal supply line lengthens at the rate of 15 to 20 km a year.[9] Sudan's agriculture is concentrated in the Gezira, the largest area of irrigated land under single (government) management in the world, in the narrow band of irrigated land along the Nile and in a limited area of rain-fed lands in the south. Most of the country in the north and east is desert or semi-desert thornwood and grassland, which has been the habitat over many centuries of nomadic pastoralists, between 15 and 25 million people in the mid 1980s, who regularly migrate across the Sahel.[10]

Under colonial rule, cotton was the major crop produced from the irrigated land of Sudan and most of what was very high quality cotton was exported as raw linters. The staple food crops of the people were millet and sorghum, produced mainly in rain-fed areas in the south but also on irrigated lands. The north-south divide of the country is not only an agricultural one but also reflects historic differences – the influence of Christianity in the south and of Islam in the north. Fighting between the north and the south broke out even before the British withdrew. After seventeen years of civil war and at least a million lives lost, a new president, General Nimeiri, who came to power in 1969, reached agreement in 1972 with the rebels, granting regional autonomy to the south, and proceeded to establish an Islamic state in the north. Political and military power was retained in the north and fighting continued under both Nimeiri and his successor al-Mahdi and worsened under the military rule of al-Bashir after 1988. Mass executions of southern rebels were reported by Amnesty International; and foreign studies all indicated that there would never be peace without partition between a Muslim north and a Christian south.[11]

The matter of the causal sequence of debt, famine and violence is, however, not so easily settled. Nimeiri, on achieving power, at first set out to follow a so-called 'bread-basket strategy' of emphasizing production of food rather than cotton on the irrigated land and stepping up development expenditure, especially on machinery for mechanizing agriculture.[12] It seemed to be a sensible strategy. After the great drought of 1968-73, billions of dollars of aid was poured into the Sahel from the oil-rich Arab countries and from bilateral and multilateral grants and loans. Much of it was in food aid, but the aim of the donors was to rehabilitate productive capacity. The result in Sudan of the switch from cotton to food production was disastrous: exports of cotton fell and imports of capital equipment rose; and since, at the same time, the cost of fuel imports soared as a result of the oil price hike, despite the aid the deficit on the foreign balance of payments dropped out of control. In 1976 the IMF was called in.[13]

The IMF prescription was for the government to devalue the currency – for encouraging exports and reducing imports – to liberalize control over both foreign investment and local prices, especially those paid to the tenant cotton producers, and, finally, to make reductions in government expenditure. As a result of resistance from government officials, who did not believe that devaluation would have the desired effect, the IMF package was not implemented for two years. In 1978, however, Saudi Arabia, which had been supplying oil as aid, made the offer of further aid conditional on IMF policies being adhered to. For three years trade and payments were liberalized and the currency devalued four times – to a level one quarter of what it had been. But loans and aid were spent on increasing imports, mainly of consumer goods and fuel, amounting in all to 23 per cent of GNP, twice the level in 1978.[14]

Some of these increased imports into Sudan were the illegal fruits of corruption, but they reflected the increasingly unequal distribution of income and the spending power of the 'class of merchants, traders and commission men [who] in the post-independence period took over almost exclusive control of social and political power and thus of the state for their own ends'.[15] It was not until 1983 that the IMF proposed some control on imports of consumer goods. The increased imports were not balanced by any increase in exports. With the exception of sorghum, which benefited from Saudi Arabian subsidies, exports fell, the total stagnating at around 8 per cent of GNP. The IMF continued to provide stand-by support, but in 1982 the World Bank was called in to provide loans for agricultural rehabilitation, with the aim of reviving the production of export crops.[16]

The reason for declining export-crop production was the lack of incentive for Sudan's peasants to produce. Safwar Fanos, a Sudanese economist, commented that: 'Perhaps, the one positive policy of the IMF and World Bank in Sudan was to ask the government to pay tenants the international cotton prices converted to Sudanese pounds, using the . . . market rate . . . instead of the official rate,'[17] i.e. they got a better deal for their crops. Other policies recommended by the World Bank were ineffective or otiose. Aid to Sudan in the 1970s had been concentrated on irrigated agriculture; only 4 per cent had gone to growing rain-fed food crops.[18] The World Bank continued to put its emphasis on large-scale projects, particularly in the Gezira, with 80 per cent of investment devoted to 'the "modern" areas of the centre and north of the country . . . and 80–90% of agricultural research also supporting mechanized or irrigated farms'.[19]

There was no doubt that production in the Gezira was suffering from the high price of fuel and lack of spare parts. Some of the requirements of the World Bank were, however, mistaken, especially the replacement of 'joint accounts' (i.e. of the tenants with the government managers) by 'individual accounts' between each tenant and the scheme's management. The Bank wished to control inputs of fertilizer, et cetera and to divert their use from food crops to cotton; but the result was that the tenants had individually to carry the risks of reduced earnings, from falling prices or poor harvests, while still paying the government for their inputs. The government gained, but poor tenants after a bad year would not have the credit to buy inputs for the following year and would either run up debts or have to sell their tenancy rights to richer tenants. The more affluent, however, were not necessarily the more dedicated farmers.[20]

Cotton yields in the Gezira increased, but a landless peasantry grew and production outside the Gezira stagnated, so that overall cotton and other agricultural exports rose for a time and then fell away in the late 1980s. Other large-scale projects of the World Bank proved equally ineffectual. The areas of land under sugar and wheat were greatly increased and large-scale sugar mills and silos built, to meet growing urban needs.[21] For a long time the government maintained the wheat subsidy while ending subsidies on millet and sorghum, which are more drought-resistant cereal crops and are the standard diet of the rural people. When drought conditions returned in 1984–5, wheat had to be imported, with or without aid, in order to feed the urban population and also the one to two million refugees who were fleeing from the famine and fighting in the south to find refuge in temporary camps around Khartoum–Omdurman.[22]

The conclusions of the agronomists who have studied the Sudan are that the recommended export-led growth of the IMF and the World Bank has not occurred and that growth, while it may be 'a necessary condition for the alleviation of food insecurity', is not a sufficient condition if 'growth strategies are targeted mainly on larger producers in the modern sector'.

All accept that growth of irrigated or mechanized rain-fed agriculture increases agricultural production and therefore helps to lower prices; it also provides employment and incomes for poor people. All suggest, however, that the trickle-down strategy implicit in the growth model is inadequate as a solution to food security; and all recommend a poverty-oriented development strategy, focused largely on rural development in the traditional rain-fed sector . . .

[where growth] yields better consequences for the poor than growth in the modern irrigated or mechanized sectors.

'Similarly,' other experts conclude, 'the activity injections through the public utilities and construction have the most powerful income effects on the most food insecure urban groups.'[23]

Professor Al Abdel Gadir Ali, a Sudanese economist, has summed up his view of IMF and World Bank policies in Sudan as follows:

Over the period 1978–April 1985 the Sudan economy was managed to all intents and purposes by the IMF in collaboration with the World Bank, the two institutions experimenting with almost all kinds of structural adjustment measures. The end result of the IMF–World Bank management of the Sudan economy was a deepening economic crisis which in turn precipitated declining social welfare and increasing human misery.[24]

The result, he says, was the overthrow of the Nimeiri regime in the April uprising of the people in 1985. But the situation of Sudan only deteriorated thereafter, as the civil war intensified.

Hunger and Land Capacity

In their major study of hunger in the modern world, Drèze and Sen emphasize, as key factors in the creation of famines, the distribution both of food and of support for food production. It is not just that they found much food aid in Sudan going to those who needed it least but other aid policies actually counteracting peasants' food-growing capacities.[25] Famine, as distinct from hunger, is a crisis of livelihood rather than a crisis of food. A Save the Children Fund worker who was in Sudan throughout the famine years of 1984–7 wrote, 'People are quite prepared to put up with considerable degrees of hunger, in order to preserve seed for planting, cultivate their own fields or avoid having to sell an animal.'[26] But they must not lose all these resources and must, in the first place, either own or have access to such resources, which the landless peasant or migrant to the shanty town inevitably lacks.

The Chinese proverb, which the distinguished French authority on African agriculture, René Dumont, loves to quote: 'Give the people fish and they will not starve today; give them the means to catch fish and they will not starve for the rest of their lives,'[27] needs to be updated by adding: 'Give them fish and it may destroy their incentive to catch fish.' It is not, of course, only in Sudan, as we have already seen, that

imported grain sold at low prices to urban dwellers spoils the market for
local food producers.[28] Drèze and Sen quote a report on earlier disasters
claiming that: 'A shift from a "communal" to a "market" economy
does in general . . . mark a shift toward greater vulnerability to and
severity of famine.'[29] They go on to instance other Sahel countries
which did not suffer the same degree of famine conditions as Sudan in
1984–5, where the shift to a market economy had been less pronounced.[30] This is a finding of great importance.

One of the main elements in the creation of famine and of refugee
movements in the Sahel (as distinguished from normal migrations) is
the relative change in the prices of cereals and livestock, since these are
regularly exchanged between their respective producers. If cereal prices
rise, cattle have to be sold and increased numbers of animals coming up
for sale lead to falling stock prices. In famine conditions, with higher
animal mortality rates, herders are forced to sell younger males and
then even their reproductive stock to buy grain.[31] Timberlake claims:

There is little evidence that herds *permanently* degrade the dry Sahelian
grasslands, [but] there is considerable evidence that overgrazing damages it at
least temporarily over vast areas, so that carrying capacity drops quickly and
animals die of hunger rather than of thirst. The 1968–73 Sahel drought, for
example, killed hundreds of thousands of grazing animals. But it had no real
effect on rising livestock trends.[32]

The 1984–5 drought appears to have been more damaging, partly
because of the movement of refugees fleeing from the war who joined up
with the movement of herds, partly because of the neglect by governments of the basic needs of pastoralists. There have been many UN and
World Bank projects for land management, to rotate years of grazing
and fallow, and for group ranching, and they even include a grandiose
scheme entitled SOLAR (Stratification of Livestock in Arid Regions)
but 'the picture that emerges', as an American expert reports, 'is one of
almost unrelieved failure'.[33] And why should that be? The answer is
that there was no consultation with the pastoralists and no understanding of how they operate, and this was as true among local decision-
makers as among the foreign 'experts'. According to another American
consultant, speaking of ranching projects in the Sudano-Sahel region,
'with the exception of Mauritania in the Sahel and of Somalia in East
Africa, the ruling élites in these states are drawn from groups which are
not only not pastoral, but which have viewed pastoral people with
ambivalence at best, and often outright hostility.'[34]

Famine and War

The association of famine and war has a long history. In the apocalyptic revelation of St John, the four horsemen signifying conquest, war, famine and pestilence ride over the earth.[35] A British geographer remarked ironically in 1984, 'The only early-warning system you need of famine is lists of which governments are spending disproportionate amounts of their GNP on military activities: look at Ethiopia, Sudan, Chad, Angola and Mozambique.' And Lloyd Timberlake, after quoting his words, adds: 'The year 1984 saw massive amounts of grain shipped to Africa, but it was also the first year that the value of arms imported by Africa outstripped the value of imported grain.'[36]

It is a tragic fact that at least a half of all African countries in the 1980s had military governments. The supply of arms by the major industrialized powers to support their African clients and raw material suppliers is well documented.[37] It makes depressing reading. 'The single most potent force in the trade in arms to Africa,' according to *Arms for Africa*, 'has been the demand for them by African rulers.'[38] It is an African professor, writing in honour of the silver jubilee year of the Organization of African Unity, who has dug up this quotation for us; and he goes on to present us with three long tables of statistics, detailing the arms supplied to African governments from the USA, Western Europe, Eastern Europe, the USSR and China in the 1960s and 1970s. The tables would need to have been longer still to cover the 1980s. The resultant reductions in African government expenditure on health and education have been documented by the World Bank. In the Bank's report on *World Development, 1991* there is a list of twenty-five sub-Saharan African states which spent more than 2 per cent of their GNP on the military in 1987, and seven of these spent less than 2 per cent on health and education.[39]

It is inevitable that the finger of censure should be pointed at the governments in question. As Claude Aké has commented, writing about Nigeria:

When the military comes into government it cannot help acting like a fighting machine. As a government, it tends to think in terms of allies and enemies, patriots and subversives ... Military rule displaces not only democracy but also participation and replaces them with legitimation by force ... military rule is often a confusion of discipline and arbitrariness; the arbitrariness arises from the dissociation of power from accountability and the heavy emphasis on obedience.[40]

Such an attitude of mind sits easily with commands that come from a recognized higher authority, which expects the conditions of aid to be dutifully fulfilled. It is an ironic fact that military regimes have been more prepared than less authoritarian regimes to implement the requirements of the IMF and the World Bank.[41] A neo-liberal economist, who worked in the World Bank's research department in the early 1980s, is quoted as having suggested that

a courageous, ruthless and perhaps undemocratic government is required to ride roughshod over ... newly-created special interest groups. Democratic governments are seen as the source of irrational economic policies forced on them by their need to placate competitive interest groups.[42]

A series of correlations drawn up by another World Bank economist at the end of the 1980s showed no evidence in the African countries he studied to suggest that the introduction of structural adjustment policies facilitated a transition to more pluralistic and democratic systems of government. It was found that, if existing per capita income was already high, this was associated with both high government spending and a high degree of political pluralism.[43]

In summarizing the argument about the relation between hunger and war, Drèze and Sen take an even-handed approach which allows for the influence of forces outside of Africa itself in determining the issue:

Angola, Chad, Ethiopia, Mozambique, Somalia, Sudan, and many other countries have been transformed to a greater or lesser extent into veritable battlefields. Quite a few of these wars have been directly or indirectly associated with global conflicts and the cold war, with the African governments falling in line with one international side or another. The big powers have also been remarkably tolerant of regimes on their respective sides despite persistent violations of the very principles of democracy and socialism on behalf of which the big powers allegedly wage their respective battles. It is a story in which there is little honour – either locally or in the distant capitals from which many international conflicts have been pursued with such vigour and lethal arms pushed with such energetic cunning.[44]

Armed Intervention from Outside

The arming of African regimes by the industrial powers has had both a strategic and an economic rationale. The chief example was South Africa's military engagement in occupying or destabilizing countries on her borders and in the so-called front-line states, which supported the opposition to the apartheid regime in South Africa. These southern African states, and especially Angola and Namibia, also contain rich mineral resources, in which South African companies have investments.[45] The losses sustained by the front-line states as a result of South Africa's destabilizing policies have been estimated at US$ 10 billion in the five years 1980–85, more than all the foreign aid these states received in this period.[46]

For the same mix of reasons, the hideous regime of Mobutu was established and sustained by the United States in Zaire – as a rich source of copper and as a base for the rebel armies in Angola. 'There is all the pressure in the world for capitalist governments to support Zaire's economy,'[47] was the judgement in 1977 of Dr Irving Friedman, senior vice-president of Citibank, who had held previous positions in the IMF and World Bank. In that year Dr Friedman negotiated on behalf of thirteen leading US banks to raise '$250 millions in new money [which] would not be used to repay old debt, but would be used to develop the nation's [Zaire's] mineral resources'. Doubts had been raised among the creditors for Zaire's vast debts about the creditworthiness of the Mobutu regime, but Dr Friedman was able to answer for that:

any country that has lost its creditworthiness has the ability within itself to restore it ... I had had a long relationship with Zaire before coming to Citibank, so I was able to approach [Zairean central bank] Governor Sambwa as a friend, on an informal basis.[48]

Other countries in southern Africa were not so lucky to have such a friend. Throughout the 1980s Zaire received exceptional grace periods for repayment and approval of further loans, and when, in 1987, an unprecedented extension of repayment terms was granted to Zaire by the Paris Club, it was made clear that the same terms would not be extended to other debtor countries.[49]

The case of Angola parallels that of Zaire. When, in September of 1992, a left-wing government was duly elected in Angola under the watchful eye of UN observers, the US government decided to give it formal recognition. The rebel forces of UNITA, financed and armed by South Africa, as well as by the USA, refused to accept the result and continued to challenge the government's rule in large parts of the country. By the end of 1994, Zaire remained a base for Angolan rebel movements, and, despite growing Western disenchantment, Mobutu survived local attempts to unseat him as Zaire's dictator.[50] The rich reserves of oil in Angola remain a prize to be held on to by the giant oil companies, while two million Angolans are threatened by hunger, poor crops and disease as a result of rebel military activity.[51]

The Gulf War should have given warning enough to African governments of the continuing military–economic importance of oil supplies. The massive intervention of military might by the industrialized powers against Saddam Hussein together with US military intervention in Somalia perhaps indicate what the future may have in store for Africa. In world economic relations the continent may be increasingly marginalized, but, where a major economic or political interest of the industrialized powers requires it – the protection of oil supplies, of essential mineral production or of a naval or military base – crisis management will take a particularly violent form.

The results of the Gulf War were a serious reduction of income for African states, from lost remittances of African workers in Kuwait, from costs of the resettlement of returning workers, from lost tourism and export markets and from the raised price of oil imports. The total losses have been conservatively estimated at an average 2 per cent of the national product and 10 per cent of the export earnings for fifteen sub-Saharan African countries, with Sudan suffering a loss of some 3 per cent of GNP and 50 per cent of exports.[52] Sudanese officials put the figures much higher, at a level equal to the whole value of Sudan's annual export earnings.[53] Of the African countries affected, only Egypt received any realistic compensation – and this was for her contribution to rallying Islamic support for the attack on Iraq. In addition to compensation of $5 billion towards estimated losses of about that amount, Egypt had $20 billion of debt forgiven. Sudan backed the wrong side and was penalized, but, while the participants in the allied invasion from industrialized countries including the USA received massive subsidies, sub-Saharan African countries received minimal sums. These mainly comprised the advancing of promised loans from the World Bank for those countries which had structural adjustment programmes.[54]

In the TNI study, *The Debt Boomerang*, the links connecting outbreaks of violence and civil war with the continuing drain of debt and the failure of the IMF/World Bank development model are convincingly demonstrated. But the authors of *The Debt Boomerang* are altogether too sanguine in their expectation that fear of war in Africa, spreading via terrorism and refugees to Europe, will persuade governments of industrialized countries to forgive the debts of the least developed African countries. 'To do nothing,' the TNI team concludes, 'to remove the conditions which create war and brutality in the third world is, very simply, to risk waking up to find that war and brutality have, like all boomerangs, come home.'[55] Boomerangs are, however, designed to hit their target before they come home.

Fear is not perhaps the best motive for taking a new approach to Africa's problems. Fear is a bad guide to action except in the first moment of response to danger. Fear leads to continuing defensiveness against retaliation, to beggar-my-neighbour actions, a fortress mentality, fascist-type regimes and ethnic cleansing. Hope is a better guide in the longer run, hope that builds on confidence in human beings' capacity to cooperate as well as to compete, hope that is nourished by the ability to listen to what people themselves are saying about their condition and how they might improve it. To such voices the peoples of Africa are now calling us to turn our attention and this we must do after the sorry failures of those from outside Africa who offered solutions to Africa's problems based only on outside experience and on outside interests.

TABLE 6.1 African Countries' Foreign Debt Ratios, 1980 and 1988–91

Countries ranked by debt service/export ratio	Outstanding debt % of GNP		Debt service % of exports of goods and services	
	1980	1988–91	1980	1988–91
Averages				
North Africa	38	66	16	34
Sub-Saharan	21	88	9	25
Above average debt service/export ratio, 1988–91				
1 Algeria	38	67	28	67
2 Guinea Bissau	99	276	40	66
3 Uganda	48	84	5	66
4 Côte d'Ivoire	48	150	25	60
5 Somalia	124	235	10	47
6 Madagascar	26	131	13	45
7 Burundi	16	59	8	43
8 Ghana	28	60	7	43
9 Egypt	64	107	23	37
10 Sudan	59	103	10	37
11 Morocco	41	83	40	36
12 Niger	24	69	14	36
13 Ethiopia	17	118	6	35
14 Congo	75	153	17	34
15 Kenya	31	70	16	34
16 Zaire	30	112	18	33
17 Mozambique	18	309	11	33
18 Tanzania	34	151	15	30
19 Senegal	32	76	20	29
20 Nigeria	6	87	4	28
21 Malawi	66	88	22	28
22 Cameroon	31	43	12	27
23 Mauritania	112	191	15	27
24 Djibouti	9	45	3	26
25 Guinea	68	85	23	26
26 Rwanda	14	36	2	25
Below average debt/export ratio, but greater than GNP				
27 Zambia	53	135	19	24
28 Mali	43	106	6	19
29 São Tomé	–	270	–	17
30 Gambia	53	118	3	17
31 Liberia	50	150	7	14
32 Equ. Guinea	(25)	152	12	14
33 Sierra Leone	36	(100)	16	12

TABLE 6.1 *continued*

Below average debt but evidence of major conflict

Angola, Burkina Faso, Chad, Comoros, Lesotho, Namibia, Togo, Zimbabwe

Low debt: no evidence of major conflict

Benin, Botswana, Cape Verde, Central African Republic, Gabon, Libya, Mauritius, Namibia, Réunion, Seychelles, Swaziland, Tunisia

Notes: figures in brackets are for Equatorial Guinea 1975 and for Sierra Leone 1980. Figures for São Tomé not available for 1980 or 1975.

Source: UNCTAD *Handbok of International Trade and Development Statistics, 1993*, Table 5.14. For evidence of conflict see text and Dan Smith 'Conflict and War' in Susan George, *The Debt Boomerang*, Pluto Press, 1992, Tables 6.1 and 6.2.

PART II

WHAT AFRICANS ARE SEEKING

In the absence of *credible alternative visions*, prevailing forecasts about Africa's future, extrapolated from current trends and conventional analysis, but leaving no scope for unanticipated events, could become self-fulfilling prophecies.

Chinua Achebe, et al. (eds), *Beyond Hunger in Africa: Africa 2057 – Conventional Wisdom and an African Vision*, Nairobi, 1990 and James Currey, 1991.

CHAPTER 7

Africa Must Unite: The Alternative Vision

The organization shall have the following purposes:
    (a) to promote the unity and solidarity of the African states;
    (b) to coordinate and intensify their cooperation and efforts to achieve
a better life for the peoples of Africa;
    (c) to defend their sovereignty, their territorial integrity and
independence;
    (d) to eradicate all forms of colonialism from Africa.

> From Article II. (1) of the *Charter of Unity* of the Organization of African
> Unity, signed at Addis Ababa, 25 May 1963.

'Africa must unite' was the impassioned cry of Kwame Nkrumah, 'or perish!'[1] With that vision before their eyes, the leaders of Africa's peoples, some free and some still under colonial rule, met in Addis Ababa in May of 1963 and founded the Organization of African Unity (OAU) and signed a Charter of Unity, which included the commitments listed at the head of this chapter. A month before this meeting, there had assembled in London a gathering of delegates from twenty-six African student unions in Europe and Africa. The resolutions of this student assembly had included the demand for 'a political constitution' for Africa, with a 'Pan-African Parliament, a Pan-African Executive and Public Service ... a Pan-African Army under joint high command'.[2]

The Pan-African ideal, nurtured by black Americans like W.E.B. Du Bois ever since the first Pan-African Congress held in the United States in 1900, had struck a deep chord, especially among Africans living outside Africa.[3] Amilcar Cabral once suggested that emphasis on the cultural unity of all Africans in expressions of Pan-Africanism or *négritude*, and equally in black Americans' insistence on their African 'roots', revealed their sense of loss of cultural identity. It was an ambiguous claim, because it left them without any specific cultural homeland.[4] Most of the students who met in London were to hold high office in the newly independent states of Africa over the years to follow. They did not entirely forget their youthful enthusiasm when they returned to their homes, but they had to forge links there with their own people.

Nkrumah had been the leading spirit in creating the Organization of African Unity, with the enthusiastic support of many of those students. Yet, in a collection of essays in honour of Nkrumah, twenty-five years later, the editor, Kwesi Krafona, felt bound to declare that, 'in the silver jubilee year of the OAU, there is nothing to celebrate, [nothing] but misery to harvest'.[5] What had happened?

Nkrumah's warning at the OAU's formation had come true.

To go it alone will limit our horizons, curtail our expectations, and threaten our liberty . . . Unless we meet the obvious and very powerful neo-colonialists' threats with a united African front, based upon a common economic and defence policy, the strategy will be to pick us off and destroy us one by one.[6]

Whether or not we call the policies of the IMF and World Bank neo-colonialist, the fact is that these policies have treated each of the fifty-six individual African states in isolation. No support has been given for regional, let alone continental, economic cooperation. And the equally unpalatable fact is that the African leaders have come to prefer it that way. The OAU charter of 1963 accepted the colonial borders as the natural boundaries of the newly independent nations. They have not been changed since; and the commitment in the Charter to coordination and intensified cooperation has rarely been honoured.[7]

Unity in Diversity

The Charter of Unity of 1963 was a long-term commitment of Africa's new leaders to common defence of the continent – economic, political and military – but it was to be a unity of diverse nation-states. Nkrumah was convinced that political unity was the only defence against the continued exploitation by outside powers of Africa's rich resources.

The foreign firms who exploit our resources long ago saw the strength to be gained by acting on a Pan-African scale . . . The only effective way to challenge this economic empire and to recover full possession of our heritage, is for us also to act on a Pan-African basis through a Union government.[8]

This quotation comes from Kwame Nkrumah's book published in England in 1965, *Neo-Colonialism: The Last Stage of Imperialism*. In it he reiterated the declaration he had himself drafted at the Pan-African Congress held twenty years earlier in Manchester, England.[9] Yet, in the years between, Nkrumah had returned from Europe and North America to his native Ghana. There, he accepted the British and French model of territorial decolonization state by state and thereby in effect the balkanization of Africa. He had rejected a merger with Guinea and Mali when Ahmed Sékou Touré, the nationalist leader of Guinea, the first state to break away from the French empire, had proposed it.[10] The seduction of nation and nation-state proved too strong.

In a prophetic passage in his *Journey to a War*, the English poet, W.H. Auden, had written in 1939 of the allure of state power:

> By wire and wireless, in a score of bad translations,
> They gave their simple message to the world of man:
> Man can have Unity if Man will give up Freedom.
> The State is real, the Individual is wicked;
> Violence shall synchronise your movements like a tune,
> And terror like a frost shall halt the flood of thinking.[11]

Nkrumah was not, of course, the only one to believe that freedom would come through the nation-state. Sir Abubakar Tafawa Balewa, prime minister of Nigeria, was quick to respond in 1963 to talk of a United States of Africa: 'Oh surely, it is very premature to start talking about anything like that. Nigeria has not the slightest intention of surrendering her sovereignty, no sooner than she gained independence, to anyone else, including other Western African countries.'[12] This was a clear dig at Ghana and Nkrumah.

There were continuing deep divisions between the African nation-states in their attitudes to the ex-colonial powers, the expatriate companies and to regional groupings.[13] There was the division of language between anglophone, francophone, lusophone and Arabic Africa, with ties respectively to British, French, Portuguese and Levantine companies, and there was southern Africa, with even closer ties to South African companies.[14] There were deeper divisions still between those states which were in effect client states of United States or European capital and those which received the support of the Soviet Union, some of them self-styled Marxist states. Massive supplies of arms were provided on either side and even listed in an OAU report.[15] And these divisions were a running sore right into the late 1980s and early 1990s, with the example of US support for a beleaguered Mobutu in Zaire[16] and continuing commitment on the other side, at least until 1989, to the role of 'Soviet support for African revolutionaries and progressives'.[17]

Even to distinguish the differences in the official language of the states – whether English, French, Arabic, or Portuguese or Spanish – and the differences between Marxist and non-Marxist states does not begin to encompass the full diversity of Africa's nation-states. Apart from Hausa, Swahili and Yoruba, which are spoken by very large numbers of Africans, there are over a thousand separate African languages, some of them recognized as official languages in their nation-states. Most are members of the four main language families in Africa, Afro-Asiatic in the north and north-east, Nilo-Saharan around the Nile valley, Niger-Congo in the catchment areas of the two great rivers, including Bantu in central, southern and eastern Africa, and Khoisan in the south. In addition, there are many hundreds of local dialects.[18]

It is an important fact about Africans that, unlike Europeans or Chinese, the majority can speak at least two languages – French or English, Portuguese or Arabic – *and* their mother tongue. This fact implies a much greater capacity for unity than the diversity of the tongues would suggest, although it also emphasizes the importance of the four main groupings based on *non*-African languages and the hegemony of *non*-African over native languages. This continuing cultural imperialism remains a major obstacle to African unity and to indigenous African political and economic initiatives. It serves, in particular, to emphasize the separation of the educated élite from the African masses.

Amilcar Cabral, the revolutionary leader of the liberation of Guinea Bissau from Portuguese rule, recognized better than most the ambiguous influence of European culture on the African middle classes – both attracting and repelling. But he instanced the tiny proportion of Africans who were assimilated (0.3 per cent of the population, he claims, in his native Guinea Bissau) after 500 years of Portuguese 'civilizing presence' as proof of 'the indestructibility of cultural resistance to foreign rule by the mass of the people'.[19] This important insight should not be underestimated in any attempt to comprehend the role of nations and ethnic groupings in Africa's post-colonial development.

The distinction between Marxist and non-Marxist is not much more helpful than language differences in characterizing the political typology of African states. The representatives of many of those which called themselves Marxist states attended the meetings of *non-aligned* countries in Lusaka in 1970 and they continued to do so when the meetings were held in Georgetown in 1972 and Algiers in 1973 and subsequently every three years, as did Liberia and Zaire, which were firmly committed to the United States.[20] Table 7.1 reveals this fact and also the distinction which can be made between states which had single-party rule and those with multiparty polities.

By no means all those states with single-party rule are or were Marxist. They ranged, moreover, from despotic rule through varying degrees of authoritarianism and tolerance of opposition. A majority of African states have at one time or another in the three decades since their independence been brought under military rule, and many still are. In some but not all cases, military rule is associated with the dominance of one party. Multiparty rule itself does not necessarily bear much resemblance to that adopted in most European countries. It may better be described as populist rather than pluralist. The judgement of the experts is that only three states – Botswana, the Gambia (until 1994) and Mauritius – can be said to have 'retained competitive multi-party systems since achieving independence'.[21] And they are amongst the very smallest on the continent.

Growing Authoritarianism of the Nation-states

One characteristic almost all African states had in common – and it was not conducive to the building of unity – was that within their own state boundaries governments moved steadily away from democracy towards authoritarianism. The shift began in the 1960s as part of the process of nation-building in states with deep internal ethnic and communal divisions, and as a result of the apparent need for a strong central state to achieve economic modernization. By the 1970s many states which had semi-competitive one-party systems, like Kenya, Tanzania and Zambia, became increasingly authoritarian. The scope for opposition was reduced and the independence of cooperatives, trade unions and other interest groups was curbed. Ruling parties became entrenched in the system of clientelism.[22]

The result of this system of ethnic privilege has been an unmitigated disaster for the African people. In the words of Fantu Cheru, an Ethiopian-born, American professor: 'The virtually unlimited power of those at the top has allowed them to plunder the natural riches of their country and to amass great fortunes.'[23]

Some of the reasons for this evolution towards authoritarianism must lie in the corruption of power and the absolute corruption of absolute power. A more generous explanation may undoubtedly be found in the ethnic diversity and sometimes in the long-standing mutual hostility of the different populations gathered together within the old colonial state boundaries. For this resulted in uncontrollable competition for political dominance and thus in outbreaks of fighting and actual civil war. Much of the reason, however, must be sought in the steadily worsening economic situation resulting from the decline in world prices for African products and the rising burden of foreign debt. Outside forces – in the shape of the ex-colonial powers, the USA, the USSR and South Africa – aided and abetted the maintenance of power by authoritarian regimes even to the extent of assisting them to defeat popular insurrections against arbitrary rule. The motivation for such intervention was either their interest in continuing the exploitation by foreign companies of Africa's resources or, in the Soviets' case, their perceived need for naval bases in Africa as part of their claim to global power.[24]

From the moment of independence, then, Africa's new leaders embarked upon the task of nation-building within the confines of the old colonial states. Any merging of these would at once undermine the base of their political power and privileges. But for many of them this insularity was reinforced by the much stronger bonds that they enjoyed with their one-time colonial masters than any they experienced with their next-door neighbours. 'These élite groups,' the same Ethiopian professor was to declare, 'will not support regionalism and South–South cooperation . . . because they are aligned economically and politically with the First World.'[25] This, in effect, meant continuing the colonial role of each individual African country as a supplier of one or more primary products for the factories of the industrialized lands.

The rhetoric from the African nationalists was different, but the outcome was the same as under the rule of the European colonial powers. Despite the fact that most African states comprise two or more ethnic groups, whose presence is not confined to that state, the boundaries were adhered to and ethnic differences to some extent accommodated. In most countries, according to Saadia Touval, 'norms and procedures [were developed] enabling the maintenance of an ethnic balance within the political and administrative institutions'. Where these failed, as in Sudan and Ethiopia, wars broke out and secession occurred. There were, moreover, widespread border disputes – in the cases of Niger, Benin, Mali, Burkina Faso, Libya and Chad as well as in the better-known cases of the Biafran secession and the Eritrean and Somali wars. The OAU held to its charter that borders were sacrosanct and its attempts at mediation generally failed. 'Maintenance of the status quo,' Saadia Touval was forced to recognize, 'came to be associated with the self-preservation of the state. It was feared that to grant any group or region the right to secede, would stimulate secession demands from others and thus be conducive to disintegration of the state.'[26] It was for this reason that Eritrea's struggle for independence from Ethiopia was never recognized by the OAU.

State-centred Government

The forms of government which African rulers have adopted in tackling their economic problems have not been all the same, but they shared one general characteristic: they approached economic activity as a state-centred operation and not a society-centred affair. The reasons for this are clear. Their power depended in the first instance on taking control of the natural resources which had been developed. If they were agricultural resources, the marketing boards inherited from colonial rule provided access to these. If they were mineral resources, then joint state–transnational company ventures could be established with the mining concerns of the ex-colonial powers. Once the new rulers had the necessary resources under their control, the task of government consisted, as it had the world over from time immemorial, in allocating incomes and jobs in the first place to supporters, but with something to spare to pacify rival groups. Parliamentary assemblies gave the opportunity for offering prestige and place without real power.

In a wide-ranging review of the literature on African governance, two researchers from the British Overseas Development Institute (ODI) in 1991–2 found little evidence of a correlation between economic success and different political systems. The sheer size of the state sector appeared to be 'negatively correlated with growth';[27] and this was a basic assumption in the World Bank's requirement from loan recipients, that public spending should be cut back. But other research by one World Bank expert suggested that it mattered very much what form the state's expenditure took. Expenditure on education and health appeared to be conducive to growth; subsidies, whether on food or on local consumer goods, by contrast, had a negative effect.[28]

The ODI researchers discovered what they saw as an important distinction among potential beneficiaries of state expenditure between 'ethnic/regional groups' and the 'class interests' of employers and trade unions. They saw this in part as a rural/urban divide.[29] They took much of their evidence from an American study, *State and Society in Africa*:

The main focus of ethno-regional interest groupings tends to be distribution of services such as health care, education, transport and communication, investment, targeted development funds and civil service recruitment. The economic/class interest groups are more likely to focus on tax policy, credit lines, subsidies, and protection.[30]

The form of patronage most available to governments was the gift of jobs – in the public service and in parastatal bodies dealing with imports and exports. As the resources at government disposal declined with the falling value of Africa's crops and minerals in world markets, competition sharpened. It was not surprising that the pressures of urban groups, and especially those nearest to the centres of power, should come to predominate. But among these groups there were many separate interests, which became more clearly identifiable when World Bank policies began to bite. The urban masses might get cheap imported bread grains, but protected jobs in government and industry for the middle classes disappeared and so did the overvalued currency exchange rate which allowed the élite to maintain their purchases of European consumer goods and to invest profitably outside Africa.[31]

Structural Adjustment, Liberalization and the Elites

African governments one by one accepted the IMF and World Bank conditions for loans and other financial support, because they had allowed other alternatives to go by default. Whatever their apparent differences, these governments shared two common failures. The first was the failure to nourish a pluralist society in which alternative policies could be discussed and criticisms raised against misconceived enterprises before they collapsed. The second was the failure to create a technocratic civil service capable of challenging governments and designing economic policies. These were needed not only to rescue collapsing economies but to discover forms of organization – both regional and sub-regional – which would give some united strength to a disintegrating continent.

The civil service in most African states is not a bureaucracy in any sense of a class independent of state power. The dominant class in Africa is a state élite of politicians and civil servants, which has 'used state power to acquire capital and resources'.[32] One American scholar in the 1960s with some percipience described it as a 'bureaucratic gentry'.[33] The absence of a landed gentry, even of any organization of large-scale farmers, other than the white settlers of Kenya, Rhodesia or

Mozambique, combined with the slow growth of an indigenous industrial bourgeoisie to present no challenge to an élite based on commercial activity and on the rent from the control of exports.

The attempt by the World Bank to cut back state power in Africa and encourage market forces had thus the result only of creating confusion and anarchy, because, while the power of the old rentier élite was undermined, there was no class of large farmers or of local industrialists to create a new centre of power on the basis of a free market. The 'retreat of the state' could in time make space for new forms of association among groups previously excluded from power. This could well involve all those women and both rural and urban households who, excluded from the formal economy, have taken refuge and found a living in the informal economy. Opening up of this space may prove to have been the most valuable contribution the World Bank has made to Africa, but outside support, as will be shown later, is needed to assist such development from the grass roots.[34]

The first result of the conjuncture of a worsening economic climate and the erosion of living standards with the disintegrative effects of the World Bank's policies was the turmoil of 1990. An almost universal explosion took place throughout the continent in challenges being made everywhere to the continuation of despotic and single-party rule. Table 7.1 reveals that most states with single-party rule prior to 1990 had either moved to multiparty rule during the early 1990s, or else the move had been attempted and the issue was in doubt. The ODI research reaches a clear conclusion:

Internal pressures for political reform have been of paramount importance in promoting a process of political liberalization in Africa ... Opposition ... movements are primarily urban-based and represent a coalition of interests in civil society. Students, trade unionists, intellectuals and professional organizations (principally lawyers and teachers) have been in the forefront of protest.[35]

Until these groups can find a common cause with the 'forgotten Africans' in the rural areas and the urban underground economy, the sustainability of the current reforms must be questioned. The World Bank should not take all the credit. Reform by African leaders from above had started prior to the intervention of the IMF and the World Bank, and was only taken up more strongly as World Bank policies failed.

There were three or four lifelines that African leaders could grasp in the approaching deluge. They could begin to work out policies which a united Africa might pursue in a long-term haul; they could begin building sub-regional blocs which, short of actual federation, might buttress their position as representatives of nation-states; they could work together to raise the prices of their export commodities in world markets; and they could seek to incorporate into their own structures the movements of protest.[36]

The Organization of African Unity

Until 1990 all of Africa's leaders saw development as something to be achieved from the top downwards and this is how the workings of the Organization for African Unity must be understood.[37] While the charter of the OAU accepted the colonial boundaries of the African states, the violence and the killing in almost all parts of the continent that have marred the last three decades of Africa's history cannot, however, be laid at the door of the OAU and its charter, without recalling how the continent was divided up into artificial states under colonial rule. It is even more important to remember that, where the burden of foreign debt was not overwhelming, African countries have been able to settle their internal differences in relative peace. Economic cooperation, if not on a continental scale at least on a regional basis, offered a clear alternative to dependence on the World Bank; but for long it was not the path that was taken.

After the OAU was founded the African heads of state met regularly every year at each other's smart new capitals. They talked and dined and agreed to protest about the surviving areas of colonial rule in the continent, including the apartheid regime in South Africa. Their foreign, finance and other ministers met between heads of state meetings to discuss common problems and to settle disputes. The OAU was not the decision-making African parliament for which Nkrumah had once hoped, but a secretariat *was* created and also an African Development Bank with a capital equivalent to US$ 2 billion by 1980 and an African Development Fund.

Robert Gardiner, the Ghanaian-born, first executive secretary of the UN Economic Commission for Africa (ECA), regarded the setting up of the Bank as the single most important achievement of his ten years at the ECA.[38] The sums supplied for financing projects were not large, even after the Bank opened its membership to non-African countries in 1982. But the Development Bank continued to provide support for the projects of small-scale businesses and joint ventures between states, which the World Bank persistently neglected. The main limitation on the use of the Development Bank's funds was the lack of hard currency, which is what most African countries were short of, to service their debts and maintain imports of oil and other inputs for their industries. When the Bank's total lending had reached the equivalent of just over US$ 2 billion in 1988, Africa's hard currency debts were approaching US$ 200 billion.[39]

By tying themselves to the markets and sources of manufactures in the lands of their old colonial masters, the new nationalist African leaders failed to develop trading links either with each other or with the rest of the non-industrialized world. Some African leaders had in the 1960s sought to develop economic relations among the non-aligned states. Nkrumah had believed in a wider non-aligned 'third force' as well as in African unity. The beginnings of planned trade exchanges among the non-aligned states had already been established in the 1960s, but one by one the populist regimes of the non-aligned bloc had fallen to internal coups supported by external forces.[40] Nkrumah, Sékou Touré and Ben Bella were the African non-aligned leaders who fell in this way. It was not until 1980 that the OAU became convinced that the situation had deteriorated so far that some common economic measures were required. As a result, what became the Lagos Plan of Action was discussed, first by the fifty or so planning ministers meeting in Monrovia in 1979, and then agreed upon by the OAU heads of state meeting in Lagos the next year.

The Lagos Plan of Action

The need for common action after 1979 arose more from anxiety among African governments at the withering away of private foreign investment and overseas development assistance for Africa than from any conviction about the need for increased self-reliance. One sympathetic critic of the OAU suggested that nothing but 'recognition that their own legitimacy was at stake', after so many failed programmes designed to deliver what had been promised to the people on independence, had brought Africa's leaders to the point of signing.[41]

The analysis and programme advanced at Lagos were none the less important recognition of the need for an African alternative to what had up till then been offered from outside. Some of the ministers present may have regarded the exercise as largely rhetorical; others probably saw the proposals as a warning to their masters of what would happen if aid was not stepped up. If that was the intention, it was certainly successful. The Berg Report from the World Bank followed immediately after, offering a clear alternative to African joint action. There was a promise to individual African governments of further aid – conditional on internal reforms. These reforms were to make it possible to re-establish 'export-led growth through increased African integration into the world capitalist system', as Fantu Cheru put it.[42] The Lagos Plan was pre-empted but just to have presented an alternative vision at Lagos, based upon an African perspective, became an important benchmark for future discussion of African development between African governments and outside bodies, whether donors, investors or international institutions.

The Lagos Plan of Action was deliberately presented as a long-term plan, committing members to nothing less than the establishment by the year 2000 of an 'African Economic Community, so as to ensure the economic, social and cultural integration of our continent'.[43] Philip Ndegwa, economic adviser to the president of Kenya in 1979 and later governor of the Central Bank of Kenya, commented in a remarkable understatement that among the African countries there did 'indeed appear to be general acceptance of the fact that weaknesses exist, and that alternative strategies are necessary'.[44]

The long-term objectives of the Plan have been summarized by Onimode as:

* achievement of regional food self-sufficiency through domestic food production – not just food security that can be achieved through volatile food aid and food imports;
* satisfaction of critical needs for food, safe drinking water, clothing, housing, health care, education and transport;
* elimination or alleviation of poverty; and
* achievement of effective regional integration through national and collective self-reliance.[45]

At the same time, the Plan emphasized that there was to be less dependence on traditional exports and markets. The global strategies offered from the North, far from improving Africa's economy, had contributed to stagnation and crisis; the exploitation of the colonial era had been continued by 'external forces'.[46] Expanding exports of raw materials at declining prices would only perpetuate the decades of dependence. Foreign aid and external trade were not to be rejected, but to be greatly reduced to the level of a supplement to Africa's own efforts towards economic and political liberation. Dependence on food imports in particular was to be ended. The achievement of a major shift of resources into agriculture was given high prominence.

At the root of the food problems in Africa, is the fact that Member States have not usually accorded the necessary priority to agriculture, both in the allocation of resources and in giving sufficient attention to policies for the promotion of productivity and improvement of rural life.[47]

It was a bold statement for African governments to make, and it was important that the self-criticism was made, but the Plan itself was a good deal stronger on principles than on practical ways to implement them. As two American experts commented, the planners 'simply specify a destination for Africa, but provide only a sketchy outline of the directions for getting there'.[48] In the event, Africa's leaders did little or nothing to implement the Lagos Plan until the 1984 drought and famine revealed their negligence and many African governments found themselves facing food riots and even armed resistance. Something had by then to be done urgently to combat drought and desertification.

In 1986 the OAU adopted Africa's Priority Programme for Economic Recovery (APPER) but this time, while African governments acknowledged their mistakes and emphasized the need to pursue self-reliant strategies, and for the first time recognized officially the important role of women in food production, many of them had already turned individually to the World Bank for support and agreed to programmes of structural adjustment. The measures proposed to increase food output and peasant productivity and generally to strengthen the agricultural sector came to be increasingly those recommended by the World Bank's advisers, although many of these measures had already been shown to be the very cause of Africa's food crisis.[49]

The Bank's policies for improving Africa's agricultural performance included in particular the raising of prices paid to farmers for export crops and for food imported for the towns (e.g. wheat and maize, which were competing with the locally cultivated food crops, like millet and sorghum); the reduction of farm subsidies, including fertilizer subsidies, although intensive use of 'improved input packages' was recommended; and a much increased number of irrigation schemes to be initiated. From the African side, despite the rhetoric about self-reliance and technical and financial support for small farmers, there were no proposals in the Lagos Plan or in APPER for a major shift of resource allocations towards agriculture or of any involvement of the grass-roots village associations, cooperatives and other collective groups in determining how policies might be applied, let alone in making decisions on priorities or crafting the reports for the OAU.[50]

When the OAU prepared its submission to the UN General

Assembly's Special Session on Africa in 1986, which was adopted as the UN Programme of Action for African Economic Recovery and Development, 1986–90 (UNPAAERD), even the rhetoric of partial delinking from dependence on 'external forces' was dropped and the aim of regional self-sufficiency was relegated to the long term.[51] This was unfortunate because one of the major strengths of the Lagos Plan of Action had lain in its elaboration of 'wide-ranging policies for regional and sub-regional cooperation among African countries on the basis of a planned programme of drastic reduction of Africa's external dependence'.[52] These were to include expansion of intra-African trade, exchange of industrial products, sharing of technological data, common training and research programmes and joint ventures to improve intra-African transport and communications, such as the Trans-African Highway. Such measures would have made possible some integrative planning at regional and sub-regional level and the advance to collective self-reliance of African countries, at least in food supplies. But, all this was lost in the mad rush of the several nation-states for aid from the IMF and World Bank.

TABLE 7.1 African States Political Orientation, 1970s/1990s

Colony of	Country	Non-aligned, or attended Lusaka	Group of 77, 96* or later**	Onetime 'Marxist' states	Type of rule 70s/90s
	North Africa				
F	Algeria	yes	yes	no	one/?
F	Libya	yes	yes	no	despot
F	Morocco	yes	yes	no	despot/?
GB	Egypt	no	no	no	multi
F	Tunisia	yes	yes	no	one
	Sub-Saharan Africa				
P	Angola	guest	no	yes	one/war
F	Benin	no	no	yes/no	mil/multi
GB	Botswana	yes	yes*	no	multi
F	Burkina Faso	no	yes	yes	mil/multi
G/B	Burundi	yes	yes	no	mil/one
G/F/GB	Cameroon	yes	yes	no	one/multi
P	Cape Verde	no	no	yes	one/?
F	CAR	yes	yes	no	despot
F	Chad	yes	yes	no	mil/?
F	Comoros	guest	no	no	multi
F	Congo	yes	yes	yes	one/multi
F	Côte d'Ivoire	no	yes	no	one/multi
F	Djibouti	no	no	no	one
S	Equ. Guinea	yes	yes*	no	mil/?
I	Ethiopia	yes	yes	yes	mil/multi
F	Gabon	yes	yes	no	one/multi
GB	Gambia	yes	yes	no	multi
GB	Ghana	yes	yes	no	mil/multi
F	Guinea	yes	yes	yes	mil/multi
P	Bissau	no	no	yes	one/multi
GB	Kenya	yes	yes	no	one/multi
GB	Lesotho	yes	yes*	no	mil/?
US	Liberia	yes	yes	no	mil/war
F	Madagascar	no	yes	yes	one/multi
GB	Malawi	no	yes*	no	despot/multi
F	Mali	yes	yes	yes	mil/multi
F	Mauritania	yes	yes	no	mil/?
GB	Mauritius	no	yes*	no	multi
P	Mozambique	guest	yes**	yes	one/multi
G/SA	Namibia	no	no	no	–/multi
F	Niger	no	yes	no	mil/multi
GB	Nigeria	yes	yes	no	mil
F	Réunion	no	no	no	Fr. départ.
G/B	Rwanda	yes	yes	no	mil
P	São Tomé	no	no	yes	multi/?
F	Senegal	yes	yes	no	one/multi

TABLE 7.1 *continued*

Colony of	Country	Non-aligned, or attended Lusaka	Group of 77, 96* or later**	Onetime 'Marxist' states	Type of rule 70s/90s
GB	Seychelles	no	no	yes	one/multi
GB	Sierra Leone	yes	yes	no	despot/mil
I/GB	Somalia	yes	yes	no	one/war
GB	Sudan	yes	yes	no	one/mil
GB	Swaziland	yes	yes*	no	monarchy
G/GB	Tanzania	yes	yes	no	one/?
F	Togo	yes	yes	no	mil/?
GB	Uganda	yes	yes	no	despot/one
B	Zaire	yes	yes	no	despot/?
GB	Zambia	yes	yes*	no	one/multi
GB	Zimbabwe	guest	yes**	yes	war/multi

Notes: B = Belgium; F = France; G = Germany; GB = Great Britain; I = Italy; P = Portugal; SA = South Africa; S = Spain; US = United States.

The Lusaka meeting of Heads of State of Non-aligned countries was in 1970.

The Group of 77 was formed in 1964, the 96 was the count of the Group in 1972; it was 128 by 1990.

Guest means that national liberation movements were invited. one = one-party, mil = military; multi = multi-party; ? = unclear how it will turn out; / divides 1970s and 1990.

Sources: M. Barratt Brown, *The Anatomy of Underdevelopment*, Spokesman 1974, pp. 11 and 56, and for 'Marxist' states, Barry Munslow, *Africa: Problems in the Transition to Socialism*, Zed Books, 1986, p. 64.

J. Grace and J. Laffin, *Africa Since 1960*, Fontana, 1991 and Keesing's *Record of World Events*, Annual Reference Supplement, vol. 39, 1993.

CHAPTER 8

Regional Groupings in Africa

The PTA (Preferential Trade Area) was created as a first step towards the establishment of a Common Market for Eastern and Southern African States. It is an institution whose aim is to assist Member States to attain economic transformation and social advancement and to address the problems of economic dependency on external institutions, mass poverty and general underdevelopment. It also seeks to jointly attain higher rates of sustainable growth through the 'promotion of cooperation and development in all fields of economic activity, particularly in the field of trade, customs, industry, transport, communications, agriculture, natural resources and monetary affairs with the aim of contributing to the progress and development of the African countries.' PTA is, therefore, not a mere trade promotion organization. It is an institution for enhancing sustainable growth and development in the Member States.

Quoted from 'Why the PTA was Created' in *PTA Trade and Development Strategy*, adopted by the Heads of Government of the Preferential Trade Area at the Tenth Summit held in Lusaka, Zambia, 30–31 January 1992, p. 4.

Regional grouping had always been a basic policy prescription of African economists. In the charter of the Organization of African Unity the governments of all the African states committed themselves to inter-state cooperation and in the Lagos Plan of Action they confirmed their support for effective regional integration. But not all African politicians or economists agree about the purpose of regional groupings or even about their value. The views expressed in the quotation at the head of this chapter from a manifesto by the Preferential Trade Area (PTA) represent the pragmatic approach of the UN Economic Commission for Africa, which launched the PTA within the general framework of the Lagos Plan of Action published at the same time.

Regional Integration and Development

The PTA was not the first regional grouping to be established. The Economic Community of West African States (ECOWAS) and the Southern African Development Coordination Conference (SADCC) had already been formed in their respective areas. These sub-regional groupings, and the PTA in particular, emerged from the creation by the Fourth Conference of Ministers of the ECA in 1977 of what were called Multinational Programming and Operational Centres (MULPOCs).[1] There was much optimism at the time about African prospects in general and the potential for growth in regional economic cooperation, if the correct lessons were learned from the recent collapse of the East African Community. There were dissenting views. Some either decried the whole concept of regional groupings or regarded them as no more than trade promotion organizations. At the other extreme, some expected much more from them, to provide, in effect, the building blocks for a united Africa.[2]

Most of these alternative views were expressed at a seminar of African scholars called by the African Association of Political Science in Harare in 1984.[3] By this time much of the earlier optimism had waned and the consensus of the papers presented at the seminar was that attempts at regional cooperation were likely to be unsuccessful. This was because of the continuing historic links of the separate states with Europe and North America and the undiminished 'ambitions of imperialism' in the form of neo-colonialism. The view was most sharply proposed by Profesor Dan Nabudere from Tanzania, in summarizing studies of 'the new force [in the transnational corporation] for integration of production, distribution and finance on a world scale'.[4] He concluded:

What the study was saying was that regional integrated production and marketing was impossible in the face of the foreign ownership, management, and productive control over industry, commerce and agriculture. In short, the region was integrated externally, so intra-regional cohesion was impossible.[5]

Dr Ibbo Mandaza suggested a further difficuty, quoting from Thandika Mkandawire's observation of SADCC projects:

They are not only foreign aid-funded and technical in nature, but they are also purely national in character, therefore lacking both a regional framework and tending to divert the region from embarking on the more politically loaded developmental and distributional issues.[6]

Others took a more moderate view. Mandaza quoted Professor Jinadu, speaking of the experience of ECOWAS: 'We cannot take it as self-evident that regional integration will promote or facilitate regional development. It may or it may not.'[7]

Dr Mandaza, who wrote up the seminar for the United Nations University Studies in African Political Economy, was himself somewhat more encouraging, as perhaps befitted a one-time lecturer at the universities of Dar es Salaam and Botswana who became the Secretary to the Ministry of Planning in Zimbabwe. While recognizing the 'pressures of transnational corporations and international finance capital' and the 'harassment of the World Bank and the IMF', he was still able to write, in 1986:

Yet it would be both unrealistic and even ahistorical to conclude that Africa's efforts at regional economic cooperation are doomed to fail in the circumstances that she finds herself in at this historical conjuncture. There is the need not only to identify the positive way out of this apparent failure, but also to recognize that these efforts have developed a degree of political unity and coordination among African states, at both regional and continental levels. To many, such unity might appear fragile and even *ad hoc*. But, given the nature of the African terrain and the history of the continent, political unity today might be the basis of the goal of economic cooperation and autonomous development tomorrow.[8]

In such a diverse terrain the economic logic for regional groupings will tend to vary from region to region.

The Different Regions

After almost another decade of experience of regional cooperation it may be possible to judge better the views of the optimists and the pessimists. The first thing to notice is that the regions are very different in their geographical characteristics, populations and incomes, as well as in the forms of regional organization that have been adopted. Taking the whole of sub-Saharan Africa to be a region, five or six sub-regions have formed themselves over the years: the countries of francophone Africa, all tied to the French franc; UDEAC, founded in 1964 (the Customs and Economic Union of Central Africa); MARIUN, founded in 1973 (the Mano River Union of Liberia, Guinea and Sierra Leone); CEAO, founded in 1972 (the West African Economic Community); ECOWAS, founded in 1975 (the Economic Community of West African States – which includes CEAO and MARIUN); CEPGL, founded in 1976 (the Economic Community of the Great Lakes); SADCC, founded in 1980 (the Southern African Development Coordination Conference); PTA, founded in 1981 (the Preferential Trade Area for East and Southern Africa), which also admits neighbours as members; and SACU, which has a long history of customs union between South Africa, Botswana, Lesotho and Swaziland.[9]

The states included in these sub-regions are listed in Table 8.1. A few countries belong to more than one grouping and some of the Indian and Atlantic Ocean islands – Réunion, São Tomé, Seychelles and Madagascar – belong to none. The groupings vary in size of population from MARIUN's 11 million to PTA's 150 million and in income per head from CEPGL's $240 to UDEAC's $1000. There are, in effect, two powerful groupings south of the Sahara – ECOWAS, including CEAO and MARIUN, in the north and west, and the PTA, in the south and east, with SADCC in part overlapping the PTA. UDEAC, a francophone group at the centre of the continent, and CEPGL, the three countries with Belgian links around the Great Lakes, are relatively small in population and income, although relatively large in area.

It is of significance that each grouping has one very large state and several surrounding smaller states – Nigeria in ECOWAS, Zaire in UDEAC and CEPGL, Tanzania in SADCC, and the PTA has Kenya and Ethiopia, and in economic terms, Zimbabwe, as well as Tanzania competing as its larger member states. It is also an important fact that each of the main groupings contains member states which had different colonial rulers and therefore these have different official languages. This must make for problems in the secretariat and should, if the colonial influence were not so strong, suggest greater use of common African languages in place of European. In fact, the one recent claim that has been made for an additional language for official all-Africa meetings is that Portuguese should be added to English, French and Arabic. Cultural imperialism dies hard. These differences and inequalities are bound to make regional integration difficult, but similar problems are being overcome in the European Union.

Comparative Advantages and Poor Communications

The main benefit of such sub-regional cooperation is generally believed by economists to derive from the widening of markets and from the opportunities for specialization in production by each country developing its comparative advantages. There are additional benefits to be had from the pooling of information and research and the exchange of experience.

The economists' model of what they call comparative advantage implies that each country produces what it is best at and exchanges these products for what other countries are best at. This is, however, a static model. It is the basis for the quite artificial division of labour, which we have already observed, by which African countries are confined to primary production for export to the industrialized countries for them to work up into manufactured goods. African primary producers found themselves in a weak and ever-weakening bargaining position in relation to the manufacturers. It is not enough to start from where African countries now are and hope that by opening up regional markets an expansion of activity will automatically take place, as it did for example in the European Community.[10]

One of the arguments for regional cooperation in Africa and throughout the South has been that regional and sub-regional markets are needed to make up for declining markets in the North. But such a switch is not as easy as it sounds. Many African countries produce just the same goods as each other – coffee, cocoa, tea, sugar, groundnuts, cotton, fuel oil, copper, bauxite, diamonds, et cetera. Many of these products are not consumed in large quantities in Africa. In world trade, manufactured goods make up by far the greater part of the exchange between countries, but Africa's contribution to this trade is very small indeed. Most of Africa's exports are of primary products. As one African writer has put it, 'Colonialism programmed African countries to produce what they do not consume and to consume what they do not produce.'[11] This position is not likely to be changed very quickly. 'There is,' as another African economist said, 'just simply very little to trade.'[12]

Where there are economic possibilities of exchanges being developed within Africa, there are major technical difficulties of transport. Since Africa was deliberately opened up for the production and export of raw materials to Europe, the main roads and railways, such as they are, run from the mines and other sources of primary production to the ports. Internal communications barely exist. Outstanding examples are that there is no coastal shipping service linking the major African ports; Gabon has no major road going into the interior; the route from Chad to the Congo involves transshipment from road to river to rail to sea; there is no bulk transport link between Douala, the capital of Cameroon, and Lagos in Nigeria, although they are only an hour apart by aeroplane.[13] It is, moreover, often quicker to fly from one African capital to another via Paris or London than to travel direct, although the capitals may be only a few hundred miles apart.

Even if it were possible, however, for these transport difficulties to be overcome by movement of goods along the coast and by improvements in inland transport – the building of the Trans-African Highway, for example, had already got from Mauritania to Lagos by 1989 – there remain two quite crucial problems to be settled. The first is that governments must agree on which sectoral markets in a regional grouping should be opened up to encourage specialization and the second is that they must decide on how to ensure that the benefits of the opening up of such markets are equally shared by all the parties or that compensation is paid for losses.

Regional Common Markets

It must be evident now why regional cooperation in Africa will not happen 'while ministers are sleeping', as it was said to do in Europe, just because agreement is reached to open up a common market. Each of the states which joins a regional grouping will have policies in place such as tariffs and non-tariff measures to protect particular producers in their country against outside competition. This is particularly true of industrial production, where it is necessary to protect an infant industry against more advanced producers. One immediate result of establishing regional and especially sub-regional common markets is expected to be that the most advanced producers capture the whole business and less advanced producers go to the wall.

There are lessons to be learnt from the single market in the European Union established in 1992. Major losses of business are taking place, but these are justified in this Union by the belief that countries which suffer a decline in one industry will be able to develop others, and that all will benefit from the greater efficiency of the more advanced producers. There is some reason to doubt whether this will work in Europe; it certainly would not work in Africa. This is perfectly well understood, and as a result it has been necessary in devising common policies for regional groupings of states to take positive measures to ensure that there are mutually beneficial results which will flow from them.

In creating common markets, it will also be necessary to agree on some common external protection, or the expanded market will immediately be occupied by more advanced producers from outside. Enlarged markets are just what large transnational companies are looking for, since they can take most advantage of economies of scale in production and marketing. Ann Seidman and her colleagues working in Ghana and later in Zimbabwe have made detailed and comprehensive studies of this aspect of the role of transnational corporations in Africa.[14]

Regional cooperation in Africa is, thus, a matter of taking positive action towards integration and not simply of removing barriers to trade. Positive action means people to act and there is an inevitable danger that each sub-regional organization builds up a large secretariat, which makes plans and proposes schemes, but without the power to implement them. Looking at the experience of the several groupings in Africa over the last two decades, it should be possible to judge their success or failure. It must be said that they have certainly tried to take positive action; and they have not been without support from the OAU and more particularly from the ECA, which has regarded itself as the 'Platonic guardian' of African regional cooperation and economic integration.[15]

The West and the Centre: ECOWAS and UDEAC

ECOWAS is the largest and richest grouping, with a population of some 170 million and combined GDP of US$ 78 billion. Within this grouping and rather uneasily connected to it are the two smaller West African groupings of CEAO and MARIUN. No external tariff has yet been established to create a single common market, but much attention has been given to providing a framework of harmonized policies in respect of customs and trade. A compensation fund has been set up to finance the fiscal losses which should result for any party from measures of liberalization. The actual state of progress of regional cooperation in the late 1980s was judged to be something between 'moribund'[16] and 'encouraging'.[17]

In the years from 1970 to 1984 the share of West African imports which originated in West Africa rose from 5 to 8 per cent and this increase appears not to have been at the expense of trade with other parts of Africa.[18] It is not much to show for a great amount of secretarial work. Much of this must be reckoned as largely counter-productive because of the contradictory effect of having both the CEAO and MARIUN inside ECOWAS but with their own common external tariffs and liberalized internal trade, at least in unprocessed agricultural products. Only one 'Union' industry can be claimed to be the result of regional specialization – the manufacture of glass bottles in Sierra Leone.[19]

Some members of ECOWAS do indeed show much larger figures for their intra-trade than the average. Exports of manufactured goods from Nigeria, Côte d'Ivoire and Senegal and imports of these into Ghana make up the greater part of this trade.[20] The smaller countries have probably gained little, as a result of the identical nature of most of the produce each would have to trade. This does not mean that swaps do not occur. The real figure for intra-West African trade will be very much greater than appears in the statistics, as it is surmised that an almost equal amount of goods crosses inter-state borders illegally as that which is recorded by frontier guards and customs officials.[21] This is particularly the case with CEAO and MARIUN, where there are virtually no restrictions on the movements of people across the borders.

The main claim to success for ECOWAS lies, in fact, not in any expansion of intra-trade, but in the development of regional communication systems and road transport (the Trans-African Highway), which were promoted by the secretariat with support from the ECOWAS regional fund. This has become an important conduit for outside aid, mainly from the European Community.[22] ECOWAS has some further potential for development. As a result of exchange rate liberalization, moves in ECOWAS towards monetary union were being envisaged in 1990 by Ghanaian economists, but a major obstacle has lain in the already existing convertible currency union among the francophone countries.[23] ECOWAS has, significantly, moved into the political sphere through establishing its joint peacekeeping force in Liberia since 1990.

The UDEAC is described as 'the latest grouping of equatorial African states which have been forming associations since 1910'.[24] Its experience has revealed the same limitations in trade generation as ECOWAS. The aim was to establish a common external tariff and to reduce internal tariffs and promote harmonized development policies. The reality is determined by the overwhelming position of Cameroon, Congo and Gabon, which are all oil-producing states with their exports oriented almost entirely outside Africa. The single tax on products coming from within all the countries of the region and a small compensation fund should have resulted in some specialization within the region, but the absence of specific projects to encourage such development meant that nothing happened.[25] All the countries of this region are in the franc zone and this of itself gives them a certain coherence, but also a strong outward orientation. It is a fact that they have performed rather better than the sub-Saharan African average in economic growth, but this is arguably more due to their resources of oil than to their success in regional cooperation.[26]

The South and East: SADCC and the PTA

The two regional groupings for the south and east, SADCC and the PTA, were founded in the early 1980s and not, as the others, in the 1970s. It had always been intended by the ECA that there should be four sub-regional bodies – for the north, west, east and south – but SADCC in the south has been regarded as the 'ugly duckling'.[27] Unlike the PTA, SADCC was not founded on the initiative of the OAU or with the aid of the ECA. It is not primarily a trade-based organization and not concerned with trade liberalization like the PTA.[28] It was established in Lusaka shortly after Zimbabwe achieved independence in 1980, with the explicit aim of reducing southern Africa's dependence on the Republic of South Africa and of strengthening the security of the front line states in their resistance to South African pressure. Most of southern Africa's mining enterprises were controlled by South African companies,[29] South African forces were supporting rebel armies across their borders and the cost to its neighbours of South African aggression and destabilization was estimated in a confidential SADCC paper of 1986 to have exceeded US$ 10 billion in the previous five years.[30]

Thus, the liberation movements in South Africa and SWAPO in Namibia all recognized that 'SADCC and the national liberation struggle are two sectors of a single front in action'.[31] The task for SADCC was to strengthen the southern African economies. To this end, it was proposed that each of the nine members (Namibia was added in 1990) should take responsibility for developing priorities and for formulating plans and projects for particular sectors of the regional economy. For example, Zimbabwe took responsibility for food security, Zambia for mining and development, Angola for energy, Mozambique for transportation, Tanzania for industrial development, Botswana for livestock research and Swaziland for training.

By 1985 some 400 projects had been approved by SADCC and funding of over $1 billion obtained for them with another $1 billion under negotiation. Projects included repairing the Mozambique to Zimbabwe railway line, which had been disrupted by South African-backed rebels; establishing a satellite communication network between the ten member states and early warning systems for weather and crop predictions; creating a twenty-five-year agricultural research programme on drought-resistant varieties of sorghum and millet.[32] In the longer term it was intended step by step to build *de facto* indicative planning for sectoral specialization.[33]

The opening up of the possibility of a change of regime in South Africa with the release of Nelson Mandela from prison in 1990 and the ending of hostilities in Mozambique and Namibia gave to SADCC a new potential. Links between black southern Africa and a democratic South Africa would be likely to create an added dimension of great importance for regional economic integration. However, much of the pressure was relaxed which had brought the front line states to act together. More than this, some member countries, like Zimbabwe, which had resisted overtures from the World Bank to engage in structural adjustment programmes in exchange for loans, had changed their minds in the face of the debt crisis. This meant an intensification of policies oriented towards overseas trade and some reduction of interest in regional collective action, unless it could provide another way of earning hard currency.

The imminence of the establishment of a democratic South Africa concentrated minds wonderfully in southern Africa. The big South African mining companies took defensive action in two ways: on the one hand, by siphoning profits out of Africa through transfer pricing, estimated at an outflow of US$1 billion a year from 1990 onwards; on the other hand, by breaking up their conglomerate empires, as GENCOR was the first to do.[34] This last process, which had the support of the African National Congress (ANC), has the effect of making joint ventures with governments in southern African states very much easier.

The response of SADCC to the changing position in the Republic was to change its name to the Southern African Development Community (SADC) and to agree to concentrate on trade exchanges both amongst existing members and with an eye to anticipated post-sanctions expansion of trade with South Africa, which would be invited to join, once a democratically elected government was in place.[35]

In the meantime, the same problem with intra-trade arose in SADC as in the other regional groupings. One or two of the larger or more economically advanced countries came to dominate, at the expense of the smaller and less advanced. In the case of SADC it was Zimbabwe and, to a lesser extent, Botswana that were taking the major shares in the expansion of trade. Until the drought in 1992, Zimbabwe was a supplier of food to the rest of the region, mainly of maize and sugar to Botswana, but the region also provided an important market for Zimbabwe's iron and steel, paper and other manufactured goods. In exchange Botswana supplied meat and textiles and nickel to Zimbabwe, and also manufactured goods to other members.[36]

The danger for the southern African states as they face an opening-up of trade with South Africa is that the pattern of African trade with Europe could easily be repeated – that the industrialized partner supplies the manufactured goods and in exchange purchases the raw materials for its industries. The non-industrialized partners remain without industries and in a weak bargaining position because they are unable to diversify out of primary production. The southern African economies would become, in effect, satellites of the Republic.

By 1993 the new SADC was expanding its personnel and resources in consultation with the ANC to meet such a situation as we have described. SADCC had previously prided itself on the small size of the secretariat upon which its activities were based. This certainly made it different from the other African regional groupings, but it also reduced the resources available for coordinated sectoral planning. Simplification and harmonization of trade documentation and a much expanded exchange of trade information were certainly regarded as important achievements of SADCC, but, while the actual expansion of trade exchanges inside the region was not the main aim, a much more consistent promotion of joint projects was needed after the initial 400 had been launched. To do this required more technical staff, finance for SADCC institutions and funding for projects. Both Zimbabwe and Botswana had been willing to give support to the projects of their poorer neigbours, but without a major boost to the image of SADCC among the several government ministries, its influence on policy was limited.[37] All this was bound to change after a new government was established in Pretoria.

South Africa's Regional Policies

An indication of how a more integrated economy in southern Africa might develop after the ending of apartheid can be found by examining the economic and financial relationships already established by South Africa with Botswana, Lesotho and Swaziland. The Southern African Customs Union (SACU) between South Africa and these three countries goes back to 1903, but a new agreement was signed after the three achieved independence in the late 1960s. The Republic continued to set the duties and to be the custodian of the common revenue pool from customs and other duties collected on goods entering or being produced in the common area; but the new agreement provided for a more equitable distribution of the pool between the parties. The three peripheral states nevertheless continued to regard the agreement as oppressive because it limited their discretion in fiscal and monetary policy, and this was of particular importance since a major part of their state revenues came from customs and other duties. The agreement also had the effect of preventing the three from developing their own manufacturing industries behind protective tariffs, and indeed provided South African industries with a captive market.

Some modification of SACU is bound to follow political changes in South Africa, but if there is not to be a local repetition of European protectionism, the modifications will have to be considerable.[38] The African National Congress, in preparing its case for the first democratic elections in South Africa in 1994, had an economic programme prepared in advance by a macro-economic research group. This included a paper entitled 'Reconstructing Relations with the Southern African Region: Issues and Options for a Democratic South Africa'.[39] In the paper the authors recognized the million lives lost and $60.5 billion damage inflicted on the economies of the neighbouring states in the 1980s and reiterated the ANC's commitment to 'seeking actively to foster greater regional cooperation along new lines which shall correct the imbalance in current relationships'. After reviewing in detail the nature of these relationships, they arrived at rather sombre conclusions. They envisaged three possible scenarios – continuation of current neo-mercantilist policies, a more sensitive hegemonic bilateralism and a wholly new path of full and active partnership on regional programmes.

The authors of the paper did not conceal their expectation that the first, and at best, the second, was the most likely to ensue, but they spelt out what would be involved for South Africa in pursuing the third course: not just discussion but partnership in formulating a regional programme, subject to negotiation and re-negotiation; membership of organizations established by the rest of the region, while recognizing the need for institutional reform; contributing to the development of an agreed mutually beneficial programme, combining elements of cooperation, coordination and integration; recognizing that any such programme would have to include significant counter-polarization measures with a strong developmental focus.

Just to look at these implications is enough to make one realize the unlikelihood of any such path of development. South Africa's relations with her closest and smallest neighbours, Lesotho and Swaziland, reveal the chief problem – the overwhelming relative strength of its currency, based on the South African economy, with a GNP equal to more than twice that of all the SADC countries combined.

Lesotho and Swaziland have for long had a monetary agreement with the Republic. The Rand Monetary Agreement of 1974 was changed in 1986 into a Common Monetary Area. The South African rand provides backing for the two local currencies, which gives them added strength, but at the cost of following South Africa's monetary polices. In theory, the aim is to sustain the economic development of the area as a whole; in practice, far from being a strength, South Africa's increasing financial difficulties have been visited on the other two.[40] Lesotho would probably fare better within a new federation.

For many years the overriding influence on African government policies has come from the IMF and the World Bank; and the refusal of these institutions to think in terms of support for regional development in Africa has been an insuperable obstacle to African unity. Funds from the African Develpment Bank to promote regional integration have been limited in amount and largely restricted to East and West Africa.[41] The tragedy of African governments' relations with the World Bank and IMF is that they have never been coordinated. When governments have broken off from dependence on the international financial institutions, as Zambia did in 1987, others were at the same time increasing their dependence. Even without a common line of policy among African governments in any single region, some synchronizing of activities would have been helpful.

To take but one example: at the very time that President Kaunda was serving as chairman of SADCC, imports were pouring into his country from South Africa, as a result of the IMF-mandated trade liberalization programme in Zambia and the devaluation of the currency. When Zambia finally abandoned the IMF recovery programme, Zimbabwe had agreed to accept a World Bank structural adjustment programme. Zambia's declaration of 'unilateral bankruptcy' left it isolated, unless it could reorient its trading pattern towards SADCC, and, with Zimbabwe's new policy reorientation in the opposite direction, this was that much more difficult to accomplish.[42] Finally, the ousting of Kaunda in 1990 brought Zambia back into the fold. It is somewhat ironic that a regional grouping built around a democratic South Africa might be a much more attractive proposition for support from the World Bank, which normally prefers to deal with individual states.

The Preferential Trade Area

The PTA (Preferential Trade Area for Eastern and Southern African States) was founded on the initiative of the ECA to complement ECOWAS and, as the last of the regional integration organizations, to provide the missing regional framework for the east and also for the south of Africa. It thus overlaps with SADCC, having Lesotho, Malawi, Swaziland, Tanzania, Zambia and Zimbabwe as members in common, and this overlapping has created problems of divided responsibilities. Such problems may be increased as the PTA's constitution allows for neighbouring states to be added. This would allow Sudan and Zaire, Angola, Botswana, Madagascar and the Seychelles all to join. As its name implies, the main aim of the PTA is to encourage the expansion of regional trade exchanges, and this was never SADCC's main aim. However, the PTA has wider aims, as the quotation that heads this chapter indicates. It has also been developing projects for transport corridors for the land-locked states, for airline mergers and for early-warning weather systems, all of which have also been the concern of SADCC projects.[43]

The measures adopted by the PTA to expand trade exchanges within the region comprise preferential tariffs moving towards a common market, a clearing house for merchandise trade with settlement of balances in hard currency, relaxation of import licensing among members, and the operation of a trade finance bank.[44] It is perhaps too early to judge the results of measures taken only in the later 1980s. After some expansion in the 1970s the share of intra-trade in Central and Southern Africa appears to have declined in the 1980s to a level of 10 per cent of total trade, but that is above the proportions in North and West Africa, always remembering that as much trade is unrecorded smuggling as is formally recorded.[45]

It would seem that once again the traditional economist's beliefs have to recognize that the liberating effect of opening up markets to free trade does not of itself lead to trade expansion. Where entrepreneurs are lacking for industrial development and agricultural exports have been confined to a limited range of primary products, both crops and minerals, for export to overseas markets, trade expansion requires positive action to encourage specialization on a collective basis. The PTA has not provided this. Countries which already had some industrial development, such as Kenya and Zimbabwe, have been able to take advantage of wider markets, as have the oil producers in the region, but the less favoured and less industrially advanced economies have gained little or nothing.[46] Tanzanian economists have complained that sub-regional programmes and projects have been poorly integrated with national plans and budgets.[47]

The attempt in the PTA region to establish a clearing union for trade in merchandise emphasizes the importance of the role of international payments in developing trade exchanges. The PTA's Clearing

Union required that the settlement of balances should be made in hard currency. But this was just what the member countries were lacking and to overcome which they were seeking to expand trade, and particularly sources of supply, inside Africa, where they did not have to pay with hard currency. With such sources available they could then conserve their hard currency earnings for paying off their debts and for essential imports from the industrialized countries of supplies which could not be found in Africa.

A Parallel Clearing Union

The governments of African countries which faced such onerous debt payments in the 1980s found themselves in much the same situation as the countries of Europe in the 1950s, trying to rebuild their war-shattered economies with the only resources for doing so in the United States, where dollars were needed to buy anything. The Marshall Plan had supplied most of the dollars, but the Plan had recognized the need for regional cooperation as a central development strategy. This itself required technical assistance in equipment and personnel, but also financial support for a regional payments union, if it was to create the conditions for an expansion of regional trade through the relaxation of trade barriers.

It had to be that way round: finance before trade. The trade barriers could not or would not be lowered until there was financial support for industrial reconstruction throughout Western Europe. The analogy between Africa's condition today and Europe's forty years ago has been forcibly argued in an academic study of 'Intra-Regional Trade Growth in Africa' by Chandra Hardy, a one-time senior official of the World Bank, in a 1992 volume, *Alternative Development Strategies in Sub-Saharan Africa*, edited by Frances Stewart and Sanjaya Lall and the Tanzanian economist, Samuel Wangwe.[48]

The European Payments Union, which was created in 1951, permitted members to exchange their own currencies in the process of trading with each other, without resort to gold or dollars. The Union provided credit at current rates of interest and only as an accounting device were balances valued in dollars. After a number of years of successful operation, the balances could be exchanged for convertible currencies or for gold, but by that time Western Europe was well on the road to recovery.[49] The subsequent evolution of the European Community itself has also been examined for lessons to be learned by Africans, but the high proportion of extra-African exchanges in most African countries' trade has been assumed to preclude similar advantages accruing from customs unions in Africa.[50]

The analogy of the European Payments Union is worth recalling not only for its own sake, but for a further reason. In 1964, at the start of ECA's exploration, under the leadership of Robert Gardiner, of the possibilities of developing sub-regional trade groupings in Africa, a proposal for a payments union was given serious consideration by the ECA. It came from a Hungarian economist working with FAO, Dr Andreas Goseco.[51] This proposal has even greater relevance for the situation in the 1990s, when the African regional groupings find themselves at a dead end because of the burden of foreign debt.

The Goseco proposal was for a multilateral trade clearing agency. This would make it possible to settle payments for trade exchanges between several countries without requiring gold or hard currency. Countries in a regional union would agree to expand their trade with each other, in the first instance payments being made by means of a credit note exchangeable against other products and denominated in a common currency. After an agreed period, these notes might be changed into gold or dollars or they could be held as a reserve for future trading. Expansion of trade exchanges by increasing specialization could be encouraged by each country making offers of goods which they could hope to produce and making bids for the products offered by others. These could be matched by brokers in a central clearing house operating like a commodity exchange. Today this could be effected by computer as it is in the money market.[52]

The proposal for an African Trade Clearing Union was not taken up by ECA. This was partly because the 1970s witnessed a boom in primary commodity prices. It was also because of the strong prejudice of the international financial and commercial institutions of the North against any trading system which sought to bypass them. By the 1980s, African countries were being encouraged to orient their entire export potential to the North in order to earn the hard currency to pay off their accumulating debts. Their chief concern was to maintain these earnings by acting together to check the fall in primary commodity prices.

As the 1990s proceed, the proposal could well be revived. If it were possible for a major programme of debt relief to be applied in Africa, aid for reconstruction might begin to flow into the continent once again, and a structure for such financing on a multilateral basis would then be required. But that is to anticipate what will be discussed in the last part of this book.

TABLE 8.1 Regions and Sub-regions of Africa, 1988–9

Country and Region	Population (millions)	Density (pop/km²)	GDP Total ($m)	per head ($)	Exports (US $ billions)	Imports (US $ billions)
Mahgreb						
Morocco	23.8	53	22.4	922	3.3	5.5
Algeria	23.7	10	39.8	2284	8.6	8.4
Tunisia	7.8	48	8.9	1287	2.9	2.9
Other North Africa						
Libya	4.2	2	22.9	5417	6.8	5.1
Egypt	50.1	50	31.6	681	2.6	7.4
Sudan*	23.8	10	–	461	0.7	1.2
Sub-total or average	133.4	15	125.6	2050	24.9	30.5
UDEAC						
Gabon	1.1	4	3.4	3030	1.2	1.0
Cameroon	11.1	23	11.1	1136	0.9	1.3
Congo	2.1	6	2.3	1007	0.9	0.5
Equ. Guinea*	0.3	14	–	438	–	–
CAR*	2.9	5	1.1	388	0.1	0.2
Chad*	5.4	4	1.0	169	0.1	0.4
Sub-total or average	22.9	9	18.9	1000	3.2	3.4
ECOWAS **Mariun**						
Liberia*	2.4	22	–	484	0.4	0.2
Guinea*	5.4	22	2.7	446	0.4	0.5
Sierra Leone*	4.0	55	0.9	297	0.1	0.2
Sub-total or average	11.8	33	[3.6]	407	0.9	0.9
CEAO						
Côte d' Ivoire	11.2	35	7.2	876	3.0	2.4
Senegal	6.9	35	4.7	717	0.6	1.2
Mauritania*	1.9	2	0.9	522	0.2	0.2
Benin*	4.4	39	1.6	410	–	0.3
Niger*	7.3	6	2.0	329	0.3	0.4
Mali*	9.7	7	2.1	223	0.3	0.5
Burkina Faso*	8.5	31	2.5	218	0.1	0.4
Sub-total or average	49.9	20	21.0	490	4.5	5.4

Table 8.1 *continued*

Country and Region	Population (millions)	Density (pop/km²)	GDP Total ($m)	per head ($)	Exports (US $ billions)	Imports (US $ billions)
Other ECOWAS						
Ghana	14.1	59	5.3	369	1.0	0.9
Nigeria	101.9	110	34.8	296	9.0	3.6
Cape Verde*	0.3	87	–	748	–	0.1
Togo*	3.3	59	1.3	408	0.2	0.5
Gambia*	0.8	72	–	271	–	0.2
Guinea Bissau*	0.9	26	–	159	–	0.1
Sub-total or average	121.3	80	[41.6]	350	[10.2]	5.4
CEPGL						
Zaire*	33.5	14	9.6	193	1.3	0.8
Rwanda*	6.8	258	2.2	340	0.1	0.3
Burundi*	5.2	186	1.0	211	0.1	0.4
Sub-total or average	45.5	150	12.8	240	1.5	1.5
SADCC						
Angola	9.5	8	7.7	610	1.4	0.5
Botswana	1.2	2	2.5	1654	1.4	1.0
Lesotho*	1.7	55	0.3	232	–	0.4
Malawi*	8.2	69	1.4	146	0.3	0.5
Mozambique*	14.9	19	1.1	84	0.1	0.7
Namibia	1.7	48	1.6	1030	–	–
Swaziland	–	–	–	–	–	–
Tanzania*	25.5	27	2.5	123	0.3	0.8
Zambia*	7.9	10	4.7	346	1.4	0.9
Zimbabwe	9.1	23	5.2	690	1.3	1.1
Sub-total or average	79.7	26	27.0	490	[6.2]	5.9
PTA						
Burundi*	5.2	186	1.0	211	0.1	0.2
Comorosi*	0.5	237	–	402	–	0.1
Djibouti*	0.4	18	–	589	–	0.2
Ethiopia*	46.1	38	5.4	121	0.4	1.1
Kenya	22.5	39	7.1	375	1.1	2.1
Lesotho*	1.7	55	0.3	232	–	0.4
Malawi*	8.2	69	1.4	146	0.3	0.5
Mauritius	1.1	568	1.7	1843	1.0	1.3
Rwanda*	6.8	258	2.2	340	0.1	0.3
Somalia*	7.0	11	1.1	239	0.1	0.1

Table 8.1 *continued*

Country and Region	Population (millions)	Density (pop/km²)	GDP Total ($m)	per head ($)	Exports (US $ billions)	Imports (US $ billions)
Swaziland	–	–	–	–	–	–
Tanzania*	25.5	27	2.5	123	0.3	0.8
Uganda*	17.5	74	4.5	243	0.5	0.7
Zambia*	7.9	10	4.7	346	1.4	0.9
Zimbabwe	9.1	23	5.2	690	1.3	1.1
Sub-total or average	159.5	90	31.9	360	6.6	9.8
OTHERS						
Réunion	0.6	230	–	3930	0.1	1.7
Seychelles	0.1	300	–	3510	–	1.2
Madagascar*	11.3	19	2.3	167	0.3	0.3
São Tomé*	0.1	120	–	548	–	–
Sub-total or average	12.0	170	–	2000	–	2.2
Grand Total or average	570	19		650	55.1	60.5

Notes: * = one of the least developed countries; – = figures not available; [ ] = incomplete totals.
Source: M. Barratt Brown and Pauline Tiffen, *Short Changed*, Pluto Press, 1992, Table A.1.

CHAPTER 9

Common Defence of Common Resources

The African countries were a major pillar of support for the Integrated Programme for Commodities and their firm commitment to the Common Fund was a political necessity of the highest importance.

The negative influence of foreign trading interest groups and their local associates in the capitals of developing countries should not be underestimated.

Gamani Corea, one-time UNCTAD secretary-general, *Taming Commodity Markets: The Integrated Programme and the Common Fund in UNCTAD*, Manchester University Press, 1992, pp. 86 and 147.

Africa was not united by the 1990s, not even in regional groupings. What had brought the leaders of Africa together in the mid 1970s was the catastrophe of sharply falling commodity prices after the euphoria of booming prices in the 1960s continued into the early 1970s. This common interest was to be reinforced by the shared experience of accumulating foreign debt resulting from the adverse terms of trade – falling prices of Africa's primary product exports and rising prices of imported oil and manufactured goods. It was later to be confirmed by the collapse of the Soviet Union and the ending of the arms race.

Taming the Commodity Markets

Anxiety about unequal trade exchanges had already in the late 1960s led several African leaders to discuss their common problems in the forum of the United Nations with leaders of Latin American and other developing countries. They were particularly dissatisfied with the workings of the General Agreement on Tariffs and Trade (GATT), which had replaced the proposed International Trade Organization (ITO) as part of the post-war international economic settlement reached at the Bretton Woods conference. ITO was intended to have a positive responsibility for encouraging trade development. GATT had a largely negative role of establishing free trade. As has been mentioned, to the developing countries GATT appeared to be providing what an Indian delegate called a one-way street in free trade. The goods of the industrialized lands flowed freely down to the South, but getting any goods except traditional unprocessed primary products up into the North proved to be as impossible as it had been in the colonial era.

Without the alternative of diversifying their exports, the countries of the South were put at a great disadvantage. The governments from these Southern countries sought to strengthen their bargaining position by forming the Group of 77 developing countries.[1] By acting together they successfully obtained the establishment in 1964 of the UN Conference on Trade and Development (UNCTAD). It was not an International Trade Organization, but it was expected to serve as an information centre and pressure group for the interests of the South in world trade.[2]

The African countries had a very special interest in UNCTAD, because of the heavy dependence of their trade on exports of primary products. There were thirty-one African countries in the Group of 77 from the start and another eight joined in 1972, when the Group total was brought up to ninety-six. The role of the African delegation was an important one from the formation of the Group, and it was in Algiers that the first meeting of prime ministers was held, which adopted a common line of action and a document known as the Algiers Charter. This committed the 77 to act together and agree on common policies in advance of each UNCTAD session. The major problem facing nearly all of them, but especially the African members, was that each of the primary commodities entering world trade was the subject of separate treatment and, moreover, of treatment in commodity markets over which the producers had little or no influence.[3]

There had been international agreements about commodities before, having the aim of stabilizing prices in the interests of both producer and consumer countries, but these had always been agreements concerning a single product between the major producers and the major consumers of the product. Prior to the Second World War, most producers had been expatriate companies in colonies of the industrialized countries and the consumers were also mainly companies in the industrialized countries. Bargaining was, roughly speaking, between equals. After decolonization, however, the commodity producers were mainly the individual farmers and their organizations or the governments of the poor, developing countries and they were facing the much richer and more powerful business consumer organizations in the industrialized countries.[4]

The ten core commodities, identified by UNCTAD as requiring action, were cocoa, coffee, copper, cotton, hard fibres, jute, rubber, sugar, tea and tin. All but two – jute and tin – were key African products, on which the whole livelihood of many African states depended. It was a trade of the poor with the rich. Taken together, 84 per cent of these products came *from* countries with per capita incomes in 1976 below US$900, while 79 per cent went *to* countries with per capita incomes of over US$1500. At the extreme, about 60 per cent came from those with incomes below US$500, while about 50 per cent went to those with incomes over US$2500. The commodity problem was, as the first secretary-general of UNCTAD, Raul Prebisch, insisted, at the centre of the dynamics of underdevelopment. The poor had less bargaining strength than the rich and the demand for primary products was falling relative to the demand for manufactured goods in world trade. This last relationship came to be called the Prebisch effect.[5]

A number of new commodity agreements had been reached in the 1950s and 1960s – for coffee, olive oil, sugar, tea, tin and wheat – and these covered four of UNCTAD's selected ten commodities. But none of these agreements was regarded as satisfactory by the producer countries, because there were often four or five or more competing producers of the particular commodity coming from widely separated regions and facing a powerful and often associated group of business consumer organizations from the industrialized countries. Moreover, there were six commodities on the UNCTAD list without any agreement, and many others of importance to African economies not even listed.

As a result of much lobbying, at the second session of UNCTAD in 1968, the secretariat called for 'an integrated commodity policy' to be embodied in a 'general agreement on commodity arrangements', in order to overcome the problem of fragmented case-by-case treatment, and to go beyond price stabilization to long-term diversification of products. The second and third sessions of UNCTAD II in 1968 and 1972 failed to get further than a revised sugar agreement and a cocoa agreement.

A Common Fund for Commodities

The idea of an integrated programme, however, was combined at this time in the UNCTAD secretariat's thinking with the evident need for financing buffer stocks of commodities, when supply exceeded demand. The combination led to the concept of a Common Fund and a multi-commodity stock under international ownership. This was indeed a revolutionary idea and required a formidable effort of explanation and advocacy to convince not only the governments of developing countries but also those of the industrialized lands too that it should be given support. The task fell to a new secretary-general of UNCTAD, Gamani Corea of Sri Lanka, appointed in 1974, and to the head of the commodities division, Bernard Chidzero of Zimbabwe, who was later to become UNCTAD's deputy secretary-general. That the idea received a new degree of acceptance from both producer and consumer country governments was due in part to the energy and persuasiveness of these two men, but chiefly to the action which had been taken by the oil-producing countries in 1973 in raising the price of fuel oil.[6] This had shown other primary producers what could be done by combined action and had considerably frightened the consumer countries with the prospect of such action being applied in the case of all commodities.

Gamani Corea, in his book *Taming the Commodity Markets*, has traced the intricate details of the negotiations, which took place at the Nairobi session of UNCTAD IV in 1976 and at the four sessions of the Negotiating Conference on the Common Fund in 1977, 1978, 1979 and 1980, leading finally to agreement in 1981 on establishing a Common Fund for Commodities. What emerged was not what many representatives of the developing countries had hoped for. The Fund was to be much smaller, $500 million and not $6 billion as originally proposed, but it had powers to borrow. It was not the independent instrument for intervening in world markets that some, especially the African delegates, had hoped for; it had to operate through the separate International Commodity Organizations; but the number of commodities covered was enlarged from the original ten. It could not provide compensation for falling prices, as some had wished; but it had a 'Second Account' or 'Second Window' which could be opened to provide finance for research and development and product diversification. In providing for its future management, the developing countries had not won a majority voice, despite their overwhelming populations; but they had gained a much greater say than in any other international institution, based on the principle of each country's contribution to the Fund qualifying for an equal basic vote, with extra votes given according to the larger or smaller contributions determined by national income.[7]

The agreement on setting up a Common Fund was regarded with varying degrees of satisfaction or dissatisfaction by delegates, viewing it from widely differing positions. The industrialized, consumer countries felt that, by agreeing to share the costs of stockpiling with the producer countries, they had prevented a dangerous precedent emerging in the granting to developing countries of the power to spend the industrialized countries' money with impunity. Some of the spokesmen from the developing countries were euphoric, describing the agreement as 'one of the most glittering prizes of the New International Economic Order'.[8] Some small developing countries did not know how they would find the minimum subscription of $1 million and, if their products were not included in existing commodity agreements, did not see what benefits they would receive. Most of the delegates, both from the developing countries and from the so-called 'like-minded' smaller Northern industrialized countries of Canada, Scandinavia, the Netherlands and elsewhere, felt that the best that could be got had been won, and that the Second Window was a particular victory, even though government contributions to meeting its opening funds were to be voluntary.

One of the most interesting features of Gamani Corea's report was his frequent reference to the strong support from the African group for the Fund and for its progress throughout the negotiations. 'They were,' he avows, 'a major pillar of support.'[9] They had accepted the necessity for the Fund to work through the International Commodity Agreements, because they recognized the suspicion of Latin American producers towards an African lobby operating outside the purview of the commodity organizations.[10] The determination of the African delegates to obtain an African voice in the world arena sometimes made them embarrassing allies, but their success in marshalling effective arguments in favour of complex propositions won universal recognition. They acted as a cohesive group and much of the success of carrying the Integrated Programme of Commodities and the Common Fund through to final agreement must be attributed to their efforts. It was not their fault that in the end so little was gained by the whole exercise.

The agreement on the Common Fund had laid it down that the Fund would come into operation when ninety members had subscribed and two-thirds of the capital had been assured. It was eight whole years before this was achieved. Most of the developing countries ratified in 1981 and 1982, although some of the smaller African countries delayed.

The 'like-minded' group ratified early, as did the UK, but some of the big subscribers held back, and the USA made it clear that it did not intend to ratify. It was only when West Germany and then the Soviet Union signed up, along with Cuba, in July 1988 that the agreements made in 1981 came into force. By that time, nearly all the International Commodity Agreements upon which the Fund depended for its operation had collapsed. This was the result of the gathering slump in world demand for primary commodities during the 1980s, which had left the managers of buffer stocks overloaded and unable to halt the decline in prices.[11]

Africa and the European Community

Baulked by the long delay in the launching of the Common Fund and overwhelmed by the falling prices of their staple commodity exports, the governments of African countries had to look elsewhere for help. They turned first to their old colonial masters in Europe. In 1973 the UK had joined the European Community, accompanied, as a result of long historic ties, by her one-time colonial suppliers of primary products for the British home market. These had to be accommodated within the Common Market, which otherwise imposed tariffs or levies at various rates on outside suppliers. The chief exceptions were generalized preferences (GSPs), which had been granted to developing countries, mainly for certain manufactured goods. Beyond that the French and Belgian governments had also won concessions for imports from their ex-colonies, which were designated as Associated Territories under agreements signed at Yaoundé and Arusha in 1968–9. Similar arrangements had clearly to be made for the one-time British colonies, but there was some jealousy encountered here. The French government was determined that imports from ex-French colonies should not have to face competition from ex-British colonies, and won this protection at least insofar as the French market itself was concerned.[12]

The African countries which had been British colonies were particularly anxious to hold on to their traditional European markets and were prepared in exchange to concede entry to their own markets for European goods and capital, together with the sweetener of a promise of economic aid. A new convention for all the ex-colonies of the European powers in Africa, the Caribbean and the Pacific (ACP countries) was agreed at meetings in Lomé in 1975, and became known as the Lomé Convention. Under this Convention special arrangements were made for the entry of certain products into the European Common Market from the ACP associated countries for a limited number of years. A second Convention (Lomé II) was signed in 1979, a third (Lomé III) in 1984 and a fourth (Lomé IV) in 1989, each of which prolonged the arrangements and increased the measures of aid.[13]

This aid from Europe increasingly took the form of compensation to producing countries for a fall in commodity prices, to be paid in respect of specified primary products when export earnings fell by 7.5 per cent below a moving average over the previous four years. The sums were not large, even in the worst years of the late 1980s, when lost income from primary products for African countries was calculated to exceed $100 billion. Payments of the equivalent of $234 million (repeat million) were made under the STABEX scheme for agricultural products in 1986 and another $5 million (repeat million) under the SYMEX scheme for minerals in the same year, when losses from export earnings among African countries in this one year were reported to amount to $19 *billion* (repeat *billion*).[14]

Far larger sums were obtained by African countries from the IMF, to which one African government after another turned in the 1980s. The IMF compensatory finance schemes (CFS) had already made available over $1 billion by 1986 and much larger sums were to follow. These payments from the IMF came out of each country's existing quotas in the Fund, carried conditionality clauses and had to be paid back quickly. They did not go chiefly to the poorest, the so-called least developed countries, most of which are in Africa.[15] They did not prevent Africa's debts from rising and more and more of Africa's export earnings having to be assigned to debt repayment. To meet this situation the World Bank stepped in with its structural adjustment loans. Had the African governments' proposals in UNCTAD for taming the commodity markets been accepted, none of what followed need have happened. What Gamani Corea called the 'negative influence of foreign trading interest groups and their associates in the capitals of developing countries' proved to be too strong.[16]

Alternative Commodity Agreements

As African experience with the World Bank and the IMF became increasingly unsatisfactory throughout the 1980s, the argument in favour of an 'African alternative' grew steadily stronger. By the end of the decade a whole quiver full of alternatives was being considered by African governments at the suggestion of the ECA. Most involved some degree of self-reliance in place of dependence on export markets and some kind of economic transformation from the Western model imposed by the international financial institutions under structural adjustment programmes. But some countries in sub-Saharan Africa did give consideration to alternative ways of managing their commodity exports in world markets, and of making use of the UNCTAD Common Fund.

The first possibility was to make use of the Common Fund in cases where International Commodity Agreements were still operational. After 1990 this was only true of rubber and cocoa but, even in these cases, stocks were so high that intervention was not feasible. This was the direct result of the World Bank's simultaneous investment in extending the export capacity of several producing countries, especially of new hybrid cocoa trees in Malaysia and hybrid coffee trees in Indonesia.[17] Given the need to increase export earnings, reduced prices were not having the effect of reducing output, but rather of encouraging competitive planting of higher-yielding trees. But world demand was simply not growing in line with supply. The same situation applied in relation to palm oil, where bio-technology was enormously increasing yields.[18]

For African coffee growers the situation was even more dire. The International Coffee Agreement collapsed in 1989 when stocks rose beyond the capacity of the manager to keep prices up by retaining stocks. Prices were almost halved over the next three years and reached a level where they did not even cover the costs of the growers' labour. Yet production continued because the millions of small-scale growers had no other crop to sell for cash and because governments still looked to coffee sales to find the hard currency to pay back debts on foreign borrowing. At the same time, most African coffee is of the robusta variety, which was becoming less and less popular with consumers.[19] All efforts to revive the International Coffee Agreement in the early 1990s failed, and the price in late 1992 reached the seeming rock-bottom low of $900 a tonne compared with $2400 in 1984.[20] The sudden sharp rise in coffee prices as the result of frosts in Brazil in the spring of 1994, exaggerated by market speculation, showed the absurdity of a commodity marketing system which brings prices so low as in the end to reduce production and new planting and then results in stocks running so low as not to cover a single bad crop.

If African producers could not hope to benefit from the First Window of the Common Fund, was there nothing to be had at the Second Window, that is from the Fund's Second Account? The new secretary-general of UNCTAD, appointed in 1987, was a Ghanaian, Kenneth Dadzie, who, in that year, still had high hopes that the Fund would give 'a new impetus to producer-consumer cooperation and international policy in the field of commodities'.[21] But a cartoon in *South* magazine of June 1987 revealed the real situation. It showed him painting out 'UNCTAD' above his shop window and replacing it with 'DADZIE'S MARKET'. Underneath this, there were stickers on the windows showing 'Prices Slashed', 'Coffee at Knock-down Prices', 'Sugar Marked Down Today', 'Special Offer – Tin' and 'Many More Bargains Inside'![22]

The Second Window had been intended to provide producer countries with funds for improving the quality and the marketing of their products and for crop diversification. But this had to be done through the International Commodity Organizations. The only one of these to adopt a policy of such non-trading support was the International Jute Organization which, in 1991, provided funds for diversifying the market for jute products.[23]

Africa is not a jute-producing region, and applying this idea to other commodities came up against the fact that just two or three giant transnational companies, like Nestlé and General Foods in the case of coffee, control the marketing of up to 90 per cent of the final product.[24] None the less, there were reports in 1993 of attempts still being made to make use of the funds deposited with the Second Account of the Common Fund. It had not escaped the notice of a number of African as well as Northern NGOs that there were still quite large funds in this Account which had never been drawn upon. At least one successful application has been reported – from Ghana.[25]

Organizations of Small-scale Producers

If African governments had failed through UNCTAD to improve their bargaining position in world markets, what could African producers themselves do to take common defensive action? Two suggestions were being canvassed in the early 1990s. The first was a desperate proposal to repeat the solution applied to excess stocks in the 1930s – burn them. The weakness of producers in the market today is that the big consumers hold the stocks and the many separate producer countries cannot easily agree among themselves to hold back production, although coffee producers in 1993 were moving to such an agreement.[26] This is what the oil-producing countries had agreed to do in 1973 and the result was the huge rise in oil prices. Such action was not easily replicated. The number of oil producers was not as great as in other fields of primary production and they had a common enemy in Israel to unite them.

There are literally millions of coffee producers in the world, exporting from over sixty countries, with twenty-five in Africa alone. Nothing unites them except that they are coffee growers and generally view each other as competitors. The International Coffee Agreement, while it existed, tended to be dominated by Brazil and Colombia as the largest producers and by the United States as the largest consuming country. They could reach deals on prices, which the others had to accept. Neither Brazil nor Colombia was prepared in the 1990s to burn coffee, as Brazil did between 1936 and 1943 – to an amount then equal to five years' average Brazilian exports or two years of world consumption at that time.[27] Yet all the other coffee growers would have been better off today if they had done the same after 1989, when the coffee agreement collapsed. And this would have maintained planting to meet the coffee shortage when it came after the 1994 frosts in Brazil.

There was a much more imaginative alternative: they could have established their own coffee auction, to which all coffee had to be sold, fixed their own minimum prices for different qualities and then instructed their own auctioneer to order the destruction of all coffee that did not make the price. Such a proposal was in fact circulated in 1992 to a number of the chief coffee-exporting countries' national marketing boards, but there was too much competitive manoeuvring for position in the allocation of quotas, in the event that a new International Coffee Agreement were to be reached, for the proposal to be taken seriously.[28] In the meantime, all the several million coffee growers suffered, and the big companies profited, without passing on much of the benefit to the consumer in the shops.

The second suggestion is somewhat less draconian and had already been put into practice on a small scale in the early 1990s. This was that the small producers should agree together to sell coffee directly through their own associated organizations established in the consumer countries at prices in the shops somewhat above the norm, explaining to the shoppers that they were engaging in 'fair trade'. This idea was launched in the Netherlands by a charity taking the name of a Dutch novel of the nineteenth century, which exposed the poor conditions of Indonesian coffee growers. The eponymous hero was a certain Max Havelaar, and this is the name of the brand of coffee, which is franchised by a charitable company drawing upon a number of small-scale coffee-growing organizations in Latin America. These organizations then use the income they receive for improving the lives of the families in their communities. The Max Havelaar brand has captured about 2 per cent of the Dutch market; that is nearly a quarter of what remains after the giant companies have taken their share. By 1992 similar coffees had won the same share in the supermarkets of Switzerland and Germany and also in the UK.[29] Purchasers know that the price is above that of other coffees, but are prepared to pay over the odds to give a better deal to the growers.

The most important aspect of these initiatives was that they had already involved some thirty organizations of small-scale coffee growers from twenty different countries, representing nearly a million coffee-growing families. They met in London in 1992 to set up a Small Farmers' Cooperative Society, and thereafter established a full-time staff in London engaged in arranging markets in Europe for coffees from member organizations. Plans were in hand for further offices to be opened in New York and Switzerland. African coffee growers from Tanzania, Kenya, Uganda and Zaire were represented and support was being given to organizations in these countries to improve the quality of their product, specialize in organic coffees and add value by roasting and packing in the country of origin.[30]

It is a somewhat ironic fact that these organizations had the World Bank's loan conditionality requirements – which had done so much damage in their countries – to thank for their freedom to trade their coffees without having to pay commissions either to a local government marketing board or to a parastatal jointly owned by a foreign company. The same 'freedom' has been established for the growers of many other African primary products – cocoa, cotton, tea, palm oil, tobacco – and new opportunities exist, therefore, for associations of African growers to take advantage of.[31]

As in the case of the coffee growers, other small-scale farmers will need the technical and financial help of organizations like the Max Havelaar Foundation and Twin Trading to get started. Winning 1 or 2 per cent of the market may seem to be a small thing, but for the growers it means much more than that. It means greatly increased knowledge and self-confidence to hold the giant companies and the local middlemen at bay and maintain alternative outlets for their products in place of a single buyer who can set the price. The next stage in producer cooperation is to establish storage, packaging and processing facilities so that more of the value added stays in the producing country. None of this will be realized without a whole new desire for cooperation between the governments and the growers of Africa's various primary products, so as to develop a common defence against the exploitation of their resources.

Smallholders and Plantation Workers

It is not an unambiguous advance for smallholders in Africa that they are now being viewed by the World Bank as the agents of agricultural development to be freed from state restrictions. After years of support for large-scale agribusiness as the key to modernization in Africa, the Bank, without apology, let it be known in 1989 that it had changed its mind. In its *Cameroon Agricultural Sector Review, Confidential Report*, the Bank reported the low labour productivity on the large Cameroonian plantation estates and recommended the government to concentrate attention not on middle-sized estates but on the smallholders:

The focus on smallholders is justified by their dominant role in production systems for both food and export crops, and by their relative efficiency in using resources. Smallholders *produce more per hectare, use land more fully, and face fewer labour constraints* (an important consideration given Cameroon's high labour costs). Smallholders also use labour more intensively ... absorbing increases in the labour force ... [and] since smallholders make up 90 per cent of the rural population ... [they] will assist in efforts to raise incomes generally (emphasis in the original).[32]

This new-found ideological attachment to smallholders and their cooperative associations became official policy in the Bank's *Strategy to Develop Agriculture in Sub-Saharan Africa*, published in 1993 as part of its privatization policy.[33] The Bank's technical advisers might perhaps have noticed the importance of 90 per cent of the rural population rather earlier. The fact that they have come in the end to recognize the particular importance of smallholders today cannot be unrelated to the decision not only of African parastatals but also of the big plantation owners like Unilever to shift from direct estate production to indirect subcontracting to smallholder production.[34]

The shift from estate labour to farm contracts is the result of a combination of pressures – falling world commodity prices and failure to increase labour productivity on the estates. Smallholders may well be able to increase ouput per hectare and use land and labour more productively, but they can also be more easily exploited. Since they grow their own food as well as a cash crop, they can survive on a price for cash crops that a plantation worker could not live on; and as individual farmers they cannot so easily organize to defend themselves. There was a specially long history of strike actions by unionized workers on the rubber and palm oil estates of the Cameroon Development

Corporation, which became intensified as falling world commodity prices led to downward pressure on wages. The workers became conscious of the power of their position in the labour-intensive operations of rubber tapping, palm harvesting, tea plucking and banana cutting.[35]

At the same time, there was also as much resistance to the Corporation's contracts among the smallholders. Although these farmers held on to their land rights, which were the envy of plantation workers, they soon found that all the risks of poor harvests and price fluctuations fell on them and that inputs of fertilizer and agricultural services supplied on credit had to be paid for together with interest when payment was received against crop deliveries.[36]

The Dutch agronomist, Piet Konings, has made a major study of labour resistance in Cameroon to successive attempts to modernize the production of agricultural materials. He quotes from a 1988 report of the effect of contract farming on the autonomy of the peasantry:

Contract farming is a form of disguised proletarianization: it secures the farmer's land and labour while leaving him/her with formal title to both. The control exercised by the company is indirect but effective; the farmer's control is legal but illusory. In this sense s/he is a 'propertied labourer' – on the one hand a landlord, and on the other a labourer who cares for corporate plants.[37]

This description reveals the dilemma of governments which wished to maintain the support of a middle layer of the peasantry through contract farming and of the expatriate companies which wished to obtain a regular supply of agricultural commodities for their rubber factories and oil mills at relatively little cost. Some of the larger farmers may have been able to benefit from the contracts since they did not need to borrow in order to purchase inputs and had some power to bargain about prices. The great majority of smaller farmers are reported in Cameroon to have 'regularly engaged in a variety of collective and informal modes of resistance which have seriously impeded the progress of the schemes'.[38]

Such peasant resistance to modernization has an important bearing on the issue of African governments' attempts to get a better deal for their natural resources in the world market. A major reason for the failure of smallholders' development programmes is said to be lack of government support.[39] Yet a unified approach to agricultural modernization from governments and peasant organizations is essential if improved earnings are to be realized. Unfortunately, most African governments do not value at all highly the worth of their small peasant farmers. This has been true both of governments with a capitalist orientation and of those which described themselves as Marxist. Their commitment to the Soviet economic model was only equalled by their transposition to African conditions of Marx's belief, drawn from his studies of capitalist Europe, that the sole potential agent of social change must be the wage-earning proletariat.

Only a few lone voices among African intellectuals saw the peasantry as a revolutionary force. Claude Aké, the Nigerian philosopher, in a nonconformist essay on *Revolutionary Pressures in Africa*, saw no hope for African revolution if it was not peasant based.[40] A much more typical analyst of Africa's political trajectory, Bade Onimode, at the end of his study of the *Political Economy of the African Crisis*, comes almost reluctantly, as it seems, in the last of over 300 pages, to recognize the existence of the African peasantry.[41] Yet, even in the 1990s, this class comprises at least two-thirds of the whole population throughout the continent.

In speaking of the need to mobilize the peasantry into 'a meaningful class alliance' for revolutionary change, Onimode draws upon a rather ambiguous statement of Amilcar Cabral that 'peasants are a great physical force but a reluctant revolutionary force'.[42] Onimode would have done well to ponder Cabral's detailed analysis of African class structures, in which he emphasized the need to build upon the strength of peasant resistance to oppression in forging a revolutionary alliance.[43]

Failure to understand Africa's structures of class and occupation, and to work with the grain of them, must be seen as the outstanding characteristic of all the nation-building and manoeuvring from the top downwards, even in the noblest of causes, that have marked the first thirty years of African independence. The overwhelming majority of the population remain small-scale primary producers on the land, whose skills and opinions have never been properly acknowledged. If African countries are to make common cause to defend their resources, it can only be done on the basis of the fullest possible mobilization of all the skills and opinions of the men and women in rural Africa.

CHAPTER 10

Transformation and Self-reliance

Successive structural adjustment programmes are rending the fabric of African society . . . The preference for foreign experts, foreign models, standards and goods is a consequence of Africa's imitative modernism and constitutes a barrier to experimentation, innovation and self-reliant development. But not all aspects of Africa's cultural milieu are negative and problematic. There are many that are positive and could be exploited successfully for development. Examples are the implications of African perceptions of human beings as the fulcrum of development, extended family for the cooperative spirit of self-help development and traditional sanctions on leadership.

> From the Economic Commission for Africa, *African Alternative to Structural Adjustment Programmes (AAF–SAP): A Framework for Transformation and Recovery*, Addis Ababa, 10 April 1989, pp. 1.7–8.

In rejecting the claim of the IMF and the World Bank that the structural adjustment programmes of these institutions in the 1980s had been to any degree successful, African leaders were thrown back on the ideas of self-reliance which they had begun to explore in the Lagos Plan of Action. They had to ask themselves what was wrong with the World Bank's concept of structural adjustment and what the alternative might be. The first results of this re-exploration of the ideas of self-reliance were presented by the Economic Commission for Africa in its 1989 report, entitled *African Alternative to Structural Adjustment Programmes (AAF–SAP): A Framework for Transformation and Recovery*, from which the passage that heads this chapter is taken.

This 1989 report from the ECA was no hastily prepared riposte to the World Bank. It followed from the African Priority Programme for Economic Recovery (1986) and it derived from a whole range of initiatives made public before and after 1989, emanating from the Commission itself and from the OAU. These might be referred to as the 'two As', the 'four Ks' and an 'AEC'. The two As are for the 1989 Abuja Declaration on Women in Development in Africa and the 1990 Arusha Charter for Popular Participation in Development. The four Ks are for the 1988 Khartoum Declaration on Human Resource Development, a Human-focused Approach to Socio-economic Recovery, the 1989 Kilimanjaro Plan of Action on Population Control, the 1990 Kampala Agenda for Action on the Environment and, with some licence in the spelling but not in pronunciation, Common Markets in the sub-regions; and the 'AEC' is the decision in 1990 by the heads of state of the OAU to establish an African Economic Community by the year 2015 (in the Lagos Plan of Action it was to have been by the year 2000).[1]

Human-centred Development

The significance of these charters, declarations, plans, agendas and commitments by the heads of African governments in the late 1980s was very great. African leaders were recognizing that the choice they had made at independence of Western-style modernization and nation building within the narrow confines of their separate nation-states had been mistaken. No less a person than General Olusegun Obasanjo, one-time Nigerian head of state, was conceding in 1990 how mistaken their choices had been:

In the past, African leaders were interested in little more than survival and the accumulation of power. The bald fact is that we have squandered almost thirty years with ineffective nation-building efforts. Our policies were far removed from social needs and developmental relevance.[2]

In the AAF-SAP of the ECA, the proposed 'framework for transformation and recovery' was not just a statement of economic policy measures and mechanisms for implementation and monitoring; it was also a statement of profound change in the philosophical commitment of Africa's leaders. This recognized the 'necessity', in the words of the conference of ministers, 'for a new African transformation ethic that incorporates, rather than alienates'.[3] The controlling element in this ethic was stated to be 'human-centred development'. It seemed in 1989 to be either stating a truism or a flight of rhetoric to insert such phrases into an economic report. But by 1991 Professor Adebayo Adedeji, who had been the Executive Secretary of the ECA, felt able to write:

Since the ECA came out with AAF–SAP and the Charter on Popular

Participation, no one now disputes the centrality of popular participation and the human factor as the only viable development paradigm for Africa. This new consensus on a human-centred development strategy is a quiet revolution in economic thought. The orthodox development paradigm anchored development to things not people. The central emphasis was placed on capital, particularly foreign capital. Even its 'export-as-the-engine-of-growth' hypothesis saw export as the source of foreign exchange earnings or as liquid capital for the import of physical capital and other 'things' for development.[4]

Professor Adedeji has made it clear that this means going back to Africa's pre-colonial history. In a review of Basil Davidson's book *The Black Man's Burden: Africa and the Curse of the Nation-State*, he writes:

Africa . . . owes . . . Davidson [whom Adedeji calls the 'doyen of African pre-colonial history'] a world of gratitude for reopening discussion on this fundamental issue which lies at the heart of the continent's persistent crisis . . . Davidson has argued convincingly that until the Africans rediscover their roots and build on them their own political, economic and social order, the process of alienation will persist and socio-economic and political crises will remain unabated . . . The tragedy has been that when the opportunity came to cast aside the yoke of colonialism, no effort was made to reassert Africa's self-determination by replacing the inherited foreign institutions and systems of government and the flawed European models of nation-states with rejuvenated and modernized indigenous African systems that the people would easily relate to and would therefore be credible.[5]

It was one thing for Africans to decide to go back to their roots, after thirty years of faithfully and fatefully copying the model of their erstwhile colonial rulers; it was quite another to decide what those roots actually were. We have seen in earlier chapters something of the way that these had been neglected and overlaid by alien growths. But, as African scholars explored along the paths that historians had pioneered, the outline of an indigenous African political economy became clear enough for essential conclusions to be drawn from this rediscovery of the past which could be applied to the future. The conclusions were summarized in a statement by the Ghanaian economist, George Ayittey:

The indigenous African economic system, by strict economic definition, is emphatically capitalistic. In the sense that the means of production were not owned by the chiefs or tribal governments, but by peasants or private individuals, capitalism was not 'invented' by Western colonialists. The type of capitalism practised in Africa was of a different variety, however. Profit was not appropriated by a single individual or by corporate owners, as in the West. Nor was it appropriated by the state, as in the East. In indigenous Africa, profit was shared between the owners and the workers. For want of a better term, we may characterize this as cooperative capitalism. The indigenous political system was democratic. Democracy was also not 'invented' by Western colonialists. Participatory democracy and confederate types of government existed in Africa . . . The true challenge of development is how to build upon and use the existing indigenous systems.[6]

Africa's Indigenous Strengths

Claude Aké, another African scholar, but working in the Marxist tradition, would be less than happy with the concept of 'cooperative capitalism'. In the later 1970s, inspired by the successes of popular movements against the Portuguese colonial power and against white minority rule in Rhodesia and South Africa, Aké had committed himself in his book, *Revolutionary Pressures in Africa*, to a highly optimistic prognosis. 'Capitalism in Africa,' he wrote, 'is on the way out and revolution against capitalism will increasingly be the order of the day.'[7] Aké then saw the revolutionary struggle of the African proletariat, and particularly, he insisted, of the peasantry, as but one part of the global struggle between what he called 'bourgeois countries' and 'proletarian countries'. In the latter, especially in Africa, the local ruling class acted as clients supplying political power to support the economic power of their patrons from the ruling class of the bourgeois countries. And, because they could not do this without coming up against the pressures of an increasingly disaffected proletariat, he concluded that

the dynamics of social forces in Africa . . . are moving Africa towards socalist revolution . . . As the global class struggle develops, and the contradictions between bourgeois and proletarian countries deepen . . . mutual alienation of client and patron classes will increase accordingly.[8]

We shall see!

In looking back to pre-colonial Africa it is well to be reminded of this aspect of the global economic forces within which African development has been taking place. What is all the more remarkable is that coming from a quite different intellectual tradition, Claude Aké had later reached the same conclusions as George Ayittey. By the end of the 1980s Aké was writing enthusiastically about 'Sustaining Development on the Indigenous' and insisting on understanding the indigenous as an 'authentic expression or outcome of Africa's history, social evolution and culture'.[9] Aké makes a clear distinction between 'traditional' and 'indigenous', since so many traditional African institutions and values were the result of interaction with other social forces.

Aké sees indigenous values and institutions being determined by what 'the community considers most important as reflected in popular attitudes and behaviour'; and he draws the most profound lesson from this concept of the indigenous:

The people and all those things that make them what they are – their culture, values and interests – are never an obstacle to their own development. This is so for two reasons. First, the task of development is to help people to move forward (by their own values) given all they are and not what they might become . . . Secondly, only what the people accept as the real or potential betterment of their lives can properly constitute their own development.[10]

There are four factors, in Aké's view, that give the indigenous in Africa its sustainability, not just economically and environmentally but in human organization also, in continuously generating local capabilities. The first is that 'in Africa the sense of community remains strong . . . Africans seem more interested in communal rights than individual rights . . . [This is] especially evident in the constant surge and role of ethnic associations, often called voluntary associations.'[11]

Aké gives as an example of voluntary association the Harambee projects in rural Kenya, which in the past supplied the whole range of local government services on the basis of self-help. Unfortunately, the government bureaucracy, fearing that its managerial role was being threatened, moved in to regulate and control these projects, thus greatly reducing their development potential. So it has come about that, having this strong sense of collective identity, Africans regard the state as a threat to be contained not as a protection to be preserved. As a result, Aké believes that today the African 'state is at once inordinately powerful and pitifully irrelevant'.[12] To harness the development potential of the community, Aké concludes that decentralization has to be political, administrative and economic, 'to coincide with natural communities where primary loyalties are strongest'.[13]

The strong sense of community among Africans has important implications for development. 'If the development potential of African communality is to be realized, it is desirable,' Aké argues, 'to give scope to cooperative relations in production.'[14] These are seen as being not only an important motivating force for economic development but also as ensuring that development is sustainable. Aké quotes a World Bank study on sustainability to show that 'a major contribution to sustainability came from the development of grass roots organizations, through which project beneficiaries gradually assumed increasing responsibility for project activities'.[15]

The second factor in African indigenous culture and institutions to which Aké seeks to draw attention is the role in the African economy of the extended family or household:

In the African context there is an indigenous production unit that deserves special mention because it is important in the lives of the people. It is the household economy; that is the household as an economic system ... It is an economy concerned with reproduction rather than production and it follows the law of subsistence rather than the law of value [i.e. of the return to capital]; it is tendentiously independent because its members own their means of production ... The household economy has not found much favour among the managers of development in Africa ... it hampers the capitalization of agriculture and it perpetuates a scale and technical level of production that is not conducive to very high increases in productivity. The model of the household economy might have helped us to avoid one of the appalling contradictions of the development experience in Africa – the food dependence of an overwhelmingly rural population with land of acceptable fertility and adequate grazing.[16]

The third factor which Aké proposes for consideration in building development upon indigenous African roots is linked to commonalty.

An important aspect of African social life that the development effort has not come to terms with is the profoundly participative character of African culture ... Africans do not generally think of themselves as self-regarding, atomized beings in competitive and potentially conflicting interaction with other such atomized beings. Rather, their consciousness runs in the direction of belonging to an organic social whole [in which] the point is to find one's station and its duties, not to assert one's interests and claim rights against others.[17]

Aké suggests that the universal prevalence in Africa of the informal sector reflects the communal and participative tendencies of African culture. But he comments that 'far from taking advantage of this participative culture, current development thinking and practice in Africa tended to assault it. And yet it is becoming increasingly clear that there is a positive correlation between development and participation.'[18]

Some will feel that there is a certain element of romanticism in Aké's picture of the African peasant, but he makes a convincing point in his defence. Where the state is regarded as a hostile force, there is simply no alternative for most Africans except to work together in associations where they feel comfortable. Participation for Africans is a process, not the exercise of a right. It is a 'matter of sharing tangible things, namely the rewards and sacrifices of community membership'. And since men and women will support what they perceive to serve their interests, participation will always be linked to sustainability.[19]

This link between African culture and what is sustainable lies at the very heart of Aké's argument. If no other arguments prevailed, the appeal to the conservationist instincts of the subsistence farmer must carry weight. This is where Aké believes that most attention must be concentrated by those who would help Africans to emerge from their current problems. Because the margin between death and survival is narrow in a generally hostile natural environment, African peasants will be, more than others, 'sensitive to the realities on the ground, especially ecological factors, which [they] seem even more concerned about than economic factors'.[20]

Ecological sustainability implies devising what Aké calls 'mini-development plans for localities'. Thus, the last words in Aké's paper contain an appeal to the agents of development that 'they will have to learn to suspend belief in the validity and superiority of their knowledge and values. And they will have to learn to think "small", very small, and act democratic.'[21]

Aké draws a sobering conclusion from his study of the indigenous in African society. 'The lesson is,' he concludes, 'that Africa can no longer look to the wealthier nations, international agencies, or even African governments for their development. This leaves us with the "forgotten alternative" – the ordinary people of Africa.'[22] Without taking too literally this admonition, it provides a salutary warning and it suggests something of the depth of the reappraisal which informed the ECA's proposals for an African alternative to structural adjustment. In fact, the ECA does not propose delinking and complete self-reliance. In the *Framework for Transformation and Recovery* there is a place not only for African governments, but for aid from wealthier nations and international agencies. Indeed, some measures of structural adjustment are only in part to be modified, while others are to be replaced completely.

There is a certain irony in the importance that is being attached here to the writings of George Ayittey and Claude Aké, because the two papers from which their evocations of Africa's indigenous strengths have been taken were both commissioned and published by the World Bank itself in the Background Papers that accompanied the Bank's Long-Term Perspective Study of Sub-Saharan Africa. In a Preface to these Papers, the editor, the distinguished Indian economist Ramgopal Agarwala, claimed that 'they helped the Bank to move to a "high ground" that is not only intellectually sound but that can also lay the foundations for an improved consensus among the partners in Africa's development'.[23] The irony lies in the fact that, despite the rhetoric about 'taking the human element into account', the Bank's recommendations lie entirely in the economic realm. The policy prescriptions from the Bank continued to stress economic liberalization and 'export-led growth' for the continent following the Western model. It was seen earlier, in the Bank's *World Development Report, 1991*, in a section headed 'Trade Routes to Growth', that the authors were still to be found writing: 'The industrial countries of today grew prosperous through trade. No effort should be spared to ensure that the developing countries can follow that same path to progress.'[24]

Modifying and Transforming Structural Adjustment

Whatever may be understood from the World Bank's publication of these and other background papers, there is no possibility of understanding the ECA's 'Alternative to Structural Adjustment' except in the light of the reappraisal of Africa's indigenous strengths, which have been considered here. The thoughts expressed by George Ayittey and by Claude Aké inform its whole approach. The *African Alternative to Structural Adjustment Programmes* (AAF–SAP as it is known) comprises a list of 'Policy Instruments and Measures to be Modified', *and* an outline of 'Proposed Policy Instruments for *Adjustment with Transformation*' (emphasis added). But it starts with an Introduction on 'Human-centred Development'.

In proposing 'human beings as the fulcrum of development',[25] the African Alternative has been criticized as being strong in philosophical commitment, but weak in practical application. The answer to this charge lies in the detail of the proposals that follow, but the philosophical commitment is an essential part of the reality, as the Introduction to the Framework makes clear. The key paragraph deserves quotation in full:

It should be emphasized that the urgency of alleviating mass poverty and increasing the welfare of the African people is rooted not simply in the humanistic or altruistic aspects of development. It is predicated, above all, on the rational proposition that development has to be engineered and sustained by the people themselves through their full and active participation. Development should not be undertaken on behalf of a people, rather it should be the organic outcome of a society's value system, its perceptions, its concerns and its endeavours. As such, to achieve and sustain development, it is necessary to ensure the education and training, health, well-being and vitality of the people so that they can participate fully and effectively in the development process.[26]

The African Alternative Framework proposed in the ECA paper consisted of two main parts. The first was concerned with policy instruments and measures already in force under structural adjustment programmes which needed to be *modified*; the second comprised the *new* policy instruments and measures which were being proposed. These were presented in four sections, dealing respectively with strengthening and diversifying production, raising and redistributing income, switching expenditure patterns towards satisfying needs, and the necessary institutional support for adjustment with transformation. The several sections were summarized in the ECA paper and listed together with a brief statement of their expected effects.[27] They can be further summarized here in important detail:

MEASURES TO MODIFY SAPs

Modifications to be made to:

1. the drastic budget cuts in social expenditure, which have been undermining human potential for development;
2. the indiscriminate promotion of traditional exports through price incentives, which have been undermining food production and leading to over-production for export;
3. the across-the-board credit squeeze, which has been reducing output and capacity utilization;
4. the generalized devaluation of the currency through open foreign exchange markets, which has raised import prices of basic goods, generated inflation, increased the flight of capital and worsened income inequalities;
5. the unsustainably high interest rates, which have encouraged speculative activities and discouraged productive investment;
6. the total liberalization of imports, which has jeopardized food self-sufficiency and the survival of infant industries;

7. the excessive dependence on market forces to get 'prices right', which has created inflation and further distorted income distribution;
8. the doctrinaire privatization, which has restricted growth and undermined social welfare.

FOUR GROUPS OF POSITIVE MEASURES

A. For Strengthening and Diversifying Production Capacity:

1. land reforms and enhancement of women's rights and role, to increase production and employment opportunities and alleviate poverty;
2. investment in agriculture – up to 25 per cent of total public investment, to improve rural infrastructure and raise agricultural productivity;
3. increased devotion of foreign exchange to vital inputs for agriculture and manufacturing, to increase domestic output, inter-linkages of agriculture and industry and to satisfy critical needs;
4. allocation of priority credit to the food sector and to essential manufactures for food self-sufficiency and increased employment;
5. investment in small-scale industry, to encourage local entrepreneurs;
6. discrimination in interest rates, to discourage speculation and to mobilize savings for productive activities;
7. creation and strengthening of rural savings banks, to mobilize rural savings;
8. rehabilitation and improved maintenance of underutilized installed productive capacity, to increase output and save imports;
9. utilization of multiple exchange rates, to encourage capital inflow and discourage outflow, so that the balance of payments is improved and critical needs are met;
10. creation of a special development fund at subsidized interest rates for innovative producers.

B. Improving the Level of Income and the Pattern of Distribution:

1. improvements in tax collection to increase government revenue;
2. reduction in state spending on defence to release resources for productive investment and reduce unnecessary imports;
3. removal of subventions to parastatals other than those in the social sector and in strategic industries to release resources for productive investment;

4. realistic use of deficit financing to sustain selective growth;

5. guaranteed minimum prices for food crops through use of strategic reserves to sustain increased local food production for the needs of the people.

C. Pattern of Expenditure for the Satisfaction of Needs:

1. switching 30 per cent of government expenditure to education, health and the integration of women, and maintaining this proportion ahead of the population growth rate, in order to raise living standards and invest in human capital;

2. selective subsidies on essential commodities to meet the needs of the poor and ensure intermediate inputs to industry;

3. selective trade policy to ban luxury imports and raise taxes on conspicuous consumption so as to enlarge markets for domestically produced goods;

4. strengthening intra-African monetary and financial cooperation to increase African self-reliance;

5. limitation on debt service ratios to free resources for productive activities and to improve the balance of payments;

6. specific export incentives for selected processed products, to increase diversification in export earnings and to reduce vulnerability to commodity price falls;

7. differential export subsidies and encouragement of intra-African barter trade to reduce external dependence and to strengthen African economic integration;

8. seeking bilateral and multilateral commodity agreements to establish improved and more stable balances of payments.

D.   Institutional Support for Adjustment with Transformation:

1. creation of adequately funded 'supervised food production credit systems' in rural areas with easy access for farmers to sustain increases in food production and the adoption of new technology;

2. strengthening agricultural research and extension services, to create self-sufficiency in basic foods – maize, sorghum, millet, rice and tubers;

3. creation of rural institutions to support cottage and small-scale industries, with indigenous technology, domestic finance and strong women's participation, to promote integrated rural development and to enhance the attractiveness of rural areas;

4. provision of a clear legal framework of ownership for small-scale

artisans' cooperatives, et cetera, so as to increase popular participation and to strengthen the informal sector with a view to its ultimate integration into mainstream development;

5. establishment of community development institutions, especially involving indigenous NGOs and self-help programmes, to encourage community labour on the rural infrastructure of roads, health centres, schools, small irrigation schemes, et cetera;

6. greater mass participation in decision-making and in the implementation of programmes to mobilize human resources and win popular confidence in the development process and greater commitment to the sacrifices required.[28]

Responses to the African Alternative

No one can say that the philosophy at the beginning of the ECA paper is not supported by a balanced package of practical measures and policy instruments after reading through the list of twenty-nine proposals which have been summarized here. How far governments will be able to implement them is another question, but some indications are encouraging. The report 'generated a very lively debate, both within and outside Africa', was the comment of the retiring executive secretary of ECA, Professor Adebayo Adedeji.[29] A widely attended conference of African scholars organized by the Institute for African Alternatives and the Institute of Development Studies of the University of Dar es Salaam at the end of 1989 adopted what came to be called the Dar es Salaam Declaration on Alternative Development Strategies for Africa. This declaration ended with an important warning: 'that the most basic problem with alternative development strategies in Africa is their implementation. This requires that development documents in Africa must become political documents that should be widely disseminated and debated.'[30]

The publication in Addis Ababa in 1990 of Adebayo Adedeji's *African Alternative* showed that the process of dissemination and debate had started. The book was followed by the founding at the end of 1991 of a new African Centre for Development and Strategic Studies (ACDESS) in Ogun, Nigeria, with Professor Adedeji as first Executive Director. The Centre was, in the words of its first Bulletin of July 1992, 'a continental institution', its aim 'to create a think-tank in and for Africa'.[31]

African governments, which had always dealt individually with the

IMF and the World Bank, for the first time persisted, in relation to the ECA report, in acting and negotiating collectively. Support for the report was obtained from the churches and leading African NGOs; and the report, which came to be known simply as the 'African Alternative', was endorsed not only by the OAU and the Non-aligned Movement, but by the General Assembly of the UN itself.[32] The United States was the only country to vote against and to veto a proposal for the UN to adopt the plan, the US delegate arguing that the adjustment programmes arranged by the World Bank and the IMF were more suitable for country-by-country negotiations.[33]

The most remarkable response to the African Alternative came from the World Bank itself. By the end of the year in which the ECA report was published, the Bank produced its Long-Term Perspective Study, *Sub-Saharan Africa: From Crisis to Sustainable Growth*. In the Introduction, it is claimed that the study

is the result of an intensive collaboration with both Africans and donors and, as such, tries to reflect the evolution in African views from the Lagos Plan of Action in 1980 to the program of action presented at the United Nations in 1986, the Abuja Declaration of 1987, the Khartoum Declaration of 1988, and the UN Economic Commission for Africa [ECA's] 1989 report *African Alternative Framework to Structural Adjustment Programmes*. The attention to human resources, technology, regional cooperation, self-reliance, and respect for African values that informs these African policy statements provides the main focus of the strategy proposed in the following chapters.[34]

As a supplement to the Long-Term Perspective Study, the Bank commissioned and published four volumes of Background Papers, in which African scholars made the main contributions.[35] They explored specifically indigenous African roots as a base for the construction of Africa's future. They took part in a workshop on regional integration and cooperation. They presented a wide range of African views on economic and sectoral policy issues as well as on particular country perspectives. Whatever may have been the Bank executive directors' intentions, the papers provide a rich resource of the thoughts and aspirations of Africans on the future development of their continent.

African governments through the ECA had also begun to make their own individual country studies, as part of what had been deliberately called a '*Framework* for Transformation and Recovery'. Bade Onimode, speaking for the ECA, insisted from the start that the AAF–SAP report was not a programme to be applied to all countries at all times, regardless of their special circumstances. Rather, it is a framework or conceptual basis for formulating national programmes from the *menu* of policy directions and measures in AAF–SAP, from which countries are to select their policy packages according to their national peculiarities.[136]

The World Bank, in its turn, responded with an African Capacity Building Initiative. This was co-sponsored by the Bank with the UN Development Programme (UNDP) and the African Development Bank. The aim was to end the massive brain drain from Africa (50 per cent of all African professionals work outside Africa) and to establish a long-term development approach in place of short-term measures. But there had to be jobs to come back to, and these would have to be mainly in the public sector. The fact was that 'grafting bits and pieces on to already failed orthodox SAPs', as Bade Onimode put it, could not work.[37] There had to be a clear reversal of the budget cuts and credit squeeze across the board, but especially those in health and education, which had been required under structural adjustment programmes. The doctrinaire demand for wholesale privatization along with import liberalization had to be ended and more relevant programmes put in their place. Few would doubt that in many African states the role of government was too large, but to go to the other extreme and cut it right back was to create chaos.

Professor Adedeji in his *African Alternative* drew the obvious conclusion:

While the Alternative is pragmatically affirmative on the role of the public sector, it is equally affirmative on the pivotal role that the private sector must play in the process of adjustment-with-transformation. The African Alternative distances itself from dirigism and dogmatic public intervention as much as from doctrinaire privatization and excessive reliance on markets and prices as allocative mechanisms. The Alternative's central aim in this area is to find an objective, non-ideological balance between the public and private sectors to ensure efficiency and dynamism in national economic management. In conclusion, AAF–SAP does not advocate fat government in Africa (what the Spanish call *estado adiposo*) but muscular government (*estado musculoso*).[38]

ECA Criticized

Academic authorities outside Africa did not receive the ECA report with favour. Professor James Pickett, a Scottish professor of overseas development studies and an adviser to the African Development Bank, was scathing – rather surprisingly in a volume of essays in honour of Robert Gardiner: 'Since it has something of a shot-gun approach, it cannot be said that the ECA document is all wrong,' wrote Professor Pickett. 'It mostly is, however, and it is dangerous.'[39]

The professor discerned two main flaws. The first, he argued was 'the assumption that African countries are poor because of the weight of subsistence agriculture, primitive technology and narrow markets ... On the contrary, they have little in the way of modern techniques, small markets and most of their workers in agriculture, precisely because they are poor.'[40]

This might sound like the chicken and the egg, but the professor went on to explain that what he meant was that structural characteristics cannot be changed by administrative solutions, but only by solving economic problems, that is to say, by removing obstacles to economic growth. The second flaw was said by the professor to follow from the first. The ECA sought to solve economic problems by what he called 'the stubborn advocacy of extensive contra-market economic management in face of all the evidence of recent history and regardless of resource requirements'.[41]

In plain words, Professor Pickett went on to state his firm belief that governments should 'get off the back of the peasant' and leave economic development to the free working of market forces. 'In the event, the spontaneous growth that would have resulted largely from free markets would almost certainly have been positive and so greater than that actually secured in many countries.'[42] 'Even with respect to income distribution – the frequently cited "Achilles heel" of the market – supply and demand are likely to do better by the mass of the African poor in rural areas than governments have done to date. Moreover, *at its best* the market is completely impartial' (emphasis added).[43]

Professor Pickett turns for authority by quoting Adam Smith: 'What is called for is a policy that deals "equally and impartially with every sort of industry". It just happens that in most of sub-Saharan Africa that would deliver much investment to peasant agriculture.'[44]

On that basis, the professor believes, industry also could be developed as the 'offspring of agriculture'.[45] Such wholehearted faith in the efficacy of market forces fairly takes one's breath away. There is a tell-tale qualification of the market in the phrase 'at its best' and this appears elsewhere in a reference to the role of 'well-functioning' markets.[46]

'Spontaneous growth' is espoused by Professor Pickett in the light of Adam Smith's supposition that it was the division of labour resulting from barter and exchange which encouraged the steady extension of specialization and thus the development of the productive forces of labour. Apart from the fact that there are widespread doubts about Adam Smith's reading of economic history,[47] there really is no such thing today as a 'well-functioning market' which 'deals equally and impartially'. Some people enter the market with more money, resources and bargaining power than others. We saw in earlier chapters the weakness of the millions of small-scale primary producers in the face of the few big dealers in the commodity markets and of the dozens of small states producing minerals in face of the few giant transnational mining companies.

Professor Pickett does not accept that increasingly adverse terms of trade could be a major explanation for the weak performance of African low-income economies.[48] Asian countries, he argues, were able to survive the same adverse trends.[49] The run of figures for commodity prices which he quoted stops at 1986 before the really disastrous collapse for African products in 1989; and he failed to explore, as we had to earlier, the complex reasons for the switch of investment in new technology by the big companies from Africa to Asia and Latin America. The African complaint of the encouragement of excessive export cropping he called a 'contentious issue'.[50]

There is much more besides. Professor Pickett dismissed as irrelevant the limitation of the small size of national markets in African countries,[51] and gave credence to Hayek's claim that European aid should be blamed for encouraging Africans in having large families.[52] Most of the responsibility in his arguments, however, is laid upon African governments, for their interference in the free working of the market, for their flawed agricultural policies and their state-driven industrialization. This is but to echo the World Bank. Professor Pickett is not entirely consistent. He recalls that Adam Smith allowed the state three functions – defence, justice and the *provision of public goods* (emphasis added)[53] – and, when writing jointly with Hans Singer, Pickett makes a crucial concession:

Economic historians confirm that, historically, increased agricultural productivity has come as much from increased investment as from a rational price structure [i.e. market determined]. Moreover, much of the investment has had a public good character and so would only have come from the public sector.[54]

It is not the intention here to whitewash African governments, whose inefficiencies, corruption and ruthlessness have already been exposed. But, given the disastrous results of the World Bank's measures of structural adjustment, it is necessary to welcome in the ECA report and the supporting resolutions of African governments' recognition of the urgent need for changing their ways. Thirty-five African governments had been prepared to go along with World Bank policies more or less willingly. The ECA report was a real attempt to find a new way forward; it was not, as Professor Pickett had it,[55] a return to the flawed reliance on state decision making, which even philosopher kings could not make efficient, let alone, one might add, the 'assassins' whom the archbishop of Kinshasa felt obliged to castigate for their exploitation of the people and riches of Zaire.[56]

Far from relying on 'contra-market economic management', the ECA report did recognize an important role for the market and for private enterprise, but within a framework of state regulation that would encourage both cooperation and competition. Adam Smith in fact believed in both. His 'invisible hand', that is so much quoted as if it were an almost mystical force, was in his view the force of 'moral sentiment'.[57] For Smith, in his day, as for any intellectual in an aristocratic society, this was the force of sympathy which led the rich to advance the interest of the whole society and thus provide the social foundation for what he called 'modern civility', what we might call solidarity. In a democratic society today we should look for bonds of civility in the involvement of the many representative institutions that make governments and markets accountable.

Democratizing the Decision-making Process

Underlying the ECA programme lay the absolute necessity of establishing democratic governments in Africa. The design of all national programmes was to be based on the central role of government to create an enabling environment for popular participation and to give vigorous support for grass roots initiatives. The accountability of all executive agencies and public sector enterprises to organs of popular representation was to be assured. All available modes of mass media were to be utilized to disseminate information and to popularize programmes so that the widest possible discussion and debate could take place before measures were enacted.[58] When these brave resolutions are compared with the reality of governance in most of the African states before 1990, they appear as nothing more than the mouthing of pious devotions. But what has happened in Africa since 1990 shows that they might still be realized.

The only states in sub-Saharan Africa which could be counted as even remotely resembling a pluralist democracy prior to 1990 were Botswana, Gambia (though lost to the military in 1994) and Mauritius, although Senegal might just claim that distinction. Within two years of the first weeks of 1990, there were thirty-three states in which promises of multiparty elections had been made, and fourteen where they had successfully been held. In the other nineteen, elections had been stopped, postponed, challenged by the opposition as fraudulent or had led to continuing virtually single-party assemblies. That leaves nine states where violence or open warfare rendered elections void or unthinkable (see Table 10.1).

The defeat of a number of established presidents – in Benin, Madagascar, Mali and Zambia – and the overthrow of Mengistu in Ethiopia were indeed cause for celebration. What changes will follow from multiparty assemblies and coalition governments cannot yet be predicted. Nearly all the new governments were still committed in 1993 to policies dictated by the World Bank's conditions for the receipt of financial facilities to cover essential imports and debt servicing. Some leading figures in the old regimes have lost power along with their presidents, but the commercial class and the governing élite which have always benefited from the foreign trade connections of the African states remain largely untouched. The dissolution of marketing boards and the privatization of state and parastatal companies open up some space for new enterprise. If this is not, however, to be filled by the old élite in a new capitalist guise or by foreign transnationals creaming off the milk, and is to give real new openings for small- and medium-sized private enterprises and producer cooperatives, there will need to be a framework of state support and probably also help from outside.

If words were enough to create a democratic society, Africa would be democratized. Alongside the African Alternative Framework to Structural Adjustment Programmes for Socio-economic Recovery and Transformation (1989) and the African Priority Programme for Economic Recovery (1986), there was mentioned earlier the Khartoum Declaration on a Human-focused Approach (1988), the Arusha Charter for Popular Participation in Development (1990) and the Abuja Declaration on the Integration of Women in Development in Africa (1989).

The Charter for Popular Participation and Development was prepared at an international conference of NGOs and grass roots organizations, representatives of African governments and UN agencies in
Arusha, Tanzania, in February 1990 and immediately adopted by the
OAU.[59] The aim of the Arusha Charter was to create a framework for
effective popular participation at all levels in a new partnership between
government and people.

Government was to yield political and social space to enable the popular
forces of workers, peasants, women, youths, students and professionals to
participate more actively in the adjustment with the development process.[60]

Bade Onimode, writing in 1992, suggested that the response had been
enthusiastic:

Many Africans have already warmly embraced the African Charter. Most of
them, their NGOs and grass roots organizations see the Charter as a major
political blueprint around which to organize their campaigns and for which
they must mobilize and struggle. Thus, the Organization of African Trade
Union Unity (OATUU) organized a joint regional conference with ECA on
Popular Participation and AAF–SAP in Addis Ababa, Ethiopia, in March
1992. A network of environmental NGOs in West Africa are also planning an
international conference on Popular Participation and the Environment in
Lagos, Nigeria, during the first half of 1992. Similar conferences have been
organized by different NGOs and grass roots organizations on the themes of
democratization and recovery across Africa.[61]

Onimode, in his *A Future for Africa*, from which the passage above is
quoted, clearly recognized that there is a practical and ideological
conflict between those who believe that transformation must involve
delinking Africa from the whole logic of the capitalist world division of
labour and those who see possibilities of transformation without delinking. There has in fact never been any official endorsement of delinking
as an African collective position, a fact that Onimode has emphasized.
He was able, moreover, to find common ground between the 'delinkers'
and the ECA/OAU officials in an 'inward looking strategy', that
emphasizes 'national and collective self-reliance, internalizing the engine
of Africa's development'.[62] Both groups reject the latest prescriptions of
the World Bank, which imply a more participative African involvement
but only to mobilize resources for the Bank's own structural reforms.
The Bank's Long-Term Perspective Study had concluded with a plea
for

a new international compact for Africa ... a new global coalition ... to widen the scope of consultation to cover both donors and recipients ... on the full range of long-term development issues ... a forum in which African leaders (not just from the public sector, but also from private business, the professions, the universities and other NGOs) could meet with their key partners – the bilateral and multilateral agencies and major foreign NGOs – to agree on general strategies that would then provide broad guidance for the design of country programmes.[63]

This sounds like another bid to upstage and replace Africa's own voice in the ECA and in other UN agencies. The Bank's perspectives in its 'Strategic Agenda for the 1990s' led Adebayo Adedeji, as one-time Executive Secretary of ECA, to draw attention to the 'striking contrast between African and Western perspectives' and to show precisely the nature of that contrast:

The African viewpoint, particularly that of politicians, must assume a future that is economically viable and politically sustainable. It must assume industrialization and, at least, a promise of technological equality with the West (including Japan). It must encompass spiritual health and self-reliance as well as material well-being. The perspective is quite naturally Afro-centric ... The Western perspective is that of the policy-maker ... Africa does not dominate this perspective, it is only one of a panoply of global concerns. Unlike the African, the Western bureaucrat is not compelled to assume politically viable solutions within Africa, nor does he take for granted the feasibility of rapid economic progress. Quite the contrary, he is usually more impressed by the negative, short-term implications of Africa's economic crisis – particularly its effect on political stability.[64]

The contrast between European economism and African humanism could not be more strikingly portrayed.

TABLE 10.1 Sub-Saharan African Elections 1991–95

Country	Latest Election	Election to come	Results
Angola	1992		Challenged; war
Benin	1991		President defeated
Botswana	1994		Continuing multi-party system
Burkina Faso	1992		Opposition boycott
Burundi	1993		Hutu election victory challenged by Tutsi military
Cameroon	1992		Results criticized
Cape Verde	1991		President defeated
CAR	1993		Results criticized
Chad		1995	Outcome uncertain
Comoros	1992		Widely criticized
Congo	1993		Challenged by military; violence
Côte d' Ivoire		1995	First since death of Houphouët-Boigny
Djibouti	1992		Opposition excluded; rebellion
Equ. Guinea	1993		Boycotted by opposition; human rights abuses continue
Eritrea			No opposition parties
Ethiopia		1995	Boycott by opposition parties not allied to govt.; govt. victory
Gabon		1995	Ruling party unlikely to relinquish power
Gambia			1994 coup ended multiparty politics
Ghana	1992		Opposition boycott
Guinea			No multiparty legislative elections
Guinea Bissau	1994		Won by incumbent
Kenya	1992		Won by incumbent on minority vote
Lesotho	1993		Results contested by king
Liberia			Continuing civil war
Madagascar	1993		Uncertain coalition
Malawi	1994		First since independence won by opposition
Mali	1992		Won by opposition alliance; rebellion
Mauritania	1992		Boycotted by opposition
Mauritius	1991		Continuing multiparty system
Mozambique	1994		Incumbent party wins first multiparty elections
Namibia	1994		SWAPO landslide
Niger	1993		Uncertain coalition; rebellion
Nigeria	1993		Result rejected by army
Rwanda			Tutsi rebel army takes over in carnage
São Tomé	1991		Ruling party defeated
Senegal	1993		Won by ruling party
Seychelles	1993		Won by ruling party

Table 10.1 *continued*

Country	Latest Election	Election to come	Results
Sierra Leone			Military/civil war
Somalia			Civil war
South Africa	1994		ANC-led Govt. of National Unity
Sudan			Military/civil war
Swaziland			Absolute monarchy moving towards multiparty politics
Tanzania		1995	First since independence; rift with Zanzibar?
Togo	1994		Coalition
Uganda			Govt. rejects multiparty politics
Zaire		1995	Mobuto unlikely to accept pluralism
Zambia	1991		Opposition landslide
Zimbabwe	1995		Won by ZANU–PF again

Sources: *Keesing's, Africa Confidential, Whitaker's Almanack 1995.*

CHAPTER 11

An African Model of Industrial Development

The case studies of industrial development . . . show a continued failure to develop indigenous technological capacities in much of (formal sector) African industry. Complex historical circumstances are responsible. An important feature is a lack of fit between the industrialization model adopted and the environment – of factor and product markets and social structures – in African economies . . . Rehabilitation strategy is strongly influenced by the World Bank policy of export-oriented industrialization . . . [which] . . . has tended to increase the firm's reliance on imported machinery, borrowed finance and more sophisticated managerial techniques, widening the gap between the industrialization model and domestic conditions.

> Samuel Wangwe, 'Building Indigenous Technological Capacity in African Industry – an Overview' in Frances Stewart, Sanjaya Lall and Samuel Wangwe (eds), *Alternative Development Strategies in Sub-Saharan Africa*, Macmillan, 1992, p. 241.

The Need for Industrialization

At the centre of the African case for a major social transformation leading to economic recovery has lain the absolute necessity to transform completely the nature of the African industrialization process. As it is written in the introductory chapter to an authoritative study of alternative development strategies for sub-Saharan Africa, from which the quotation at the head of this chapter is taken:

In nearly all economies, manufacturing industry has been the critical agent of the structural transformation that makes the transition from a primitive low-productivity, low-income state to one that is dynamic, sustained and diversified . . . For many African countries, however, the 1980s were years of industrial stagnation and even *de-industrialization* . . . from 1980 to 1987 . . . for sub-Saharan Africa as a whole industrial production fell by 1 per cent per annum.[1]

The World Bank had always explained African countries' industrial failures by pointing to the lack of incentives for increased efficiency in government policies for industry. These were said to be inward oriented and heavily protectionist and to subject all enterprise to state intervention, distorting both internal and external prices.[2]

These policies criticized by the World Bank were, however, policies introduced to Africa under colonial rule and proposed to African governments by expatriate advisers after independence, as Professor Samuel Wangwe of the University of Dar es Salaam has emphasized. The World Bank's proposals for structural adjustment to open up African economies still further to world markets had evidently failed to improve matters.

It was clear by the end of the 1980s that, if Africa was to succeed with industrialization, fundamental changes were required. The World Bank's revised proposals in its Long Term Perspective Study (LTPS), following the publication of ECA's *African Alternative* (AAF–SAP), while embracing some of the language of the 'alternative', only recommended more of the same structural adjustment medicine, which was already proving lethal.[3] This is the Bank's prescription:

If African economies are to grow they must earn foreign exchange to pay for essential imports . . . [and] . . . increase their share of world markets . . . The prospects for significant increases in world prices for most primary commodities are poor, so higher export earnings must come from increased output, diversification into new commodities and an aggressive drive into the rapidly growing Asian markets.[4]

At the same time, the Bank was encouraging all other indebted developing countries, and particularly those in Asia, to expand their commodity exports. The inevitable result, as we saw earlier, was rising stocks of commodities and steadily falling prices. There was nothing in the Bank's perspective about encouraging industrial production in Africa for developing manufactured goods for export. This was apparently to be left to the Asian newly industrializing countries (NICs). In this connection, a 1992 report from UNCTAD, the foremost champion of the needs of the developing countries, had discouraging news for most of Africa:

In a number of developing countries manufactured exports have surpassed or attained the level of commodity exports and have become the most dynamic sector in their economies. Nevertheless, for the majority of developing countries, commodities will have to continue to form the engine of growth, in particular for those with little opportunity to diversify out of commodities.[5]

The World Bank, in its Long Term Perspective Study, recognized the problems involved in creating an enabling environment for industrial development, but failed to see the connection between the problems and its own solutions. In proposing 'A New Start to Industrialization', the Bank stated its firm conviction: 'The private sector holds the key to future industrial growth, but private entrepreneurs have often found more enticing opportunities outside industry (especially in taking advantage of scarcity rents created by controls).'[6]

The whole point about the 'enticing opportunities outside industry' is that they were to be found in commerce – in the export–import business, which was the main business in which most African countries were involved and in which the Bank was encouraging them to stay involved. Industrial entrepreneurs could not, therefore, be discovered simply by ending the regime of state controls. Something much more radical was required, and to start with a more radical critique of the nature of the industrialization process which had been introduced into Africa.

An African Critique of World Bank Policies

Such a critique was attempted at a remarkable gathering in Addis Ababa early in 1991 of African economists and other scholars. This was organized by the Institute for African Alternatives under the auspices of the ECA and the OAU to develop Africa's 'Response'[7] to the World Bank's Study and at the same time to take account of the progress of the Uruguay Round of GATT and the Fraser Report on *Africa's Commodity Problems*. More than twenty papers were presented and subsequently published together with an agreed 'Workshop Statement'. In this statement the conference noted

the admission of the World Bank in the LTPS of the failure of its sponsored policies over the last three decades and of the SAPs imposed on African countries over the last decade. The Bank has come to accept some of the concerns and policy directions of the OAU, ECA, IFAA and other organizations and critics and has borrowed their language heavily. The areas of the emerging agreement include: the need for adjustment with growth, human-centred development, regional cooperation, and democratic participation.[8]

The conference, however, rejected the World Bank's claim that African governments had no long-term perspective and it condemned the World Bank's call for a new generation of SAPs, which would continue the flawed policies of reliance on market forces, liberalization of all prices and controls, ever greater cooperation between African and industrialized countries on existing unfavourable terms, dependence on the informal sector for industrialization and the imposition of cost recovery and user charges for social services. The statement reasserted the need for support policies in agriculture, protection for infant industries and state participation in promoting intermediate and capital goods industries. It reaffirmed confidence in the value of Africa's own long-term development plans – the Lagos Plan of Action and the ECA's *African Alternative Framework* – and proposed that African governments 'abandon the World Bank/IMF imposed SAPs and LTPS and take urgent steps to implement their own programmes'.

Finally, the statement called upon the international community to support Africa's initiatives in choosing their own path of development. The statement firmly rejected the attempt by the industrialized countries to impose new trade policies under the Uruguay Round of GATT, which would entail an estimated loss to African countries of some US\$ 3 billion annually. It also rejected the Fraser Report with its continued insistence on Africa's growth being sought through expanded exports of primary products.[9]

Inappropriate Models – from West and East

It must seem an extraordinary example of disingenuousness, bordering on deviousness, that allowed the World Bank in its criticism of African governments and their failed policies in the 1970s and 1980s, especially of poor public sector management, to overlook the Bank's own responsibility for these policy failures. The nearest that the Bank comes to self-criticism in its LTPS is in the following statement:

There are countless examples of badly chosen and poorly designed public investments including some in which the World Bank has participated. A 1987 evaluation revealed that half of the completed rural development projects financed by the World Bank had failed.[10]

There was not a word about failed World Bank urban *industrial* investments, although a rather grudging admission is made:

African governments and foreign financiers (commercial banks and credit agencies *as well as donor agencies*) must share responsibility ... Governments also agreed to – and often pressed for – grandiose or inappropriate investments (emphasis added).[11]

More seriously, the World Bank never sought out the reasons for its failures, but always suggested that it was the African governments' failure to implement Bank policies that was the problem.[12]

This is where the African analysis is so important. Mistakes by African governments – of heinous proportions – are admitted. But they have been made because they followed the logic of the Bank's privatization policies, from which even the sins of corruption have largely flowed. In a presidential address to the African Studies Association in 1988, Nzongola Ntalaja made the point very clearly: 'Many African rulers have virtually privatized the state itself in the sense that state resources, including state enterprises, are used not to promote the public good but to serve private interests.'[13]

One would hardly know from World Bank criticisms that African governments had already moved a long way in the 1960s and 1970s to encourage direct private investment in industry, especially from overseas. Here is how Samuel Wangwe described what was found in the studies of industrialization that were made in Côte d'Ivoire, Nigeria and Tanzania:

First, initial planning of the sectors was undertaken by foreign experts. Their influence had therefore tended to be built-in from the start. Second, project planning and execution was carried out with little deliberate or actual local participation. The close link between foreign engineering consultants, machinery suppliers and foreign finance systematically operated against involvement of local personnel ... Fourth ... concerns with speed of project implementation were overriding; the use of foreign finance packaged with foreign personnel was deemed most appropriate ... Fifth ... experience, which was supposed to have been acquired in the process of implementing earlier or older projects, was not systematically employed in the planning and execution of subsequent projects.[14]

It was encouragement of foreign direct investments such as these which led to the wholly inappropriate industrialization plans, which the World Bank then had the gall to criticize. They were *its* plans.

Speaking of the Bank's LTPS, Khetso Gordham claims,

The report fails to recognise that the World Bank and allied international financial institutions promoted import substitution industrialization policies in the 70s by lending indiscriminately and supporting capital intensive heavy industrial projects knowing that markets were protected.[15]

Samuel Wangwe concluded from his case studies that the transfer of technology for industrialization in Africa was determined by the characteristics of the industrialized countries' culture, level of technology and scale and sophistication of markets. In other words, import-substitution industries in Africa were designed by expatriate engineers to provide a replica of the formerly imported products mainly for higher-income consumers, without any allowance being made for indigenous resources and existing products, local skills or wider market preferences. Participation of local people in decisions on design, project planning and execution was minimal or non-existent. Alternatives were simply not considered in resource use or product design, and the training of local staff was limited to middle-rank management, final decisions and initiatives remaining in the hands of expatriates.[16] The tragedy is that Africans should have allowed this to happen.

This tragedy has to be understood in the light of the unbounded faith which many African nationalist leaders had not only in Western technology but also in the applicability to African conditions of the Soviet Union's measures of industrialization – high protective walls against foreign products including intermediate and capital goods, large-scale capital-intensive projects, state ownership, especially of these large projects, artificially low interest rates, rigid price controls and other regulations of incomes, marketing, raw material purchases and foreign exchange allocation and, in effect, a tax on agriculture.[17]

Given the absolute absence in sub-Saharan Africa after independence of an indigenous industrial capitalist class, economic power lay in the hands either of a commercial élite through their grip on foreign trade or of the ruling group through their control of state enterprises. It was believed that Lenin had shown that industrialization could be achieved through the employment of Western engineers teaching their skills to local workers.[18] But the Soviet Union in the 1920s was very different from Africa in the 1960s. Russia had some small industrial tradition and a small entrepreneurial class; it held the many nationalities of the Soviet Union under one central government, leaving only very limited powers to the smaller republics. Following independence, Africa's states had no such inherited skills and no coordinating political and economic centre.

After achieving independence, most African governments sought to leapfrog from the most primitive to the most advanced stage of technology. Technologists distinguish four stages in the development of technology:

The first and most primitive stage is characterized by hand tools that are not designed according to scientific principles. The second . . . involves hand or human-powered machines, designed in accordance with scientific principles . . . The third . . . relies on scientifically designed machines, powered mechanically . . . The fourth involves the use and development of scientifically designed automatic machinery.[19]

By the mid 1980s some African countries were making their own machines at stage three, but where there was stage four technology it was but a parody of the real thing and not developed indigenously.

Modern Industry as a 'Foreign Body' in African Society

When Samuel Wangwe refers in the quotation at the head of this chapter to 'complex historical circumstances' that must be held responsible for Africa's failed industrialization, we have to go back to the early chapters of this book to understand his meaning. It came to be believed, as we saw, both by Europeans and by Africans themselves, that somehow Africans were incapable of managing anything but the simplest tasks. This was the heritage of the slave trade followed by colonial rule, which introduced Europeans or Levantines into all management positions. The belief was, of course, nonsense. African farmers are noted as being among the most skilful in the world; African craftsmen are among the most artistic; African pre-colonial states involved no less complex organizations than others of the same time. But the nonsense was believed, and now the result is the introduction of industrialization as a 'foreign body' into Africa's political economy.

This most perceptive image of a 'foreign body' in African society comes from an African expert in the French Ministry of Cooperation. He points to the Western-type society, very different from the African environment, that an African entrepreneur and even an African wage earner must penetrate on entering the formal sector of industry – Western legal rules, Western standards for credit and bank guarantees, Western-type formalities for licences and permits, Western legislation covering taxation, price controls, working hours and conditions and an environment of expatriate Western managers.[20]

Others, reporting on African industrialization, have emphasized the absence of Africans as technicians and administrators in high-level managerial positions in foreign-owned industrial enterprises. In Côte d'Ivoire and Zimbabwe more than three-quarters of all such higher posts were held by Europeans. Even in skilled and semi-skilled posts,

Europeans were significantly well represented – forming respectively 28 and 19 per cent of the total.[21] The high salaries and expenses of such a large expatriate staff were not the only disadvantage, although these have been estimated as adding considerably to the direct and indirect costs of projects.[22] Much worse was the failure to develop African capabilities, to involve African participation and to recognize the limitations of the small scale and the different preferences of African markets compared with those of the West. The result was inefficient management, underutilization of plant and subsidized industry carrying a cost to the national product and not a contribution to it.

It might still have been the case, even had Africans been more involved in the process of industrialization, that its presence would have remained a 'foreign body' in African society. Africans would have studied in Europe and North America and themselves would have been inoculated with the 'foreign body'. The point being made is a wider one that takes us beyond political economy into the realm of different cultures. It is sometimes suggested that technology is neutral, but this is clearly an insupportable proposition. Technology emerges out of a specific society and to meet specific politico-economic demands – overwhelmingly, so far, those of European and, by extension, North American societies. Robert Jungk, the author of *Brighter than a Million Suns*, a desperate warning of the threat inherent in uncontrolled European technology, still hoped that an alternative was possible when he wrote in 1973:

We are still at the beginning of the development of specifically Asian, African and Latin American variations in technology. What they have in common, despite the great geographical distances, is their desire to conform more closely to life and nature . . . They all arose in protest against the mechanical, insensitive, standardizing occidental technology, geared predominantly to speed and maximum output . . . Before the end of the millennium yellow, brown and black development advisers will be called . . . to show their former teachers how vital necessities can be produced without waste and without harm to people and the environment, without haste and without alienation.[23]

Twenty years later, it may have to be said that in East Asia and in parts of Latin America, European technology has gone too far to be stopped. This might still not be true of India[24] and – what about Africa? What chance of an indigenous industrialization there?

The Case of Tanzanian Industry

No country in Africa has tried harder on the face of it than Tanzania to develop an indigenous industrial base. As a result of the Arusha Declaration of 1967 the major means of production were nationalized. Since most of the manufacturing industries were formerly owned by transnational companies (TNCs), this brought their ownership out of foreign hands and into the state sector. Under colonial rule manufacturing had been established mainly in sisal decorticating and cotton ginning and in food and beverage processing, with some enterprises in wood working, machine repairs and certain consumer goods.

Following the Arusha Declaration, a very large investment programme was inaugurated with imported technology in the form of capital equipment, intermediate inputs and expatriate technicians. This was seen to be the only way for the country to industrialize, since Tanzania at independence had only an extremely small human resource capability, even by African standards. The literacy rate was about 25 per cent, while in a population of 9 million only some 12,000 pupils were enrolled in secondary schools. The proportion of skilled labour in the African labour force was 0.2 per cent. Out of 3,100 professional and technical jobs only 200 were occupied by Tanzanians, of whom 150 had university education.[25]

Every effort was made to create an indigenous technological capacity. A massive literacy campaign was launched, which raised the literacy rate to 80–90 per cent in the 1980s, by which time entrants to secondary education had doubled and the university population multiplied ten times from 340 to 3,400, about two-thirds of them studying science and technology. The aim of successive national plans was to raise the local proportion of human resources at every level, including the higher levels of technology and management, to achieve self-sufficiency in all fields by the 1990s.

In the event, the local proportion of higher level manpower was increased from 20 to 94.4 per cent by 1988.[26] It should have been a great success story. It was in fact a dismal failure. The annual growth rate of value added in manufacturing industry (MVA) was over 10 per cent in the years 1963–73, just over 4 per cent in 1973–9 and negative (−4.5 per cent) between 1979 and 1986. This was, unfortunately, typical of sub-Saharan African industrialization, whether this was taking place in the public or private sectors (see Table 11.2).

Every 'old Africa hand' who has been an expatriate engineer will tell you the same thing: 'As soon as the "expats" left and the Africans took over, projects that were running perfectly well soon collapsed in shambles.' They will be echoed by a chorus of World Bank complaints about state interference, state bureaucracy and general corruption. The story of collapse is not, of course, universally true. Whole new industries have developed in Kenya and Lesotho, as well as successful sugar refining and textiles manufacture; there is the knitwear story from Mauritius, meat products and drinks in Botswana, cement manufacture in Cameroon and Nigeria and Nigeria's chemical industry.[27] Iron and steel and electrical engineering in Zimbabwe are a continuing success, but still have chiefly white engineers and managers.[28] In Tanzania there is at least the radiator factory, Afro-cooling, to add to the list of successes.[29] But they are largely Western successes.

The reasons for the collapse of African industrialization are complex. Wangwe has sought to disentangle them in the case of Tanzania. He looked at four major industries – textiles, cement, farm implements and sugar processing – all under state ownership. He examined what happened in the transfer of technology at each of five stages: pre-investment planning, specification of product and process, technological capability, evolution of production and attempts at rehabilitation. Here is a summary of his findings.

The *textile* sector was surveyed by a Swiss firm which made recommendations about scale, location and technology. Despite the long history of textile manufacture in Tanzania, most of the new mills were turnkey projects, supposedly because of the need for speedy implementation. Technology was chosen according to the availability of finance from national aid organizations to pay for it. Although a local team of experts worked closely with the foreign team during installation, the local team was dissolved thereafter and high manpower turnover seriously weakened training programmes. Rehabilitation programmes were concentrated on updating technology and have simply reinforced dependence. Labour productivity actually declined.[30]

In establishing a large-scale *cement* industry, the Tanzanian parastatal company relied entirely upon foreign consultants – first Swiss, then Indian, then Danish, all financed by aid from their respective governments. It was decided that only Portland cement was to be manufactured and not any of the traditional types and the technology introduced was the most up-to-date available for large-scale production – more advanced than that used in most industrialized countries. The possibility of establishing small-scale plants using local materials was not explored. Technical problems and absence of spare parts have steadily reduced output to around a third of capacity. Training was limited to low cadre staff and the localization policy for top management was reversed because of one major accident. Rehabilitation agreements were concerned with obtaining automatic monitoring mechanisms for achieving a standard quality cement. Local management currently being paid the equivalent of $1 a day might be encouraged by higher pay and would still be cheaper than foreign managers at $400 a day.[31]

The two Tanzanian *farm implement* firms were launched by the government with technical and financial assistance provided by China and India, later supported by Swedish experts. No lessons were learned from each other's experience. Tools were produced with Indian designs and little attention to the real needs and constraints of local farmers. Machinery supplied was multi-purpose, but not needed for most purposes. Once again availability of foreign finance determined the choice of scale, location and technology, and rehabilitation programmes failed to consider the possibility of creating smaller units in rural locations[32] (Dar es Salaam, with 44 per cent of the country's total population – in 1978 – accounted for 50.3 per cent of large-scale manufacturing employment and 53 per cent of small-scale – 1 to 10 persons).[33]

The Tanzanian State *Sugar* Development Corporation is a holding company for five public sector sugar estates and associated factories, although some of the estates get part of their cane from private outgrowers. Planning and implemenation of projects has been dominated by Dutch firms and Dutch consultants financed by the Dutch government. The standard product is refined white sugar, replicating what was formerly imported. No attempt has been made to diversify towards less refined types or to utilize the jaggery, which is produced in small units in some sugar-growing areas. Expatriates continue to provide the production, project and development engineers because they are said to be able to obtain spare parts more easily. There is no systematic on-the-job training. Sugar output has remained virtually stationary from 1974 onwards. Imports and exports balance out at about 10,000 tonnes a year and are determined, as with other consumer industries, by the consumption patterns of the relatively wealthy urban population.[34]

To this depressing list of failures one further example may be added, this time from the *shoe* industry, where Tanzania can boast of one of the most famous white elephants in the whole of sub-Saharan Africa; their total probably outnumbers the wild elephants.

The public sector Morogoro Shoe Company (MSC) ... was a World Bank financed project, set up to draw on Tanzania's large supply of hides and skins to manufacture shoes for the export market: an appropriate activity, in a low technology industry, using local resources, provided with ample foreign exchange for several years of production and, given the right financial incentives, to be export oriented. The project was designed and set up by an Italian consultant; there was no local investment capability to handle footwear of this scale and quality. The foreign consultant chose very sophisticated equipment, as was necessary for production for European markets. MSC came on stream in the early 1980s, never achieved even 5 per cent capacity utilization, was unable to design or manufacture shoes of a quality even acceptable to the Tanzanian market and was a disaster in every conceivable way. Most of the cases of machines were never opened, and deteriorated on the shop floor: the foreign exchange cost still has to be repaid by Tanzania to the World Bank.[35]

This Tanzanian disaster only reveals in caricature all the failings of the other flawed attempts to introduce modern industry into Africa. The technology was too advanced for the skills available, local teams were not trained to work with expatriate consultants and engineers, indigenous materials were not made use of, financial sources for sustaining production with necessary foreign inputs were not obtained, and neither home nor export markets were adequately researched.

Lessons for the African Alternative Industrialization

Faced by white elephants on this scale, it is evident that the option of muddling through by rehabilitating what exists is not available. Nor is it possible to go back to immediate post-independence expansion by obtaining debt cancellation and aid for more, and hopefully better designed, projects.[36] It is not therefore surprising that some have argued for the abandonment of the whole industrialization process. But this is not an option which receives any support in Africa itself, however enthusiastically the anti-development lobby outside Africa may advocate it.[37] There are really only two alternatives – the untried one of building up Africa's capabilities in quite different ways from those indicated in the European model and basing development on indigenous strengths; or its very opposite, the World Bank's well-tried but failed attempt to open up African economies to international competition from the North and to eliminate all measures of state intervention in market prices and exchange rates.

It may seen tiresome to repeat that such economic liberalization is quite wrongly said to have been the way of industrialization that was followed successfully by the newly industrialized countries (NICs), such as South Korea and Taiwan. In fact, in their industrialization, import controls, export subsidies and state intervention on a massive scale were at the heart of these countries' development. The measures taken were specific, carefully timed and rigorously planned – and they took into account local cultures, a far cry indeed from the World Bank's favoured prescription of incorporation in the world markets freed from all state regulation and controls.[38]

African countries did, however, face two quite specific handicaps on the day of their independence, as compared with the East Asian countries. Wangwe and his colleagues have drawn attention to both of these. The first was the low level of human capital in Africa. In the 1960s both South Korea and Taiwan had universal primary school education and enrolment ratios of about a third at secondary level. For sub-Saharan Africa as a whole, even by 1986, the primary school ratio was 73 per cent and the secondary ratio only 20 per cent. The second handicap was the small size of most African economies – thirty-four with populations below ten million, twenty with populations below five million. Taiwan and South Korea each had in excess of forty million.[39]

In the African alternative view, both the task of correcting the previous policies of the World Bank and that of establishing a framework for an 'African Alternative' are seen in the light of the need to build up African capabilities on the basis of indigenous strengths, using both public and private enterprise and developing the regional groupings. The emphasis is on cooperation between the public and private sectors.

World Bank Technical Discussion Papers are often more honest than the Bank's political reports. Thus, a World Bank paper on *Public Enterprise in Sub-Saharan Africa* concluded:

In most African countries the internal markets are so small that large manufacturing firms frequently acquire a monopolistic or oligopolistic position . . . A basic fact must be faced: even if every conceivable candidate for divestiture were sold or liquidated in the near future, a substantial Public Enterprise sector would still exist in every sub-Saharan country. It is within the realm of possibility that traditional Public Enterprise activities such as utilities might be transferred to private ownership in the long run, but it is not at all likely. African governments regard the provision of many services as 'strategic' natural monopolies.[40]

Ironically, the result of the World Bank's prescribed destruction of much of the state apparatus and parastatal enterprises of African economies has been to open up an empty space, which will not be filled by local capitalists, since they do not exist, and may not be filled by foreign capitalists, since it will not seem to them to be worth filling on the limited scale of any single state. The space created might just be filled by new local forms of popular organization, if they received some minimal outside assistance to start up. For any large-scale development regional cooperation is essential.

In the short run, African industries, including parastatals, will have to overcome their managerial inefficiencies and low capacity utilization, or be closed down. In that case, investment will not just automatically transfer to places where it is needed. For this, we have the very considerable authority of Sanjaya Lall, writing about the structural problems of African industry:

It is not enough to rely on removing disincentives. Positive action is needed and policies reformulated to focus on upgrading industrial capabilities . . . Getting the right price signals and releasing competitive forces will not evoke the proper supply response if the necessary skills and know-how are lacking . . . The ability of firms to respond to incentives depends on their initial base of capabilities and their access to skills within the economy.[41]

Lall emphasizes that 'Entrepreneurial capabilities, like other capabilities, have to be developed and this takes time.'[42] Such development not only takes time; it would take a whole panoply of supportive measures, which Lall, Stewart and Wangwe have laid out in a series of necessary steps:

1. to moderate the privatization programme since the dogmatic pursuit of this only leads to the creation of a vacuum which is filled by foreign investment or not at all; instead, the parastatals will need to be reconstructed and their efficiency built up;
2. to 'structure' markets by applying resources to support small- and medium-sized firms, so that large commercial firms do not hog all the credit and foreign exchange available;
3. to end the across-the-board liberalization of tariffs and introduce selective (temporary) protection for the following:
a) industries of relatively high labour intensity;
b) industries agreed upon for development through regional specialization arrangements;
c) export-oriented industries;

d) industrial schemes to develop skills training, infrastructure provision and research;

4. to reform state intervention rather than abandon it, so that support is given for regional specialization, product diversification of exports, research and training, transport and communications;

5. to reverse the policy of cuts in state spending in order to balance budgets in the short term and, in fact, to step up spending in priority areas and in particular on health and education, training and research, and infrastructure in rural areas; while making cuts in military spending;

6. to seek to organize common action among all particular commodity producers, not only in Africa but worldwide, to obtain the common writing off of foreign debts and secure commodity price improvements through agreements to limit excess production.[43]

Lall believes that a start can be made 'in the foreseeable future . . . with small-scale and large-scale production of products that need relatively simple processing technologies, enjoy natural protection because of transport costs and rely largely on domestic raw materials'.[44]

Lynn Mytelka and others, from studies in the Côte d'Ivoire, have emphasized that it is not so much simple technology that is needed – that would only be a recipe for continuing African uncompetitiveness – but the decentralization of production units. A survey of four main Ivorian industries concluded with a statement of what is 'needed to enable African industry to develop on a sound basis':

On the demand side . . . greater attention to domestic market needs and real learning by doing. On the supply side, smaller, more decentralized units . . . first, they would rely less on massive transportation and storage networks and be closer to local inputs. Second, they would also be closer to markets and this would reduce the need for planning and computerized techniques to speed throughput. Third, they would require a more limited use of sophisticated capital goods and hence a lessened reliance on imported parts and components and the international lending mechanisms required to finance these capital goods. Fourth, such firms would be less vulnerable since with a smaller debt burden the break-even point of the firm would be lowered, allowing for greater flexibility in adjusting to fluctuations in demand. Fifth, new forms of articulation to the informal sector would be possible within such an organizational structure.[45]

The 'Missing Middle'

The links to the informal sector will be examined in the next chapter. There remains the problem of the 'missing middle' between modern technology and the most primitive craft activities which only partly occur in the informal sector. The World Bank reported in its LTPS:

In other regions, especially in Asia, a middle ground of enterprises between the largest and smallest firms has developed during the past thirty years. The products and services of these enterprises are well suited to the conditions in many developing countries: surplus labour, scarce energy, foreign exchange constraints, lack of technical information and skills, scarce investment capital, variable weather and soil. Small and medium-sized enterprises create jobs at a lower cost and use local resources more intensively. These enterprises also contribute to equity by producing goods and services that are widely afford-able. They foster entrepreneurship through learning-by-doing.[46]

In the concluding chapter of the LTPS, the Bank emphasized that 'there can be no growth without entrepreneurs' and continued:

Much can be done to foster African entrepreneurship by recognizing the role and vitality of the informal sector – replacing discriminatory legislation, by unshackling businessmen from unnecessary and unhelpful regulations and controls, and by facilitating access to credit and markets ... Despite recent policy reforms, entrepreneurial initiative is hampered by regulation and limited consumer demand for local products and services.[47]

Regulations by government can and no doubt should be relaxed in some cases, but the lack of consumer demand is unfortunately the result of the low productivity and low incomes of the very informal sector which the Bank is depending upon. Moreover, a 1987 study of Kenyan experience with small-scale African enterprises in the Kenyan industrial estates revealed that:

More advanced small-scale manufacturing does not generally draw on simple informal activity for entrepreneurship – a gulf exists between the two that few entrepreneurs bridge, and thus the relative absence of 'graduation' ... Interme-diate and subsistence parts of small-scale industry are heavily over-represented in indigenous private enterprise ... this 'missing middle' leads to a shortage of opportunities for entrepreneurial development. The medium-to-large-scale industrial sector has practically no private African entrepreneurship. Where the state has taken over the entrepreneurial role (and expatriate experts have been given limited roles), the underdeveloped nature of the indigenous capabilities deployed has caused inefficiency. Administrative fiat cannot by itself create the foresight, experience, organizational know-how, financial acumen, and leadership qualities that large-scale industry needs, and adverse exogenous shocks and mistaken policies have added to the malaise of African industry.[48]

Some authorities have questioned the general absence of a middle sector in Nigeria,[49] although Lall's evidence just quoted from Kenya is confirmed from other parts of Africa, by Carl Liedholm's studies of Ghana, Sierra Leone and Zambia[50] and by Lall himself from a wide range of country studies.[51] This apparent absence of a small-to-medium modern business sector in sub-Saharan Africa had led the authors of World Bank reports to advocate a development strategy based on the informal sector. The implications for productivity increases of a more rapid growth of employment in the informal sector than in the modern sector were, however, so disturbing that further inquiries were launched. All the evidence from East Asia and even from Africa shows that economic growth is fastest where the share of *waged* employment in the total labour force grows fastest. The informal sector almost entirely consists of self-employed persons with very low rates of productivity increase.[52] An ILO study made in 1988 was not encouraging about development through the informal sector and concluded that it 'can only be a partial solution if not marginal to the current unemployment problem in African countries'.[53]

The World Bank inquiry was made in 1990 to review the progress of businesses in sub-Saharan Africa which had been receiving support from the Africa Project Development Fund (APDF), an offshoot of the International Finance Corporation, which is a World Bank affiliate promoting development through finance and investment in the private sector. In the four years from 1986 to 1990, sixty-five projects in eighteen countries obtained APDF finance and another 250 were receiving technical advice. This was out of a total of 2,000 requests received. Independent assessments were made of eighty-three projects in twenty-two countries and these were found to show an average projected internal rate of return of about 30 per cent. Many of the projects were associated with foreign companies as suppliers of machinery and as outlets for sales, but they were all independent African companies. Some had obtained government support with grants and tax concessions. This was especially the case in Botswana. But complaints about government bureaucracy were almost universal. Most had received some help from bilateral aid agencies as well as from APDF. Yet in almost all cases the scarcity of financing – both loans and credit – was regarded as a severe impediment.[54]

Six countries with varying levels of development and growth strategies were selected for study in depth and thirty-six entrepreneurs were interviewed – six from Botswana, five from Côte d'Ivoire, four each from Ghana, Kenya and Malawi and two from Tanzania. The conclusion of the survey, edited by Keith Marsden, was that: 'Far from being what was described as the "missing middle" these [modern African] entrepreneurs can be the true pioneers of development in sub-Saharan Africa.'[55]

The thirty-six entrepreneurs who were interviewed were not lone pioneers; nearly all stated that they had numerous domestic competitors in the same field. Yet it did not appear that foreign investment had blocked African entrepreneurship. Rather the opposite: the relationship between foreign and indigenous enterprise was shown to be complementary rather than just competititve. Many of the African entrepreneurs interviewed had acquired their basic technical or managerial skills working for foreign-owned companies. Numbers of small-to-medium-sized firms were reported to be growing. Chambers of Commerce and Industry which were visited during the inquiry reported recently increased memberships, but it was not suggested that this was at all the result of any new policy of foreign companies to subcontract production to local suppliers. Several of the APDF-assisted entrepreneurs began their businesses on an informal basis. Only two of the whole sample had failed. The entrepreneurs were all individualists, but their backgrounds ranged from self-educated sons of peasants and workers to Oxford graduates and dissatisfied higher civil servants. There were four women among them, one in fishing, two in garments and knitwear and one in hair-dressing products.

Twenty of the interviewees were concerned with processing local agricultural materials, ranging from flowers and horticulture to knitwear and tanning. Industries represented which were not closely related to rural production were printing, metal furniture, pharmaceuticals, construction, transport and tourism. Most significantly, sixteen had most of their business in export markets, but these did not include the ones which were *un*related to the processing of agricultural produce.[56] The conclusion of this study must be that there are many small- and medium-sized entrepreneurs in Africa but they will not necessarily emerge from the informal economy or succeed without the positive support of public agencies, whether from outside, like the APDF, or from the local state.

The Importance of Export Markets

The adverse exogenous circumstances in the 1980s referred to by Lall are a continuing problem, in particular, the collapse of commodity export prices and the rising cost of debt servicing. Together these rendered the dependence of many African industries upon imported inputs of fuel, materials and spare parts quite unsupportable. Even a country like Côte d'Ivoire, which had the most diversified 'export basket' – including base metals and machinery, textiles, chemicals and food products – and was 'the fastest growing exporter among major non-oil economies',[57] received a stark warning in 1988 from an expert study of its economic future:

The Ivory Coast will remain structurally vulnerable to external shocks as long as its income remains so dependent upon commodity exports with erratically fluctuating prices . . . One remedy is clearly the diversification of the productive structure oriented towards a deepening of the domestic market . . . but . . . as long as we import intermediate inputs, machinery and equipment, we must export.[58]

Over-dependence on commodity exports was the great fault in the World Bank's promotion of export-led growth for African economies. Exposure of this fault should not lead, however, to ruling out all commodity exports, nor to failing to give an important role to exports of manufactured goods based on local materials to neighbouring African countries as part of specialization agreements; additionally these should find overseas markets where niches can be discovered. Lall argues that 'The ideal set of incentives thus combines some competition (of the right sort, ideally from world markets) with protection for the period of learning when costs are high and quality low.'[59]

Roger Riddell, in his magisterial study of *Manufacturing Africa*, reflecting on his seven country case studies, recommends, in the end, 'an approach which blends elements of both [import substitution and export-oriented industrialization] . . . (although probably in relation to different industries and sub-sectors)'.[60] This is an unnecessary caveat, as he makes clear elsewhere, when he rejects the options for Africa's manufacturing sector of either trying to go back to public sector development, or doing nothing, or opening up the economy in the manner proposed by the World Bank. He concludes that 'such past approaches – long-term protective, high cost, internationally uncompetitive, domestically focused manufacturing – have been a drain on national resources.' He therefore opts for 'interventionist measures . . . to accelerate the growth, expand the exports and deepen the inter-linkages of the sector through selective import substitution'.[61]

The measures which Riddell proposes are not concerned with 'tinkering with tariff levels'. 'Even the Botswana experience,' he believes, 'shows that a liberal trade regime is inadequate, in isolation, to create a strong manufacturing sector capable of competing internationally.' His measures are concerned rather with raising productive efficiency. They are not minor:

more appropriate machinery, 'new' management techniques, research and technological capabilities, innovative ways of raising labour productivity, systematic attempts to enter new non-domestic markets with higher quality products, packaged more attractively, attempts to reduce comparative transport disadvantages, the provision or extension of export credit guarantees and facilities to minimize foreign exchange risks.[62]

Riddell is able to give examples from Zimbabwe and elsewhere, just as Marsden did in his survey, of technological advance occurring as the result of the challenge of entry into export markets. The Zimbabwe example of Central Africa Cables is particularly striking because, as Riddell notes, 'while almost all exports are to the regional markets, these markets have been secured by overcoming both South African and overseas competition'.[63] Both Botswana and Lesotho have taken advantage of the proximity of the South African market for their manufactured goods exports, but without facing outside competition. Lesotho in particular has simply supplied a cheap labour resource and tax haven for international companies from the US, Europe and Taiwan to gain privileged access for their shoes and clothing in the South African market.[64] The benefits for the people of Lesotho have been negligible.[65]

Blending Technologies

If African industrialization cannot sensibly be limited to meeting domestic demand, nor can it be limited to relatively simple processing technologies. Zimbabwe need not be regarded as a special case. Zimbabwe's industrial managers are mainly white settlers, and Zimbabwe is more advanced industrially than most of sub-Saharan Africa, but the country shares the economic environment of the other states. It is not alone in exporting manufactured goods successfully and in demonstrating that there are 'dynamic technological innovators and entrepreneurs working in the [SADC] region with success'.[66]

This claim for local African innovation comes from the Preface to an 1992 OECD study of *New Technologies and Enterprise Development in Africa*. The authors of the study looked in depth at industrial development in six of the SADC member states and examined the potential for exploiting the strength of the resource industries, and especially of offshore petroleum, mining and forestry. They went beyond a simple concern with modern technology to look at the applicability to African conditions of the new and emerging technologies (NET), which are revolutionizing the economies and societies of the industrialized countries, and which could build upon indigenous African strengths.[67]

From their case studies, they arrived at some important conclusions:

SADC countries were already significantly involved with NET[68] . . . Technological innovation and technical entrepreneurship occur . . . by building on niches that form natural bases for setting up dynamic, profitable and locally controlled technological development . . . many [of which] are to be found in the natural resource industries forestry, minerals and petroleum [and in] biotechnology and environment services.[69]

The authors of this study looked only in part to bureaucratic push to advance NET in Africa; they looked chiefly to the private sector 'to initiate aggressive, fast and unfettered action'. There was need, however, of a balance between demand pull and supply push. They were less interested in the contribution of expatriate companies than in 'upgrading traditional small-scale activities for the production and delivery of basic needs'.[70] They insisted that 'local initiative must prevail . . . initiative must be decentralized [but] . . . open interaction with the world techno-economic community is essential'.[71]

African countries have no possibility now of getting into the business of microelectronic chip manufacture or the assembly of related sub-systems. However, in areas like bio-technology . . . the barriers to entry are low.[72]

The OECD team's findings were reinforced at a United Nations Transnational Centre workshop in Harare in mid 1988, which concluded that 'NET would undoubtedly have major impact on African economies, and it was necessary to undertake a comprehensive programme to tackle the issues posed'.[73]

The researchers of NET advocate a 'blending' of technologies. 'All or nothing' is not the rule in adopting NET; it is necessary to be selective. The recommendation to African countries to add value by processing their raw materials has often been challenged by pointing out that most processing plants are capital intensive. The extra value is returned to the capital invested, and not to labour. NET offers the chance for developing countries to produce better products and use better processes for augmenting their natural resources, without large capital investment.

Several examples given by the OECD team incorporate modern bio-technology: improvements in traditional fermentation techniques for local brewing; better grades in tea production; plant cloning in growing pest- and disease-resistant cocoa and coffee trees; bacterial leaching to stretch the lives and capacities of deposits of copper and other mineral resources.[74]

None of these examples of the application of bio-technology requires large-scale operations. That happened to be the way bio-technology was introduced to cocoa and coffee growing in Malaysia and Indonesia by the giant firms which had developed the technology, but the same technology can be used by small-scale growers. None of the applications observed in Africa reduced the employment of labour. Indeed, it was increased by the greater use of labour in the nurseries and in planting, as in the Malawi tea plantations, where labour employed was actually increased by 25 per cent. Foreign exchange requirements were reduced because of less use of imported fertilizers, pesticides and herbicides (with attendant environmental benefits). At the same time, export earnings were increased because the superior, often organically grown, products fetched higher prices in world markets.[75]

Selectivity in the use of NET and the blending of new and traditional technologies are essential if many of the mistakes made in introducing mechanization into Africa are to be avoided. While there is room for new technology in sugar processing, for example, mechanization of the cane cutting is to be avoided. A report by Booker Agricultural International Ltd on the Côte d'Ivoire sugar industry concluded: 'When compared with manual harvesting the system of mechanical harvesting is more costly in financial terms and even more costly in economic terms. It is also less satisfactory from a technical standpoint.'[76] There are, moreover, dangers in leap-frogging technologies to the latest ones available. The Tanzanian experience, where the requirements of infrastructure and of skilled manpower were not met, is likely to be repeated in the case of most African countries. Blending of technologies is an intermediate stage that enhances learning by doing.[77]

Technology Networks

Technology transfer in this context is different from its usual connotation. It is no longer the transfer of 'organized sets of skills about the design, operation and maintenance of industrial plants or equipment ... often huge scale and highly complex and sophisticated, which cannot be absorbed into the local techno-industrial cultural environment',[78] often also designed only to produce luxury or semi-luxury goods. With NET it is, instead, a two-way process of learning and adapting, to make innovative linkages between existing supply and demand in the market. It can be applied not only to final products but, more importantly in the African context, to intermediate goods and services for supplying to the big resource-exploiting and processing industries.

Innovation, the OECD authors insist, is not the same as research and development. It thrives on information networks such as those which bring together for a specific project the contributions of university researchers, government laboratories, production and equipment engineers, construction firms, technological societies and venture capitalists.

In presenting their report to SADC, the OECD authors made recommendations for the SADC region, but by implication for other regions in Africa as well, or for the larger countries on their own. The central message was that SADC should establish a number of 'cooperative alliances' for different fields of economic activity.[79] In using this concept, they were drawing on Japanese experience, applied also in Canada, of creating a framework of cooperation within which individual firms can compete even at the most advanced levels of technology. They suggest that a new approach to donor funding is required, one that looks for such alliances and helps to found them, but requires full financial responsibility from those – whether private companies or parastatals – which undertake specific NET projects.

Encouraging examples of NET in the SADC region are described in information technology in the petroleum sector in Angola; in a road-heading machine for open cast chromite mining in Zimbabwe; in hydroponic tree nurseries and in environmental service programmes, also in Zimbabwe; in bio-technological services supplied by the Biotech Laboratory at the University of Dar es Salaam, ranging from environmental protection and forest regeneration to brewing, wine and bio-gas production.[80]

All these projects have been pulled by industrial demand and have paid their way, but the original networks, training programmes and project seed money came from the push of donor agencies.

To the OECD examples I can add, from the experience of TWIN and Twin Trading, the introduction of computers for the use of peasant organizations: in Senegal, for analysing data for a large number of irrigated vegetable plots to study yields and sales prices in relation to a range of variables – type of seed, sowing and harvesting times, weeding, application of water and fertilizer; in Uganda and Tanzania for coffee growers to gain access to E-mail for obtaining up-to-date information on markets, prices, orders and delivery consignments; and in Ghana for spreadsheet budgeting and accounting in a cocoa farmers' cooperative.[81]

The crucial issue in technology transfer is that it cannot be a gift; it can only be an act of cooperation between the technologists and those who will use the technology, in which both parties learn from each other about what is appropriate for the particular circumstances. Ian Smillie's comprehensive study for the Intermediate Technology Group, *Mastering the Machine*,[82] includes studies of inappropriate technologies, but also of many that were appropriate: vegetable oil presses designed in Tanzania and in use in Ghana, Kenya, Lesotho, Mozambique, Tanzania and Zambia; the Sri Lankan wood-burning stove in use in Zimbabwe, Kenya and Niger; lime production in Malawi; brick and tile making in Botswana and Ghana; machine-tool making in Ghana and Zimbabwe.[83]

At the end of his book he draws a conclusion that the more dogmatic enthusiasts for 'small is beautiful' should bear in mind:

Although this book has focused mainly on technology that is small, simple, cheap and non-violent, it is not intended as an attack on higher technologies. Many apparently simple technologies are derived from intensive high technology research and development. The bicycle, for example, which was not commercialized until after the typewriter and the sewing machine, combines specialized techniques of thin-walled drawn steel tubing, modern rubber processing technologies, ball bearings, sprockets, roller chains and complex gear-changing mechanisms. The question for developing countries is not a trade-off between 'high' and 'low' technologies. It is a choice between appropriate and inappropriate technologies.[84]

TABLE 11.1 Sector Shares in GDP, sub-Saharan Africa, 1987

Income category	Country	GDP per cap. $ 1986	Shares in GDP (%)				
			Industry incl. Mf'ing & Mining	Mf'ing	Mining	Agric.	Services
Above Average Industrial Share							
M	Botswana	997	57	6	4	3	40
oil	Nigeria	473	43	8	–	30	27
M	Zimbabwe	583	43	31	8	11	46
Oil	Gabon	2882	41	–	3	11	48
L	Zambia	257	36	23	15	12	52
L	Zaire	180	33	7	24	32	35
Oil	Congo	870	33	10	–	12	55
Oil	Cameroon	1071	32	13	–	24	45
M	Mauritius	1365	32	24	–	15	53
L	Guinea	267	32	5	21	30	38
M	Swaziland	628	30	20	–	24	46
L	Lesotho	181	28	15	–	21	51
L	Liberia	723	28	5	14	37	35
Average (excl. Nigeria)			28	10		34	39
Below Average Industrial Share							
M	Senegal	564	27	17	2	22	52
L	Burkina Faso	205	25	15	3	38	38
M	Côte d' Ivoire	920	25	16	–	36	39
L	Niger	294	24	9	8	34	42
Oil	Angola	495	23	3	–	46	31
L	Rwanda	297	23	16	–	37	40
L	Mauritania	413	22	–	12	37	41
M	Cape Verde	353	20	4	–	19	60
L	São Tomé	347	19	–	–	30	51
L	Kenya	333	19	11	–	31	50
L	Sierra Leone	309	19	4	13	45	36
L	Ethiopia	119	18	12	–	42	40
L	Chad	178	18	15	–	43	39
L	Malawi	170	18	–	–	37	45
L	Togo	322	18	7	7	29	54
Oil	Seychelles	2680	17	9	–	6	77
L	Madagascar	259	16	–	–	43	42
L	Ghana	407	16	8	2	51	33
L	Sudan	382	15	11	–	31	48
L	Burundi	268	14	9	–	59	27
L	Benin	335	14	4	–	46	39
L	Comoros	356	14	4	–	36	50
L	CAR	391	13	8	–	41	46
L	Mali	188	12	6	–	54	35

Table 11.1 *continued*

Income category	Country	GDP per cap. $ 1986	Shares in GDP (%)				
			Industry incl. Mf'ing & Mining	Mf'ing	Mining	Agric.	Services
Above Average Industrial Share							
L	Gambia	213	11	6	–	35	55
L	Somalia	351	9	5	–	65	26
L	Tanzania	214	8	5	–	61	31
L	G. Bissau	185	6	–	–	61	33
L	Uganda	278	5	5	–	76	19
All World Low Income			27	12	na	33	40
South Asia			28	18	na	31	41

Notes: – = No figures available; L = Low income; M = Middle income; Oil = Oil-producing.
Source: World Bank, *Sub-Saharan Africa: From Crisis to Sustainable Growth*, Washington, 1989, Table 1, p. 221 and Table 3, pp. 224–5.

TABLE 11.2 Sub-Saharan Africa: Public and Private Sector Growth Rates of Manufacturing Value Added 1963–86

Country	1963–73	1973–79	1979–86	Sector
Above 5% 1973–86				
Botswana	6.2	10.3	11.7	Private
Burundi	13.8	5.7	8.7	Public
Cameroon	2.5	6.4	24.6	Private
Congo	0.3	2.5	6.2	Public
Gabon	10.9	13.0	2.9	Private
Gambia	3.5	1.1	13.9	Private
Kenya	8.6	10.8	4.9	Private
Lesotho	34.3	4.0	12.9	Private
Mauritania	5.1	7.8	8.4	Private
Mauritius	2.8	4.3	7.6	Private
Nigeria	7.6	13.2	1.6	Private
Rwanda	15.5	6.0	9.1	Public
Somalia	21.5	4.6	6.9	Public
Swaziland	18.1	7.1	2.9	Private

TABLE 11.2 *continued*

Country	1963–73	1973–79	1979–86	Sector
Below 5% 1973–86				
Angola	10.2	− 16.8	− 1.7	Private
Benin	6.0	− 7.4	− 3.2	Private
Burkina Faso	18.3	4.6	− 2.2	Public
Cape Verde	9.0	0.8	2.6	Public
CAR	6.6	4.3	− 1.4	Private
Côte d'Ivoire	10.7	5.8	− 0.4	Public
Chad	5.4	− 4.8	− 12.1	Private
Comoros	7.2	− 8.9	3.6	Private
Equatorial Guinea	5.1	− 16.8	− 0.8	Private
Ethiopia	8.2	1.0	4.8	Public
Ghana	6.9	− 1.9	− 2.4	Public
Guinea	3.3	3.2	4.1	Public
Guinea Bissau	8.4	4.2	− 1.0	Public
Liberia	12.8	7.2	− 6.0	Private
Malawi	14.9	5.4	2.7	Private
Mali	4.8	3.3	2.7	Private
Madagascar	19.0	3.4	− 6.3	Public
Mozambique	13.6	− 11.2	− 5.5	Public
Niger	8.0	0.0	0.2	Private
Senegal	4.2	4.5	3.6	Private
Sierra Leone	4.5	1.8	1.7	Private
Sudan	5.6	− 3.1	1.5	Public
Tanzania	10.2	4.3	− 4.5	Public
Togo	14.0	− 1.7	1.3	Private
Uganda	5.3	− 12.1	− 0.8	Public
Zaire	12.5	− 5.9	− 0.7	Private
Zambia	12.7	− 2.2	1.0	Public
Zimbabwe	10.9	− 1.3	4.5	Private

Note: Public and Private Sector imply predominantly one or the other up to the early 1980s.
Source: Roger C. Riddell, *Manufacturing Africa*, James Currey, 1990, Table 2.3, p. 18–19.

CHAPTER 12

The Informal, Second Economy

The second economy is here defined as economic activities that are unmeasured, unrecorded and, in varying degrees, illegal.

Janet MacGaffey, *The Real Economy of Zaire*, James Currey, 1991, p. 12.

There are many words used to describe the sector of the African economy which is not recorded in the statistics and is unregulated by state controls and taxes. It is a grey area, when it is not actually part of the black market. It is a parallel economy, informal in the sense of unstructured. It could be transitional. It is certainly concerned with petty production, using very simple, labour-intensive techniques with a minimum of capital. Skills are improvised rather than traditional. Wages are generally low and irregular, especially for the 'apprentices'. This element in the economy may or may not be monetized, but it provides goods and services chiefly for low-income consumers, not necessarily on a small scale. It frequently involves women as the entrepreneurs and, according to ILO reports, women make up at least half of the total numbers involved.

The second economy is not by any means limited to urban areas and often provides a link between rural and urban small-scale activities. There is a tendency for such producers to congregate together, but there is little intra-trade within the sector, although there are frequently trading links with the formal, first economy. In African converse, this second economy is often called *jua kali*, literally 'hot sun' in Swahili, because much small-scale manufacturing and repair work is done out in the open. V. Jamal calls it the 'unconventional economy', but here we shall follow MacGaffey in calling it the second economy, except when quoting others.[1]

Jacques Giri, the French environmentalist, has described the essentially heterogeneous nature of this second economy in the provision of both goods and services:

Some can be classified as rackets, such as watching cars in the street, or are legally or morally reprehensible, such as prostitution or the illegal drug trade. Others make an essential contribution to urban life, such as supplying wood or charcoal for households, a trade that today is entirely informal. It also includes activities such as the repair of bicycles, motor cycles, cars and radios – activities that sometimes include the manufacture of parts that are unobtainable on the market. Craft activities – some of which are highly developed, such as cast iron or aluminium foundries – are also included. The informal sector also provides passenger and freight transportation in the cities. It provides services to neighbourhoods to which access is difficult and other services that the formal transportation sector does not provide; it sometimes competes fiercely with the formal carriers. It also provides public services such as water distribution (15 per cent of Abidjan's water is distributed informally). Finally, the informal sector includes financial activities, such as informal banks that collect small savings and make loans for segments of the population that have no access to traditional bank credit.[2]

Despite the length of this list, many important parts of the second economy have been omitted, in particular cooking and brewing, the whole range of tailoring and shoe making, watch repairing, 'bush' garages, wood working and metal working, house construction and every kind of carrying, including import and export business, which is generally, in effect, smuggling.[3]

A Growth Sector

Many observers of African economic development have commented on the very strong growth of the second economy in marked contrast to the weakness, and recent decline, of industrial development.[4] By definition, it will be difficult even to estimate the scale of such an informal second economy. Janet MacGaffey believes, on the basis of household surveys, that 'the real economy of Zaire may well be as much as three times the size of the official GDP'.[5] If this is typical throughout sub-Saharan Africa, it would explain the extraordinarily low levels of official GDP per capita, in half of the states falling below the average $330 per year in the late 1980s. Given the unequal distribution of incomes in Africa, this figure would give an income for the poorer households on which it would seem to be impossible to survive. Official statistics already include, as well as information on monetized exchanges, an estimate for the value of the non-monetized rural subsistence sector (i.e. self-consumption of farm households), so that what MacGaffey is talking about as the 'real economy' is quite vastly in excess of what the statistics reveal as the national income.

The GDP of most African countries in the late 1980s was declining in real terms at the rate of at least 1 per cent a year. Of course, the official statistics cannot be relied upon, but the decline in rural earnings of those recorded as employed during the 1970s and 1980s was at annual rates exceeding 10 per cent and sometimes 20 per cent. This decline was combined with a great increase in non-employment of new arrivals in urban areas during this period; and it might have been expected, 'there being no official welfare system,' as Basil Davidson has commented, to 'indicate a widespread condition of, or imminence of, sheer starvation. But, somehow or other,' he goes on, 'this is seldom what is seen. Corpses are not being carted off the streets of large African "cities" in anything like the numbers that the statistics would lead you to assume.'[6]

Two Tanzanian sociologists writing in 1990 saw the growth of the second economy as both 'a reflection of the weakening of state control' and a 'challenge to the state legitimacy of many African countries'.[7] J-M. Servet has called it 'a form of social disobedience'.[8] MacGaffey, writing in 1991 about Zaire, saw 'a huge expansion in the number of second economy transport, construction, trading and manufacturing enterprises' and quoted studies from the mid 1980s describing 'an informal transport system . . . in Kinshasa that carries almost as many passengers as the parastatal bus company . . . [while] the informal construction sector of the city accounts for 70 per cent of the growth in the residential area and houses two-thirds of the population'.[9] A survey by the ILO in Zaire in the mid 1980s reported 12,000 manufacturing, retail and service enterprises in the city of Kinshasa's informal sector.[10]

This burgeoning of the second economy has not only been taking place in the capital of Zaire, but in rural areas also. Nor is such growth confined to Zaire. ILO studies report figures for the urban labour force engaged in the informal economy ranging from 20 per cent to 80 per cent, with examples from major cities – 30 per cent in Abidjan, over 50 per cent in Dakar and Lagos, 73 per cent in Ouagadougou, 80 per cent in Accra.[11]

In what he calls a 'trialist model', Jacques Giri has distinguished three sectors in African cities. First, there is the modern sector composed of large enterprises, either state owned, foreign owned or jointly owned, plus a few medium-sized enterprises with private African capital. The second is an intermediate sector of small enterprises, a few medium-size, supplying goods and services using little capital but all locally owned. Some of these enterprises come within the legal and fiscal frameworks of government; some ignore them or are excluded from them and are therefore part of the second economy. Thirdly, there is the subsistence sector, composed essentially of households or one-person enterprises. These are operating with virtually no capital and are entirely informal.[12]

This categorization appears to suggest a continuum, with individual entrepreneurs of ability rising up the ladder of formality. The fact is that such promotion is rare. Access to the formal sector is restricted – by legal barriers (registration), by financial barriers (credit), by administrative barriers (licences), and above all by fiscal barriers (taxation and price controls) and by legislation (governing minimum wages, working hours, safety standards et cetera). Even if the typical informal entrepreneur could overcome the barriers, the additional production costs would be prohibitive.[13]

In some countries, the informal sector producers have had their workshops bulldozed along with shanty-town houses, as in Nairobi, or forcibly removed to the outskirts, as in the Magaba suburb of Harare. It is city zoning and licensing that make so much of the second economy illicit, if not downright illegal, and nearly always neglected by the planners.[14] But in this last respect things are changing.

The World Bank has stated its belief that 'the informal sector (with low capital intensity) would be the dominant source of growth' in manufacturing industry in Africa.[15] The Bank asserts that it can 'make a significant contribution to long-term growth by building upon the seed bed of experienced entrepreneurs, from which the "missing middle" of small and middle-sized enterprises (SMEs) can emerge, grow and generate the successful inventors and managers of larger enterprises in the future'.[16] It only requires 'less restrictive (state) regulations [to] facilitate the dynamic process of informal firms becoming SMEs'.[17]

Such optimism is typical of the Bank's naïve faith in the sovereign remedy of freeing the market. The facts of the origins and workings of the second economy in Africa do not suggest any such easy solution of what are long-standing economic and social disorders. Lall, Giri, Riddell and others all doubt whether the transition from informal to formal, or from small- to medium-scale, can be made without increases in productivity, which would require finance from the state or from outside and other support for introducing machinery and even minimal capital equipment such as is now wholly lacking in the second economy. And for this they believe that a much higher level of education and training would be required of the informal entrepreneurs.[18] Marsden was more optimistic.[19]

What are the facts? To start with education: most men and women, and especially the women, who are working in the second economy are very poor people with their families, and are generally either illiterate or have minimal education.[20] This is only to be expected since they either come from rural areas, where educational opportunity is very limited, or are new arrivals in Africa's burgeoning cities, where educational provision has failed to keep up with the growth of population. There is evidence in the last decade of an actual decline in school attendance, particularly for girls, as the result of the introduction of school fees, or what the World Bank's recommendaions call 'cost recovery'.[21] Even with training programmes in place, absence of formal education may be the most serious obstacle in the way of a progressive development from the second economy.

Savings Clubs

In contrast, informal access to finance appears to be widespread. Reports of local savings clubs come from all over Africa – *susu* in Ghana, *tontine* in Cameroon and Niger, *sande* in Sierra Leone, *upatu* in Tanzania, *sanduk* in Sudan, *hagbad* in Somalia, *pisces* in Kenya, the 'Six S' in Burkina Faso, Mali and Senegal.[22] A survey of five countries in West Africa revealed that 28 per cent of households participated in a *tontine*, while only 13 per cent had a bank account.[23] Many of these savings clubs are run by women and for women, since in most African cultures women have no assets in land ownership and do not receive the income from cash crops. Men monopolize these rights and therefore the access to cash and credit.[24] Savings clubs are organized in a very simple manner, drawing upon the small sums that women earn in the second economy. Here is a description of a *susu* in Ghana:

a group of people coming together and saving a mutually agreed amount of money on a predetermined day at regular intervals (market days). The money realized after one or more collections is given on a rotating basis to a member of the group and the process is repeated until everyone in the group has had a turn.[25]

Under another system, also in Ghana, contributions are not uniform. The size of contribution qualifies for a loan of a certain size after six

months and the total is returned at the end of a year, less a fee where
there is a *susu wara*, a *susu* man (it is nearly always a man) who collects
and keeps accounts and generally takes one day's contribution in a
month, i.e. about 5 per cent.[26]

The Moroccan sociologist, Hassan Zaoual, has written about the
'*tontine* economy' in Africa, which he sees as the key to any African
model of development.[27] Western economists are accustomed to the
concept of individual savings building up in banks to finance
development.

The low level of such savings in Africa implies for them a major
constraint on increased productivity. Zaoual draws upon a number of
studies in French West Africa to show that there is a strong resistance to
what people call the 'cold money' of anonymous circuits of formal
finance, including most international aid.[28] *Tontine* money is, for such
people, 'warm money'. It is from a communitarian group ethic, and not
from individual economic logic, that the money is collected and put into
circulation. It has what Zaoual calls a 'social consistency' that gives it a
priceless strength of 'confidence capital'.

Zaoual understands *tontines* as elements in his concept of 'symbolic
sites' in African economy. These are, as we might say, the motherlands
or fatherlands of African kinship groups. They are not necessarily wide
or even specifically demarcated territories. They have the same meaning
as English people intend when they begin an explanation of their
customary practices with the words, 'Where I come from'; and you may
be sure that where they come from, 'things are done properly': we help
each other out. There is a group ethic, which has its own rituals of
celebrations and exchange of gifts. There is a high degree of mutual
trust. In Britain it is a relic of an earlier pre-commercial society, which
in Africa has not yet been overlaid by economic rationality.

It is a question of great importance whether such savings systems as
the *susu* and *tontines* can be built upon to finance increased productivity
in agriculture and industry. It is asserted from the studies by French
sociologists all over francophone Africa that banking systems imposed
from outside have failed where, in the words of one writer, J-L. Lespes,
they 'forget the cultural dimension and replace it or disturb it with
exogenous rules that have no organic and dynamic links with the living
springs of the *tontines*'.[29] One successful linkage has been established in
Kenya by PRIDE (The Promotion of Rural Initiatives and Development Enterprises). Members subscribe to a Loan Insurance Fund. Five
members can form an Enterprise Group (EG) and ten EGs can choose
to form a Market Enterprise Group (MEG). Loans start at $200 and if

repaid can go up to $1000. The key to success is that any loan to an individual member or EG must be guaranteed by all the others.[30]

Charles Magubre, a Ghanaian working with ACORD, a consortium of European and African NGOs engaged on long-term development in fourteen African countries, has argued that Northern NGO finance generally swamps and kills off local savings.[31] In many parts of Africa today, however, there is such deprivation and poverty that savings are virtually non-existent. Many savings clubs are limited to quite narrow kinship groups and, from hearsay, there is increasing evidence that they are exploited by the leading members of the families. Magubre gives examples of Rotational or Revolving Savings and Credit Associations in Senegal, Sudan and Uganda which deployed quite sizeable funds, but these were believed by ACORD to need topping up.[32] Some of the problems involved for NGOs in supplementing local savings will be discussed in the last chapters.

In all of these schemes, defaulting is unheard of. Group social control ensures that members pay regularly. Where companies like the Bamask company of Nigeria have built up a banking system on the *susu* tradition in Ghana as well as in Nigeria, there have been defaults, but this is where they went beyond the bounds of *susu* and made loans without assets to meet them.[33]

The success of informal credit clubs like the *tontines* and the *susu* has encouraged not only companies but governments in many African countries to introduce official *tontine/susu*-type schemes. This has happened not only in Ghana but also in Cameroon, Côte d'Ivoire, Togo and Zimbabwe.[34] In Ghana, a life insurance scheme was introduced by the State Insurance Corporation, called 'Money-Back' – so-called because contributors can get their money back after a year. According to the size of daily contributions, loans of appropriate size are payable after six months' contributions or to a beneficiary at death, if this takes place within the year. The loans enable informal, generally single-person, enterprises to make purchases for trading or for materials for manufacture. Larger sums would be required for capital equipment. The proliferation of small savings groups suggests the possibility of accumulation of finance for larger-scale development. But Sena Gabianu, who tells the story of the Ghanaian *susu*, comments that 'what is lacking is a certain amount of networking. Each unit stands on its own and operates separately.'[35]

Origins of the Second Economy

There has probably always been a second economy in African countries, but it appears that the scale and spread of informal activities have increased greatly in the in the 1970s and 1980s. One set of studies of the second economy in the 1970s covered eight different sub-Saharan African countries. The studies were limited to manufacturing and excluded mining, construction, trading, transport, finance and social and personal services. They showed a marked growth in small-scale industry, particularly in the rural areas, but an actual decline in *formal* one-person businesses. Small enterprises above the one-person level did grow in size as local incomes rose, although hardly as far as to qualify as medium-sized.

The editor of these studies, Carl Liedholm, argued from his experience outside Africa as well as inside that this was a natural progression.[36] Data for his African studies end in 1986, after which incomes declined sharply in most African countries.[37] If the converse of his argument applies, then, as incomes fall, one-person enterprises would be expected to increase; and that is certainly what appeared to be happening in the informal, second economy in the 1980s and early 1990s. The 1990 Kenya study referred to 'the informal sector as a last resort for people without alternatives, as a residual urban labour sponge'.[38]

There seems to be no doubting the numbers. Côte d'Ivoire was said to have 23,000 informal enterprises in manufacturing in 1990, that is not counting those which were only trading and not producing.[39] In Kenya it was estimated that 43 per cent of employment in the mid 1980s was in the informal urban and non-farm rural sectors.[40] What then explains this remarkable growth of a second economy that seems to be, if not peculiar to Africa, very much more pronounced there than elsewhere?

It would be quite natural to suppose that this wholly endogenous growth is a relic of traditional African society; and there is no doubt that there is a long tradition of informal trading. The market mammas of Ghana, the *Nana Benz* of today in Togo and elsewhere, have a history going back far beyond colonial times. Without rights in the land, with their men taken in slavery or absent for long periods in the mines, women were left behind to live by their wits. Small-scale enterprises at home, like tailoring and brewing and buying and selling in the market, provided obvious coping activities. Such relics of a past world would not be expected to die of isolation in modern society, nor to become just a marginal activity, but their growth needs explanation. It appears that many of those working in the second economy are 'happy with their situation and have no plans to work in a formal company, large or small'.[41]

Giri believes that the growth of the second economy is a result of Africa's rapid urbanization.[42] It has certainly been rapid. Urban populations have grown in the last decade at more than twice the rate of the population as a whole.[43] And the proportion of the urban population of sub-Saharan Africa in cities has grown even faster. There were three cities with half a million population in 1960 (two in Nigeria). By 1980 there were twenty-eight (nine in Nigeria). The city of Kinshasa, capital of Zaire, reached three million by 1986, more than three times its population twenty years earlier.[44] It appears that the magnetic force of the cities is the wide range of income-earning opportunities.

Studies in several African countries in the 1970s and early 1980s showed, however, that informal activities were as prevalent in the rural as in the urban areas. Indeed, some studies at that time suggested that the vast majority of small-scale industries examined were located in the rural areas, and 'employment in small rural manufacturing often exceeded that generated by all urban manufacturing firms'. In Zambia and Sierra Leone local studies at the same time showed that rural manufacturing employment was twice the official estimate.[45] The definitions here are important. 'Rural' is defined as 'localities with fewer than 20,000 inhabitants'.[46] 'Small-scale industry' evidently excludes much that is 'invisible', even concealed, in urban areas, and so in fact much of the second economy.[47]

It may be concluded that the massive growth of the second economy in Africa in the last two decades has to be understood as the product of a complex interaction of factors: traditional barter and informal exchange in a subsistence economy; the special position of women in Africa – not legally recognized but effectively heads of households because of the continued reliance on large-scale migrant male labour for mines and for seasonal work on plantations; growing rural poverty in the late 1970s and 1980s as the price of cash crops fell and manufactured goods prices rose; the adverse incidence of structural adjustment programmes on the poorest members of society; the subsequent search by households, especially by women, for coping strategies: all this leading to an exodus from the rural areas into the towns – not to the promise of formal jobs in manufacturing industry or in services, but to the hope of finding some way of making a livelihood.

The second economy is, in effect, a response to Africa's crisis. 'In the everyday struggle of survival in Africa, the majority of rural and urban households survive through juggling a myriad of activities.'[48] This is the conclusion of Fiona Mackenzie's study of Africa's *Development from Within: the Struggle to Survive*. The fact that these activities are barely legal or openly illegal is the direct result of the effective breakdown of government in much of sub-Saharan Africa.

Without the informal economy, it seems that most people would not have an income on which they could survive. We need simply to compare the movements of African incomes and consumer prices during the decade of the 1980s. At least half of the population in African countries gets an income from the land. World prices for African agricultural commodities were halved in the decade in relation to manufactured goods' prices.[49] Inflation inside African countries, averaging between 10 and 20 per cent a year (nearly 50 per cent in Ghana), reduced purchasing power even further.

Only a small proportion of Africa's population earns a wage from manufacturing industry – on average about 15 per cent, much higher in Zimbabawe and Zambia – but where they did so in the 1980s, wages almost everywhere rose by less than prices. The only exceptions were Cameroon and the Seychelles. In many countries wages fell even before allowing for price increases – in Tanzania and Madagascar by over 10 per cent a year, leading to an annual real earnings decline of around 30 per cent (see Table 12.1). Miners' wages in Zambia fell by amounts ranging from 60 to 80 per cent between 1981 and 1986.[50]

Salaries in the African public services, affecting a further proportion of the population, were hardest hit of all. In Zaire, as early as 1983, in the 'public services, salaries in real terms represented less than one-fifth of the 1975 level'.[51] In 1984 the National Institute of Statistics estimated that an average monthly food budget in Kinshasa for a family of six would be over 3,000 zaires, while the base monthly salary for a medium-level civil servant was 750 zaires.[52] Salary increases in subsequent years totally failed to keep up with prices.

The ending of subsidies and the cuts in public expenditure required by World Bank structural adjustment policies made matters much worse for poorer groups, greatly widening the disparities between social classes. In Tanzania, the Economic Recovery Programme was said in 1989 to be 'squeezing the majority of the peasantry who were previously protected by policies which accorded priority to food security'. The removal of the maize subsidy in Zambia in 1987 and improved prices for maize farmers, but not for the majority of farmers who grow cassava, millet and sorghum, hit most rural farmers and also the lower income groups in urban areas. These last had come to rely on maize and were found to be spending 77 per cent of their monthly income on food. In Ghana in 1988 the minimum wage was estimated by UNICEF to be enough to cover 2.9 per cent of a minimum 'socially acceptable household budget' for a family of five; the salary of a middle-level civil servant would cover 5.9 per cent.[53]

How then did families survive? The answer is partly through sharing houses, partly through changing consumption patterns – from fish and meat to cereals – but chiefly through supplementing salaries or wages by informal activities. A 1986 survey of households in Zaire revealed that managers were actually spending three times their formal salary, skilled workers only a little less and others over double their formal wages.[54]

Zaire was by no means untypical of collapsing economies. In Conakry, Guinea, in 1985 salaries supplied an average of only 10 per cent of household income. In Lusaka, Zambia, in 1990 a government worker's monthly wage lasted the family for five days. In Uganda by 1988 the minimum monthly wage bought one and a half bunches of bananas, the staple food. A senior civil servant could afford to buy two bunches a day on his salary. He needed to make three times his salary to establish a modest standard of living. In Angola the price of a chicken in 1985 was the equivalent of an official's whole salary for a week. One egg cost half a day's pay for a worker. And yet there was a thriving market in the second economy.[55] There were few countries in Africa where this was not the picture in the late 1980s.

How the Second Economy Works

It is hard to understand how income could be made by informal activity, if no one has an income. The first explanation lies in the grotesque inequality of incomes – between a small élite with huge wealth, manipulating a corrupt state machine, and a large impoverished population being slowly driven out of cash cropping and even out of subsistence farming. Studies of urban income distribution in fifteen African countries in the 1970s showed the top 20 per cent of households receiving on average thirteen times that of the bottom 20 per cent. Follow-up studies made ten years later showed that the gap between rich and poor had greatly widened. Even in the countryside, the gap was wide. Again in the 1970s, studies in Botswana showed the bottom 40 per cent of rural households to be receiving less than 12 per cent of all rural incomes. Among cocoa farmers in Ghana the bottom 20 per cent shared 5 per cent of the income, in Nigeria the bottom 40 per cent only received one-quarter as much as the top 10 per cent.[56]

From these great disparities, two opportunities followed for earning extra income. The first was from the spending of the urban élite, not only on services but also on luxury goods. Much of African industrialization has been devoted to supplying substitutes for imports of consumer goods for the élite.[57] When these goods needed to be repaired or maintained, or when imports became more costly as exchange rates were devalued, a market for servicing and spare parts opened up. When imports of luxuries were subjected to banning or to high customs duties, a black market soon established itself for smuggled goods.

The next income-earning opportunity created by increasingly unequal incomes, combined with the ending of state purchasing and of price controls on foodstuffs, was the opening up of markets in the cities for rural producers to enter directly or through ethnic connections. Products from the countryside – grains and vegetables – were cultivated, processed and transported considerable distances and distributed among relatives or friends in the towns in exchange for products from informal urban workshops.[58]

Most of this carrying and trading is done by women who have used the informal economy to get access to money denied to them by their husbands, and this can be regarded as a second major reason for the growth of this second economy. To feed their families and make up their men's incomes, the women and their children have engaged in all the money-making activities to which they could put their hands – tailoring, cooking, brewing, running cafés and bars, selling fuel, carrying – anything and everything.

The women, particularly those in the rural areas, are not the ones who make most of the money in the second economy. The money is made by the traders and truckers who make advances against standing crops and pervade the whole peasant economy in Nigeria and Zaire. In numbers involved, the women and children certainly predominate in the second economy, but the value of their activities is in no way commensurate, most of these being no more than extended systems of barter.

MacGaffey has argued from her studies in Zaire that, as informal activities have grown, money has begun to circulate more generally inside the second economy. More and more people in urban and rural areas began to produce goods and to provide services without registering or declaring their activities to the authorities. Clandestine links began to be forged with the formal sector. Factories and offices found that they could obtain supplies of materials, spare parts, repairs and other services much cheaper from the second economy than from the first; they did so and kept quiet about it.

Jobs which people held in the formal sector came to be valued not for the direct income they gave but for access to the profitable opportunities they offered of doing informal business. In Zaire, President Mobutu actually encouraged the population to fend for themselves in this way. 'Débrouillez-vous personnellement,' became his motto. 'Everything is for sale,' he is reported to have said, 'everything is bought in our country. And in this traffic, holding any slice of public power constitutes a veritable exchange instrument, convertible into illicit acquisition of money or other goods, or the evasion of all sorts of obligations.'[59] Mobutu should know. With the largest slice of public power he is reputed to be one of the world's richest men, his wealth steadily accumulating in Swiss banks while his people perish.

It is, then, in great part as the result of the breakdown of state power and state provision that the second economy has grown to its present dimensions in so many African countries. Not only the simpler forms of cleaning, maintenance and repairs can be had in the second economy but also, increasingly, all forms of transportation, the ordering of plant and equipment from overseas, replacement of parts and spares are available only in ways that are outside the purview and control and, therefore, outside the taxation of government. With the cutting back of public expenditure, informal services have begun to replace formal provision in health and education as well as in other forms of social service.

The growth of the second economy in Tanzania is seen as a reflection of the weakening of state control, and not only the inability of the state to provide the basic needs of the masses but also its ineffectiveness in controlling and coordinating its excessive interventionist programmes.[60]

Such is the conclusion of two Tanzanian economists writing in 1990. By the end of the 1980s, there was emerging throughout most of Africa what MacGaffey calls a 'parallel commercial system developing in the heart of the state'.[61] And this was the nation-state which had been taken over from the colonial rulers and built up after independence with the central purpose of providing a framework for public enterprise.[62]

Smuggling – Across All the Borders

The third explanation for the growth of a second economy in Africa follows also from the creation of nation-states out of colonial territories. With the boundaries of fifty-six states drawn up on a map with little or no logic and frequently dividing ethnic groups between two and even three different states, it was not surprising that movements of peoples and goods should take place across borders without regard for customs duties and other state regulations. The sheer length of many of the frontiers and the fact that they are often unmarked in tropical forest make a nonsense of border patrols.

African trade flows still follow pre-colonial patterns. Many towns are nearer to the capitals of neighbouring countries than to the state capital to which they belong.[63] There are two particular reasons for the increase in smuggling today. The first is the shortage everywhere of hard currency, which a few of Africa's products can always buy. Gold and diamonds are obvious examples. The second is that in each state prices and tariffs, taxes and subsidies differ widely. Carrying goods across state borders can therefore be extremely lucrative.

Headloading of goods frequently takes the place of vehicular transport because of the lack of roads and the failure to maintain even those that exist. Reports of unrecorded trade collected in 1989 included the following:

* the share of unrecorded trade in the total trade of the ECOWAS region may be between 20 per cent and 30 per cent;
* the unrecorded trade between Togo and Ghana is several times the amount of recorded trade;
* over 60 per cent of Ghana's imports of essential commodities is smuggled away;
* more than half of Uganda's exports take place outside of official channels;
* 30 to 60 per cent of Zaire's coffee production is smuggled out annually;
* the amount of cocoa smuggled out of Ghana in 1982 was enough to meet the needs of an underground economy nearly two-thirds the size of the official economy.[64]

From these figures it was estimated that the actual total of intra-African regional trade amounted to at least twice the recorded share of 5 to 6 per cent in the recorded total of country imports and exports.[65]

Zaire appears to be a major centre of smuggling. This is partly because it has borders with nine other African states – five of them land-locked – and because it lies at the very centre of the continent, linking north and south, east and west. It is partly because of the scale of foreign investment in the rich copper belt; but it is partly also because of the piratical nature of the Zairean government, which permeates the whole economy. In the Zairean smuggling business, MacGaffey's studies show that we need to distinguish between informal petty trading, the small-scale carrying of rural produce – maize flour, sugar, cooking oil, vegetables and cash crops like coffee – across the borders, often between members of the same ethnic groups, on the one hand, and, on the other, the large-scale smuggling of gold, ivory, diamonds and precious stones, vehicles, fuel oil, spare parts and products of the copper mines, the last being mainly stolen goods.[66]

Small-scale movements of rural produce were especially prevalent between Zambia and Zaire during the years when, in Zambia, sales of maize, sugar and cooking oil were subsidized to maintain the living standards of the workers. The difference in price in Zaire made it possible for a smuggler with a bicycle to earn the equivalent of two-thirds of the monthly minimum wage in one day, even after bribing the frontier guards.[67] Large-scale operations often involve armed gangs and are said to have the participation, not only of dishonest customs officials, but of politically powerful persons. The chains of trading connections reach out from Zaire north into Sudan and Nigeria and south into Botswana and South Africa. Along these routes flow concealed loads of gold, diamonds, ivory, coffee, cobalt and malachite and, in exchange, vehicles, motorcycles, fuel, pharmaceuticals and luxury goods into Zaire.[68]

All this illegal trade involves big money and implies a market that is not just grey but black. Goods destined for sale outside Africa or in South Africa earn hard currency. For many years nearly all African governments maintained their currencies well above the open market rate, so that a black money market flourished. Much of the ill-gotten gains found their way into Swiss bank accounts and property investment in Europe and the USA, but some stayed at home and this provided the lubrication for the workings of the second economy everywhere, but especially in Zaire.

The scale of Zairean smuggling can only be estimated, but from several reliable reports it appears that the operations involved have been massive – 30 to 60 per cent of the coffee crop between 1975 and 1979, diamonds valued at $59 millions in one year, 90 tonnes of cobalt in 1985 valued at $15 million, 90 per cent of the ivory exported in the 1970s, until Zaire's herds of elephants all but disappeared.[69]

Zaire may have been the centre of African smuggling, but its experience is not unique. Because of the low prices paid to the farmers, four-fifths of Ghana's cocoa crop was smuggled into Togo in 1980. Twelve per cent of Ghana's gold and diamond production is reported to have been smuggled out in the 1970s and early 1980s. Two-thirds of Senegal's peanut crop went over the border into Gambia unrecorded in 1985, as well as a flourishing illegal export of medicines, arms and drugs. In Sierra Leone diamond smugglers took two-thirds of annual output in 1983–4, valued at between $50 million and $60 million. The Angola diamond company reported in 1984 losing as much as 50 per cent of its revenue to smugglers. Cameroon lost an estimated $285 million (CFA 85 billion) in the late 1980s because of the smuggling of food crops into Nigeria in exchange for manufactured goods. Coffee and gold were smuggled out of Uganda in the 1970s on a huge scale. And so it goes on and on.[70]

Transition from the Informal to the Formal?

It was MacGaffey's view in 1987, drawn from her studies, that a

local capitalist class is in process of formation in Zaire, to which wealth accumulated in the second economy has been a contributing factor ... profits from smuggling and other second economy activities have been one source of capital for investment in substantial manufacturing, and in agro-business producing for the local market as well as for export, in commerce and in real estate. The nascent bourgeoisie enjoys a middle-class lifestyle, educates its children through university, and passes on wealth to them; it is thus beginning to reproduce itself as a class.[71]

This is an extreme position which others have questioned. Davidson expects 'the pincers of the actual and existing economic order ... to nip any such useful development in the bud ... [since] the subordinate nature of these ex-colonial (or "neo-colonial" in a much used term) systems of exchange has ensured that the transfer of real wealth to ex-imperial (or "neo-imperial") economies in North America and Europe has continued'.[72] Mackenzie makes the same point from a different perspective, that the emergence of a local *industrial* bourgeoisie would confront a securely entrenched *commercial* bourgoisie firmly integrated into the 'actual and existing' economic order. Present 'ruling groups' are not to be expected to 'commit political suicide'.[73]

MacGaffey's more hopeful expectations are open to question on grounds that her own studies have revealed. Smuggling, black markets and illicit trading withhold from the state the resources for providing the essential framework of law and order, the basic infrastructure of roads and communications, the utilities of power and water supply and sewerage and the security of state finances, which nascent industry must have. Individual capitalists cannot be expected to supply these on their own, although in some cases both they and the expatriate companies are forced to do so, at considerable cost. A World Bank survey in 1990 of 179 firms in Nigeria found that 92 per cent had their own electricity generators, 63 per cent their own boreholes for water, 37 per cent their own radio and telephone equipment.[74] How they disposed of their effluent was not recorded.

Industrial linkages, forward and backward, downstream and upstream, are essential for cumulative development. Open communication is a necessary requirement for the diffusion of technology, skills, market information and finance. 'Inter-firm or inter-industry linkages do not occur through market forces,' Lall has argued. 'These require the deliberate establishment of sustained extra-market relationships between buyers and sellers of industrial products, vital to the development of modern small-scale industry.'[75] This is what the state has had to supply in all countries that have successfully industrialized.[76] But it is just what the World Bank has been discouraging African state governments from supplying.

The very essence of the Zairean secondary economy is that the state is itself working the black economy. Many individual enterprises are disparate, even secretive, linked together only within family or wider kinship ties. There is a distinction to be made here between the more profitable operations based on accumulation of wealth outside the law, upon which MacGaffey places her expectation of a capitalist development, and the smaller-scale trades and services in the second economy. These are everywhere lacking in financial and other resources.

The agglomerations of similar trades in one place, as in Magaba in Zimbabwe or in Kisumu in Kenya, do go some way to advance the division of labour which should lead to larger-scale production. In Magaba, however, few of the 300 or so stalls of painters, welders, carpenters, vehicle repairers and tinsmiths have electricity or access to machine tools. They were all forcibly moved by the government into a fenced-off area in this suburb of Harare in 1989. Despite the belief of the Confederation of Zimbabwean Industry that 'they will form the nucleus of a large number of small new companies',[77] the several bodies established by the government to assist small-scale business never reach down to the informal sector at the level of Magaba.[78]

In Kisumu the 700 or 800 metalworkers, carpenters and furniture makers do have electrical tools and lathes and sewing machines and other equipment which can be rented. Orders are subcontracted to neighbours, ideas for new designs are diffused, customers are attracted to a well-known site. The next stage in Kisumu could be the establishment of production lines, use of common facilities on the site, discounts on local and regular purchases, lockable stores, improved infrastructure and the extension of mutual trust credit groups. Kenya has good roads and the access of rural people to such sites gives to these small-town artisans their market.[79] Yet there is no evidence of 'graduation' from one- or two-person enterprises to larger establishments. Growth in the 1980s was taking place only in the number of small enterprises.[80]

The report which describes this development in Kisumu and in other towns in Kenya suggests that the reason for the failure of enterprises to grow is that 'the market may be quite circumscribed . . . it is a middle-income clientele of teachers and other public employees'. The abysmally low living standards of the mass of the rural population, and equally of the shanty-town population on the edges of the new cities, in Kenya as elsewhere in Africa, does not offer the purchasing power for developing industry.[81] There is some evidence of the formal sector of industry in Kenya drawing supplies and services from the second economy. This was noted by the ILO report in 1972, and the conclusion twenty years later must be the same, that it is only the ultra-cheap labour of the second economy that supports the cheap labour industries of the formal economy.[82] This need not mean that no increases in productivity take place. The World Bank IFC report showed that they do.[83]

The Absence of State Support

The subsequent failure of industrialization in Kenya suggests that the critics were right in 1972. Exploitation of cheap labour does not guarantee economic development. Yet one should not rule out the possibility. This is how British industry emerged. But it was in a world without competitors. Nigeria is always quoted as the exemplar of capitalist development in Africa. While most of the commercial élite started off well-heeled, it is indeed reported that in Nigeria some petty traders have risen to be medium-sized traders and even large-scale capitalists.

In one case this is said to involve a major export business in motor parts linked to Taiwanese companies, but it has to be noted that the exports are 'currently indirect and *unofficial*' (emphasis added), that is to say, smuggled out of the country, presumably with official connivance.[84]

The trickle-down effect from the wealth of a few very rich members of the élite in each African country, most of whom are involved in trade and not in production, cannot be any guarantee of capitalist development. The banking system is almost wholly oriented towards trade rather than production. State finance for small-scale development of industry is largely absent. A recent study showed that in Nigeria, 98 per cent of financing for *productive* enterprises, as opposed to trading, was family based. In Tanzania the figure was 93 per cent.[85]

The future relationship of the state to the second economy in Africa must be regarded as highly problematic. In some places, informal activity has evidently been encouraged by state officials and even by highly placed political figures. But if it grows, it can hardly continue to be encouraged, since it offers a direct challenge to the authorities. If it developed beyond a largely parasitic association with the formal economy, it is likely that pressure would be brought to bear from the formal sector on government to bring it under control.[86] Anything less would be to invite ruling groups in effect to carry the reduction of state intervention as part of structural adjustment to the point which indeed involved their own 'political suicide'.[87]

The crucial question concerning the future of the second economy in Africa is not so much whether it can be translated into formal development or, in the words of the World Bank, become the 'seed bed of development', to be recognized and cultivated by government,[88] but rather whether it can become a centre for strategic challenge to undemocratic government. When the president of the World Bank stated that the Bank was proposing measures for

empowering ordinary people, especially women, to take greater responsibility for improving their lives – measures that foster grass roots organization, that nurture rather than obstruct informal sector enterprises and that promote non-governmental and intermediary organizations,[89]

Ben Turok gave Africa's response:

Was it really intended to reduce the power of Africa's élite, who bear so much responsibility for the wrong path taken since independence . . . or rather to bring to power governments which will be even more pliable to Western pressure?[90]

It is a fair question, and can only be answered as the struggle against such élite governments, which was begun in 1990, begins to unfold.

Political action by ordinary people involves the 'realization of strategic needs', as one sociologist has described it, 'which go beyond those of "coping mechanisms" or "practical needs", reorders social relations' and is thus bound to challenge not only local interests but also state power.[91] T.L. Maliyamkono and M.S.D. Bagachwa concluded a study in 1990 with the warning that 'although the "informal sector" has always been regarded as non-threatening, in its new excessive form, however, the over-expansion of the sector poses a challenge to the state legitimacy of many African countries'.[92] In Zimbabwe it is reported that 'the very success of the savings movement . . . attracted so much attention that the government found it necessary to intervene . . . By 1987 the government was able to force changes in the governance of the savings movement by installing their own appointees on the Board of a reconstituted and renamed Self-Help Development Foundation.'[93]

The response of the African state to the growth of the second economy has tended to combine both incorporation and repression. In Cameroon, while efforts were being made to bring smuggling under control, the government established a National Centre for Assistance to Small and Medium-Size Enterprises (CAPME) and, when this achieved 'mediocre results rather expensively', assisted the promotion of NGOs like the Association for the Promotion of African Initiatives, which were 'more effective and less expensive'.[94] In Kenya, while Harambee projects were incorporated into state structures, centres like the Kamiriithu Community Education and Cultural Centre in Limuru were closed down, the latter for performing a play which exposed the 'stark realities of the social origins of the wealthy who control the government'.[95]

In spite of the generality of these two types of response from the state to the growth of the informal economy, there does appear to be just a chance that, in the words of one African scholar, 'the spontaneous mobilization of a powerless group to defend itself against destruction may yet contain the latent seeds of organization for multiple new development actions'.[96] The emergence of new cooperatives rising from the grass roots, after the total discrediting of so-called 'cooperatives' which had for long served as controlling arms of the central state and party, was being reported in 1993 from many African countries, including Tanzania and Kenya, Ghana and Uganda.[97] This must give grounds for new hope. The new growth of cooperatives from the grass roots is the subject of a later chapter, but, since women are reported to be at the heart of much of the new mobilization in Africa, it will be sensible first to estimate the chances of such new growth surviving, by looking at what the women have been doing.

TABLE 12.1 Changes in Real Earnings in Manufacturing (Mf'ing) Industry, Sub-Saharan Africa, 1973–87

Country	Mf'ing, % of GDP 1980	Mf'ing Earnings 1973–80	1980–86	Price increases 1973–80	1980–87	Real Earnings 1973–80	1980–86
Low Income							
Ethiopia	11	−7.3	−3.1	5.7	2.6	−11.8	−5.6
Tanzania	11	−	−11.5	15.4	24.9	−	−29.2
Burkina Faso	(15)	11.7	2.6	11.2	4.4	0.4	−1.7
Madagascar	(11)	−0.9	−12.9	10.2	17.4	−10.1	−25.8
Gambia	4	19.2	4.4	13.5	13.8	5.0	−9.3
Burundi	7	−9.0	−	15.4	7.5	−21.2	−
Zambia	18	−5.3	0.2	8.9	28.7	−13.0	−22.2
Somalia	5	−6.1	−8.6	17.6	37.8	−20.2	−33.7
Togo	7	4.2	−	8.2	6.6	−3.7	−
Kenya	13	−2.5	−3.7	11.6	10.3	−12.6	−12.7
Lesotho	5	−16.1	−	11.3	12.3	−24.6	−
Nigeria	9	−0.4	−	16.2	10.1	−14.3	−
Ghana	8	−20.0	−	45.5	48.3	−65.0	−
Middle Income							
Senegal	15	−4.9	−0.2	8.8	9.1	−12.6	−8.5
Zimbabwe	25	0.6	6.1	10.6	12.4	−9.0	−5.6
Swaziland	(20)	3.3	−	13.3	10.2	−8.8	−
Côte d'Ivoire	11	−1.3	−	16.0	4.4	−14.9	−
Cameroon	8	5.6	12.6	10.4	8.1	−4.4	4.1
Botswana	4	2.6	−4.2	11.6	8.4	−8.1	−11.6
Mauritius	15	2.9	−3.1	12.5	8.1	−8.5	−10.4
Seychelles	7	9.2	5.3	19.3	3.7	−7.7	1.5

Notes: Figures in brackets are for 1987; − = no figures available.
Real earnings changes are the result of discounting earnings changes by the rise in prices.
Source: World Bank, *Sub-Saharan Africa: From Crisis to Sustainable Growth*, Washington, 1989, Tables 1, 10 and 27, pp. 224, 238, 268.

CHAPTER 13

Let the Women Lead!

Men are always slow in taking things up. They want to wait and see.
When there is progress they come.

> A member of one of the ORAP women's clubs in Zimbabwe reported in
> Lloyd Timberlake, *Africa in Crisis*, Earthscan, 1991, p. 185.

The local people thought of the idea (of a women's group) because of
their needs, so they wanted to get together to solve their problems and
meet their needs. There was no support from outside.

> A member of Kundi ya Kuela Mbesa Women's Group, based in Kisuini
> village, Machakos District of Kenya and started in 1983, reported by
> Peter O. Ondiege, 'Local Coping Strategies in Machakos District, Kenya'
> in D.R. Fraser Taylor and Fiona Mackenzie, *Development from Within:
> Survival in Rural Africa*, Routledge, 1992, p. 135.

At a conference on Alternative Development Strategies for Africa held
in Dar es Salaam in 1989, one of the few women delegates reported that
a leading specialist from the WHO had given a doomsday warning
about the spread of AIDS in Africa. 'The women of the continent,' he
warned, 'would have to face a new situation, when there would be no
men to do the work in very many communities.' 'What's new?' was her
ironic and bitter riposte. 'We already do the work.'[1]

That women do double, and often treble, shifts each day, in the
house and outside, in unwaged and waged work, is recognized as a
worldwide phenomenon, but that the woman is so frequently head of
the household is a peculiarly African characteristic. The men have gone
away ever since the Atlantic slave trade took mainly male captives.
Thereafter, the mines took the men away for long periods. The plantations and seasonal contracts for harvesting took others; and this pattern
of work has continued to this day. The women stayed behind caring for

the land as well as for the children. They still do. Half of all African farms are managed by a woman. In the Congo and many other countries which have always been labour reserves the proportion is nearer 70 per cent.[2] It is 90 per cent in Nyeri in central Kenya.[3]

In the World Bank's Long Term Perspective Study, it was estimated that in Africa over 60 per cent of agricultural production and 70 per cent of staple food production are carried out by women.[4] If the children's work were added in, the proportion would be higher.[5] Even where there is a man in the household, the woman puts in more hours of actual production than the man – between 60 and 70 per cent of the total according to four country studies recorded by the World Bank.[6] One survey of a representative group of Ayirebi households in Ghana showed that the women's daily activities averaged over several weeks in each of three periods of the year – post-harvest (January–March), lean season (April–August) and harvest season (October–December) – totalled two hours more than the men's in the first two periods and three and a half more in the last, the harvest season.[7] As well as doing all the child caring and food processing, the women did nearly as much of the outside farm work and non-agricultural production as the men, more of the fetching of firewood and water, washing, cleaning and transporting goods to market. ILO studies suggest that these figures for women's participation in the labour force are underestimates.[8]

In the division of labour between men and women, only building, including well construction and house repairs, were found to be almost entirely men's work. Some men hunted and went out to do waged work, but if they were living at home these activities were counted in their totals.[9] The division of labour is fixed by tradition, and is related to the man's rights as owner of both the land and the house. Ownership extends to trees, as it does to wells. Since it gives title to land, the planting of trees or cutting trees down is the man's prerogative, although the women collect branches for firewood, just as they draw the water from the well or work the land.

The supply of fuel wood is a good example of the problem facing African women, as forests are steadily cleared for permanent crops or for logging. There are schemes everywhere to grow more trees in Africa. Most of Africa's farming communities already grow trees for shade, for fruit and for scaffolding. Firewood comes traditionally from the forest; and schemes for growing trees just for firewood have generally failed, especially if the wood is to supply the towns. It has not seemed to be worth the time involved. The women would see no advantage since they would not receive the income from the sale and the men would have no interest in planting trees that were not on their land. New trees, moreover, take time to grow – up to ten years – and there are too many other more urgent jobs to be done.

Women farmers are often criticized for failing to take the long view and for degrading their environment, but it is the pressure of extra work, with men away and lower prices for their produce, that forces women into this position. And they see all around them whole regions of forest being cleared for large-scale cash crop projects and the traditional fallow years for forest recovery being abandoned.[10] Yet there is widespread evidence that women are quick to respond to incentives and to innovate where opportunities of training, credit, extension services and other inputs are available.[11]

An interesting example comes from Côte d'Ivoire, where a Swiss NGO carried out a project of participative research with the women of two villages in the western part of the country. The object was to introduce a small-scale palm oil press to replace traditional manual methods. The oil of the palm grape plays an important part in local nutrition, representing at least 80 per cent of the fats consumed, and is also an important export to neighbouring areas, mainly through informal channels. Although the young married women were the chief participants, care was taken to involve the men and the older women. The cost was within the ability of the women to save up for – about $5 a month among thirty persons over a six-month period. The press was simple, strong and reliable and could be produced locally.

The women were involved in all stages of trials and adjustments to the raw materials available. The result of the improved technology was not only a higher yield (by about 11 per cent) and better quality (less water and acids) compared with traditional methods but a great reduction in the use of water and fuel wood (63 and 28 per cent respectively) and in the tedious nature of the work. Within two years 95 per cent of the women in the villages were using the new technology for an average of about a third of their output. The local manufacturer sold two presses in the first year and eight in the second. This story illustrates not only the capacities of rural women in Africa, but the fact that quite small investments can make for quite large productivity increases.[12]

The Invisible Woman

Emy Siganga was the representative of Kenya's Association of African Women in Research and Development at a 1991 IFAA workshop on the African response to the World Bank's Long Term Perspective Study (LTPS). This is what she had to say:

I cannot see how the committees which produced the LTPS and the Fraser Report failed to find a single woman on the entire continent of Africa to serve on them and represent the interests of women. This was a terrible mistake. That is why we have such weak recommendations on the well-being of the silent majority.[13]

The women have not in fact been so silent, but to most outsiders it must seem that until recently they remained invisible. The World Bank for long failed to recognize their existence until it prepared the LTPS, in which, for the first time, it accepted that 'women are perhaps the most important, and the most neglected, rural people'. The authors of the LTPS went further, writing in their Introduction and Overview:

In Africa women are generally lead managers within the household; they are responsible for feeding the family; for providing water, education, and health; and for family planning. They are also active in production of food crops and in trade. Their role should be more explicitly recognized in design and implementation of human resource development programs.[14]

But there they leave it. What does this mean in terms of consultation and participation at all levels – from drawing up reports to running local government? So far, very little, or so it appears.

The problem starts with women's rights. In most African traditional cultures, women may be allocated their own fields (usually from their father's or their husband's land) and be responsible for specific crops and operations, from which they enjoy a separate income. Under traditional law, women often had the right to use land belonging to a close relative. This right is being eroded in many places as a result of population pressure. Land registration generally means that the man registers as sole owner. At the same time, with the spread of waged work for men, more and more of the family farm work is being done by the women. The result is not only excessive burdens of work on the women, who still have all the household work to do as well, but it means inevitably the neglect of conservation measures and other invest-ment in the land to maintain crop yields. Land preparation, planting and weeding are delayed or scrimped, so that yields have been reduced by up to 30 per cent in many places.[15]

There are many examples. Sadly, in a village irrigation project in Senegal, it was the women's vegetable plots which showed the worst results. Why? Because they had least time to spare for work on them.[16] It was the same in Kenya, where cotton growing was introduced in Nyanza. The project failed because the women gave precedence at harvest time to their food crops.[17]

The problem of women's rights is compounded by the associated problem of women's lack of access to credit, since they have no title to land or security of tenure. This reduces their ability to purchase inputs for agricultural production and improved tools for working the land and for food processing – hand grinders, for example. Women generally cannot have bank accounts without the husband's permission, which is often withheld. This is the main reason for the large number of women's informal savings groups and credit unions. Rural organizations of women, however, go far beyond the pooling of savings.

Women's Oppression

During the 1980s, Peter O. Ondiege, of the University of Nairobi, studied the local coping strategies of women in Kenya's semi-arid Machakos district, known since colonial times as a 'problem district' because of overstocking, soil erosion and, later, of overpopulation. He found the formation of large numbers of women's groups and concluded that they were the result of an attempt by the women to gain access to and control over resources that had historically been dominated by men.[18] As individuals the women were powerless, but united they could challenge the men. Paul Harrison visited Machakos district and was greatly impressed by the women's work in terracing to contain the tropical rainfall and in tree planting in the gullies to stop further soil erosion.[19]

On the basis of wide experience throughout Africa, Harrison suggested what may be the background to the role and status of women in Africa.

In many respects the African rural household does not act as a single unit, but with husbands and wives competing to maximize their own incomes or minimize their labour inputs. Because of this, the usual approach of targeting official assistance at farm households on the assumption that this will benefit

all the family members can have perverse effects in Africa. The benefits . . .
usually flow to men, while women are often left worse off.[20]

This situation is confirmed from many parts of Africa. All the women
who attended a conference in 1988 on African Women in Cooperatives,
organized by the Institute for African Alternatives, had the same story
to tell. The main constraint on women's involvement in organized
economic activities was shown to be 'male attitudes'.

These include restrictions on the mobility of women; negative attitudes towards
women holding cash; fear of women's increasing power if they gain economic
strength, and that women will reject marriage; competition in starting projects
and getting employment; and resistance to women's independent ownership of
land or other resources. Male leaders have even taken over women's projects
that have proved successful.[21]

One particular complaint of the women was that the introduction of
mechanization nearly always involved the men only, the hand labour
being left to the women. Margaret Anstee records a project in ground
water exploration in West Africa. This project

benefited immensely . . . from the decision to train local women in the basic
maintenance of village pumps . . . [not only did they] keep the water flowing
. . . [but also] as a by-product the women achieved higher recognition of their
status by showing that they could acquire the skill.[22]

Associated with the general appropriation by the men of any mechanical aids introduced into African agriculture, there is the absence of
women extension officers.[23] The take-up of agricultural training is
overwhelmingly by men (83 per cent is the figure given for all African
schemes), while the women who are in fact predominantly the farm
managers are left out. Male extension workers, according to one report
from Kenya, 'find that their contacts are generally women . . . [and
these are] more interested and more committed than the men'.[24] Where
special efforts to organize women are made by extension workers, as in
Burkina Faso, the number of groups grows rapidly.[25]

The conflict between men and women in African households should
not be thought to be universal. Studies by George J.S. Dei of 'indigenous
responses to seasonal food supply cycles and socio-environmental stresses
in the 1980s' in south-east Ghana involved a sample of 400 households
among the Ayirebi community. The region had suffered not only from
the national economic crisis, but also from drought, bush fires and an
influx of Ghanaian deportees from Nigeria. Dei found

a remarkable degree of cooperation between the genders to find solutions to common problems both within the household and community and on the farms . . . [Far from finding, as others had suggested, that] sharing, hospitality and generosity will go by the board in times of scarcity . . . largely through self-help, mutual aid, sharing and generosity, the local population was able to cope with ensuing hardships. There was a cultural awareness and acceptance that the main causes of the environmental crisis were human induced. The crisis was widely attributed to the breakdown of respect for customs including one's obligations to kin and neighbours.[26]

The link to African cultural traditions must be noted here. It is a fact of some importance that this Ghanaian community had a tradition of matrilineal descent of family land inheritance and had resisted the alienation of land by some chiefs and lineage elders to use for cash crops and especially for cocoa. Ayirebi was fortunate also in having a ready market by road for food crops and vegetables in the nearby urban centres of Akyem and Accra.[27]

Changing gender roles and shared decision making in the family were found also among the Akamba in Machakos district of Kenya. Mary Tiffen and Michael Mortimore of the Overseas Development Institute in London, who made a study jointly with seven members of the staff of the University of Nairobi in 1990 of land resource management in Machakos, found a change to the nuclear family from the extended family where land was becoming scarce. They comment:

A positive aspect of the change to nuclear families is that men no longer confine themselves to clearing land for new farms and caring for livestock, but, if their main role is farming, like the women, they may contribute to all stages of crop production. Now, one woman leader in Mbooni told the study team, 'men have become more helpful'. The farm labour force has become more flexible.[28]

Literacy and Numeracy

The exclusion of women from full citizenship in much of Africa remains a serious obstacle to both urban and rural development. One of the most damaging forms this takes is the disparity in educational attainment. Literacy rates for women remain at not much more than half those for men. In some countries – Chad, Niger, Sudan, Guinea, Gambia, Sierra Leone, Somalia, Mali – less than a fifth of the women can read and write. Enrolment in primary schools greatly improved in the 1980s, but in the countries just listed this still left less than half of the girls enrolled. Indeed the average for all the low-income countries is only just a half, and in many more countries the proportion of girls at primary school was under two thirds.[29]

The situation in secondary schools was worse. In 1985, just as in 1965, the girls still on average had half the opportunities of their brothers. By the later date this meant that 10 per cent instead of 2 per cent of girls were still at school at twelve years of age in Africa's low-income economies.[30] There is, moreover, evidence after 1985 of a serious decline in the proportion of girls studying at all levels, which is said to have followed the introduction of school fees.[31]

One result of the women's lack of education we noted earlier is the fact that women's savings groups often have to depend on men to keep their accounts – and the men have been known to abscond with the funds. The alternative for many women's groups is that they fail to manage their businesses efficiently.[32] Some of the Kenyan women's groups, including the one quoted at the beginning of this chapter, were found to be suffering from problems of late payment of contributions and poor records of repayments.[33] The absence of links with the formal banking system increases the risks of exposure without insurance against a crop failure or other local disaster. Their marginalization by government left women's organizations with absolutely no resources but their own. Indeed, in Tanzania, women's organizations, other than official Party bodies, were actually outlawed during the 1970s.

Reading the stories, however, of the way the intervention of government and of formal credit unions have operated, it could be that it was perhaps best for women to remain invisible. Outside intervention often helped only those who were already privileged. Jacob Songsore of Ghana University made a study in 1988 of the Cooperative Credit Union Movement in north-western Ghana. He noticed

(a) a skewed distribution of credit in favour of the urban and rural centres where the credit unions are located as against the wider catchment areas; (b) a further polarization of capital in the hands of the local dominant classes; (c) a distribution of credit in favour of male members of the respective credit unions ... and in many cases ... farmer traders have seized control of the management of the unions and as a result have begun to appropriate a larger share of total loans to themselves.[34]

Alice Nkhoma-Wamunza of the University of Dar es Salaam studied the informal sector in an *ujamaa* village in the Mbeya region of Tanzania in 1990 and had a sad story to tell. Some women came together in the late 1970s to set up a beer club to retail the product of their home brewing activities. They improved the premises, built latrines and ran the club according to the rules they had laid down themselves. They succeeded too well, arousing the attention of a local businessman, who felt threatened and used the local health officer to condemn the premises as unhygienic and ensure withdrawal of the support of the village government, which then promptly appropriated the club and handed it over without compensation to the businessman.

Undeterred, the women still brewed the beer and went on to make enough money to start up a second club. Once again they aroused ill will, this time among the husbands of some of the women who felt threatened by their wives' independence and picked on the poor book-keeping of the club's accounts to complain to the village leaders. The leaders were men. They felt that the women were becoming 'bigheaded' and this time took over the club themselves as a village project, again without compensation. The women complained to the Tanzanian Women's Organization (Umoja wa Wanawake wa Tanzania, UWT) and, when an official of UWT paid a visit to a number of villages in the area, she appealed to the village government to return the clubs to the women. As there was no follow-up to the visit, nothing happened.[35]

Taylor and Mackenzie conclude their collection of studies of survival in rural Africa with the following comment: 'In many situations local initiatives succeed because they remain invisible to those outside. A grey or parallel economy often fares better in the shadows.'[36]

Market Women Traders

If it might just be possible to claim that women were invisible in the African countryside, where they may be spread out in the fields or concealed in the family compound, no such excuse can be offered for failing to notice them in the towns. The markets are full of them, not only buying but selling on every stall. There is a long tradition here of the market mammas, and we have already noted the market women's practice of pooling their savings through *susu, tontine* and other credit systems, which protect women's earnings from their husbands.

During colonial rule, MacGaffey tells us from Zaire, 'Official restrictions discriminated against employment of women in the movement to the towns; the only means for them to make money was by selling domestic services, including sex.'[37] Women's opportunities for education hardly existed at that time, and the women lost, in coming to the towns, the role they had enjoyed in rural life, hard as it was, and the control they then had over any food surplus left over after the family was fed.

With independence from colonial rule, the chances for women in the towns to get an education did greatly improve, but within a decade job opportunities and real wages declined. MacGaffey writes:

It became imperative that women contribute to household expenses. Given their lack of skills and the discrimination which, though against the law, they face in the formal market, they have found that their best opportunities lie in second economy trade. They have taken it up everywhere in Zaire's towns and cities. The result of this change is that women have once again become the major food providers for households.[38]

MacGaffey quotes Joseph Houyoux and Kinavwuidi Niwembo's studies of incomes in Kinshasa in 1969, 1975 and 1986 to show the proportion of household income represented by income from formal salaries falling steadily – from 99 per cent for officials and 70 per cent for other wage workers to 33 per cent for officials and 37–40 per cent for different categories of wage workers. Houyoux assumed that a large part of the unknown source of household income came from informal family enterprise.[39]

Data from interviews carried out in 1987 by Walu Engundu of Kinshasa's *Centre de Recherche en Sciences Humaines* showed that such family enterprise primarily consisted of 'women's trade'. This trade was largely unlicensed and evading tax, and was used to pay for the food consumed by the household.[40]

Here is a summary of how Walu Engundu tells the 'traders' tales' of eighteen market mammas in Kinshasa, told during three months of participant observation and interviews:

The sample was taken to comprise women from a range of income, education and social status. Only five were licensed, four who sold beer, itself illegally brewed at home, and one who rented a market stall. Six others paid for a sublet of a market stall. The rest operated with varying degrees of illegality, the richest selling from their own homes, the poorest from stands in their courtyards, for which they had to make small payments (bribes) to the officials. Twelve of these women received gifts from their kin in the countryside but only three relied on such kin for their supplies, plus one whose husband in the army bought local foodstuff in rural areas and transported it to Kinshasa by military or civilian aircraft. Apart from those who brewed the beer, four others sold what they had themselves produced – doughnuts, cooked fish and meat, soft drinks and bread, and clothes made in a factory and purloined. Produce from the countryside often included goods brought over the border from the Congo and even wider forays were made into Nigeria for blouses, shoes and medicine, household appliances and kitchen utensils. From further afield still, Belgian jewellery and perfumes were being imported with the help of friends who were air hostesses. Dutch wax for batik prints appeared to be the most remunerative import, partly because it was banned by government, to encourage sales of (inferior) local wax.[41]

Income from these varied activities, not surprisingly, ranged widely, from a few hundred zaires a month to over 100,000 (US$ 1000 in 1987). Diamonds and gold and French hard currency (CFA francs from Brazzaville) passed regularly through the hands of the more affluent of these market mammas. Only women of high socio-economic position had the contacts and the capital necessary to carry on the more profitable commerce.[42] Walu Engundu reports that 'Most money changers seen operating on the streets are women' and she adds, 'Renowned for their resplendent physiques, informants affirm that they are protected by men in the political system.'[43] Women are reported by another investigator from Zaire to be the main carriers from Kenya via Uganda into Zaire of smuggled high quality women's accessories, for which prices double or treble in transit.[44]

Thus do women in Zaire find opportunities that did not exist for them before. And not only in Zaire. A similar situation was reported in 1988 to be developing in Tanzania. Studies by Bertha Koda and Aili Mari Tripp in Dar es Salaam in 1988 showed that 66 per cent of urban women were self-employed. Moreover, 65 per cent of those who started up small businesses between 1982 and 1987 were women.[45]

The majority of women were engaged in vending processed food, fuel, vegetables and fruit. A few, however, who belong to the middle- and upper-income brackets, engage in more lucrative business like raising chickens, pigs or dairy cattle; some are even engaged in export and import trading (exporting prawns to Botswana, Zimbabwe, Burundi, et cetera and importing chicks from Zambia).[46]

Aili Tripp adds an interesting comment on the origins of these women traders:

Many of the women have left professional or semi-professional jobs as secondary or vocational school instructors, nurses, accountants, secretaries to become the main breadwinner in the family through their projects, while their husbands retain their formal jobs and the status and connections that go along with them. Not more than five years ago it was virtually unheard of for women to be managing ambitious private enterprises.[47]

It all sounds very exciting and remunerative. It is for a few. But for most it only adds a 'double day' to the demands of frequent child bearing and the heavy burdens of daily domestic duties; and, as Walu Engundu concludes, 'the result of continuing gender inequality is that, with rare exceptions, women's contributions to household economies do not bring corresponding improvement in women's status in household and community'.[48]

The fact remains that support of husbands for their wives' trading activities is rare. It seems to be less rare in Ghana and Tanzania than in Zaire. Although half the women surveyed by Walu Engunu in Kinshasa had obtained their first finance from their husbands, such support did not necessarily survive the wife's becoming a too successful trader. Living on the wrong side of the law is an anxious business for man and wife. And such business is frequently complicated by the fact that it may involve the wife granting sexual favours to officials, with the attendant risk of acquiring AIDS as well as a jealous and resentful husband.

Market trading undoubtedly provided women with some solution to their economic problems in the 1970s and 1980s, but, as the formal economy declined, informal enterprise was squeezed too. Women who had made money earlier by their trading projects were hardly surviving in the early 1990s. Walu Engundu's Kinshasa collaborator, Claude Schoepf, had already drawn a bleak conclusion from earlier studies in 1981:

Complacency about the ability of the urban 'informal sector' to provide people with the means of subsistence is especially pernicious for women and children ... The vast majority are forced to eke out an insecure existence in petty trade and/or prostitution. The outstanding success of a few women in these occupations should not be allowed to obscure the misery that is the lot of most.[49]

By 1990, Engundu and Schoepf were warning that, while only two of the households surveyed were poverty stricken in 1987, a follow-up survey showed that 'seven were in serious trouble in 1989'.[50]

Women's Organizations in Africa

The main feature of the operations of women traders in Africa is that they are individualistic or based on the family and close friends.

Aili Tripp reports from Tanzania

elaborate mutual support networks . . . which offer much to women in terms of sharing skills, responsibilities, capital, information and even markets . . . Friends, relatives and spouses . . . offering loans, running the project, providing important information, and minding children while the mother is away from home. It is common, for instance, for a friend or sister to specialize in cooking beans or pastries while the other person cooks rice or prepares tea. They then sell together.[51]

Most of the women interviewed by Walu Engundu contributed their savings to a *likelemba* (a kind of *susu*).[52] This too is a personal action, to avoid the grasp of husbands; it is not an action of collective organization.

Organized women's groups are, however, widespread throughout Africa. Many of the women in Dar es Salaam worked together as households or neighbourhood groups. A few formed formal cooperatives – for fishing, growing and selling vegetables, flour milling and fish smoking – but cooperatives were not the women's first choice for organizing their projects.[53] Kenya is reputed to have the strongest women's organizations – or perhaps it is just that they have been more fully recorded there. A survey of one district in Kenya with a population of 1.5 million revealed that there were over 500 women's groups formed in the 1980s.

These Kenyan women's groups were made up as follows:

115 self-help groups and women's groups were engaged in ecological activities – terracing, dam and water tank construction and afforestation. 96 self-help groups, 249 women's groups and 73 cooperative societies were involved in goat, poultry and bee keeping, ranching, dairy farming, fishing and craft work; also in construction work for houses, schools, shops and barns and in running bookshops, nurseries and restaurants. There were 19 specifically savings and credit societies, but many of the self-help and women's groups combined these activities with their other interests.[54]

It is possible from this information to calculate the relative importance of these women's organizations in this one district of Kenya. The size of these groups varied from twenty to thirty members to several hundred.

Taking an average of sixty members per group, this would mean 30,000 members in the 500 women's groups. Assuming that there were 300,000 households in the district, we arrive at a figure of just one tenth of all women being organized in these various ways.

More important, perhaps, than their numbers was the range of their activities. Far from these women engaging in purely coping strategies, they were responding to land shortage, population pressure and drought by taking positive measures of conservation and enhanced food production. Trees were being planted and bench terracing constructed against soil erosion, while at the same time production of crops and of beef and milk was being greatly increased, to meet a ready market in the nearby city of Nairobi. Horticultural produce – tomatoes, onions, cabbage and citrus fruits – was enormously boosted and even found a place in the export market.

Such successes have encouraged the women to think of the revival of local crafts and cottage industries – sisal basket making and wood carving. These products reached markets in Europe and North America and led to the formation of new institutions – cooperative societies for handicrafts and group enterprises (like the Yatta South Women's Group Enterprise Development) with several women's centres and participation in the Machakos District Cooperative Union.[55]

Forming their own cooperative has for many women in Africa been seen as a way of circumventing male dominance. This is certainly the view of Bukola Oni, the former head of the Home Economics Division of the Nigerian Federal Ministry of Agriculture. She made the point quite clearly at a workshop on Management for Women in Agriculture and Rural Development held in Ilorin, western Nigeria in 1988.

Women in some parts of the country have found it extremely useful to form themselves into groups. Some of the reasons advanced are that if they own crops collectively it is very difficult for their husbands to lay claims to such crops as traditionally women are not supposed to own property.[56]

This argument was put forward by Gloria Thomas-Emeagwali, a Nigerian contributor to an all-Africa workshop on Women and Sustainable Development held in Dar es Salaam in December 1989, but she was anxious to set the argument within the framework of the long history of what she called 'the spirit of cooperation in Africa that has been cultivated and had been expressed among its people spontaneously in different sorts of collective institutions of credit, mutual aid and work'.[57]

This need in Africa to build on the cultural strengths of the people was emphasized by Claude Aké in his World Bank paper as the basis for all African development, but it is the women who have seized upon it. *Ukhuluma usenza* (discussing/reflecting while you work) is the philosophy of ORAP (the Organization of Rural Associations for Progress) in Zimbabwe, whose members claim that 'ORAP people use their culture as a tool for social analysis and self understanding'.[58]

Women in Cooperatives

At a conference in 1988 of African Women in Cooperatives, however, it became clear that there was almost universal discrimination against women in African cooperatives. It was reported:

In most countries, the majority of women were excluded from membership of agricultural production and marketing cooperatives in the state sponsored sector, because of membership regulations which only recognize one member, the 'household head', per family . . . this excludes married womem.[59]

Women in cooperatives, where they have been admitted, have generally been treated as less than full members and their labour has often been exploited. This is said to be the reality of Harambee, the widespread cooperative movement in Kenya.[60] In some places, such treatment has led to the collapse of the cooperative, since the women simply reduced their work input in response to their poor reward.[61]

For women to form their own cooperatives, none the less, requires experience and resources. There are reports of successful women's cooperatives in Mozambique, Botswana and Angola, where women play a major role in agriculture because of the migration of men to the towns or to South Africa and because of government encouragement of women's political involvement.[62] To take just one example, women living in the suburbs of Maputo, Mozambique, began in the mid 1970s to form 'Green Zones', under the personal supervision of the President, Samora Machel. From these zones they helped to overcome food shortage in the city. By the early 1980s, 181 producer cooperatives had joined a Union of Green Zone cooperatives, with the support of an Italian priest, Father Prospero (sic), who had helped Frelimo in the liberation struggle.[63] The Union received finance from the State Development Bank, and similar Green Zones came to be formed around other Mozambiquan cities.[64]

Successful cooperative projects have also been reported from Cameroon and as elements of integrated projects in Tanzania, Kenya,

Senegal and Cameroon (MIDENO), 'which are known to have provided women with resources and inputs, extension services and training and income'.[65] Cooperatives of small-scale farmers in Zimbabwe include a growing number of women's cooperatives. They are reported to be producing 50 per cent of the nation's marketed maize, the national staple food.[66]

Most of these examples are of rural agricultural cooperatives, but in Tanzania women's cooperatives in Dar es Salaam have been established in tailoring and soap making with government assistance, and in Uganda the new government is said to have 'contributed much to the development of women's cooperatives by, e.g. funding their purchases of new inputs, espicially machinery and spares'.[67]

Women in Zimbabwe can show more success than elsewhere in Africa in winning equality with men in agriculture. Women farmers have gained equal status with men in training in Zimbabwe's National Farmers' Association 'Master Farmers' clubs. By 1988, there were 4,500 of these clubs, with a membership of 70,000 and 150,000 associates. These were sponsored by government but were largely initiated by the farmers themselves. In two communal areas which were studied by a Zimbabwe university lecturer, Lovemore M. Zinyama, most of the farmers were found to be women, generally as wives of absent migrant workers, but sometimes as owners (respectively 14 and 21 per cent in the two areas). As well as their membership of the Master Farmer clubs, many of the farmers had formed mutual help groups and savings clubs, which Zinyama believed 'could be the basis for the development of cooperative agricultural productive units, in line with government policy for the socialist transformation of the economy and society'.[68]

Women were still, however, not being treated as equals in the cooperatives. Zinyama reported that the women took less part than the men in decision making in the clubs, not only because of their domestic work loads, but also because of male prejudice.[69] This inequality was very strongly expressed in an earlier inquiry by the Zimbabawe Women's Bureau into the working of Master Farmer clubs. The women interviewed said that they still had to do most of the work, not only in the home, including the fetching of the water and fuel, but also in the fields and in transporting produce to the market. Husbands kept the earnings and some would not pay the fee for the women to join the clubs.[70]

One of the most successful rural cooperative organizations in Africa is ORAP in Zimbabwe's Matabeleland. This began outside Bulawayo, as a series of women's clubs, but grew to take in men as well as women.

Each group consists of 50 to 100 families in a village and these joined together in an association of three or more groups which came under an 'umbrella' of up to 14 groups, finally bringing together by 1989 some 650 village groups. ORAP's motto is 'Putting the last first' and the village group remains the centre of power. Bodies at higher levels are supposed to have only advisory functions and consist always of equal numbers of men and women. Advisory services include advice on propagation and use of indigenous seeds, rain-water catchment, inter-village food marketing and community grain stores.[71]

ORAP has not entirely avoided the dangers of over-centralized administration or of dependence on donors, according to a highly self-critical evaluation made in 1990. But ORAP membership has genuinely sought to reach down to the poorest and most disadvantaged, whom so many projects fail to mobilize. This they have tried to do through the elaboration of their two key concepts of *amalima* and of *zenzele*. *Amalima* are the small family groups who work the land together. *Zenzele* is an active word, meaning 'be the main actor yourself!' Together the two concepts form an encouragement to self-help, including collective think-ing and planning, as well as collective action.

But what does this mean at the level of umbrella associations and larger projects of irrigation schemes, grinding mills and development centres? Sithembesi Nyoni, one of ORAP's founding mothers, posed the dilemma in a discussion paper for ORAP's tenth anniversary in September 1991:

– to keep the same spirit of *zenzele* as demonstrated by *amalima* at these (higher) levels in which outside aid confronts people's self help efforts;

– to empower rural people against the most powerful and aggressive economic and market forces of which the recently introduced structural adjustment programmes are part.[72]

Failures as well as Successes

The ORAP experience in Zimbabwe is of particular importance both because it emphasizes the value of grass roots democracy in rural development and because it shows how women's projects can be inte-grated into larger-scale agricultural development. In other countries, where women's projects have been components of larger integrated development schemes, many failures have been recorded. The chief reasons for failure, according to Joyce Endely of the University Centre of Dschang, Cameroon, appear to be the following:

(a) refusal to identify women as equal participants with legal rights;

(b) stereotyping of women's work, e.g. vegetable gardening, child care, sewing and baking, with no access to machinery;

(c) lack of women advisers, extension workers and managers;

(d) no consideration in project design of the whole life of a woman as mother, housekeeper as well as worker outside the household;

(e) neglect of the potential of women for training in new skills;

(f) dependence of projects on outside government or NGO management and initiative.[73]

As a result of all the limitations on women's contribution to rural cooperatives, many projects focusing specifically on women, far from narrowing the existing gender gap in rural life, have served only to widen the gap still further.[74] This often appears to be the deliberate intention of government aid for women's cooperatives. One example comes from the Sudan, where the Productive Family Programme encourages women to engage in handicrafts and backyard gardens, explicitly 'to keep them working within the home sphere'.[75]

Another example comes from Mali. The *Ton villageois* in Mali has its origins in village associations of a mutualist nature freely joined by the villagers, but under the UDPM (Union Démocratique du Peuple Malien), *Ton* development committees were established in 1979 as 'instruments of execution for decisions taken by the administration including the levy of a "development tax"'. As a response and with overseas aid support, FEDEV was established to promote income-generating activities for women, mainly through market gardening and craft products but including soap making, livestock rearing and dyeing. Numbers were still small in 1988 – twenty or so rural groups of 60 to 100 woman each.[76]

The major handicap for African women farmers developing their full potential remains their neglect by government agencies in the provision of extension education and technological support. Women farmers have been shown in several country surveys to be most desirous of extension contact and to have established contact as much as men. Improvement in results does not always follow. The reasons are several. The educational level of women is generally lower than that of men. If improvements involve the use of animals or machinery, that is men's work and not women's. Most agricultural research is done by men and many of the technical recommendations concern crops that are regarded as men's responsibility – maize and other cash crops – and not the vegetables and food crops like cassava, sweet potatoes, millet and sorghum which are in the care of the women. Most extension agents also are men and, although in the inquiries made both in Nigeria and Kenya women said that they preferred male agents, this could be because the male agents talked mainly about farming and the women agents about home economics.[77]

The technology needs of rural women in Africa are immense, even though the level of technology that would greatly increase productivity is very low, not even involving animal or machine power – simple manual ridgers, planters, rotary hoes and fertilizer spreaders on the land; hand grinders, dehusking, threshing and cleaning tools, cooking stoves and proper storage facilities in the home; bicycles and wheeled carts for transport. Such work-time saving measures are essential if higher yielding varieties of plants are to be introduced, because all such varieties are more demanding of timely cultivation, irrigation, fertilization and weed control.[78]

A major finding of the World Bank surveys was that the presence of buying and selling cooperatives was crucial to the take-up of new technology, and fewer women than men were found to be members of cooperatives. On the other hand, women's own groups were often at the root of the success of women farmers making use of extension provision. This was especially the case in Burkina Faso, where a 1988 seminar organized by the Extension Department resulted in raising the number of women's groups from 20 to 1394 and the number of women directly contacted by extension from 15,000 to 299,000.[79] It is one of the tragedies of the cuts in public spending as part of structural adjustment that these have led to reduced funding for extension work in many countries just as governments had begun to make facilities available for training women agents.

Women's Groups Everywhere

Given women's subservient position in African society and their lack of experience and resources for establishing formal cooperative organizations, it is not surprising that nearly all women's associations in Africa are informal, although not necessarily in what we have been calling the informal, second economy. Some commentators have described these as 'pre-cooperative', but this is to imply that they might lead to more formal organization; and this is far from being the case.[80]

Rau in his study of grass roots remedies for Africa's food crisis gave a wide range of examples of informal women's groups. In Central Nigeria women had developed 'an exciting but totally unreported example of economic innovation in soybean production and processing'. They established an 'informal extension service of their own' to share seeds and experiences. The soybean was used as substitute in soups and stews for locust beans, which required longer to process and were controlled by the men, since they came from trees.[81] In western Cameroon and elsewhere 'working bees', or rotating labour-sharing arrangements, allow women to contribute to agricultural work and draw upon friends and neighbours to complete the tasks.[82]

Sometimes, women's groups do develop into formal cooperatives. A women's nutrition club in southern Zambia started out by purchasing dried fish, beans and milk from the National Food and Nutrition Commission for resale to its members, but decided to grow and market their own, transforming itself in the process into the Chikuni Fruit and Vegetable Producers' Cooperative Society. After some years they were operating two vegetable processing plants and a Chikuni Credit Union.[83]

Much prejudice remains against women's organizations and their methods of work. A good example of the failure of the experts to recognize women's traditional knowledge comes from Sierra Leone. Farmers in the high rainfall areas are mainly women. They produce rice by the method called 'minimum tilling', designed to reduce labour inputs. This was at first decried by the agronomists as a lazy and ignorant practice and condemned as 'unsightly' because of the mix of weeds and crops that came up. But, later, the experts had to accept that the women's traditional practice was an efficient use of women's scarce labour time and one which did not greatly reduce the crop yields.[84]

Senegal is said to have the 'general reputation of backing big projects at the expense of peasant agriculture'. Examples are the US Bud Company's groundnuts scheme and the big dams on the Senegal river. Both have proved to be disasters.[85] Senegalese women, however, in the Casamance area have been taking the lead with 'gardening groups' which have become 'a major force for development'. Each woman has her own plot but there is a communal two-hectare plot they share. The groups are democratically run and, although they have had help from UNICEF and other technical advice from PIDAC (Integral Project for Agricultural Development in Casamance), there is reported to be 'little indication that they intend to surrender much power to any centralized organization'. The over 10,000 members have, however, formed a 'federation' and run a truck to market their produce. Men have even begun to join, although the groups are still called 'women's gardening groups'.[86]

Women have also taken the lead elsewhere in Africa in other branches of food production and processing – in goat and sheep projects in the dry lands of Niger and Kenya, with help from Oxfam and Catholic agencies and from government extension workers; in natural resource projects, protecting forests and marking contour lines against soil erosion in Burkina Faso;[87] in fish processing in Togo; in fishing, transporting and marketing in Ghana and Togo, where 95 per cent of the 100,000 people involved are women (Ghana's attempt to establish a fish processing industry on the Cape Coast based on male entrepreneurs collapsed).[88]

A new perspective for women's organizations in Africa has been opened up by the egalitarian ethos of the liberation movements both in Tigray, Ethiopia and in Eritrea, particularly in the latter. Even under the Mengistu regime in Ethiopia, there was some rhetorical encouragement of cooperatives, but women formed only about 7 per cent of the membership of the producer and service cooperatives in the 1980s.[89] Yet groups of mainly Christian immigrants in Addis Ababa with much larger women's representation were able to take advantage of government encouragement to make a success of food-growing cooperatives as a 'coping strategy' in the city itself.[90]

In Eritrea, probably more was done for women by the EPLF (Eritrean People's Liberation Front) than can be found anywhere else in Africa. The EPLF not only redistributed land to nearly 100,000 families even while the war was raging, and encouraged the formation of cooperatives and mutual aid groups, but started a revolution among the women. For the first time in history, women were given rights to land ownership and inheritance and to divorce. Women formed one-fifth of the fighting forces and were given equal pay, such as it was, and equal opportunity in education and training. Eritrean women during the long struggle for liberation became not only active organizers, teachers and health workers, but engineers, electricians and mechanics and provided one in ten of the national delegate congress.[91] The implications for the future of Eritrea and indeed for all African women could be considerable.

Women in Power?

Women's initiative and organizing capacity at the grass roots of African society seem hardly, if at all, to be represented at the centres of power.[92] African governments have accepted the UN Charter on Women's Rights, and they initiated the Abuja Declaration of 1989 on the Integration of Women in the Development of Africa. Making declarations is one thing; implementing them is another. The ECA Training and Research Centre for Women was closed down in 1987 for lack of funding because, it was said, it was not an integral part of other ECA activities.[93]

Several African governments have a Ministry for Women. In Zimbabwe it was headed until her tragic early death by Sally Mugabe. By contrast in Gambia, the president, Sir Dawda Jawara, and not his wife, held the portfolios of National Defence and Women's Affairs until relinquishing them after twenty years in what was called a 'significant concession' in 1992 to the vice-president, Mr Saiho S. Sabally.[94] No comment is needed!

Other governments have women's organizations associated with the leading party, like Tanzania's UWT and Nigeria's National Commisson for Women (NCW) and the women's branches of the Ghanaian CDR. The presence of women in the higher ranks of government is exceedingly rare. One of the two women members of Botswana's parliament is a cabinet minister and there are 'women presidents of urban customary courts, councillors, ministers and directors' as well as thirty-three women (one-third of the total) on the top management of Botswana's wide-ranging cooperative movement.[95]

The Organization of Angolan Women has a remarkable record of struggle for their own emancipation and for the liberation of their country.[96] The OAW has 1.9 million members; and women form 90 per cent of the membership of the peasant associations. Its principal function is said to be 'to discuss with the government all matters concerning women'.[97] In Mozambique, as in Eritrea and Angola, women were fully engaged in the freedom struggle. They have demonstrated considerable interest in political participation and in 1980 held 40 per cent of the positions as elected judges in the local justice tribunals. But many women claim that 'while they make up 79 per cent of all the economically active people involved in agriculture, they are not consulted in production planning and decision-making'.[98]

Outside of the African countries in which independence was achieved through a long armed struggle, women are still battling for political representation. In Nigeria the state-funded NCW, with the support of many women's organizations, the National Council of Women's Societies and the Nigerian Association of University Women, campaigned in the 1991 elections for women candidates. The result was two women deputy state governors, three women local government 'chairmen', two women appointed secretaries to state governors, one woman deputy clerk and a clerk in the legislative arm of government – perhaps 1 per cent of the total jobs at this level. Neither party gave any commitment to the ending of gender subordination in Nigeria, which in the Islamic north means almost total purdah.[99]

Women's Resistance to Oppression

The oppression of women in Africa is only now being documented.[100] Much of what we have seen in this chapter and in the last shows women ignoring or secretly challenging the state authorities. In some cases they have openly resisted. Women took part in movements of peasant resistance to the construction of large-scale dams in Mali, Nigeria and Senegal; to protest the failure of 'Green Revolution' in Zambia, where packages were not delivered anywhere and crops were not collected; and to end the cheating over weights and prices by the Malian cotton company.[101]

The 'Ondo Women's War' in south-west Nigeria in late 1985 followed upon an increase in tax revenues imposed on market sales. The women shut down the market and rallied tens of thousands of their sisters to protest the government's action. The governor agreed to a compromise which protected those women who were on lower incomes.[102]

Women cassava growers in eastern Zaire protested on their own against official corruption and unjust tolls levied at three points on their road to the local town, when they found these payments were not being used for road and bridge repairs but went into the local officials' pockets. From resistance they went on to elect sympathetic candidates at the next elections and had the tax and tolls abolished – an extraordinary achievement in 1983 in a police state like Zaire, pervaded as it is by violence and corruption.[103]

The relationship of the women's movement to the state in Africa is, as elsewhere, an ambivalent one. Most of the more educated women are employed by the state. They are 'in and against the state'. In the many demonstrations and acts of protest that led to the fall of several African governments in 1990–92, women were often to the fore. It was a woman teacher who was shot in Gabon in March 1992 in protests which led to a general strike demanding new elections.[104]

The many women's groups and cooperatives which appear in the studies made by Taylor and Mackenzie's team of African researchers have shown that those which succeeded – in Ghana, Kenya, Tanzania, Zimbabwe – did so with state support. This was true also in Sierra Leone and Zambia and most particularly in Eritrea and Mozambique. Elsewhere, the support of foreign NGOs has been crucial. World Bank reports have made a particular point of this fact.[105]

In this matter of support for women's organizations, the role of the foreign NGOs has been ambiguous: on the one hand, there is no doubt that they have helped women to get organized; on the other hand, we noted in an earlier chapter a tendency for expatriate personnel to impose their own solutions and to stay on in responsible positions after initiating schemes, thus depriving Africans of responsibility.[106] Moreover, when NGOs give aid, there is not only the possibility of jealousy among others being aroused as a result of seeing the special treatment granted to particular groups, but also of antagonism developing among local authorities and representatives of the central state.[107]

The World Bank in its new look has begun to explore the relations of NGOs and the state with particular regard to women. In the LTPS, 'developing farmers' associations' and 'recognizing the role of women' are placed together in one section in the chapter on agriculture and much is made of the importance of 'the neglected role of women farmers' in Africa.[108] Women reappear in the Study in providing the delivery of social services[109] and in the mobilization of community savings, thus 'using free resources to meet the community's most urgent needs'. This comes in the chapter entitled 'Sustainable Funding for Development'.[110]

The Bank is open to criticism on at least four grounds, which Mackenzie has distinguished. The first is the assumption of an undifferentiated historical context for communal solidarity as if there were no class or gender differences; the second is the supposition that there are 'free resources' – presumably women's unpaid labour – to mitigate cuts in state spending on social services; the third is imagining for one moment that local empowerment will provoke no response from those holding power at the state level; finally, there is a wanton failure to connect the interests of different groups in society at different levels in projects for economic development.[111] To be effective it is necessary for women's organizations to be integrated into the whole range of measures that Africans are proposing for developing human resources.

CHAPTER 14

Developing Human Resources

Participating . . . is the key word. In contrast to the many theoretical interpretations circulating today, African society has age-old experience of what it means. The challenge to planners and practitioners is to maintain wherever possible the vitality of this cultural legacy and of traditional support systems during this period of social change . . . Redressing the social ills of African society and improving the distribution of social services can be achieved only in the context of social planning. And I am not afraid to use the word planning . . . The ultimate purpose of development, it should not be forgotten, is to improve the well-being of people – all people.

> Margaret Joan Anstee, Director General of the UN Office at Vienna, as the UN Under Secretary-General responsible for UN activities relating to social policy and development, writing on 'Social Development in Africa: Perspective, Reality and Promise' in James Pickett and Hans Singer, *Toward Economic Recovery in Sub-Saharan Africa: Essays in Honour of Robert Gardiner*, Routledge, 1990, pp. 203–4.

In 1987, the Nigerian writer, Chinua Achebe, called together a group of African writers to look seventy years on 'Beyond Hunger' to the year 2057.[1] In a marvellous evocation of Africa's 'age-old experience', the vision which they saw was not one of some miraculous economic growth or political change; it was quite simply the emergence of healthier and better-educated people rejecting counsels of despair and turning around the current perspective at every level. They received sponsorship from African institutions – the African Academy of Sciences, the Council for the Development of Economic and Social Research in Africa (CODESRIA) and the World Hunger Project. They sought to demonstrate, first, 'the need to create new, magnetic images of the future that can shape policy, action and research' and, second, 'the need for a more pluralistic policy environment'.[2]

These African writers started from two assumptions, which reflected the importance they attached to Africa's cultural traditions:

Africa is a continent whose culture has for centuries been denigrated . . . The self-esteem and self-confidence that turn human beings into agents of change will only come about as a result of greater respect for and recognition of the role culture plays in society.[3]

Here is the outline which they drew from the comparison they made between the present and the future as part of the discussions which they had at their meeting at Kericho in Kenya:

TABLE 14.1 Differences between the African Vision and the Current Perspective on Africa[4]

Level	Conventional Wisdom	African Vision
Conceptual	unilinear	dialectic
	crisis oriented	beyond crisis
Methodological	surprise-free	surprise-rich
	deductive	inductive
	predictive	retrodictive
Institutional	state-centred	grass roots oriented
	concentrated	multiple/dispersed
	monopolistic	pluralizing
Operational	donor-fed and controlled	locally owned/initiated
	directive/pre-emptive	supportive/nurturing
	capital intensive	people intensive
Financial	massive transfer	seed money
	project specific	matching funds

At each of these levels what differentiates the African vision from the conventional wisdom is the central position which is accorded to the human cultural dimension. The development of human resources is seen not as the hoped-for product of measures of economic development, but as the very means of development. The disastrous effect of structural adjustment programmes in Africa in the last decade has been that they have been 'implemented at high human cost and sacrifices', to the point that they have been 'rending the fabric of African society', weakening the very capacity of the people to engage in socio-economic recovery and development.

These words are taken from the Khartoum Declaration of 1988, which emerged from the International Conference on the Human Dimension of Africa's Economic Recovery and Development, held under United Nations auspices.[5] It is a tribute to the uniting force of Africa's new vision that, within a year of the launching of the Beyond Hunger Project, African governments of many different colours and persuasions were endorsing its central theme.

Health and Education as Investments

More than a score of the papers, mainly by African experts, which were contributed to the 1988 Khartoum conference have since been published. Their conclusions were summarized in the Khartoum Declaration:

Regrettably, over the past decade the human condition of most Africans has deteriorated calamitously. Real incomes of almost all households and families declined sharply. Malnutrition has risen massively, food production has fallen relative to population, the quality and quantity of health and education services have deteriorated. Famine and war have made tens of millions of human beings refugees and displaced persons. In many cases the slow decline of infant mortality and of death from preventable, epidemic diseases has been reversed. Meanwhile, the unemployment and underemployment situation has worsened markedly.[6]

Adebayo Adedeji, at that time Executive Secretary of the Economic Commission for Africa and Under-Secretary General of the United Nations, added as a further conclusion:

The situation has been severely aggravated by the structural adjustment measures that have been pursued, which emphasize short-term financial and fiscal adjustment concerns rather than long-term balanced development . . . neglect for the human dimension is not only counter-productive from the point of view of well-being, but is also detrimental to the economic process.[7]

Since the Khartoum Declaration of 1988, detailed studies have been made by African experts from ten sub-Saharan countries to assess the implications for education, health and employment of the impact of structural adjustment. The studies were part of a research project entitled 'Population, Human Resources and Development in Africa' at the African Institute for Economic Development and Planning at Dakar, Senegal, and were funded by the United Nations Fund for Population Activities (UNFPA). This is their conclusion:

In most countries, despite economic improvements in a few areas, there has been a decline in the extent and the quality of education and health care, and formal sector employment has fallen, sometimes drastically. Much of the blame rests with the economic crises that preceded structural adjustment, but clearly the adjustment measures themselves contributed significantly to this decline.[8]

In fact, 'there is consensus among the authors of this volume that, in the [ten] countries surveyed, one does not find a strong association between adjustment policies and economic performance', and they confirmed the views of UNICEF, ILO and ECA that the cuts in public expenditure required by structural adjustment programmes have fallen most heavily upon the most vulnerable sectors of society – the poor, the women and children and the aged. In particular, the effect of introducing school fees and health service charges has been to exacerbate inequality and poverty. More than this, these measures have gravely weakened the human resources upon which recovery and development depend.[9]

So rarely is this last point given its due weight that it is necessary to repeat here the sombre warning of UN Under-Secretary General Margaret Joan Anstee:

The impact of recession and adjustment in the 1980s has been dealt with by economists and policy makers, within a framework of macro-analysis that pays scant attention to the people directly caught up in these economic events. These trends were inexorably leading to an ominous deterioration of sub-Saharan Africa's scarce human capital, which can be replaced only at great cost. They were also setting the stage for an accelerated spiral of decline in the continent's future development.[10]

It is necessary to remind ourselves of the connection between the economic crises that preceded structural adjustment and the adjustment measures themselves. The chief aim of these measures was to ensure that African governments were enabled to service the debts that they had incurred by borrowing for industrialization programmes when the prices of their primary product exports were still high. All the other aims and objectives claimed by the IMF and World Bank for their policies for Africa have been secondary and on occasion fraudulent.[11]

It had become absolutely essential by the late 1980s to halt the decline in Africa's human capital. Resources going into debt repayment had somehow to be retained for development in African. Once more, we have the authority of Under Secretary-General Anstee:

Here it is sufficient to say unequivocally that, without significant alleviation of this burden [of the foreign debt], Africa will not be able to achieve the recovery and renewed growth, combined with improved living conditions for the poorer segments of its population, that it so desperately needs. But even that is, in itself, not enough. Another key to the problem is that Africa has not had sufficient confidence in itself, in its ability to produce African products, build on African institutions and cultivate African values.[12]

Adjustment with a Human Face

When, in 1986, the government of Zambia announced that it would restrict debt servicing to 10 per cent of net export earnings, President Kaunda asked rhetorically of the IMF,

which is a better partner for you in the long run, a nation which devotes all of its resources to paying the debt and, therefore, in the long run grinds to an economic and political halt, or a stable nation capable of sustaining the repayment of its entire debt?[13]

This is a question which Kaunda's successors in Zambia may ponder, as they return to the treadmill of debt repayments in return for new grants and loans of over $1 billion – on conditions, which include not only deregulating foreign exchange but boosting exports and cutting public expenditure.[14]

The judgement of the University of Zambia's professor of economics, Venkatash Seshamani, will have to be noted, that much state spending in Zambia as elsewhere was wasteful, low priority being accorded to 'those sectors such as health and education which provide the necessary inputs for the building up of human capital'. But the professor insisted, 'the solution lies in the development and improvement of indigenous managerial skills [and not in] selling off parastatals into private hands, whereupon most of their social objectives would be thrown to the winds.' Nor was there any solution to be had in making drastic reductions in social services. 'It is . . . essential,' he went on, 'that the levels of real per capita social service expenditure should be at least maintained, if not increased.'[15]

The professor, writing in 1989, called upon a recent UNICEF report on the situation in Zambia to support his argument that reductions in such expenditures reduce the quantum of public service. This is what the report said:

Absolute poverty is correlated with lack of adequate access to public services. This is largely because of the relative geographic isolation of many absolutely poor rural families, and because most absolutely poor urban households are in squatter or other peri-urban areas which are ill-served, especially if they were established or grew rapidly during the post-1979 years [post-1975 in the case of Zambia] of constrained public budgets.[16]

The professor concluded with the following warning:

By denuding the existing meagre stocks of human capital the country has, it [a reduction in public spending] acts as a long-term constraint on development.[17]

Another African university professor, Akilagpa Sawyerr, the vice-chancellor of the University of Ghana, writing on 'The Politics of Adjustment Policy' for the conference that led up to the Khartoum Declaration, listed four programmes to put a 'human face' upon structural adjustment or at least to cushion its impact:

a) . . . the introduction of nutritional support programmes for special target groups such as children under five years old, and lactating and nursing mothers, with UNICEF playing a very active role;
b) . . . an increase in resource flows into the social services – education, health, rural water and sanitation, etc. – specially directed at the poorer sections of society;
c) 'food for work' schemes aimed at putting unemployed and underemployed people, especially the youth, to work on projects of special community value, such as improved water supply, schools, clinics and feeder roads; and
d) schemes aimed at increasing income generation among lower-income households.[18]

This may appear to be an obvious list of absolutely basic requirements in any programme of recovery, but the vice-chancellor goes on to comment wryly:

The fact of the matter is that the proposals outlined above run counter to the basic thrust of structural adjustment programmes, namely the market-determination of prices and the allocation of resources and the reduced role of the state in the specific management of the economy.[19]

Absolute and Relative Poverty

The most striking result of structural adjustment programmes through-out Africa, which the vice-chancellor believed had most urgently to be corrected, was the widening gap between the few rich and the many poor. As he put it succinctly, 'the poor in society thus become poorer, both relatively and absolutely, under the austerity measures'.[20] This is not just a matter of a number of small vulnerable groups at the bottom of society and a tiny élite at the top, but of the overwhelming majority of the whole population of many African countries being reduced to absolute poverty. World Bank estimates of the numbers of people below country-specific poverty lines reveal 'rural poverty . . . to be as high as 65% of the rural population in a sample of twenty-one sub-Saharan countries'.[21] By 1985 60 per cent of rural children under five were estimated by the UN Population Division to be living in absolute poverty. The corresponding estimate for urban areas was 29 per cent.

The UNICEF report recording these figures commented: 'These estimates of poverty and income are not expected to improve under current conditions in many African countries' since by 1995 'per capita incomes were forecast to be 20% below 1980 levels' and 'in the lower-income non-fuel primary exporting countries at least 10% below their levels in 1965'.[22]

One of the causes of this advancing wave of poverty engulfing something near to half the whole of the African people is the rising rate of unemployment as structural adjustment measures have cut into state spending. The UNFPA study of 1990 reported that:

Unemployment rates have increased in almost all the countries covered because of contractionary fiscal and monetary policies which resulted in retrenchment of workers. Urban unemployment rates rose to 14.8% in Sierra Leone, over 60% in Zambia between 1985 and 1990 and . . . to 12.2% in 1987 in Nigeria.[23]

The World Bank has argued that 'the poor as a group would probably have suffered considerably more if no adjustment programmes had been in place'.[24] This type of statement cannot be proved or disproved. Everything depends on the other factors involved, but the claim could only have been true if it is assumed that debt repayments would have continued without any rescheduling agreement with the Bank or other financial institutions.

It cannot be repeated too often that the burden of African countries' debts to the industrialized countries is the fundamental cause of Africa's anguish. The fact is that cuts in public spending are bound to hurt the poor more than the rich. Even if the rich do not evade payment of taxes (as the African proverb has it, 'The cobweb catches the fly and not the elephant'), they can buy all the services they need, while the poor must depend on public provision. For this reason, the ECA *African Alternative Framework* included proposals for a reduction in defence spending and in subsidies to public enterprise, but insisted on retaining state support for social services, and especially for education and health.[25]

Income Redistribution before Growth

The essential point that African scholars have been arguing is that redistribution of the national product cannot be regarded as something that is left aside until *after* economic growth has been achieved. It has to be an essential part of the process of development itself. Venkatash Seshamani has drawn upon a number of North American development studies to demonstrate the advantages of redistribution as a *prior* requirement of growth:

First, a better distribution of the major asset whose productivity is about to be improved, together with more equal access to markets and to opportunities for improving the productivity of that major asset, will obviously diminish the adverse effects of unequal asset distribution on income distribution. Second, the redistributed asset is not as valuable before improvements in productivity as it is after. Redistribution with full compensation would, therefore, be possible, at least in principle.[26]

In simpler language, it is both cheaper and economically more efficient to redistribute assets before rather than after measures are taken to improve their productivity.

As an illustration of this thesis, Professor Seshamani takes a proposal for land reform in Zambia, which had earlier been published by the Economic Development Institute attached to the World Bank. The authors of this proposal stated that 'not more than 250,000 ha of land (only 5 per cent of Zambia's total arable land) would be required to provide the food to all those in the urban areas who face the risk of food security.' And they went on to say:

Given that vastly more than that much land [i.e. more than 250,000 ha] on large commercial farms (239 farms of over 2000 ha in 1976/7) is left fallow, in pasture and not classified, the problem of urban poverty is solvable if even modest amounts of land could be transferred to poor settlers from urban areas. Probably, too, relatively poor and 'emergent' rural households could use land more intensely than it is on large farms. There is, at least, a case for land reform of some sort, and given the deteriorating urban economy, it is perhaps quite a strong case.[27]

Land tenure is a crucial issue in Africa. This is most serious in the case of the denial of women's rights on the land they work. The World Bank survey found only about a third of women farmers had the right to rent or mortgage land, let alone to sell it, compared with two-thirds of men farmers.[28] Land in most African countries, as Paul Harrison describes it, is in

the transition phase between communal and individual ownership. It is a no-man's land in which farmers have permanent rights over an area, without legal title to it. Their tenure is uncertain. They cannot offer their holding as collateral for loans, because it is not fully theirs to forfeit if they default. They cannot be sure they will still be farming the same areas in ten, or twenty years' time, and so they are more reluctant to invest in permanent improvements to the land, from tree planting to soil conservation works.[29]

Paul Harrison cites the success of conservation and tree planting in Kenya as being due to the fact that most farms are privately owned, and owner-occupied; and this situation he compares favourably to 'communal ownership with shifting cultivation, landlordism, and state ownership'. At the same time, he concluded:

Even within these systems farmers can be given lifetime security of tenure of their farms, rights to plant trees, rights to pass on property to their children.[30]

Such measures of redistribution could be relied upon to encourage increased food production and productivity.

Working Together – in Rural Areas

Increases in productivity of both land and labour depend essentially on reform of land ownership, especially in favour of women, and on supplementing human labour with draught animals or mechanical power. Surprising as it may seem in a continent with soaring birth-rates, there is an acute shortage of labour in rural Africa. This is especially serious in the growing season – for preparing the land and weeding. 'Animal power,' according to Harrison, 'supplies only 13% of power inputs to crop production in Africa, well below the Asian level of 31%; machinery supplies 3%; human labour supplies the other 84%.'[31] F. Ajayi and others give even lower figures in 1990 for animal and mechanical power available to farmers.[32]

Large-scale mechanization does not offer a solution in African conditions. It has been tried in many places and generally failed.[33] Much more success has attended farmers' schemes for working together, sharing tools and draught animals. Paul Harrison cites the case of Zimbabwe: 'Only a third of farm families in Zimbabwe own draught animals and more than half of them have at least one member away, working in cities, mines or on white farms.'[34]

Harrison regards the farmers' groups which sprang up all over the country as the major cause of the bumper crops in 1985. Two million tonnes of maize were harvested, more than double Zimbabwe's own needs. There have been disastrous harvests since then, mainly due to drought; and the small farmer programme still does not involve mass participation.[35] The success did, however, encourage Harrison to make an optimistic observation: 'If smallholders can be helped, the problems of insufficient food production, of malnutrition, and of widespread absolute poverty are attacked simultaneously.'

Even without large inputs of artificial fertilizer, he claims, but using organic inputs, improved seeds and water conservation, with shared use of draughtpower, very large increases in output can be achieved, amounting to returns of 60 to 140 per cent on the farmers' investment. 'Returns of this order,' Harrison comments, 'are essential for success in Africa. People at subsistence level will not take a gamble for less.'[36] World Bank studies confirm that such returns are well within the bounds of possibility.[37]

A Story from Burkina Faso

It is not only in agriculture that Africans working together in the rural areas have shown what can be done to make the great changes that are needed for Africa's social and economic recovery. Harrison lists three success stories of projects which have a nationwide reach and may even go beyond the national scale. The first has just been described in the Zimbabwe food production programme, with which Harrison links Zimbabwe's successful family planning programme; the second is the Kenyan women's drive for tree planting for timber and soil conservation;

the third is Burkina Faso's 'commando' operations in health.[38] This is a story well worth the telling.

In 1984 Burkina Faso launched a blitz attack on the three major endemic diseases from which the children have always died – measles, meninigitis and yellow fever – and which had led to a mortality rate of nearly 20 per cent for children under five. Within three months of the decision being taken and after a two-week campaign of immunization, three-quarters of the children at risk had been inoculated. This would be a remarkable story anywhere, but Burkina Faso is almost the poorest country in Africa, with one of the lowest doctor/population ratios in the world. How did it happen?

In 1983 a new, revolutionary government decided that it had to do something for the people of the rural areas who had for long been neglected by urban-oriented regimes. The secret of the campaign's success lay in the determination of the government and the participation of the people. The government ensured that the vaccine was available, that it was kept cool, that injectors were supplied and people trained in their use. The injectors chosen with the advice of UNICEF were pedojets, without needles, since the use of needles could have caused side-effects, which would have lost people's confidence in the whole programme. The government also carried out a saturation propaganda campaign by radio and posters in all local languages and by travelling theatre groups encouraging parents to have their children vaccinated.[39] This use of popular theatre is in line with a strong African cultural tradition.[40]

The response to this campaign was overwhelming, reaching far beyond the organizers' expectations. People flocked in from even the most remote areas, including families from border provinces in Mali, Nigeria, Togo, Ghana and Côte d'Ivoire. About two million children received at least one vaccination each. And the usual annual epidemics of measles and meningitis did not take place in 1986. The lessons for other African governments were obvious and many successful campaigns of vaccination and of nutrition and health education have followed. Paradoxical as it may seem, reducing the infant mortality rate is one of the surest ways to control the high birth-rate in Africa, since multiple pregnancies then cease to be needed to ensure the survival of children to help their parents on the farms.[41]

Harrison concludes his story of twenty years of work in Africa with his view of the prospects for what he calls a 'quantum leap', and sums up with the following words about minimizing the damage from the temporary rise in population growth:

The most effective strategy here exactly parallels the approach in agriculture. First, create a network of village health agents and trained midwives, with village committees and community groups to back them. Then, use these to spread ultra-lowcost techniques focused on self-help, requiring a minimum of outside or imported inputs: teaching people to monitor their children's growth using growth charts, to make oral rehydration from salt, sugar and boiled water, and water filters from charcoal, sand and gravel, and to dig household latrines.[42]

It is this mixture of practical action and visionary aspiration, both founded in African tradition, that informed the prospect of Achebe and his friends in looking 'beyond hunger'. It was the source also of the Khartoum Declaration.

The Khartoum Declaration

When 200 African delegates met together in Khartoum in 1988 under the auspices of the UN to study the papers of some thirty-nine different experts on the 'Human Dimension of Africa's Economic Crisis', they not only agreed on a vision of an African renewal, but they set down certain first steps to be taken to realize that vision.

The Khartoum Declaration spelt out five distinct areas to be focused on:

1. 'structural adjustment programmes must be designed, implemented and monitored as part of the long-term framework of Africa's development';
2. 'the human dimension must be the fulcrum of the adjustment programmes';
3. 'the structural adjustment policies must incorporate the relevant adjustments of the social sector';
4. 'consideration must be made of the consequences of macro-policies on the poor and vulnerable, not only so as to design temporary and independent compensatory additional programmes, but to make the alleviation of absolute and relative poverty and the elimination of gender biases *integral parts and factors* of the adjustment programmes (emphasis added)';
5. 'the entire process of monitoring the stabilization and structural adjustment programmes must incorporate the social aspects and criteria'.[43]

These general principles were expanded into detailed recommendations in the Declaration. They were enough to evoke a response from the World Bank in the form of the Programme of Actions to Mitigate the Social Costs of Adjustment (PAMSCAD), unveiled first of all for Ghana at a meeting in Geneva in 1988.[44] Such 'tag-on' poverty alleviation measures, as they have come to be called, have been applied also in Senegal and other African countries where structural adjustment measures have had a strong negative impact on the most vulnerable sectors of society. They fall very far below what the Khartoum Declaration had called for in requiring that the human element must be central to the entire development process.

Even the most besotted advocate of growth *before* distribution has to recognize that a society debilitated by sickness cannot be productive. Records for the year 1988 from Ghana, Côte d'Ivoire and Mauritania reveal that adult workers had an average of two to three days ill each month with a loss of a day and a half at work and over 6 per cent of normal earnings. These figures may be compared with similar records from the Philippines, Indonesia, Peru and Jamaica, where losses were less than half as great, let alone with the United States, where losses were half as great again.[45]

Yet it is reported by the World Health Organization that in sub-Saharan Africa in the late 1980s:

The hospital fees introduced as a result of the SAP (Structural Adjustment Programmes) cost recovery strategy resulted in declines in hospital attendance. Spending on health declined in most countries. In Zambia it fell at an average annual rate of 18%. Health expenditure as a percentage of the budget also declined. In Nigeria, budgetary allocations for health fell short of the 5% of national budget advocated by the WHO.[46]

The World Bank has argued that moneys should be shifted from hospital provision to preventive primary health care.[47] And much illness is undoubtedly the result of poor nutrition, contaminated water supplies, open sewers. But the problem is the low level of total spending on health and the rising numbers of patients per doctor during the 1980s in many African countries, including Ethiopia, Senegal, Mozambique, Ghana, Uganda, Gambia, Niger.[48]

The continued rapid growth of population creates a permanent pressure on health provision, but is itself the result not only of the lack of health education and of contraceptive supplies, but also of the *expectation* of infant mortality and of a generally insecure future. Africa's high fertility rates are not expected to fall markedly in the 1990s and will still be well above an average of two births per woman into the middle of the next century.[49]

AIDS and Education for Health

On top of all the other health problems in Africa comes the HIV virus pandemic. WHO estimated in 1989 that 'more than a million people in Africa were infected by the HIV virus and that 30% of these would evolve into AIDS cases in a few years'. The most seriously affected areas are in the central belt of the continent, where sero-positive rates of 5 to 20 per cent are to be found, with higher rates among high risk groups – 59 per cent among prostitutes in Kenya, for example. Just to finance the cost of AIDS treatment would require a doubling of current health budgets.[50]

Without help from outside, increases in African health budgets are truly inconceivable. But the cost of treatment is but a very small part of the loss from the spread of AIDS. Even more serious is the loss in productive capacity of men and women in the prime of their lives. Education about the causes and preventive measures for AIDS has become literally a matter of life and death in Africa.

It is widely reported from Africa that women, however ill-educated, are quicker to learn than men.[51] One example from a kwashiorkor clinic in a village near Kampala in Uganda may suffice to support the claim that health education will not be wasted in Africa. A Western agronomist visiting the clinic noted:

Obviously, this clinic provided a valuable service in improving the health of the children, but the really interesting thing was that no mother who had been brought into the clinic and taught the rules of simple child nutrition ever returned with a child having the same complaint.[52]

Education, supported by good health and adequate nutrition, must be placed at the head of all the priorities for the development of human resources. It is a terrible fact that in 1987, despite much that had been done since independence in African countries to expand educational provision, some 30 per cent of the children between the ages of six and seventeen, that is 70 million children, did not attend school, and of those that did, a quarter fell out before grade four. Even on past trends the number of children missing any schooling would rise to 85 million by the end of the century, as the population increases.[53]

There is growing evidence that the educational situation in most African countries has greatly deteriorated since 1987.[54] Charging school fees has been required under structural adjustment programmes, and this has simply meant that parents cannot afford to send their children to school and if they send the boys they keep the girls at home. What is more, if African countries were to maintain a pupil–teacher ratio of 40 to 1, four million teachers would be needed, more than twice the number teaching in 1983.[55] Yet many teachers cannot afford to continue their profession but have to take up work in the informal economy to feed their families. Others have left Africa for employment elsewhere. More than half of all professionally qualified Africans are said to be working outside of Africa.[56] Bringing them back home again, as envisaged by Achebe, is perhaps the most urgent of all tasks facing the new African governments of the 1990s.

Breaking out of the Downward Spiral

In the vision of Africa in the sixth decade of the twenty-first century conjured up by Chinua Achebe's scientific collaborators, the 'been tos' will return to Africa in large numbers, and locally trained scientists and engineers will fail to find jobs overseas any more because they are too poorly trained for foreign markets. But those who return will stay, because of growing appreciation of their role in high technology industrialization, using Africa's enormous energy potential. And this, Achebe's friends believe, will lead to the 'creation of Pan-African centres of excellence in training, research and development'.[57]

Such a welcome development is to be expected to occur as a result of what this group of distinguished African scientists describes as

the demystification and democratization of élite-oriented science and technology and also of formal higher education . . . and the slow but steady increase in local expertise and innovations replacing 'formal' technical assistance programmes . . . thus reducing the gap between the formally trained scientists and technologists on the one hand and the indigenous (informal) technocrats on the other.[58]

It is an attractive picture, and the authors give it support by the evocation of three specifically African forces – the emergence of an educated and emancipated African woman, the increasing use of African languages for intellectual and cultural communication in place of European languages and the marriage of science, culture and African-based religions.

This marriage of traditional African culture and modern science is referred to in the emergence of Kimbanguist movements. The authors describe Africa at the opening of the twenty-first century 'looking inwards to drink from the wells and springs of its own culture and religion'.[59]

Between 1995 and 2015, the grass roots movements of the previous period became the 'signs of hope' during these years and were taken very seriously by the people. Thus they became dominant in the local communities. Politically, they became respectable and in some states they were viewed as the authentic voice of the ordinary people. They started agitating for representation at all levels of decision-making in the society. In this way they formed the base on which respect and tolerance for diversity of religion was built ... In the period 2015-20 African states became reconciled to their religious diversity ... Secularization of institutions which remained from previous periods was emphasized during this era. A significant proportion of the total production in the society came from these groups and from economic institutions which had their base at the community level. These groups also started to provide leaders to other societal institutions.[60]

This utopian picture corresponds to the positive message of the Khartoum Declaration concerning the capacity of the African peoples:

no objective observer can fail to be impressed by the vitality and human creativity which strive and flourish in spite of everything. The large cutbacks and constraints of government and urban production have stimulated communities to devise their own solutions to the problem of meeting their own basic human needs. Self-help groups abound in every country; the extended family, though strained, has often provided the means of survival of many of its members; examples of community action can be found in almost every village.[61]

Is this mere rhetoric? Or is there real evidence at the grass roots of such a flourishing of community self-help that could with appropriate support become the basis for sustained economic recovery? The widespread activities of women's groups and of the informal second economy reveal an enormous vitality and creativity. But the question is whether these groups can build the links into the formal male-dominated economy such as would be necessary for their activities to become more than marginal to the mainstream of economic life.

Measuring Human Resource Development

Placing human resources at the centre of development strategy implies the availability of some measure of human development. The structural adjustment programmes of the World Bank, like all other economic strategies, are predicated on the assumption that the test of achievement lies in a measure of economic growth. This is then generally taken to be a percentage change in the gross domestic product (GDP) of each nation-state measured in relation to the growth in population over a year or over longer periods. According to this measure there was an increase in GDP per capita of about 1 per cent a year in the countries of sub-Saharan Africa between 1965 and 1980, but a subsequent decline of 1 per cent a year in the 1980s.[62] There was a slight improvement in the second half of the decade compared with the first half, in that the decline changed from just over 1 per cent to just under 1 per cent a year. For this improvement the World Bank seeks to take the credit.[63] But, within the overall measure for GDP, the decline just in private consumption per head worsened in the second half of the decade to show a doubling of the rate of decline to 2 per cent. This was the result of an increase in export volumes.[64]

There is much evidence, moreover, that during the decade of the 1980s and particularly in the later years, the distribution of incomes widened, that is to say that the rich became richer and the poor became even poorer.[65] World Bank statistics for the later 1980s show many sub-Saharan African countries with the top 10 per cent of income earners having over 45 per cent of the national income and the bottom 20 per cent having under 5 per cent.[66] Even if these figures are themselves well founded, which nobody believes, they certainly cannot be relied upon to tell more than a very small part of the story, since they exclude the whole of the informal economy and much of the value of subsistence agriculture.

These are not, however, the main weaknesses in using figures for the growth or decline in GDP as a measure of development. Many writers on problems of development, Serge Latouche *par excellence*, have questioned the standard measures of economic growth, because they exclude all the costs of what is called economic growth – in waste, pollution, destruction of the environment, unemployment, ill health, loss of freedom and security.[67] Some even question the very concept of development as any more than a mirage that offers humanity nothing but, very literally, a dead end.[68] Others insist that an index of human and social welfare needs to be constructed to replace, or at least to complement, the measures of GDP.[69]

In response to the Khartoum Declaration, the World Bank, UNDP and the African Development Bank launched a project to integrate social dimensions in the design of structural adjustment and development programmes in sixteen countries of sub-Saharan Africa. The project included monitoring poverty alleviation programmes to target the most vulnerable groups, assessing the impact of structural adjustment programmes on particular populations, implementing permanent household surveys and integrating social accounting and economic data.[70]

Social welfare indicators generally comprise the following elements:

* crude death rates (per 1000 of the population);
* infant mortality rates (under age one and under age five, per 1000 live births);
* low birth weight (per cent);
* prevalence of malnutrition (in under-fives, per cent);
* life expectation at birth (in years),
* *per capita* calorie supply;
* primary school and secondary school enrolment ratios (percentage of relevant age group);
* literacy rate (as percentage of adult population);
* numbers of population per doctor and nursing person.[71]

It is a matter of great importance for sub-Saharan Africa's future that, while most of the figures were worse than in other developing countries in the early 1980s, there had been an improvement between 1965 and 1980 equal in all respects except food supply to that in other such countries. The tragedy of sub-Saharan Africa is that after 1985 the situation worsened in almost all respects.[72]

When, in 1988, all the African states combined to issue the *Abuja Statement on Economic Recovery and Long-Term Development in Africa*, and in 1989 the ECA published its Alternative Framework, they put human resource development at the centre of their strategy. A statement from the World Health Organization and the World Food Programme offered the following comments:

Only the well nourished, healthy and literate can consistently and increasingly be efficient and productive workers ... Food aid projects and programmes can bring real benefits to the poor – especially the vulnerable groups negatively affected by structural adjustment programmes ... In addition ... there is a need to broaden the basis of raising incomes of the poor from the simple and traditional 'only nutrition' (food) input into more comprehensive 'health entitlement' and 'improved living environment approaches'.[73]

And that means involving and empowering the poor themselves.

CHAPTER 15

Rural Development from the Grass Roots

A true development process is based on a continuous series of analysis-action-reflection exercises carried out by the poor. Beginning with the awareness and analysis, poor people must gain access to and mobilize their own human and material resources as well as link into sources of external credit and technical assistance in order to initiate actions.

Stan Burkey, *People First; a Guide to Self-reliant Participatory Rural Development*, Zed Books, 1992, p. 212.

They would not think of themselves as poor people in any derogatory sense, but the great majority of Africa's population still lives in rural areas and works the land. Most of the land is farmed by peasant households, which supply not only their own needs but food for the towns and cities and cash crops for export. These are the fundamental facts of Africa's economy; and it will have to be from these peasant farmers' increased productivity that the resources for economic recovery and for social development must come.

Philemon Engongomo Tina of N'Koteng village in Cameroon was only expressing a truth that everyone in Africa knows when he told a visiting team of European research workers that: 'By himself a peasant in our country can never get rich'.[1] His use of the male gender would have made his wife agree wholeheartedly had she been asked her opinion, but what Philemon was thinking about was the need for cooperation between households. Without that, peasants would barely survive, let alone live to be 100 like Philemon's eponymous predecessor, the Greek poet of the third century BC.

Agricultural Cooperatives in Africa

Julius Nyerere put great stress on working together when he introduced the Arusha Declaration with his speech on 'Socialism and Rural Development', and he went on to spell out his conclusions:

Poor peasants working on their own are likely to remain poor.

If farmers employ labourers, the farmers may get rich but the labourers usually stay poor.

Marketing cooperatives tend to benefit farmers more than their labourers.

Voluntary production cooperatives, in which the workers are the members, are desirable because they can be productive and can divide the product equitably.[2]

Paradoxically, Nyerere went on to destroy the existing voluntary production cooperatives in Tanzania, establishing instead *ujamaa* villages. Indeed, cooperatives in Tanzania have had a chequered history that may be taken as a prototype of the successive stages through which African peasant associations have passed since colonial rule. Much the same story applied whether the post-independence regime took a so-called socialist or capitalist road. When René Dumont, the French agronomist, cried out in 1962 against the 'False Start in Africa', cooperatives under state guidance were included in the target of his attack on all top-downward organizations of production.[3]

Nyerere's thinking about socialism led him to the concept of *ujamaa* villages, in which a single corporation was made responsible for both local government and the commercial activities previously in the hands of individuals and cooperatives. Under a 1975 Act the rural primary cooperatives ceased to exist and a year later the district and regional cooperative unions were abolished. The produce of the villages had to be sold direct to the state marketing boards. René Dumont commented that he had never seen, anywhere in the world, such 'deductions [made by the colonial cooperatives], reaching half the value of the product'.[4] And the practice was continued by the new government.[5]

Elsewhere, the fate of the cooperatives was sealed by the introduction of parastatal enterprise. No village structures were allowed for between the peasant and the state. This was the case in Senegal, where the State Development Company simply assumed directly both the management and the marketing of irrigated rice production.[6] In most African countries, after an interim period of relative freedom, the newly independent governments virtually took over the colonial system of controlling cooperatives.

Under colonial rule, historic associations in one village or in grouping together a number of villages were sometimes ignored, sometimes encouraged, sometimes distorted, sometimes destroyed – depending upon the land they cultivated. If it was potentially valuable for plantation crops, the peasants were reduced to wage labourers or forced to grow cash crops for export to pay the hut and poll taxes. Other families paid by sending the men to work in the mines in the south. Cooperatives, along with other peasant associations, were enjoined under official administration to deliver primary produce for export. Each colony had to pay for the European government's costs from the taxes collected. In the British system it was reported that

the chiefs or headmen or council of elders were recognized by the [British] governor to maintain order and prevent crime by empowering them to issue orders covering a wide field of offences and regulating a number of public services.[7]

The History of the Tanzanian Cooperatives

In Tanganyika, it is recorded that: 'Regulations related to every conceivable aspect of farming practice and land use.'[8] The result was that old associations were revived, often clandestinely, in opposition to the colonial rulers and especially in protest at the diversion of land to cash crops. TANU itself was one such, formed in 1954, which came to lead the country to independence. It is all the more surprising that from 1961 to 1967 the TANU government simply continued the policies of the colonial administration, often under the same civil servants, thus rooting the new African élite more firmly in the export economy and differentiating them more sharply from the mass of peasants and workers.

All Tanzanian cooperatives came to be totally incorporated into the structure of the state marketing boards.[9] As the English principal of the Cooperative College at Moshi in the 1960s put it:

One of the main reasons why a lot of new cooperatives did not develop well after independence was that they were only rarely allowed to function as cooperatives. They were administered and controlled rather than promoted and nurtured.[10]

More than this, many cooperatives became organs of the large farmers, producing crops for export but also wheat and maize for the towns. Encouraged by the high prices for cash crops and by access to state credit, the better-off farmers began to expand their land holdings and to take on a commercial marketing role in association with the parastatal boards. Testifying to the Presidential Committee on Cooperatives in 1966, Tanzania's peasants complained of

a worse type of middleman under the cloak of cooperative societies, unions and marketing boards ... We were induced to join societies with the promise that ... we would receive a second payment when the crop is finally marketed by the Board. But now ... instead we are told every year that our societies incur losses.[11]

The Arusha Declaration of 1967 on a socialist transition for Tanzania, and the subsequent forced movement of peasants to *ujamaa* villages, thus arose from real contradictions in rural society. But the Arusha Declaration failed to solve the inherent contradictions by top-downward economic management of a peasant economy.

While the Arusha Declaration provided that

(f) ... the government actively assists in the formation and maintenance of cooperative organizations

it, at the same time, laid down that

(g) ... wherever possible the government itself directly participates in the economic development of the country;

(h) ... in order to ensure economic justice the state must have effective control over the principal means of production.[12]

The objectives were incompatible, as Alf Carlsson, the historian of Tanzania's cooperative movement, has pointed out.[13]

In the event, it was the power of the Tanzanian bureaucracy that was entrenched at the expense of the people. The State Trading Corporation, set up on the advice of McKinsey & Co., a transnational firm of management consultants, took over the whole of the country's export–import business and the allocation of imported supplies. Based on another McKinsey report, economic planning functions were decentralized in such a way as, in effect, to reproduce at lower levels whole new layers of bureaucracy.[14]

It was for this that the traditional cooperatives were abolished and it was not until the Cooperative Societies' Act of 1982 that independent cooperative associations could once more be formed. Commercial functions were separated once again from local government and passed to

Cooperative Development Committees. District and Regional Cooperative Unions could be re-formed. But many officials sought to retain the
collective village model under their control. Only when a new Act was
passed in 1991 was it possible to return to the orthodox pattern of
voluntary cooperatives and member initiative, and for many old cooperators to return to leadership in the movement.

Serious problems of cooperative structure and finance remained.
These might, in time, be solved but Carlsson, in 1992, felt bound to ask
whether, after so many distortions in the past, 'a generally growing
distrust of cooperative solutions will prove more difficult to repair'.[15]
Direct experience of working with the revivified coffee-growing cooperatives after 1993 suggests that, at least in some areas, the distrust is being
overcome and both local cooperatives and district unions are re-establish-
ing themselves, many of them with old cooperators from the Cooperative
College at Moshi involved once more.[16] But old bureaucracy, like old
corruption, dies hard.

Why Cooperatives Fail

'Why Do Our Cooperatives Fail?' is the title of an article by Manzi
Bakaramutsa from Zaire, writing in 1982 in the FAO's bulletin, *Ideas
and Action*. He lists the reasons for the failures. Most of his reasons have
been noted already – their origins under colonial rule as agencies of
cash crop production for export, their continuation under bureaucratic
control after independence, the incorporation and actual exploitation of
cooperatives by state and parastatal enterprises. But to these he adds
some secondary causes of failure, which will need to be noted if independent cooperative associations are to be successfully revived. These include
misappropriation of funds, where clan pressure no longer operates,
inadequate accounting systems, lack of training and even illiteracy
among cooperative members, which leads them to hand over responsibility to managers without democratic accountability.

Most existing cooperatives Manzi calls 'cooperative state companies',
and he concludes by recalling the strength of the traditions of mutual
aid in African villages:

In our villages mutual aid always comes into play to resolve economic
problems such as collective work in the fields, fishing, the construction of
houses. The same applies to various social activities such as marriage, birth,
sickness, death, funerals . . . Our villagers do not need cooperatives so much as

unions to defend the cultivators. Peasant members of cooperatives are often powerless, not only against the buyers, but also against their own cooperative which makes mistakes in buying or selling.[17]

Cooperatives and self-help groups are far from being the only form of peasant association in Africa. Mutual aid through the exchange of labour on the basis of reciprocity and kinship ties, 'festive labour' – sometimes called 'beer parties', which bring large numbers of workers together for a specific task – and share-contracts for cash crop production are all found in most countries of Africa. All can be used in place of hired labour for the exploitation of poorer and landless households by landlords and rich farmers, but agronomists agree that all can equally be innovative in meeting seasonal and exceptional demands for labour beyond what is available to the household or extended village farming group and in addition may help to redistribute wealth and resources.[18]

The story of the Tanzanian cooperatives explains what Manzi Bakaramutsa meant by 'cooperative state companies' and there can be no doubt that in both francophone and anglophone countries cooperatives have been 'misused, if not abused, for government purposes'. This was the conclusion of the National Cooperative Business Association (NCBA) of the USA, reporting to a World Bank seminar in 1990.[19] The process of what is called 'de-officializing' cooperatives in sub-Saharan Africa is being encouraged by the World Bank, but other contributors to the Bank's 1990 seminar made it clear that there were other reasons for cooperative failures than state control, external donor control being the most evident. Genuine cooperatives must be owned and controlled by member clients and organized to achieve specific economic goals which are not set by outside agencies. They may still need some donor finance and an enabling environment and infrastructural support from government.[20]

The World Bank seminar drew upon a wide range of contributors, mainly from donor agencies working with rural cooperatives in sub-Saharan Africa. The contributions were remarkably frank about the reasons for cooperative failures, which had evidently provided hard lessons for the donors. The first reason for failure is the old problem attending all arrangements of common property rights – the problem of the 'free rider'. Common property is nobody's property and is easily abused. Most African rural cooperatives do not in fact involve collective ownership of land. Although land may be traditionally held in common, rights to land pertain to individual families and households. Nor are most African cooperatives based on equality of contributions of funds or tools, although equality of voting rights is a necessary condition of management accountability.

Cooperatives in sub-Saharan Africa during the 1980s were operating under extremely unfavourable conditions. In the words of the World Bank report:

They exist in areas where members are poor and produce little surplus. In addition, rural cooperatives face high operating costs, low margins, low turnovers, narrow inventory stocks, fluctuating seasonal demand and trading patterns, and weak infrastructure. In many instances, private entrepreneurs have not found it profitable to break into these markets, yet cooperatives have been expected to succeed.[21]

These problems have been exacerbated by the falling prices of the crops which many rural cooperatives are involved with. Even where governments have reduced the rent they took in marketing crops, falling world prices have left producers no better off; and producer associations can still face financial difficulties when prices suddenly rise, as coffee prices did in 1994, since they must pay the farmers the new price for the current crop while only receiving the old price from sale of the previous crop.

The main requirements of a successful cooperative, according to general consensus, are full democratic participation by the members and transparency of management – open books and open accounting. These requirements imply a prior necessity – the education and training not only of management but also of the whole membership. Rates of illiteracy are high in rural areas in Africa – 80 per cent in many countries and higher even than that among the women. While training of managers has generally been taken care of in cooperatives, the importance of grass roots education has been underestimated. The NCBA was able to quote examples of membership education in projects in Niger, Mali and Rwanda and the Bank itself had organized training projects in Burundi and Cameroon, all of which proved successful in assuring active member participation.[22]

The role of donors may be crucial in providing the necessary training for rural cooperatives, but much depends on the way this is supplied. Not only is training needed at all levels, but all members need to be given the opportunity of sharing in the training programme if it is to be successful. For cooperatives involved in the export of cash crops, meticulous attention to quality control, delivery dates and record keeping has to be inculcated. While the long-term aims of social advancement, which most cooperatives espouse, need to be honoured, they cannot precede the achievement of market success. The new technologies of computers, spreadsheets, E-mail and fax messages and modern banking practices have to be grafted on to old traditions of saving and community self-help. To do this, as one old African cooperative president put it, 'We have to recompile the best pieces of past experience and create new institutional forms.'[23]

World Bank officials were evidently sufficiently impressed by the evidence presented at the 1990 seminar to embark upon a number of reviews of cooperatives and other farmers' organizations in sub-Saharan Africa, of which the studies made in Kenya were the most comprehensive.[24] These reviews largely reinforced the Bank's dogmatic conviction that the power of the state should everywhere be reduced, so that private enterprise shall be liberated, but they did also have the effect of eliciting from the Bank a modest measure of self-criticism in an African Technical Department paper on *The Development of Cooperatives and Other Rural Organizations: The Role of the World Bank*:

Bank staff in borrowing countries traditionally make contact with the government and consequently the views of representatives of organizations such as cooperatives are not adequately considered . . . The institution-building process of cooperative enterprises had not always been adequately dealt with in World Bank-financed operations.[25]

Those who made the reviews were particularly impressed with the comparative advantage of organizations which were democratically controlled and which promoted membership education as well as the equitable distribution of economic gains. They concluded, moreover, that informal self-help groups often had the advantage over formally registered cooperatives.[26] Examples were taken from Cameroon, Equatorial Guinea, Kenya, Mali, Niger, Rwanda, Uganda and Zambia. At the same time, the authors of the World Bank technical paper were concerned to see the linking together of such groups in order to strengthen them financially, to widen their range of services and, in their words,

to build a capacity to assume responsibility for promotional and development functions which have hitherto been vested in government departments.[27]

They recognized, however, that without external donor finance and a framework of government support, the linking up of individual groups will not take place. The question to which we will return at the end of this book is how the traditional grass roots initiatives of African peoples can be harnessed to a wider purpose, when all the evidence suggests that it is 'not advisable to try to officialize informal groups such as savings clubs and cooperative work teams'.[28]

Peasant Associations in Opposition

There is a long history of peasant resistance to the power of colonial and post-colonial authority. Professor Terry Ranger's comment in relation to European colonization remains true, that 'virtually every sort of African society resisted, and there was resistance in virtually every region of European advance'.[29] Nzongola-Ntalaja gives many examples in his studies of *Revolution and Counter-Revolution in Africa*.[30] Peasant struggles lay at the heart of many of the movements of national liberation from colonial rule described by Basil Davidson in his history of guerrillas in Africa, *The People's Cause*.[31]

Peasant resistance to schemes imposed from above by post-independence governments has been widespread, especially in protest against irrigation schemes which effectively denied them their land. In the case of the Kousson dam in Côte d'Ivoire, 100,000 people were displaced and troops had to be brought in to control the riots.[32] There have been successful protests by women in Zaire against road and bridge tolls, in Nigeria against market sales taxes and in Gambia against the conversion of family rice land for irrigated plots for the men.[33] The men and the young people have been no less militant than the women when their interests were threatened. The imposition of forced moves to *ujamaa* villages by the Tanzanian authorities was resisted in many places with armed force, fields were left unplanted in protest at low prices and crops were smuggled out of the country.[34]

Stories from Mali tell of dykes being destroyed in protest against autocratic management introducing a rice-growing scheme.[35] Cooperatives in Mali were formed in the mid 1970s and their members trained to resist being cheated by the parastatal Malian Cotton Company, which had exclusive contracts for exports to a French trading company. 'When the company paid the cooperatives for the producers, it is noteworthy and significant,' wrote one observer, 'that every single village decided to use its money collectively, rather than to rebate it directly to the individual families.'[36]

In northern Nigeria, farm families lost their land and farm improvements in the 1970s to a new lake south of Kano, created by a dam for the irrigation of wheat and other cash crops. Denied compensation, the angry farmers blockaded the construction site and halted work on the dam. This was only restarted when compensation schemes had been agreed and the intention to use contract labour for grain growing was modified to allow local farmers to contribute inputs from their own lands.[37]

Senegal appears to have been the centre of many peasant protests. In the east of the country in the 1960s a federation of Sarakolle villages was formed to resist the state agricultural agency, SAED, imposing irrigation systems, cropping patterns, uniform pricing policies and marketing restrictions on the peasants who grew peanuts for export. 'To some extent,' so it is reported, 'the federation's persistence has forced changes in SAED's approach and has encouraged others nearby to resist the construction of large dams to promote capital-intensive irrigation of export and cash crops'.[38]

Protests against state control of agriculture in Senegal led to the founding of one of the best-known peasant associations – the Young Farmers' Association of Walo. In the 1960s, the Senegalese State Development Company managed the irrigation system for rice cultivation in the Sahel zone, leaving the rice-growing peasants simply to tend the crop and sell it to the company for the going price less all costs incurred. In some years the costs were greater than the crop's value, in which case the company gave temporary assistance. When the land had been irrigated and drained, access had been given only to members of a specially formed cooperative, even excluding wives and sons. In 1973 young people in the area, many of them sons of cooperative members, took matters into their own hands and dug their own canal to water land allocated to them by the village elders. With vision, solidarity and patience they became autonomous farmers and established the Young Farmers' Association in Walo as a challenge both to the state and their parents.

The story has an instructive sequel. Under the New Agricultural Policy, introduced in 1984 following pressures from the IMF, the state transferred its management of irrigated lands to cooperatives and peasant associations, including that at Walo. The State Development Company ceased to receive foreign aid and ended its advance of the moneys needed for preparing the land. So, to pay the private contractors for land development, the peasants had to borrow from the company and frequently and increasingly ran into debt. The state withdrew all formal links with the cooperatives, including the provision of assistance in the event of losses. In effect, the peasants carried all the responsibilities and all the risks. Isolated individuals and small groups could not cope with a situation in which they received no aid from the state or from outside NGOs.

But the poorer peasants did not give in. Associations like the Young Farmers of Walo found a new role. On the old principle of 'all for one and one for all', they banded together to obtain credit and loans from the state bank, CNCAS. One hundred and fifteen clubs with 15,000 members in 1987 became 185 clubs with 20,000 members by 1991. But after 1988 the Bank required the clubs to break up into Economic Interest Groups (EIGs) of 10 to 20 members who commit themselves jointly to making savings and loan repayments. EIGs that fail may be helped by other members in their original club, but there is said to be a tendency for the more efficient to take over land from the less successful.

The trend is for traditional egalitarian principles to be replaced by differentiation:

a minority of efficient peasant farmers following the western production model take over all the land, water and machinery, [while] the others will become second-generation outsiders, this time excluded by their brothers, their fellow members of today.

There are quite strongly contradictory elements in the situation, however. The same report continues with the information that in February of 1991 most of the numerous peasant organizations in Senegal, including the Walo Young Farmers, sat down with representatives of the World Bank to 'work out the practical modalities of partnership' and in the event won for the first time direct access by peasant organizations to a programme of finance for small-scale projects.[39]

Those who have studied these matters most closely, albeit as foreign observers, have generally concluded that peasant resistance to schemes of national 'improvement' may often be the result of the shortcomings of the particular schemes, but it comes down to the question of 'whose interests programmes of agricultural transformation actually serve', and this quotation continues:

Peasant farmers do not perceive the advantage of complying with schemes which incorporate them into national objectives and markets from which experience tells them they have little to gain. Also, the penetration of agricultural production by state capital can lead to increased economic differentiation and like many 'green revolutions' works in favour of the already better-off farmers and urban entrepreneurs, rather than for the bulk of peasantry for whose interests the schemes are supposedly designed.[40]

David Siddle and Ken Swindell, the authors of these words, after twenty years of work in Nigeria, Sierra Leone and Zambia, sum up the variety of forms that peasant resistance takes:

We have seen that under collective systems, private plots are given preference, with the common good often coming a poor second. In other instances, peasants vote with their feet and often leave development schemes or continue to engage in non-farm employment as migrant workers, if the returns appear to be better for the domestic group as a whole. Finally, peasants on occasions resort to violence and rioting, especially when many have to be removed to make way for large dams required for irrigation schemes. Yet very rarely is resistance coordinated, cohesive and long-lasting, rather it resolves itself into a stubborn lack of interest.[41]

This appears to echo Onimode's conclusion to his chief work on the political economy of Africa. We saw him earlier, quoting Cabral in Guinea Bissau, that peasants are 'a great physical force, but a reluctant revolutionary force'.[42] By contrast, Claude Aké saw 'no case for denying the revolutionary potential of the peasantry – including the African peasantry'. He regarded it as 'most desirable to have a peasant revolution', since he feared greatly the continuing incorporation into the 'ranks of the bourgeoisie' of the urban masses and particularly the more privileged workers in trade unions.[43]

Mahmood Mamdani, whose study of the Amin regime in Uganda exposed starkly the error of the urban left in Africa in espousing military state regimes to 'make the revolution', has recognized the key position of the peasantry:

Not because the peasantry is itself capable of transforming national political life, but because no popular urban force – the working class included – can expect to influence meaningfully the direction of political events without breaking the political hold of the bourgeoisie over the peasantry.[44]

It is certainly the case that throughout Africa, the mass of the peasantry tends to be either dominated by large farmers or exploited by middlemen or both; and it is of the greatest importance, if there is to be a peasant base for economic recovery in Africa, to establish the scope and capacity of peasant associations for sustained and sustainable activity. In this search, less attention will be given to cooperatives involving actual collective ownership than to associations that have some economic function in common working, purchasing and marketing, but also have wider functions of community development, especially of health and education.

The Scope and Capacity of Peasant Associations

It is impossible for anyone to know how many peasant associations and non-governmental organizations there are in the rural areas of Africa. In the report to the Club of Rome, entitled *The Barefoot Revolution*, published by Intermediate Technology in 1988, the following figures were given for African NGOs with European or North American partners: 650 in Nigeria, 370 in Kenya, 120 in Mali, 112 in Cameroon, 35 in Togo, 23 in Gabon. The populations involved in each project were said to vary from 80,000 in Cameroon, 50,000 in Kenya to 2,000 in Gabon. These figures imply sizeable numbers that could add up to between a tenth and a fifth of a country's population. And these numbers include only those with a foreign partner.[45]

An estimate in 1986 of the total number of projects in sub-Saharan Africa involving NGOs suggested that there were some 12,000 projects, benefiting about 12 million people. This would amount to no more than between 3 and 5 per cent of the rural population, depending on whether children were being counted or only adults. Funding from outside averaged $72 per head on 107 projects that were surveyed; the projects had been running for anything between one year and twenty years. They covered a wide range of activities, including rural clinics, model farms, community centres, schools, roads, nurseries, granaries, flour mills, silos, shops, bridges, irrigation works, fishing and stock raising.[46]

Most of the many forms of rural cooperation fall far short of anything that could be described as a 'non-governmental organization' or even a 'voluntary development organization'. There will, moreover, be a much larger number of associations which have no European or North American partner. In Kenya, for example, while 130 'modern' indigenous NGOs were recorded in one report, this showed the existence of 26,000 grass roots self-help groups.[47] The so-called 'modern' NGOs will, in most cases, be in effect groupings of such smaller groups and thus present to view only just the tip of an iceberg. At the base there exist not only the extended households and systems of labour exchange and cooperation, but a great proliferation of network marketing systems. These are much more than simply market places.

In the typical African town or village, markets are held every day or every night or periodically in a sequenced ring, connecting towns and villages in hierarchies according to the goods on offer. Many such markets are based upon kinship linkages and exchanges of goods do not necessarily involve the use of money. In contrast many market networks do involve the credit and savings arrangements of the African informal economy. Markets are not only occasions for commercial exchanges and for repairs to tools and equipment, but for celebrations and other entertainments, for circulating information, for establishing political allegiances and making marriages. Markets are crucially a vent for surpluses and therefore provide an incentive to increase production and to expand exchanges between town and country.[48] These are not so easily replaced by modern marketing.

A major cause of declining agricultural output in Africa has been the suppression of traditional marketing systems by increasing commoditization of land, labour and exchange through the medium of state boards and development corporations, since these have broken the reciprocity of the informal and semi-formal exchanges of traditional African society.[49]

A number of evaluations have been made of the success of projects based upon peasant associations. From these a glimpse may be had of the capacity of such associations to serve as a base for social and economic recovery. It should not be supposed for a moment that some sort of self-help, 'boot-strap' development could produce a 'Merrie Africa' populated by self-sufficient, steady state micro-economies. Commodity production and economic differentiation have gone too far for that.[50] But a sound productive capacity in the rural areas, linked to local urban and export markets, could begin to turn around the decline that has marked African economies for more than a decade. How far can one say that such a base does really exist?

The evaluations undertaken in the late 1980s by the FAO of African agricultural modernization programmes, and jointly by ECA and FAO of participatory rural development, provide the best evidence available of the realities behind the rhetoric of small-scale, self-help projects in Africa.[51] Some of these are quoted below and they have been supplemented by drawing upon a number of other studies: the OECD Development Centre Studies 1986 publication, *Project Aid: Limitations and Alternatives* by Bernard Lecomte,[52] the ILO 1985 *Assessment of Operational Activities* and the ILO 1991 *Projects with People: The Practice of Participation in Rural Development*, edited by Peter Oakley,[53] the Intermediate Technology report to the Club of Rome in 1988,[54] the Oxfam and Action Aid 1988 report on 'Voluntary Organizations and Third World Development', *Putting People First*, edited by Robin Poulton and Michael Harris,[55] the papers presented to a seminar on *L'Autodétermination paysanne en Afrique: solidarité ou tutelle des ONG partenaires?*, organized in

1987 by the Belgian NGO, Collectif des Stratégies Alimentaires;[56] and, most recently, Pierre Pradervand's *Une Afrique en marche: la révolution silencieuse des paysans africains*, translated into English by the World Hunger Project.[57]

Cooperative Successes and Failures

Choosing examples of both successes and failures from the mass of detailed evaluations in these reports is invidious and may be misleading. There are ups and downs in all projects. This year's success may be last year's failure, and failures can provide important lessons which, if learned, create the conditions for future success. None the less, only actual examples can reveal the rich texture of the relationship of self-help groups, local and foreign NGOs, traditional authorities and government bodies. To conceal the names of the organizations and the countries would be to withhold vital evidence. Space does not allow, however, for more than two or three stories to be told, before the lessons which can be drawn from all these studies are summarized.

The first story comes from Malawi, where small-scale community-based projects have provided gravity-fed, piped water to some fifty-five different areas in all three regions, serving one and a quarter million people, about one-third of the entire rural population. The projects extended over a period of fifteen years from 1974 and were backed by the Christian Service Committee of Churches in Malawi with finance from European aid agencies. The technology used was simple and cheap, involving no machinery but a system of intake from springs, sedimentation and storage tanks, feeder pipes and communal taps in each village. The comment of the evaluator in his report is that the 'projects were remarkable for their reliance on self-help groups in the local communities for their initiation, implementation and maintenance'.[58]

The self-help groups involved formed an elaborate structure of elected local committees, section committees and branch-line committees, which led up to the district development committee of government ministry representatives, political leaders and traditional authorities. The district committee had technical staff at its disposal. 'Technical expertise and local initiatives are coordinated,' according to the report, 'in such a way that the experts and the local committees work hand in hand ... Digging for tanks, trenches and filling are done by mobilizing the community which would later benefit from free, clean water. Actual laying and joining of pipes is supervised closely by a project engineer.'[59]

The benefits of clean water supply are obvious, in the elimination of water-borne diseases, but additional benefits are the reduction in the time taken by women in fetching and carrying water and the fact – claimed in the report – that 'the traditional authorities' role has been enhanced rather than undermined by government's reliance on them'.[60] Such a linking of traditional self-help with NGO and government involvement is a central feature of all the reported rural success stories in sub-Saharan Africa. But there must be a question mark hanging over the Malawi piped-water projects. Local participation was based upon the assumption that the water would be free. Government funding would, therefore, have to be continued, and indeed increased if new projects were to be undertaken.

The second success story comes from the region of Tambacounca on the Gambia river in eastern Senegal.[61] A local NGO called OFADEC (African Office for Development and Cooperation) in the mid 1980s established twelve irrigated areas benefiting some 1,500 families, together with a programme of reafforestation and regeneration of grazing land and the construction of eighteen health stations and eight schools at village level for children and for adult training. OFADEC does not run these programmes but gives financial support to local groups which form their own self-managed cooperatives. Women have equal rights with the men and have their own council.

OFADEC provides all groups which participate with start-up food supplies and equipment (hoes, shovels, motor-driven pumps, et cetera); and the families which are settled on the new land have to build their own huts and clear the ground for cultivation. Some of the land is allocated individually, but some fields are worked collectively. A proportion of the cooperative funds is set aside for a production fund for general development of the irrigated area and for social activities, health and education.

Relations of OFADEC with Senegalese government bodies have not been easy. This is mainly because of the actions of parastatals like the SAED (National Company for Planning and Development of the Delta Region), which followed the policy of encouraging large companies producing groundnuts and other cash crops for export. After 1984 the policy was modified, the minister for rural development recognizing in parliament the need to scale down these companies which, he said, were 'suffocating the peasants'. In that year the Council of Non-governmental Organizations for Development Aid (CONGAD) organized a seminar in Tambacounda of fifty Senegalese NGOs at which the following resolution was passed:

The NGOs in Africa, and in developing countries in general, must make an important contribution to developing the will and ability of our people to take charge of their own affairs; this is only possible if they are involved at all stages of the process. It means that projects must be geared to the abilities, present and potential, of the people who will eventually be managing them.[62]

In Tambacounda, the local OFADEC official, Mamadou Ndiaye, felt able to claim on behalf of his local projects that they were well on the way to achieving these goals:

Self-reliance is for us financial autonomy. We provide material support for the cooperatives, which must gradually take charge of all the factors of production, maintenance and equipment already on the spot. Self-reliance does not mean that we shall never go near them again, to advise them or order, for example, spare parts for them. Self-reliance is the capacity of the cooperatives to manage without us. We have, for example, trained the peasants in maintenance and repair of motor-driven pumps.[63]

By contrast with such success stories comes a less happy story from the Pujehun district of Sierra Leone.[64] Self-help groups were promoted during the 1980s with technical support from the FAO and financial assistance from the Dutch government. Some, mostly men's groups, were engaged in food-crop production. The women mainly took over the vegetable gardening and soap making. At the start ninety-four groups were formed with numbers in each group varying from ten to eighty. By 1986 there were seventy-six working groups, fifty-five mixed and twenty-one women only. The group promoters not only gave technical assistance but also helped the groups to hold meetings, organize the work, keep records and plan activities for community development. Inputs were supplied at cheap rates, and loans and credit were made available to be repaid with interest after the harvest. Repayments went into a fund for future loans.

As a result of the project, group members became aware that they could tackle their problems collectively and plan and initiate action to better their conditions. A store, a school, a bridge and a health centre were built in each of six villages. A grater was bought to improve the processing of cassava. All started well, but many things began to go wrong. Inputs were either unavailable or delivery was delayed until it was too late to use them. Marketing and transport facilities were inadequate to cope with the increased production. Most serious of all, credit became scarce. Credit institutions were reluctant to become involved.

Unfortunately, the government took no interest in relating these projects to others and made no funding available. The FAO Freedom from Hunger Campaign Action for Development called a special meeting of groups working in Sierra Leone to exchange experiences and identify common needs. This was attended by participants representing fourteen national and local organizations. The chief common problems recognized were excessive dependence on outside support, or alternatively on local middlemen, and bad relations with government, especially with local politicians who tried to use the associations for their own ends.[65]

At the other extreme, some projects have failed from *excessive* central guidance and control. The Nuba Mountains Rural Development Project in South Kordofan Province, western Sudan, is an example. A pilot project was launched by the provincial agricultural division with finance from the European Development Fund and technical advice from a French firm of consultants. The aim was to provide animal-drawn implements (hoes, seeders, ridgers et cetera) on a credit basis so as to improve existing traditional agricultural practices. Extension officers at four development centres both recruited and trained village workers to assist and train participating farmers in all aspects of the newly introduced technology.

The result was not at all what had been hoped for. Between 1982 and 1987 only 2,000 farmers participated out of a local population of around 200,000. The report on the evaluation of this project describes it as

a typical top-downward project, in which a sound solution is identified and decided outside the community and transferred without consultation. Local communities were not involved in all project phases. The project adopted a single package approach which is quite inappropriate for that area . . . Only rich farmers were able to buy implements and other inputs. There was no concern for environmental aspects in an area of light soil.[66]

The picture that emerges from hundreds of pages of reports is of vibrant and resourceful people struggling, surviving and often succeeding in making improvements in their living conditions against seemingly overwhelming odds – drought and water shortage, locusts and pests and human diseases, desertification and land shortage, falling prices, violence and war. There are indeed many failures in the records, some on a very large scale. In one report it is stated that 'the failure rate of NGO water projects is simply staggering . . . 70% to 80% of new wells and pumps are no longer operational'.[67]

Learning from Failure

The reasons for such failures as these are carefully examined in the reports. An important conclusion from these reports is confirmed from the African projects of which I have direct knowledge. This is the absolute necessity to provide for learning from failure. The competitive market works on the simple principle that failure is rejected and success is rewarded. Buyers who are not satisfied turn to another supplier. But this is a wasteful system. It wastes human effort and enthusiasm, depending upon the existence of a host of entrepreneurial men and women and a thrusting competitive ethos. It does not allow for a tradition of cooperation, not competition, nor for a long history of African failure and defeat – in the years of the slave trade, under colonial rule and subsequent tyrannies.

Africa is littered with failed projects, not only because the technology was inappropriate for African conditions – which it generally was – but also because those involved were abandoned as soon as things went wrong. The market system divides and conquers. What those who have been for so long divided require is a structure for cooperation. When money is lost, whether through corruption or carelessness, when tools and machines are misused or abused, when quality control and delivery dates are neglected, when the scale of operation is too small to be efficient, when the product delivered is not what the buyers want, then what is needed in societies at an early stage of economic development is to find ways of overcoming the problem, not dropping the project. This does not mean pouring good money after bad, nor need all the tools of the market be rejected – price incentives to improve crop husbandry and product quality, market research to find new niches, quantities and packaging for ease of handling, the rigour of consumer choice. What it does mean is patient participative work in training and applying lessons learned. For this a supportive structure of institutions has to be created at every level to establish effective cooperation at local, district, regional and state levels and between states. The main reasons for failure are listed in Table 15.1, not so much as a record of failure, but as an indication of the conditions for success (the summary is my own – MBB).

The greatest weakness in the design and execution of rural development projects arises from the failure to ensure a genuinely participatory framework which involves all the people and reduces rather than increases income differentials. The lesson is that there is no such thing as a trickle-down effect – from rich to poor, from large farmers to small, from men to women. As Daniel Descendre put it in his introduction to the seminar for Collectif des Stratégies Alimentaires (my own literal translation – MBB):

The question that underlies all our work is not: 'What are the best means for developing agriculture in Africa?', but rather, 'Who gives to the peasants the power to use means of development that reinforce their economic autonomy and their social balance?'[68]

This is the question with which the final chapter concludes, and it will have to be applied not only to the peasantry but to urban working people. It is a question about empowerment, about creating frameworks for participation, and it involves, as Margaret Joan Anstee insisted in the quotation at the beginning of Chapter 14, a 'context of social planning' – and she emphasized that she meant *planning*.

TABLE 15.1 Reasons for Rural Development Failures in Africa

1. Neglect of peasants' experience and knowledge of the land and local conditions and of other available local information.

2. Rejection of peasants' priorities, e.g. of maximum calories per hour of labour, of vegetable as against animal protein, et cetera.

3. Built-in bias against the most disadvantaged households – the poorer, landless and those headed by women – e.g. in lack of access to necessary credit, lack of bullocks for bullock carts supplied, rejection of high-risk participants in group liability projects.

4. Ignorance of the demands on women's time, especially in requiring them to grow crops and supply harvesting assistance on crops with peak demands for labour.

5. Centralization of decision making and a general absence of democratic involvement, especially of women and young people, at all stages of design, execution and monitoring of projects.

6. Low salaries and lack of transport of extension workers, who have, therefore, to take second jobs and never reach out-of-the-way villages.

7. General inappropriateness of project design – wrong equipment, lack of spare parts, unpredictable inputs, poor marketing, unreliable transport, inadequate training especially in bookkeeping, lack of adequate credit.

8. Continuing dependence after initial stages on government subsidy or foreign aid, so that when these cease the project collapses.

CHAPTER 16

Urbanization and Workers' Organizations

Democratic decision making and popular organizations, particularly trade unions, stand in the way of the programmes that the IMF and the World Bank, with the collaboration of national governments, have devised for economic recovery . . . All over Africa, workplace, village-based, street-based, local-level committees have sprung up to defend the dominated classes and to advance their interests.

> From a 'thematic statement' drafted by Gavin Williams for a conference organized by the *Review of African Political Economy* at Warwick University in 1990, published in Robin Cohen and Harry Goulbourne (eds), *Democracy and Socialism in Africa*, Westview Press, 1991, pp. 10–11.

Whatever successes may be achieved by grass roots development in the rural areas, these will soon be obstructed if there is no reciprocal development in the towns. A crucially important factor in the relations between town and country in Africa is the increasing tendency of African governments to rely on imported, often subsidized, food for the urban masses. This has the direct effect of reducing the market for local agriculture. Structural adjustment programmes of the IMF and World Bank may have ensured for African farmers a better share in the price of their crops, especially export crops, but they have also opened up African markets to food imports. Local farmers cannot compete with subsidized imports from Europe and North America and cannot satisfy a taste for foreign grains, especially for wheat, which has been encouraged by food aid and by the relaxation of controls on imports.[1]

Urban Expansion and Rural–Urban Differences

The balance between urban and rural populations in Africa is rapidly changing. The predictions are that by the year 2025 about a half of the population of East and West Africa will be living in urban areas.[2] In 1987 the proportion was a quarter and in 1965 an eighth.[3] If African industry were to develop an export capacity, similar to the East Asian newly industrialized countries, and rely on buying food from outside, great parts of rural Africa would be marginalized. But this scenario, which some are advocating,[4] would seem to be an exceedingly improbable one. In all the history of industrialization, including that of East Asia, industry and agriculture have developed together.[5]

For many years in Africa living standards in the towns were higher than those in rural areas. Researchers like Michael Lipton writing in the 1970s and again in the early 1980s were struck by the urban bias of governments in developing countries and its consequences:

> The most important conflict in the poor countries of the world is not between capital and labour. Nor is it between foreign and national interests. It is between the rural and urban classes. The rural sector contains most of the poverty . . . the urban sector contains most of the articulation, organization and power.[6]

Government offices, hospitals and higher education facilities as well as manufacturing industry remain highly concentrated in and around the cities of Africa. But in the 1980s standards in the towns declined rapidly. In Sierra Leone, for example, wage income, which had been 50 per cent above farm incomes in 1970, had fallen to one-third of farm incomes by 1985.[7] As one writer put it, there ensued 'an equality of immiseration'.[8]

Part of the reason for the changing balance between urban and rural areas, both in population and incomes, lies in the earlier attraction of the cities and subsequent rural exodus. But in the cities there were in fact no formal employment opportunities.

Fortunately for Africans, the giant agglomerations of people in the cities and surrounding shanty towns rarely contain more than half of the urban population. Nigeria is the main exception, together with Angola, Benin, Guinea, Mozambique and Senegal. Elsewhere, medium and small towns predominate.[9]

The importance of the existence of large numbers of small towns in Africa is that such towns have continuing traditional links with the surrounding countryside. But these remain at a very low level of development. A.T. Salau has offered an explanation.[10] Most rural production is either for direct household consumption or for local markets and does not, in general, come into competition with similar goods produced at higher levels of productivity. Even crops for export are produced mainly, and indeed increasingly, from household farms. Imported grain sold in the towns is the only serious competition facing the rural producer, and such sales are largely confined to the cities. By contrast, everything that an urban worker can produce by hand can be made more cheaply by large-scale machine production elsewhere.

Cities as Engines of Growth

This contrast is most evident in the overflowing concentrations of population in the capital cities of Africa and their surrounding shanty towns. Historically, in Europe and North America, economic development was chiefly pulled along by the growing size of the market in the big cities, which offered a vent for surplus production in the surrounding countryside. But this process failed in Africa, where the needs of increasing urban populations were always met largely by imports from the industrialized lands.[11] It is important to note that the failure was not in agricultural supply but in urban demand. Even the World Bank has recognized that the neo-classical model of urban–rural development does not work in Africa.[12]

The history of capitalism spreading across the whole world is a long story of the destruction of native crafts by machine-made goods. The labour of the artisan has been retained only where it is driven down to a wage that barely assures survival or where there is some human skill that machines have not yet been designed to simulate. Sometimes this lies in the traditional patterns, colours and textures of what we call 'ethnic' products; sometimes it is the microscopic assembly of parts for electronic systems or the sewing together of machine-cut pieces of clothes and shoes. In each case, labour is plentiful and generally female, so that the wage still remains very low.

The fast-growing informal economy in Africa is inevitably a source of labour at the lowest possible wages to support what is already a cheap labour economy. Apart from the fact that development will, therefore, tend to be slow, if it takes place at all on the basis of cheap labour, the fact is that the place in the world market for cheap, unskilled labour in the future is now regarded as extremely limited. Production which was decentralized is moving back to the industrialized lands. Only the newly industrialized countries which have mastered advanced technology are surviving.[13]

The failure of industrialization in sub-Saharan Africa has been described earlier. Protection was given by the state against imported goods, in order to allow local manufacturing industry to produce substitutes, using local labour and materials. This was largely a failure, partly because of inappropriate plant design, partly because markets were too small for the necessary scale of production, chiefly because of the refusal of expatriate engineers to involve local people in the planning and execution of industrial projects. As a result, there has been little or no graduation of skills and experience of transfer from the informal economy to the most sophisticated.

This is why there appears to be a 'missing middle' in African industrial structures. There are some hopeful possibilities of blending technologies – hi-tech with more labour-intensive methods in different processes of production. But difficulties remain in finding the necessary finance, widening the market, training the workers, above all in creating the structures of cooperative working, which would encourage the creators of such new forms of industrial development. The role which NGOs – both African and non-African – have been playing in rural development projects is not replicated in the urban areas. Most European and North American NGOs in Africa devote their resources to the countryside. How then should urban renewal in Africa be financed?

Recapturing Mobutu's Wealth

Much more might have been done to make the cities of Africa into 'engines of growth' if it had not been for the kleptomaniac proclivities of the African élites and especially of their leaders. The case of Mobutu Sese Seko, the president of Zaire, and the gang of thieves who surround him is the best known of these kleptocracies. Careful estimates by the international financial institutions suggest that 'direct acts of theft' by these rascals in any single year amount to at least '20% of the state operating budget (of slightly over US$1 billion in 1986), 30% of mineral export earnings (worth $2000 million a year in the late 1980s) and as much as 50% of the state capital budget (US$500 million)'.[14] Yet these very international institutions continued their lending to Zaire throughout the 1980s and up to 1993 at a net rate of about US$200 million a year, taking over 40 per cent of the Zairean budget in debt servicing.[15]

Most of this stolen wealth was not spent on development, not even on luxury spending, in Zaire, but was invested in Swiss banks and European and North American real estate. Had it been invested in Zaire in health and education and in agriculture and industry over the nearly thirty years of Mobutu's presidency, Zaire would be a rich country instead of the second poorest in Africa, with an annual per capita income in 1987 of no more than US$150.[16] This is, of course, the official figure, and reasons have already been advanced for believing that the real figure may be as much as three times the official estimate. That still leaves poor Zaire as one of the low-income African economies, at about half the per capita income of the middle-income group.[17]

What was spent inside Zaire itself by the big thieves only trickled down to the masses through the informal economy and a hierarchy of lesser thieving. It is one of the bitter ironies of World Bank criticisms of African government policies, prior to structural adjustment programmes, that 'Africans spent more on imported motor cars and wine than other peoples at similar levels of economic development.'[18] Yet the effect of World Bank policies has been to bring to an end even those physical restraints on luxury imports that were in place before, and for which higher import prices are no adequate substitute. The only compensation is perhaps that the smugglers will suffer a loss of business.

Soon after President Clinton took office, the State Department opened up discussions with its French and Belgian counterparts about the possibility of freezing Mobutu's assets.[19] Although the Zairean government elected in 1992 in opposition to Mobutu had not by the end of 1993 ended Mobutu's rule as president, its members were seeking ways of recapturing the country's stolen wealth.[20] When at least some of this is returned to Zaire, a large part will be needed to repay the country's foreign debts, which amount to about twice the country's officially calculated national income.[21]

It will be of great importance for the people of Zaire, as well as for other African peoples whose rulers have been stealing from them for so long, how the repatriated wealth is spent. It was clear from the evidence offered in the last chapter that there are thousands of rural projects which could make good use of extra funds. What is the position in the urban areas? Are there similar urban projects waiting for finance?

Where are the Urban Cooperatives?

In the rural areas of Africa there are to be found a multitude of cooperatives and self-help groups. This picture is not replicated in urban areas, where the informal economy works on a largely individualistic basis and where trade unions are conspicuous by their absence. It is sometimes suggested that this is because peasants arriving in the towns and cities lose their kinship ties and become atomized and indeed alienated and subject to psychological maladjustment and other symptoms of disorganization.[22] This appears, in fact, not to be the case. According to A.T. Salau:

Kinship ties continue to exist. The extended family served as a source of shelter as well as providing for the economic, religious, legal and recreational needs of its urban members.[23]

Urban cooperatives are none the less few and far between and the record of failures is a depressing one, where they are not associated with rural producers. Malcolm Harper, one of the leading world advocates of workers' cooperatives, has reported from a 1982 conference of industrial and handicraft cooperatives in Africa a count of barely 500 such urban cooperatives in twelve countries out of a total of 25,000 cooperatives in those countries, the rest being rural. The most disturbing part of his report was that 60 per cent of the industrial/handicraft cooperatives were said to be 'dormant'.[24]

Harper tells the story of five African cooperatives, all small – with less than twenty members – made up of skilled workers, respectively tailors, welders, silversmiths, wire weavers and caterers. All had support from government or NGOs to get started. The first three failed to repay their loans and either collapsed or were taken over by a private entrepreneur. Failure was due, on the surface, to poor accounting, inadequate marketing and general lack of business sense, but lying behind that was the fact that the members came together solely because they had a common trade and not because they wanted to work together.[25]

The two which succeeded had in common that they were women's cooperatives and that they were in Zimbabwe. The support of a local NGO and of the state was certainly essential in starting them off, but the key factor seems to have been that they were made up of friends who came together in the first place to find some part-time group enterprise to overcome their financial problems. The most interesting is the case of the wire weavers, whose original venture in market gardening had failed. One of the women had had some training in wire weaving. The others were helped by the Zimbabwe Women's Bureau (an NGO) to get training and to get their first bundles of wire to weave into fencing. At first they sold fencing to their neighbours, but after a time, with help in marketing from the NGO, they were able to buy simple machinery and reached the standard quality required by a large firm. In 1990 they were self-financing and planning to buy a proper shelter, since they had been working under a tree and had to stop when it rained.[26]

They were then encouraged to move towards more ambitious enterprises, setting up sub-groups for other activities. Their success raises some questions. On the one hand it is true that their labour is being exploited by the large firm. On the other they have become a successful enterprise and are solving their financial problems and meeting a definite need in the country. It is more dubious how far their initiative could be replicated elsewhere. This cooperative is located on the outskirts of Harare, where the growth of shanty towns has been largely forbidden and with that the growth of the informal economy. The cooperative's sales are in the rural areas. This is unusual. The informal urban sector generally provides a market, albeit a poor one, for rural produce but supplies little in exchange.[27]

Most big African cities are ringed by slums, which house anything from two-thirds – Addis Ababa and Kinshasa – to one-third – Nairobi and Dakar – of the total city population.[28] It is a feature of the informal economy that there are close links between individual urban enterprises and kinship connections in the countryside. But there seem to be difficulties in making and maintaining linkages between the formal economies in urban and rural areas. The reason is that there is no framework for doing this. The informal economy works mainly outside the law, when it is not actually illegal. If licences are obtained and taxes are paid, there are simply not the resources for enterprises to survive. But the removal of state controls in itself would not be enough. One of the main lessons from the studies of small-scale industrial activity in Africa is that either government or NGO support is necessary, at least at the start.

A singular finding from inquiries into small-scale industry in sub-Saharan Africa emerged from Carl Liedholm's studies:

In most countries the vast majority [of small firms] is located in rural areas [i.e. localities with fewer than 200,000 inhabitants]. Moreover, employment in small rural manufacturing industries often exceeds that generated by all urban manufacturing firms.[29]

Figures of 85 per cent are given for Sierra Leone and 64 per cent for Zambia for the proportion of such industries located in rural areas; and it is said to be likely that all such figures are an underestimate because 'country censuses often fail to pick up the smallest of the rural industries'.[30] The definition of rural must be noted, i.e. it includes small towns. Liedholm's other main finding was that 'production linkages with large-scale industry are rather weak in Africa'. This, he suggests, 'may be due to the small markets and the tendency of foreign-owned import substitution firms to import a large share of their inputs'.[31]

It is the conclusion of several African experts that support for industrial development should be concentrated in rural areas.[32] This view is supported by those Africans who argue in favour of encouraging people to return from the cities to the countryside. In the words of Mohamed Lamine Gakou of Mali, this would mean

putting an end to the rural exodus and reducing urbanization to a level low enough not to divide economic and social policy overall. This can be achieved by creating conditions for a massive voluntary return to the countryside, where development policy will be concentrated far more than in the towns.[33]

Such a *voluntary* return would imply making the rural areas sufficiently attractive for people to want to return to them. It is a proposal that inevitably shocks experts from the North, who assume that the growth of cities is central to all economic development.

Even if this assumption is rejected, there is a problem of agency. Who will take the lead in encouraging a return to the countryside, if this is not to be the forced exodus carried out by the Khmer Rouge in Kampuchea? Rural Africa is not everywhere a happy land of cooperating peasant households. Many of those who fled to the larger towns and cities did so to escape the rule of oppressive chiefs and grasping officials or the inhuman conditions on plantations and mineworkings. Such miseries also occur in the smaller towns, and really quite revolutionary changes would have to take place in the towns and villages of rural Africa for there to be any chance of people going back to the land. Yet there are struggles taking place in mining and plantation communities which hold out indications of change, as they come to be linked up with the wider political protests that have been sweeping across Africa since 1990.

Organizing Labour in Africa's Mines and Plantations

There are many stories of African farmers defending their natural resources against foreign exploitation. They are defending the land they own or to which they have common access and the plants or trees from which they win a crop each year, both to feed their families and to get cash from sales for home or foreign markets. It is very much harder for those who work down the mines and on plantations to engage in effective defence of their livelihood. They own nothing but their labour power. Most of the plantations and mines in Africa are owned in part or in whole by transnational companies. Joint ventures of the state and foreign companies are typical of mining in Africa, and it is not at all necessarily the case that labour organizations are better treated where there is local state involvement.[34]

Organizing in the labour market is even more difficult than organizing in the commodity market. There are huge reserves of labour in Africa which plantation and mine owners can use to break up labour organizations. Dismissal is the fate of many labour organizers. For plantation and mine workers the loss of employment means hunger, since few will have access to land for growing their own food. Such problems face wage earners everywhere, but in Africa there are special problems to be overcome if labour is to join up in common self-defence.

The specific problems facing African organized labour arise from the way in which the European powers developed their African colonies, each territory supplying just one or two crops or minerals. No processing or manufacturing industry was established near to the mines and plantations. The raw material was shipped to Europe to be processed there, so that local alternative employment opportunities were non-existent. Moreover, while migration was permitted across frontiers, especially to the mines of South Africa, movement between colonies to discuss joint action was generally forbidden. It was in any case very difficult to accomplish. No inter-state transport or communication system existed. Different languages were spoken and different labour laws applied. As a result of all these factors, when independence was at length achieved, the organization of labour into trade unions in Africa was revealed as both weak and patchy.[35]

Where African trade unions had been established in industries, as in Tanzania, Zambia and Zimbabwe, they played an important part in the struggle that led to independence. In few countries, however, did industrial workers' households make up more than 10 per cent of the total, and in many the proportion was much smaller. None the less, when the International Confederation of Free Trade Unions (ICFTU) set up an African Regional Organization (AFRO) in 1960, it recorded affiliations from twenty countries representing about three million workers.[36]

The ICFTU is not the only trade union centre in Africa. It was seen by some as having unacceptable North American connections.[37] So, an All-African Trade Union Federation (AATUF) was founded in Casablanca in 1961 on a non-aligned basis. Unfortunately, very little was heard of it thereafter. During the next year, a further federation came into existence, founded by Tom Mboya, the Kenyan trade union leader, and soon claimed to have forty centres in thirty countries. But, all these federations came to nothing. By 1977 AFRO had only 700,000 members, AATUF never got off the ground and Tom Mboya had been assassinated. What became of African trade union unity?[38]

There were quite large national trade union organizations in existence in individual African counties in the mid 1970s: 350,000 members in Ghana, 800,000 in Nigeria, 205,000 in Zambia, 728,000 in Sudan, 230,000 in Kenya, 32,000 in Ethiopia, 5,000 in Malawi.[39] But they evidently did not want to federate. Either they had become incorporated into the party–state apparatus of the new nations or their leaders had been killed or put in jail.

In Ghana, Jeff Crisp, a historian of the mine workers, reported:

The state sought to control this workforce by means of co-option and by eroding the power of the union leadership. Strikes were outlawed, the mines were nationalized, while the union was induced to help increase productivity and curb militancy . . . The miners continued in stubborn defiance of immediate interests without, however, building a larger force which might transform the social system in Ghana.[40]

Likewise in Tanzania, a government official paper of 1967 argued:

NUTA's [National Union of Tanganyika Workers] wages policy should be based primarily on the needs of the national economy . . . NUTA's officials should concern themselves less with fear of exploitation and more with the sacrifice needed for nation-building.[41]

A Canadian scholar's survey of African trade union literature in the 1970s concluded that 'in contemporary Africa, national officials can more often be found stifling rank and file initiatives than articulating common grievances or coordinating industrial action'.[42] The alternative was arrest, jail without trial and even execution. Wogu Ananaba, writing from Nigeria in 1979 after surveying the trade union movement across the continent, concluded:

There are probably more African trade unionists in jail or in detention, killed or driven into exile by independent African countries than was the case during the whole period of colonial rule.[43]

All was not lost, however. In countries where the unions were not co-opted directly into the ruling party, as in Kenya and Nigeria, for example, but were none the less subject to government control and often to actual repression, unions continued to defend both the political and economic rights of their members. The Nigerian Labour Congress (NLC) was stifled by government measures and severely repressed in the wake of the 1983 military coup. And yet, Nicholas Van Hear, a historian of Nigeria's labour movement, felt able to write in 1987, 'That the NLC has survived and remained relatively independent in such parlous circumstances is no mean achievement.'[44]

The mass demonstrations of the workers at the Steyr car assembly plant in 1985, in which the manager was force-marched out of the factory, showed the potential strength of the Nigerian unions. But this plant, which assembled imported kits, was not a viable undertaking. The strike ended in total defeat and the collapse of union power. Nothing less than coordinated action with other plants and national union support could have saved them. It was not forthcoming.[45] The prospect was either outright suppression or incorporation of the unions still further into the state.

The World Bank has argued that trade union militancy was an obstacle to foreign investment in Nigeria,[46] as it had done in Ghana in 1983 in reaction to the Peoples' and Workers' Defence Committees (PDCs and WDCs). The point was nicely put to the Rawlings government:

While the PDCs and WDCs can play a useful role in increasing production and productivity, their exuberance and misplaced enthusiasm may have the potential of causing unintended harm in the economy and interfering with the efforts the Government is making towards economic recovery.[47]

The WDCs were abolished in November 1984, just a week before the Paris Club meeting of debt creditors to determine the foreign aid allocations for the next three years.[48]

The upshot in Nigeria has been a mixture of both repression and incorporation, plus a military government campaign of divide and conquer – men against women, skilled against unskilled, tribe against tribe, north against south, Christian against Muslim.[49] The attack on Muslim working women has been particularly brutal.[50] The result was a serious threat in 1993 of civil war, when a military regime held elections but refused to acknowledge the verdict of the electorate in support of a candidate for president who was unacceptable to it. Strikes broke out in 1994 throughout the country and the military government dismissed the union leaders in the oil industry and replaced them with its own nominees.[51]

Strikes and Resistance

Even where trade unions in Africa failed to maintain their independence and were either destroyed or incorporated into organizations of the state, there is much evidence both of urban protest amounting to general strikes and of continuing resistance of rural plantation workers to intensified exploitation, as is revealed in the quotation at the head of this chapter.[52] There is some argument, however, as to the political orientation of these actions. Piet Konings, of the African Studies Centre in Leiden, a historian of Ghanaian miners' strikes in the 1970s, argued that:

Miners do not want to seize political power; they do not even have a vision of an alternative socio-political order, except for some vague notions of a more egalitarian, more democratic and more prosperous society. Quite a few workers and union leaders told me that they do not bother much what kind of government Ghana has, socialist, capitalist or anything else, as long as the politicians are honest, prepared to listen to workers' grievances and demands and to deliver the goods.[53]

Richard Sandbrook, however, while suggesting a 'populist' rather than revolutionary consciousness in Africa's working class, has emphasized that workers' demands have expressed the more general demands of the urban masses:

General strikes were a major aspect of urban protest that threatened or toppled governments in Senegal in May–June 1968, Ghana in 1950, 1961 and 1971, Nigeria in 1945 and 1964, the Congo-Brazzaville in 1963 and 1968, the Sudan in 1958 and 1964, Madagascar in 1972 and Ethiopia in 1974. In all cases, the workers' solidarity depended upon the fusing of a basic economic grievance to a widespread political disaffection.[54]

Among plantation workers militant resistance to exploitation and authoritarian management has been widespread throughout Africa, but without any tendency to political action. Outstanding examples of such resistance come from Cameroon, where the Plantation Workers' Union had a long tradition of organization going back to 1945. The union was established as an independent, non-political organization, but was dissolved and replaced by a state-controlled body in 1972. Piet Konings of the Africa Studies Centre in Leiden has recorded their struggles. It is his claim that

virtually all African post-colonial regimes have been quite uncomfortable with strong and independent unions as they look upon such organizations as potential sources of political opposition.[55]

Incorporation or imprisonment of union leaders has not by any means always contained union militancy. Rank and file resistance has continued against arbitrary management, and this can best be illustrated by the case of the major Cameroon agri-business, the Cameroon Development Corporation. Protests by corporation workers continued throughout the 1970s and 1980s against the attempts made by the bosses' union to control both the workers themselves and their work processes on behalf of the Corporation.

Reasons for the extent and determination of the plantation workers' militancy and solidarity are reported by Konings to have lain not only in their intensified exploitation and in the affluent lifestyle of the managers, but in a number of other factors specific to African conditions. The first was the steady deterioration in the world prices of Cameroon products, chiefly coffee and cocoa, cotton and bananas, and the consequent pressure on workers' wages. The second was the solidarity of the workers, typical also of miners, dockers and railwaymen. The third was the continuing links of the workers with pre-capitalist social organization and value systems, which encouraged the desire to preserve a certain degree of autonomy in the labour process. There was also created the expectation of accumulating a little capital during a career of waged work in order to return eventually to settle in their home communities where they had land rights. The fourth was the labour-intensive production process, particularly in the case of semi-skilled rubber tapping, palm harvesting, tea plucking or banana cutting, where the workers could easily recognize the key importance of their labour for the plantation owners.[56]

In order to reduce this potential threat to production, the Cameroon Development Corporation attempted at first to encourage smallholder schemes feeding into the plantation supplies, but without success. Its second response was much more successful. This was to contract out to medium and small farmers the whole responsibility for production. This had the full support of the World Bank, in spite of the fact that the Bank had for long held the view that large scale agri-business was the key to modernization. In 1989 the Bank changed its mind and stated its new belief that 'smallholders produce more per hectare, use land more fully and face fewer labour constraints'.[57]

The explanation for the Bank's U-turn was not only that state and parastatal organizations in Africa had been shifting from estate to smallholder production, but Unilever, one of the giant foreign private plantation owners, was planning in 1987 to reduce plantation production to less than half of its Cameroon total. This change in policy has, in fact, proceeded much further outside of Cameroon. In all cases it is regarded as a response to labour problems.[58]

Reformist or Revolutionary Unions?

If the future of African economic development depends, as it seems it does, on forging new links between town and country, then the question is: what agency will do the forging? This raises, first of all, the issue of the potential role of urban trade unions in making economic and social change. It was the assumption of nearly all African Marxists that an industrial working class would be the vanguard of revolutionary change.[59] This belief was frustrated by the very limited extent of industrialization in sub-Saharan Africa, and by the deep divisions inside the working class itself.

It is not necessary to accept Fanon's denunciation of the industrial working class as '"a labour aristocracy" whose interests are congruent with the neo-colonial élites and not with the peasantry'[60] to recognize the division between the unionized skilled and clerical workers, mainly in transnational corporations, and the vast majority of the unskilled and semi-skilled.[61] Fanon's vision of a lumpenproletariat, 'the hopeless dreg of history', emerging as the 'urban spearhead of the revolution'[62] was absurd on two counts. It was self-contradictory and insultingly deprecatory of the hopes and consciousness of exploited miners and plantation workers.

What then were the aims of these groups of workers in Africa? In Zambia there were the struggles of the highly skilled copper miners; in Cameroon, as we have seen,

semi-skilled rubber tappers, palm harvesters, tea pluckers and banana cutters
... [were] highly conscious of their vital role in the production process [and]
... inclined to halt the process if the management refused to listen, and to
give in, to their 'justified' demands.[63]

The unions which were established in Africa were reformist rather
than revolutionary, quick to defend their rights, but slow to take action
outside their workplace. The Mineworkers Union of Zambia even held
aloof from the struggle for independence in the 1950s.[64] The failure to
hold together a united African trade union movement throughout the
1980s owed much to United States intervention,[65] but resulted chiefly
from the intolerance of African governments for any strong and independent trade union movement.[66]

The National Union of Tanganyika Workers had been one of the
strongest workers' organizations in Africa up to the mid 1960s, but was
first incorporated and then marginalized in the monopolization of
political and economic power by TANU, the ruling political party.
The unions became, in the words of one Tanzanian writer, Wilbert Kapinga, 'mockeries of industrial democracy' and 'instruments for workers'
self-condemnation'.[67]

Historians of Africa's general political development, like Chris Allen,
have drawn a clear conclusion:

Since the 1940s ... women especially, but also all subordinate strata, have
been gradually excluded from significant political participation in most African
states.[68]

Trade unions have failed to emerge in sub-Saharan Africa as a force
for change, in the same way that they have in much more industrially
developed South Africa.[69] Yet industrial workers have been at the core
of the movements of resistance to continuing colonial power in Africa.
We can take Amilcar Cabral's word for it. He was the liberator of
Guinea Bissau from Portuguese rule. Writing about the recruitment of
African people to the struggle for national liberation, he saw the
working class as an essential part of what was not only a guerrilla war
but also a political revolution. The industrial workers were too few to
play the role of an alternative dominant class to replace the Portuguese,
both because they could not bring physical might to bear on the
colonial state apparatus and because they could not provide a major
source of revolutionary class leadership. But they formed a natural
opposition.[70]

The peasantry, despite 'exploitation equivalent to slavery', were harder to convince that they were being exploited than the workers 'employed in the towns who earn, say, ten escudos a day for a job in which a European earns between 30 and 50'. They could provide the 'weight' but not the leadership. That had to come not from Fanon's lumpenproletariat, the dregs of society, but from '*déclassé* elements', especially 'young people who are connected to *petit bourgeois* or workers' families who have receently arrived from the rural areas and generally do not work'.[71]

The role of young people in making social change can be central. It is a particularly striking aspect of resistance to structural adjustment programmes in Nigeria that it has been led by the students. Kole Ahmed Shettima reports that 'while successive governments were able to disorganize and ban (at various stages) the Nigeria Labour Congress (NLC) and the Academic Staff Union of the Universities (ASUU), the ban on the National Union of Nigerian Students (NUNS) over the years has never succeeded'.[72]

In analysing the class forces involved in making a revolution, Cabral was careful to distinguish the nationalist phase – where of necessity the progressive elements of the *petit bourgeois* had to predominate – and the post-colonial phase when, in his famous phrase, it has 'to commit class suicide' and give way to the hegemony of the working class.[73] And this, of course, is what the *petit bourgeois* élite has never done.

Revolution, Military Power and Democracy

Revolutionary movements against African *petit bourgeois* ruling élites have been widespread, and it is an important fact of these movements that radical groups, often including industrial workers, have so frequently seen in military power the instrument for economic and social change.[74] In Ghana, in Liberia, in the Congo, in Sudan, in Ethiopia, even in Uganda, the military has, in the words of Peter Anyang' Nyong'o, been able to 'steal the revolution' from the popular movements.[75] Of course, there were forces with other agendas behind most of the military coups in Africa. United States capital investment in Liberia was estimated at $5 billion in 1984.[76]

It is now part of history that the principal objective of the military takeover in Liberia was to destabilize the work of MOJA [the Movement for Justice in Africa which had been organizing unions among urban workers], and *abort the struggle* of the Liberian people for democracy in Liberia. Non-military efforts directed at putting an end to the work of MOJA failed miserably: thus the resort to military means.[77]

Nyong'o, the writer of these words, concludes somewhat pessimistically about the 'practical alternative':

Thus the time for the masses to be mobilized independently of the state and to have a regime based on the genuine support of a popular democratic alliance in Liberia may yet be a long way away. That seems to be the main outcome of Doe's counter-revolution.[78]

What happens after a military coup can be compared with the situation after liberation. Not only the *petite bourgeoisie* but the military also have to commit 'class suicide', and they are reluctant to do so. In the event, in Liberia, after nine coup attempts, Doe was killed in 1990; but civil war continued thereafter.[79] Even where in other parts of Africa the military have withdrawn in a peaceful manner, to allow for the restoration of democracy, discussion among political parties legitimated for the holding of elections has been limited to consideration of central state structures. After the fall of the Amin regime in Uganda, to take an example, the various parties discussed the roles of the presidency and of parliament; but, Mahmood Mamdani insists, 'There was no discussion on whether local state structures must allow for democratic control by working people in the countryside.'[80]

Mamdani's conclusion to his study 'Class, Democracy and Uganda' may be taken as a summation of the discussion in this chapter. It follows after his statement which we quoted earlier to the effect that 'no popular urban force – the working class included – can expect to influence meaningfully the direction of political events without breaking the political hold of the bourgeoisie over the peasantry'. He goes on with three concluding sentences:

Narrow demands and top-down methods end up strengthening bourgeois rule. Broad demands and bottom-up methods end up weakening that same rule and building the autonomy of popular forces. The former will give us a sham democracy; only the latter can ensure a consistent democratic reform.[81]

Democratic Structures

Can we then find examples in Africa of such bottom-up methods? Developing structures to support such democratic aims has not proved easy. But some African producers' associations have established themselves successfully by linking urban services with rural production through marketing operations, including marketing for export. One of the few benefits we saw accruing to the smaller producers of cash crops from the World Bank's programmes of structural adjustment has been the opening up of such marketing opportunities as a result of the closing down of state marketing boards or the reduction of their monopoly positions. In general the openings have been taken advantage of by large trading companies, often from overseas. Here and there, however, small marketing organizations have been formed in towns and cities to collect and sell produce from village societies.

The Kuapa Kokoo Limited Company in Kumasi, Ghana, is an example of such a farmer-owned and oriented company. Over forty villages in 1993 began selling their cocoa through the company. The cocoa was still sold on to the state marketing board, but weighing (a crucial control over fair trading), collection, transport, labelling, storing, recording, accounting and negotiating export markets for identifiable bags had all been taken over by the company. It is an important point about cocoa processing that the first stages before export are carried out by the producers and do not require large factories as coffee milling and tea drying do.

We can learn from this story much for the conclusions which follow. The company could never have come into existence without the inspired initiative of a politically well-placed local chief and the start-up capital and technical support of three European alternative trade organizations. In particular, some outside help was needed to establish an effective structure of ownership and control between the producers themselves, their village societies and the company and to create the necessary credibility for the company with the local banks and marketing board officials. But it was the enthusiasm of the farmers and company workers which is making the venture a success and has already won official recognition.[82]

It has proved more difficult in the coffee-growing countries of Africa to establish similar farmer-owned and controlled organizations to step into the space left by the closing down of state processing and marketing organizations. Processing coffee for export standard cannot be done on the necessary scale in the villages. Hulling, grading and bulking to ensure consistency of grades are said in Kenya to require a factory with a minimum annual through-put of 20,000 tonnes. Those able to take on such a business will be either existing officials from the state companies, private traders or large farmers. However, the great majority of farmers responsible for the greater part of coffee production in Africa are small scale, farming less than 4 ha. Low coffee prices affected them more seriously than the big estates. In Kenya, Tanzania and Uganda, major efforts have recently been made by the small-scale farmers to organize themselves to be able to own and control the factories and other organizations necessary for them to compete in the processing and export of their coffees.

Small-scale producers generally belong to a primary society in their villages – there are over 200 in Kenya – and these are responsible for the reception of cherries, pulping and delivery to the mill. Although the farmers may sometimes sell to middlemen because of long delays in payment, the state has in the past had a virtual monopoly. These village societies often belong to a District Cooperative Union – there are fifteen large ones in Kenya. These unions do not generally handle the coffee but maintain records and accounts if requested by the village societies, procure fertilizers, pesticides and other inputs, provide training and representation at regional or national level. It is the national or larger regional federations of these unions that have been seeking to establish for themselves a central role after freeing themselves from state control and recognizing the opening up of the state monopoly on marketing.

We may take organizations in three coffee-growing countries as examples: in Kenya, the Kenya National Federation of Cooperatives; in Tanzania, the Kilimanjaro Native Cooperative Union and the Kagera Cooperative Union; and in Uganda, the Uganda Cooperative Alliance. All these unions have had three main aims: to take over more of the processing and marketing, including the export, of their members' coffees; to improve the quality of the coffee and the crop husbandry; and to add value to the primary product. Support in trade development has been obtained through Twincafé with start-up finance from European aid agencies. As a result, communications equipment – computers, fax and E-mail – and liquoring equipment have been supplied together with training in their use. Premium quality coffee has been sold in exchange in European markets, including contributions to the products of alternative trade organizations – Max Havelaar, Transfair and Café Direct.

The main difficulties experienced have been, first, in obtaining credit to pay producers, let alone finance for taking over the milling operations; second, in building effective democratic relations between the farmers and their village societies and the district, regional or national unions responsible for the processing and marketing. As we saw in the case of the Tanzanian cooperative movement, there is a long history of para-statal bureaucracy and peasant distrust to be overcome. Successful trading and a fair return to the primary producers offer the only way forward. But there are severe limits to the extra value that can be added at village level – hulling as well as pulping – and at the regional centres, apart from milling and grading. Roasting and grinding or the production of instant coffee are not viable propositions for long-distance export since the bulk is increased threefold in the processing and so far packaging is not up to European standards.[83]

The central message of Africa's coffee growers for all of Africa's producers in extending their primary production into manufacturing is that cooperation can be made to work at local, district and national level, and even between separate national organizations. The key to success lies in the links being forged between urban factories and services and the rural producers and the extent that they provide for democratic control by the producers and workers involved.

PART III

A FRAMEWORK FOR COOPERATION

Lessons: For the People of the North and the South

Maybe modern western culture and contemporary African cultures in
relation to economic activities and entrepreneurship are, in some aspects,
even opposed to each other and even incompatible.

> From a statement of the theme for a UNESCO research programme of
> the South–North Network 'Culture and Development' on *Entrepreneurship
> and African Cultures*, UNESCO *Courier*, no. 15 (1993).

We must continue to insist for some time yet to come that the ideas
emanating from Europe are eurocratic, partial, unholistic and
undialectical and therefore, instead of presenting as answers to Africa's
many problems, they could well compound them.

> Yash Tandon, speaking at a round table organized by the African
> Association of Public Administration (AAPAM) and the Economic
> Commission for Africa, Special Action Programme in Administration
> and Management (ECA/SAPAM), Abuja, Nigeria, December 1990.

CHAPTER 17

Cooperation on the Ground

Development is a process of articulation and participation. This is the starting point, and the end product of development is the persons themselves, knowing what they want and acting to get it.

Sithembiso Nyoni, Executive Secretary of ORAP, Zimbabwe, in *Ideas and Action*, FAO, 162 (1985), p. 14.

This is the end of our voyage of discovery. Those who have stayed the course will realize that they have scarcely begun to explore the African continent. A few points have been touched where Africans' activities have been reported and their voices recorded. There have been brief glimpses of the history of a continent, on which the first human beings evolved and which saw the emergence of the first civilizations. The initial contacts between Europeans and Africans were passed over all too quickly along with the shameful story of the Atlantic slave trade. The subsequent ways in which Africans established themselves outside of Africa and spread almost as widely across the world as the Europeans have hardly been noticed. There have been frequent references to the impact of the bare century of colonial rule in Africa, but no exploration in depth of what it meant for Africans and African culture.

The regimes established by African rulers after independence have been judged, often harshly, but only looked at in any detail in a dozen or so examples out of fifty-six nation-states. The packages of aid and advice that have been offered to Africans from the industrialized world have been analysed, and particularly those from the international financial institutions. We have found them wanting, even where some economic growth was recorded, and often actually destructive of the lives of the most disadvantaged. But their real effect on the lives of ordinary people has not been probed. We have listened to African voices, but only those selected by their access to a publisher, a researcher or a trader.

Culture and Economy

Certain economic problems for study have been discovered: the exploita
tion of Africa's natural resources, the burden of debt owed to the
industrialized lands, the frustrated attempts at regional groupings, the
failure of imported modern industry, the spread of a second economy,
the oppression of women and the undervaluation of their role, particularly in agriculture. But there has been no attempt to discuss the
differences between European and African cultures which have made
European advice so often inapplicable to African conditions. Are they,
in fact, 'in some aspects, even opposed to each other and even
incompatible.'[1]

What would that mean for the whole development project, if European experience of development was really irrelevant for African cultures?[2] Must Africans either abandon their cultures or their aspirations
for development? Is the concept of development being defined too
narrowly? There is a danger of throwing out the baby with the bath
water, seeing only the disasters of European development and overlook-
ing the advantages.[3] Yet both costs and benefits are obvious in the
spread of human communications.[4]

Only too often in this book questions have been asked at the grass
roots and answers proposed from the centres of power, without it
becoming clear how the questions and answers might be related. In
African societies, and most particularly in economic activity, there has
appeared to be a 'missing middle', not only of medium-sized enterprises,
and of a middle class, both as entrepreneurs and professionals, but also
as intermediaries to serve as a conveyor belt between the needs of the
people and the preoccupations of the rulers. Is it not possible, however,
that the assumption of something missing is perhaps a wholly Eurocen-
tric conception based on analysis of European societies by European
writers? This could apply to Marx and Engels as much as to Weber and
Schumpeter, not just to the protestant work ethic and competitive
accumulation, but also to the whole nurturing of individualism within
state structures, as against Africa's communitarian structures.[5]

Are there, then, no positive conclusions to be reached from our
studies? It would be mere presumption to claim that much can be
learned from this book by African experts. Their knowledge will be
both wider and deeper than what is revealed here. The aim of the book
was different: it was for those of us in the North who are interested to
learn something from Africans and from those who had worked closely

with Africans, so that we should understand the African condition and culture better, and thus take Africa's experience into account in considering our own future. It was hoped that this gathering of experience might be of help also to Africans. The book had a further and narrower aim: to question further the received wisdom about African economies, as preached by the World Bank, whose false assumptions have already been exposed in the world markets.[6]

Cooperation and Competition

In this chapter the situation on the ground is reviewed. In the next, Africa is looked at in the global context. The first conclusion must be that African societies seem to reflect, as in a distorting mirror, the conflicts and confusions of our own societies, but in an extreme form. It is generally assumed to be quite evident to anthropologists that the human race has survived through its capacity for cooperation as well as competition.[7] This is what Darwin would have called one of the 'grand facts' of evolution, which the economists of the World Bank have generally ignored. The problem of the human condition has always been for groups of humans to discover a social framework which allows for both of these instincts in proportions appropriate to their environment. For at least 20,000 years since the end of the Ice Age, the African continent has been a hard environment. Survival depended upon a high degree of cooperation. African societies have emerged with a strong tradition of working together. Apparently natural disasters like droughts and floods have been blamed by many rural Africans on the contravention of ancestral wisdom.

Our societies in the North have emerged from a much more benign environment. The competitive instinct has increasingly predominated, to a point in fact today where it threatens our own survival and that of the whole planet. Modern industry has evolved within a framework which encourages competition. The market system, as we call the unplanned exchange of goods and services and of the several factors of production, ensures only a necessary minimum of cooperation but maximum competition. Introducing the full capitalist market system and modern industry from Europe into African society was bound to be like introducing a foreign body into the human frame. This would have been the case, even if every care had been taken – which it was not – to ensure the presence of the requisite infrastructure, the linkages and appropriate scale of production and consumption.

The introduction of agri-business was even more harmful. It exhausted the soil and, by recruiting wage labour, as before in the mines and plantations, it deprived the household farming unit of the young men who were relied upon at home for the construction work, including terracing, well digging and dam building. Maureen Mackintosh's study of a United States company's groundnut plantation in Senegal showed how the young men going out to work for a wage, even without leaving home, broke up the whole local farming system. Advisers from the North had assumed the existence of a European family unit in place, where waged labour would have added to family income. The actually existing household farming unit was, in fact, totally disrupted by waged labour and in the end, when groundnut prices fell, the scheme failed to show a profit and was abandoned.[8] But the damage had been done.

In earlier chapters the strengths of Africa's farmers have been recognized and the appropriateness of many of their methods to African conditions, including the mix of cash crops and subsistence farming typical of the rural household economy. Their need for better hand tools and for mechanical equipment, including transport, was emphasized, so that increases could be made in very low levels of productivity. But the viability of the household unit was not questioned. Indeed, its ecological sustainability was extolled. This assumption is not without its critics, who are not by any means all self-interested advocates of agri-business.[9]

Colin Leys, in questioning Basil Davidson's evocation of viable precolonial economic and political systems in Africa, argues that these were at very low levels of development.[10] He completely ignores precolonial history: for example, that of the Creole economies in West Africa, which Davidson has unearthed for us in his *Black Man's Burden*, with their schools and universities and newspapers and theatres; and there are other examples.[11] Leys dismisses entirely the potential for increased productivity in any form of household production. His central criticism of colonial regimes is that they failed to transform the relations of production. The household unit was harnessed to the production of commodities, but no 'policies of land consolidation and proletarianization' were applied, which Leys believes would have been necessary for Africa to 'stand up to the pressure of world market forces'.[12]

One is bound to question the efficacy of such policies where they were applied – in Latin America, for example – in creating the conditions for modernization, let alone improving the lot of the people or developing sustainable forms of agriculture. And in Africa they have been disastrous, as we have just seen in Senegal. When the World Bank recognizes after thirty years the importance of the role of women and of subsistence farming in the rural areas and of an informal economy in the towns, it does so within a recommended framework of free competition. The regulation of the market by state protection and parastatal enterprise and marketing boards is then to be eliminated, to leave the field free for individual enterprise. But this is pure rhetoric, unless support systems are put in place. The great weakness of subsistence farmers and of informal entrepreneurs alike is that they work on their own without vertical or even horizontal linkages, which would give them economic strength in the market.

If this analysis is correct, it is not at all a framework for competition that Africans need, as the World Bank supposes from experience in Europe and North America. In the industrialized countries all the linkages of the market – retailers, wholesalers, bankers, insurers, brokers, agents, transporters and specialist services – and an infrastructure of public utilities are already in place. In Africa, it is rather a framework for cooperation that is needed – to create the crucial linkages and support mechanisms that in developing countries only public authorities at different levels can supply.[13]

As African countries achieved independence, the new governments, and particularly the most authoritarian among them, started out to destroy all existing local authorities and associations, cooperatives and trade unions, so that there were no other centres of power to challenge them. Thus, today, when the World Bank set about reducing the power of central government, there was no framework of cooperation left. Village communities and women's groups have tried to fill the gap by their own grass roots organizations in rural areas and the informal economy has done something similar in the towns, but they lack essential linkages with each other and with the main organizations of business and government.

Regulating Markets

During the long history of capitalist industrialization all the actors in the market system, which were listed above, established themselves by offering their services in competition with each other. Markets were formed for every commodity and factor of production. It was not, however, a free-for-all. Entry was restricted to those with adequate capital, and a framework of rules and of regulating committees was designed to prevent fraud and malfeasance. Sometimes these had to be supplemented by government regulations and prohibitions to ensure accurate trade descriptions, standard weights and measures and safeguards for public health and safety. Abuses and dereliction could be brought before the courts, but the system was fundamentally self-regulating, on a minimal basis of mutual trust.[14]

'My word is my bond' is the motto of the London Stock Exchange; and, although there have been famous examples of rule breaking, as in the cases of insider trading, where advantage is taken of inside company knowledge to make a private profit, the system works, at least for those who are members of the club. Adam Smith's 'invisible hand', which he believed was the strength of 'moral sentiment', generally prevails.[15]

Adam Smith also understood very well that much of the regulation was contrived to protect those who were already well placed in the market: 'People of the same trade seldom meet together even for merriment and diversion, but the conversation ends in a conspiracy against the public or in some contrivance to raise prices.'[16] Thus has competition between producers been regulated over the years by market-sharing arrangements, price agreements, cartels and other restraints on trade. The picture that is presented by the apologists for the free market is a quite misleading one. Most markets are in fact rigged, whatever the rhetoric of free trading may say. But the market has its rules and sets limits of impunity for their disregard. Life can be made intolerable for those who flout the rules and go beyond the limits. How on earth can these seemingly hypocritical practices, which appear so normal to Europeans, be transferred to quite different cultures?

The Meaning of Self-reliance

One answer is that the attempt should not even be made. Each region and as far as possible each nation should be self-sufficient. Trade should be reduced to an absolute minimum and people everywhere should be encouraged to follow their own traditional ways.[17] There are two fundamental objections to this argument. First, the attempt to reduce trade exchanges means freezing countries at the level of industrial development that they have so far achieved. Even if this were possible, it is not what the people of these countries are looking forward to, who have little or no industrial capacity and no mechanical means to ease the daily burdens of work. Second, such a freeze on international trade would cut off all the possibilities of extended communication between the peoples of the world, the sharing of knowledge and experience which, however much it is abused by the media monopolies, is the wellspring of human progress.

Self-reliance is not a question of reducing the area over which goods are exchanged. The condemnation of long-distance trade as damaging to the environment overlooks the fact that the fuel used to move a tonne of goods across the oceans is less than is needed to carry the same goods by road or rail across a country the size of England.[18] Self-reliance does not mean excluding computers and telephones and televisions and labour-saving tools and equipment. Nor, at the other extreme, does it mean opening up frontiers to everything that is being offered from the already industrialized lands. It means planning and regulating trade, being selective and forging measures of development on the basis of local resources, local skills and local cultural traditions.

Even the Japanese and the 'little dragons' of the Far East, who have gone furthest, and been most successful, in copying Western technology and Western lifestyles, have retained much of their traditional culture and incorporated it into the measures they have adopted for developing their industrial capacity.[19] Given half a chance, there is no doubt that Africans can do the same. How they will do it is not for outsiders to prescribe. But there are lessons to be learned from European experience and there is plenty of evidence already of innovative African ventures, which have benefited by learning from European successes and failures alike. The key question is the 'half-a-chance' that they need in order to realize the potential that is there.

Most African governments have in the past managed their economies through centralized administration by government departments and parastatals. Marketing boards for primary products, for example, managed all the business of buying and selling, supplying inputs, transporting products, monitoring quality and controlling exports. Now that the World Bank is requiring that this whole centralized apparatus should be dismantled, the assumption is that the market system of competing private businesses will take over. In some countries and in relation to some products, there are, as we have seen, local companies capable of providing such a market; in others giant expatriate companies move in; very occasionally, there are local cooperatives and farmers' associations which have the necessary skills and experience to take advantage of these new openings for their development. Indeed, the Bank is relying in part on such non-governmental organizations to fill the gap, with support from foreign voluntary agencies to provide finance and training.[20]

Linkages and Networks

In African conditions, it may not be the best solution to think in terms of establishing markets in the usual European manner. Something like networking may be more appropriate. Networks are horizontal linkages that bring together producers and consumers more directly than through either the hierarchy of administrative systems or the chains of market commercialization. In fact, many of the big retail supermarkets supply their stores through a network of contracts with independent suppliers who, while they are not their agents, produce to their specifications. Of course, these retailers' networks provide a conduit for profits to the parent company. But with government and NGO support, networking could strengthen the position of those who have little market power, especially of the small-scale producers. And it is they, in Africa, who provide the largest part of agricultural commodities for export as well as the food for local markets. I have written elsewhere about the way such networks could be made to work.[21]

Networking would be a particularly appropriate way in Africa for bringing together the craftsmen in the informal urban economy and the peasant associations of food producers in the rural areas. While they remain often isolated from each other, neither can realize their full potential. Kinship links already supply much of the rural produce for the informal traders in the towns, but these are on an individual basis. They do nothing to build organizational structures for rural and urban work groups or to provide finance for training and equipment that would step up the productivity and product quality of both. And the illicit nature of much informal trading rules out government help to support them.

Networks have the advantage over corporate structures and state hierarchies in that they enable groups and individuals to establish long-term links which still leave them free to make their own independent decisions within a mutually agreed framework of cooperation. This is how I have described their working:

Networks have no controlling centre or leadership, but this does not mean that they have no centres and no initiators. They need a communication centre and they need networkers. The role of these is to move between groups – making connections, suggesting new linkages, repairing damaged ties. Their detailed networking is what holds the network together ... Networkers are not so much themselves organizers and managers, although they must know how to organize and manage. They are what we might call 'enablers' or 'facilitators', what the French call *animateurs*. They are in some ways like a catalyst since they help others to make changes without themselves changing. They must be trusted by all parties and able to build lasting relationships. Their most important role is, in fact, that of finding groups which can work together, which are not only compatible but complementary.[22]

There are now many information networks in Africa, not only organized by non-African bodies, but also increasingly by Africans (Table 17.1). Some of these hardly extend beyond a single country, but others have a much wider ambience. FAVDO claims to have continent-wide coverage.[23] Most go no further than the exchange of experiences, but the Zimbabwe Women's Bureau has been moving towards coordination of women's actions in Zimbabwe[24] and there are church groups which have supported credit unions in Ghana and elsewhere.[25] It is both a strength and a weakness that these networks, both African and non-African, are frequently suspect by and even at odds with African governments.[26]

Most of the non-African organizations work in more than one of the African states and many work in several, and could perform a useful function in bringing together similar initiatives in neighbouring countries. It is an important feature also of some of the African NGOs that they cross the nation-state boundaries and have links with some of the regional inter-governmental organizations, and FAVDO has had a certain success in beginning to provide a coordinating forum for all African non-governmental development organizations.

The Role of NGOs in Development

NGOs in Africa are not only concerned with information networking and with famine and disaster relief, for which they are best known. Their roles are numerous and widespread and became increasingly controversial during the 1980s as they became more deeply involved in projects of African development. The 1989 World Bank report *From Crisis to Sustainable Development* explained the rationale for the growing interest of official foreign donors, both national and international, in channelling funds through NGOs, both northern and African:

A strategy of development that stresses the dynamism of farmers, grass roots communities, and other parts of the non-modern sector needs to be matched

TABLE 17.1 A List of Selected African Networks

1. Non-African

Fondation pour le Progrès de l'Homme, French–African dialogue.

FAO, Freedom from Hunger Campaign, Action for Development, seminars, workshops and the bulletin, *Ideas and Action*, quarterly 1965 to 1988, 30,000 copies per issue, now closed down by FAO.

IRED, Swiss-based International Network to Promote Development Innovations, brings together community groups worldwide, with centre in Africa in Kenya.

IFDA, the International Foundation for Development Alternatives, circulates reports from the grass roots in Africa.

OXFAM maintains links between its several projects in Africa.

RDM, the French Réseau de Développement Mondial, has the most extensive data base.

RITIMO, Réseau d'Information Tiers Monde, *Bulletin Passerelles*.

SDX, Sudan Cross-Border, regional meetings have coordinated relief logistics in the Sudanese conflict.

Six S Association, Se Servir de la Saison Sèche en Savan et Sahel, which links grass roots groups in Burkina Faso, Mali and Senegal.

TWIN issues *The Network* from London, which circulates mainly trade information.

2. African

Africa Centre for Technology Studies (ACTS) and Environmental Liaison Centre, international links to SADC.

African Association for Education for Development, in its journal *Famille et Développement,* describes traditional medical treatments.

African Women's Link has a Newsletter, based in Nigeria and produced by women journalists.

AGRIPROMO, Pour la Promotion Rurale, based on INADES, Abidjan, with circulation in ten countries.

Association of Church Development Projects (ACDEP) in Northern Ghana.

Association Villages-Entreprises and GIPATO in Togo.

Catholic Secretariat, Gambia, links with government agricultural institutions.

ENDA, Environnement et Développement Africain, based in Senegal, but also working in Ghana and elsewhere, publishes *Vivre Autrement* connecting environmental groups.

FAVDO, Forum for African Voluntary Development Organizations, based in Dakar, publishes *Echoes of FAVDO* and promotes African NGOs.

TABLE 17.1 (*continued*)

Kenya Forestry Extension Services and Kenya Energy and Environmental Organization (KENGO), NGO networking.

National Council of Women of Kenya, since 1977 engaged in grass roots struggle against desertification, deforestation, soil loss and fuel wood scarcity, has launched the All-Africa Green Belt Movement.

National Council of Women's Societies is the umbrella body for all Nigerian women's voluntary associations.

ORAP links many farming groups in Zimbabwe.

SINA, the Settlements Information Network, has 300 members in twenty-six countries, exchanging experiences in rural and urban settlements.

Tanzanian Gender Networking Programme links women engaged in grass roots struggles.

Union des Cooperatives de Kayes in Mali.

West African Economic and Social Centre in Burkina Faso publishes *Construire Ensemble* on farmers' experiences.

Work Team, the cooperative magazine from Botswana, exchanges news and criticisms of NGO activities in Southern Africa.

ZERO, sustainable energy network, linked to SADC energy programme.

Zimbabwe Seeds Action Network and MUTOKO Agricultural Development Projects.

Zimbabwe Women's Resource Centre and Network has documentation centres and coordinates regional initiatives.

For sources see references in the text.

by changes in donor financing to reflect that emphasis. The need for change has been recognized [i.e. by the World Bank] . . . This reflects a growing belief that most NGOs are committed to addressing the problems of developing societies and the needs of their poorest members in a manner not matched by government officials.[27]

It has to be added that part of the reason for the failure of governments in Africa is the reduction in government expenditure on welfare required under the Bank's own structural adjustment programmes. This, as was noted earlier, led one Northern NGO official in Africa to speak of a 'two-tier welfare system' – the failing government provision and the ever growing unofficial aid from abroad.[28] But it is a matter of some importance for the role of NGOs that official funds are increasingly being channelled through them. An estimate for 1988 suggested that '35 per cent of the total of US$6.3 million disbursed by NGOs was derived from the general taxes levied by OECD [i.e. Northern] governments' and that this could rise to 50 per cent of a total twice that figure by the end of the century.[29] Such a high and growing proportion of government support for NGOs inevitably raises questions about the independence of NGOs and whether the piper's paymaster will be calling tunes.[30]

It is necessary to distinguish different types of NGO. There is first a distinction to be made between Northern NGOs (NNGOs) and Southern (African) NGOs (SNGOs or ANGOs), although in many cases they work closely together. Below both of these there are the grass roots village- or township-level organizations, sometimes linked across a district or region, but generally with minimal institutional forms and no vertical links. There is thus, as George Baldwin has pointed out, a three-tier structure, the NNGOs funding and the ANGOs coordinating actual ground-level operations.[31]

There are different views on the relationship between the tiers. All the evidence examined in this book of successes and failures at the grass roots level indicates that top-downward organization is counter-productive. Neither ANGOs nor NNGOs would probably wish to weaken the basic strength of local groups, but often their very presence tends to have that effect. Charles Mabugre, a Ghanaian working with ACORD, whom we quoted earlier, has expressed his fears at the increasing involvement of northern NGOs in providing financial services to grass roots groups in Africa. He charges these NNGOs with being frequently incompetent, over-generous with credit, often not charging interest, failing to distinguish gifts and loans and, most seriously, undermining or at least not building carefully on the local existing informal revolving savings and credit associations, *tontines*, *susus* et cetera. He quotes an example in Uganda where local savings mobilized by more than 2,000 such associations exceeded the capital funds of the local bank in the area. Further funds were introduced by ACORD on a large scale with the aim of topping up the local savings. This involved a big expansion of staff. As a result, the original associations were largely replaced by a much more expensive system, lacking their social cohesion and account-able to the NNGO for policy on disbursal and recovery.[32]

The relationship between NNGOs and SNGOs (ANGOs) is even more controversial. George Baldwin, who is a retired World Bank economist, believes that in Africa 'the basic relations of NNGOs and ANGOs seem healthy'.[33] Yash Tandon, speaking from an African perspective, questions that assumption on two grounds: 'Western NGOs' agendas are their agendas, not Africa's'; and they are very hard to know, as these NGOs are what he calls 'a secretive lot' who are reluctant to submit their aims to the same sort of evaluation that they require of their African 'partners'. Secondly, what is clear to him is that Western NGOs 'are instruments of bringing into Africa their own value systems peculiar to European–American culture'. He gives three examples: gender issues, human rights and ecology, in all of which he claims that Africans are patronized by an approach of superior understanding. There is a further implication in Tandon's critique: that foreign NGOs' welfare provision is not only humiliating but disruptive of African development. Where it is not just 'conscience money for the continuation of 400 years of plunder of Africa's resources', it has the same aim as the World Bank – of incorporating Africa into the capitalist world economy.[34]

In considering this critique, much depends on the different roles which NGOs are playing. Mark Nerfin has distinguished four types of NGO activity (although some NGOs may be engaged in more than one):

1. relief and welfare agencies of varying sizes;
2. small-scale self-reliant, local development organizations;
3. projects for developing sustainable systems;
4. schemes of empowerment, for facilitating popular movements.[35]
(And I should wish to add a fifth – alternative trading organizations.)[36]

World Bank policies are having contradictory effects in influencing the roles of NGOs. On the one hand, the enforced reduction in government welfare spending has increased the demand for NGOs to fill the gap with or without local government encouragement. And this is how it comes about that much official aid from outside is being channeled through NGO relief and welfare agencies. On the other hand, it is widely recognized, even by the World Bank, that it is the other roles in which NGOs have a comparative advantage, and especially in realizing people's empowerment, which relief and welfare project aid does not allow for.[37] A World Bank assessment in 1990 of collaboration with NGOs identified internal Bank procedures as an actual impediment to NGOs being able to do what they are good at.[38] What then are they good at?

What NGOs are Best At

One answer to the question about NGOs' comparative advantage was given in a 1984 UN report of the 1977 Plan of Action to halt desertification:

In some respects the NGOs have been the most effective agencies in the campaign ... Their high record of success is related to the small-scale and local direction of their projects and the requirements for local community participation, as well as their flexibility in operation and their ability to learn from their mistakes. The dominance of field activities give these actions an impact out of proportion to the money invested.[39]

Lloyd Timberlake, quoting this report to emphasize the importance of 'small-scale', 'local direction', 'community participation', 'flexibility', 'ability to learn from mistakes', adds the following comment on the work of NGOs:

It is not so much because of their 'humanitarianism' that they succeed, but their humanitarianism guides them into certain methods of operation which happen to be the most effective ways of motivating people and spreading new ideas.[40]

This may be all very reassuring for those devoted people who work for NGOs, but a problem arises for the NGOs if they are to become a major vehicle for official aid. Even though an increasing proportion of aid may be provided direct to local African NGOs and grass roots organizations, the rationale for official aid is inevitably the retention of countries and whole regions within the global trading system, and particularly the repayment of debt.[41] Encouraging local independence can at best be a secondary consideration. Finance will be granted primarily for 'modernizing' projects which aim to become self-financing within the European and North American market. This may still increase African self-reliance, but it can all too easily lead to involving only the more advanced groups in society who already benefit from structural adjustment programmes, to the neglect of the poorer and disadvantaged.[42]

Most African NGOs are dependent on Northern funding whether directly from Northern governments or via Northern NGOs. This dependence carries two disadvantages. First of all, it undermines the respect and indeed the self-respect of the local NGO members. Secondly, NGOs are seen by governments as rivals for Northern aid. On the first count, it is better if the funding consists of loans and credits rather than grants; and on the second, it is better if projects can be jointly organized by NGOs with government involvement.

An example of a network where both disadvantages have been overcome is the Six S Association (Se Servir de la Saison Sèche en Savan et Sahel), to which a number of Dutch, French and Swiss NGOs have been making funds available in French-speaking West Africa. This association does not itself organize any activities but links together groups, mainly of women and young people, throughout the dry lands of Burkina Faso, Mali and Senegal. It draws its strength from the deep cultural roots of the people, especially from the Naam cooperative work associations in the Yetenga region of Burkina.[43]

By 1984 the Six Ss had twenty-one zones of activity, comprising some 400,000 people, in 1,000 groups and 500 villages. The groups send representatives to area committees and it is these committees which allocate the funds made available to the association. The funds are supplied at the beginning of the dry season to groups which are prepared to work on digging wells, culverts and dykes, clearing tree stumps and constructing community buildings. Payments are made in the form of loans for labour, at a low but guaranteed rate, and for purchase of materials not available locally; and grants may be provided for equipment and training and the payment of instructors.[44]

Management of the work and the repayment of loans is a group responsibility with agreed regulations. Such decentralization of decision-making has led to some failures, but lessons are learned and new groups are continually seeking to become associated. Extra funds would be needed from outside or from government, if further growth were to be encouraged. As it is the association's area officers have been able to establish regular discussion with local state officials about needs and priorities, and have become, in many places, an integral part of local government.[45] Some of the alternative trade organizations, such as Twin Trading, have a revolving fund which is used by producers' associations to buy peasant produce and is repaid when the produce is sold in home or export markets.

The promotion of alternative trade is an example of outside support for African organizations which has overcome some of the problems of the dependency effect and of government jealousy. Mazide Ndiaye, a leading member of the NGO RADI in Senegal, which works with TWIN, makes the point very strongly:

We do not want charity because it demeans. With the money earned from trade you can buy what you want. You cannot demand what you need from people who are helping you.[46]

The whole aim of alternative trading organizations like Twin Trading is to strengthen the market bargaining position of small- and medium-scale producers, whether peasants or craft workers. What this means will be discussed later, but the implications for NGO relations with governments are generally tricky. On the one hand, support for a better deal in world markets is welcome; on the other hand, the opening for alternative trading systems is generally the result of a World Bank requirement under structural adjustment conditions that government withdraw from the trade monopolies upon which its main income and that of individual officials have probably depended.[47]

NGOs and Governments

With world prices for Africa's primary products at all-time low levels in the 1980s many African governments came to depend very heavily on external aid, much of it voluntary – Mozambique for 60 per cent of GDP, Uganda for 70 per cent of the state budget, and similar proportions were to be found in Liberia, Malawi, Sudan and Tanzania. As was seen earlier, an increasing share of this aid is being supplied through NGOs. In Kenya, NGOs were providing 40 per cent of the health care service and almost all the family planning activities. In Tanzania, the government in 1992 returned to NGOs the hospitals taken into the state's hands after the Arusha Declaration.[48] In many countries of Africa the NGOs were, in effect, propping up governments which cannot maintain even the basic state functions of security and order. There was a great danger of competition for aid becoming sharper between governments and the voluntary sector. And there remained a gap in the linkages between government and people at the points where it is widest – between the capital city and the rural areas and between neighbouring peoples in different states.[49]

If African NGOs are to fill this gap, they will have to establish a position of strength that enables them to stand up to government on equal terms. They will need more funds to cover their recurrent costs in addition to the direct funding of projects. This point has been recognized by World Bank economists. George B. Baldwin, who has shown a strong commitment to African NGOs, has argued that the cooperative federations in francophone Africa, like FONGS of Senegal, GIPATO in Togo, the Kayes cooperative federation in Mali, but also ORAP in Zimbabwe, have been particularly effective, because they have had adequate resources for institution building as well as for project management.[50]

Another expert from the North, with long experience in Africa, is Goran Hyden from Sweden. He has written about the 'greenhouse approach', within which a whole plurality of organizations can be sheltered and encouraged to grow. But he is realistic enough to recognize the actual restrictions on growth which would first have to be removed. He places these in three categories: government restrictions on trading, marketing and urban transport; societal restrictions, especially those on the rights of women to land, property and even to income; donor restrictions on independent local decision-making in the design and management of funded projects.

Hyden gives as an example of positive measures to end such restrictions the Nairobi Statement on the Enabling Environment for Effective Private Sector Contribution to Development in Sub-Saharan Africa. This came out of an OAU conference in 1986 of representatives of governments, the private sector and NGOs from the several African regions. African governments were encouraged to permit 'the extensive resource, imagination and creativity of the private sector – both people and institutions – to participate fully in the development process'.[51] And since the conference recognized that very much private initiative and production was crowded into the informal sector, it recommended that particular attention should be paid to this sector.

Hyden gives a good example of the strengths of the informal sector:

At the first Congress of African Scientists held in Brazzaville in June 1987, one of the highlights was an exhibition by members of l'Association des Inventeurs du Congo, an association of some 200 Congolese inventors and innovators, both young and old, drawn from the flourishing informal sector of Kinshasa and Brazzaville.[52]

In the chapter on the informal second economy, some doubts were expressed about the potential of this sector to carry forward any rapid development, such as would keep up with, let alone overhaul, rising populations. More hope for raising productivity was placed in the small- and medium-scale entrepreneurs, who were believed not to be so lacking in Africa as some foreign experts had supposed. The informal economy and small and medium business are alike in lacking linkages between each other and between themselves and government structures. The 'missing middle' in Africa, as Hyden sees it, is not so much the absence of medium and small entrepreneurs as the lack of 'mechanisms for mediation between government and citizenry'.[53] Some church organizations play this role, as do a few African NGOs, but it is Hyden's view that:

In the absence of strong African NGOs a number of international NGOs will have to play this role in the next few years. Their strategy, however, must increasingly focus on servicing local grass roots organizations and indigenous intermediaries. The international NGOs can play a catalytic role in accelerating the growth of Africa's social capital by providing credit, management services and other institutional development support.[54]

Hyden gives the example of the Voluntary Agencies Development Assistance (VADA) in Kenya, which has shown that such support is best provided in the form of services to African intermediaries, but with the promoters drawn from outside the local community involved, so that they will not be tied up in feuds and factions.

Major problems will remain in establishing effective relations between NGOs and government bodies, even when actual legal restrictions on private trading and voluntary activities have been lifted, as is increasingly happening. What Hyden has to say here is confirmed by the experience of alternative trading. It is worth summarizing his argument. Where Northern NGOs are to provide linkages between African NGOs and government, great sensitivity is required. Traditional local institutions must be at the base of all development, but this does not mean that they do not need to make changes. Grass roots organizations are not necessarily democratic. At the same time, they are not necessarily at all backward and inflexible, but are constantly developing and adjusting to realities. One of these realities is the power of the state. Governments in their embrace of modern values and institutions are correct to see these modernizations as a prerequisite for fiscal and monetary policy, management of the central bank or public utilities, although small states have little power to do these things on their own. But in other areas such as health, rural credit, land reform and agricultural practice, local, grass roots values and know-how are essential elements in effecting changes.

'The international community,' Hyden concludes, 'should refrain from trying to accelerate the development process in Africa by intervening in executive action. Instead it should nudge the African governments toward greater institutional pluralism.'[55]

A report by the Northern countries' organization, the OECD, in 1988 had already argued that Northern NGOs had a positive role to play in democratization in developing countries, both by their strengthening of civil society and by their making politicians and civil servants more accountable for their actions.[56] John Clark of Oxfam devoted a whole book in 1991 to arguing for the role of voluntary organizations in democratizing development, and to this end for democratizing themselves.[57]

One crucial aspect of more democratic government in Africa would be the opening up of the separate nation-states to increased neighbourly and regional cooperation. Without the links across state boundaries between peoples of the same ethnic origin becoming legitimated, many successful grass roots activities in any one of Africa's nation-states fail to be replicated in others. This is but one result of the 'curse' of the nation-state in Africa. Colin Leys believes that Basil Davidson exaggerates. Leys perceives Africa's problem rather in the weakness of the social formations on which the state rests — as if these were a substratum and did not themselves comprise both the economic and political structure of the nation-state.[58] What is certainly true is that it will be difficult for regional cooperation to progress until the international financial institutions cease to treat only with individual states. Of course, the ruling élites prefer is that way, and will keep it that way, unless challenged from outside as well as from within.

Democratizing Government

The revolt against the authoritarian rule of African governments which has taken place since 1990 must give some hope in the future of a more positive challenge to the state from within. Of course, the challenge from without came largely from the World Bank, which had begun to demand privatization of state power as a condition for further aid. It was thus a purely negative challenge, and many of the new governments which have come to power in Africa since 1990 are pledged to carry through more rigorously the required policies of the international financial institutions.[59] But there are two reasons why even such changes can lead to positive opportunities for greater power being achieved by the people in the towns and countryside. The first is that the privatization of parastatal marketing boards and other state organizations does open up a space not only for big companies, whether local or transnational, but also for cooperatives and small-scale producer associations, given that they get the necessary finance and training.[60]

The second point to make about the challenges to authoritarian rule which have been taking place since 1990 is that these are part of a long and continuing struggle in Africa for democratic policies and systems. They did not emerge suddenly in 1990 as a response to the collapse of authoritarian governments in Eastern Europe. They came out of movements of peasant protest, women's demands, trade union organization and the radicalization of students and intellectuals over many years. Far from being triggered by events in Eastern Europe, they were triggered by events much nearer home, by the collapse of African commodity prices in world markets and the increasing burden of foreign debt afflicting so many African countries.[61] Not that the new parties have alternative policies, but the old rulers have lost their access to funds.

Pressure for the ending of single-party rule in African countries has come partly from below – from students, organized workers, women, religious groups and disaffected professionals, occasionally linking up with peasant protest. But it has also come from above, from an excluded élite, particularly under regimes where one man and his gang have operated the principle of 'winner takes all'.[62] In Zaire the various rivals to President Mobutu appear to be his long-standing collaborators, preparing to take advantage of any challenge to the dictator's hold on supreme power. For there is a combination in Zaire, as in many other African countries, of challenge from below and rivalry at the top.[63] Even in these circumstances, something may be won by the people from the establishment of multiparty rule in place of personal dictatorship.

John Healey and Mark Robinson of the London ODI, after a magisterial review of the literature on the relationship between democracy and development in Africa, end on a positive note. They fully recognize a danger of the current upheaval leading simply to the replacement of one group of predators by another. But they see the very diminution of resources available for patronage following the fall in prices and volumes of exports as a reason why African political leaders might seek to widen their political base, reinvigorating their parties at the grass roots.[64] This process, as others besides the World Bank have pointed out, should be made easier by the spread of market systems in place of state monopoly marketing.[65] Healey and Robinson see a role for donors

in assisting the weaker and less vocal sections of the population with funds and professional capability . . . Good examples should be the strengthening of organizations representing small manufacturing and trading businesses and small farmers' associations.[66]

At the same time, NGOs and other agencies which are involved in development projects in Africa will need to learn lessons from those who have had the greatest success in truly enabling African organizations to stand on their own feet and improve their conditions of life. Over years of experience in Africa, Ben Wisner formulated a check list for development projects, which Lloyd Timberlake discovered for his own use and then published. 'If the answers to the ten questions are by and large positive,' Timberlake comments, 'then the given project has the potential

TABLE 17.2 A Development Project Check List

1. Is the project oriented towards the needs of the people to be involved in it?
2. Is the focus of the project on women or on a definable group of 'rural disadvantaged'?
3. Is the control local? (The answer here must always be a compromise . . . with donors . . . and . . . national government control.)
4. Does the project make use of local human resources – knowledge, skills, cultural values and forms of organization?
5. Is the project based on local material resources – materials, energy and land?
6. Is the project sustainable in the long term (depending on what is meant by that)?
7. Is the external aid provided in sensibly limited amounts and in such a fashion that the people being helped do not become dependent on it?
8. Are new group alliances being formed through the project? (Casamance and ORAP both formed new links between men and women for mutual support. Projects which increase differences between rich and poor or between, say, pastoralist and settled farmer – as in the case of many big dam projects – divide rather than bring together rural groups.)
9. Is regional coordination sufficient, or is there a potential conflict with large-scale regional plans? (Big 'food for work' programmes often overwhelm local projects bent on helping people to become self-sufficient.)
10. Finally, is the project resulting in a shift of power in favour of the disadvantaged group? (Wisner says 'this effect is as rare as it is essential to the long-term sustainability and reproducibility' of the project. Obviously such a shift may conflict with vested interests of locally powerful people or even with the interest of the national government, as the Ruvuma Development Association did in Tanzania.)[67]

to do more good than harm.' Wisner's ten questions are reproduced above together with some comments (shown in brackets) from Timberlake.

The ODI recently completed a mammoth four-part study of 'NGOs and the State' with special reference to rural development. The volume *NGOs and the State in Africa* has sections by African scholars on Ghana, Kenya, Zambia and Zimbabwe.[68] These cover the whole range of NGO–government relations – as testers and disseminators of government technology, through networks and joint partnerships, as government agents and as influencers and trainers of government. The studies are mainly factual rather than analytical, but their common trend has informed much of the thinking that went into writing this chapter. It is summed up in the overall volume of the ODI study, entitled *Reluctant Partners*, where the authors draw the following conclusion:

The wide range of innovative features of NGOs' work in ATD [Agricultural Technology Development] should not be taken to imply that they are about to have a major impact on the livelihood of the rural poor — their efforts remain too small, fragmented and poorly coordinated. Perhaps the most significant implications of their experience lie in the lessons they generate that have potential for being scaled up by government.[69]

How far these lessons are learned within Africa depends very much on what lessons are learned outside Africa by both governments and NGOs and the nature of the links forged between African and Northern NGOs and between them both and the grass roots associations. Apart from famine relief, most of the aid to Africa from the North, as we have seen in this book, has been useless if not actually harmful. It has financed plant and equipment that was decided upon in the North and which the North wanted to sell, with wholly inadequate consultation with the African recipients. When products failed the test of local or international markets, plants were abandoned and the Africans were blamed. From the experience of projects with which I have been involved, the lessons to be learned are that aid for Africa has to be through joint ventures in which Africans have a determining voice and the aid is used to finance the necessary time required for the painstaking work on the ground by African and Northern partners in turning potential failure into actual success. What is achieved by cooperation on the ground will still need a protective framework in the wider world economy.

CHAPTER 18

Africa in the World Economy

It may well be that what threatens Africa is not so much marginalization as her negative prominence, her construction as the ultimate loser.

Claude Aké, 'The Marginalization of Africa: Notes on a Productive Confusion', a paper prepared for the Council on Foreign Relations African Studies seminar, New York, 28 February 1994.

In the first part of this book the tragic decline of Africa was traced through the centuries culminating in the disastrous fall in income and stability in the 1980s. With 10 per cent of the world's population, Africa's share in world exports was reduced just in that decade from 2.4 to 1.4 per cent; even the exports of Africa's staple non-oil primary products fell from 7 to 4 per cent of the world total, and the share of foreign direct investment similarly reduced. As the terms of trade of Africa's products declined, trade deficits and foreign debts rose until, in total by the early 1990s, the debts exceeded the combined GNPs of all the African states and debt servicing took up nearly a third of all export earnings. Ten years earlier, in 1980, the debts had only amounted to 28.5 per cent of GNP and 13 per cent of export earnings. Although the World Bank replenished much of the multilateral debt, and some debts to industrialized countries were cancelled or rescheduled, financial flows in real terms had begun to move out of Africa and not inward.[1] Africa was falling behind the rest of the developing countries and particularly those in East Asia.

What Marginalization Means

All the talk in the early 1990s was of Africa becoming 'marginalized'. Claude Aké has questioned the use of the word because it describes a condition of mind of those *outside* Africa, for whom Africa is inevitably marginal, whereas for Africans it is primary.[2] More than this, the phrase covers up the reality of the economic forces at work which have brought Africa to this condition – the historic colonial assignment of Africa to primary production of materials for processing in Europe and North America, and the declining demand for these in world markets as artificial substitutes were developed. Combined with these economic forces there was the division of the continent between the great powers into separate colonial states, each producing two or three primary products for export, their boundaries artificially drawn across ethnic homelands and adopting as official languages those of the colonial power that were none of them native tongues.

Aké does not seek to exonerate the African élites who decided, in his words,

to inherit the colonial state rather than transforming it in accordance with the democratic aspirations of the nationalist movement. Inevitably they fell out with their followers and became repressive . . . it was not the military that caused military rule in Africa . . . it was the character of politics . . . The African leaders used traditional institutions and notions of consensus to justify one-party systems without drawing attention to the traditional process of consultation and participation which produced consensus.[3]

Adebayo Adedeji, one-time Secretary General of the ECA, writes of 'the personalization and monopolization of power' in African states leading to a 'marginalization process, which has been aggravated severely by the SAPs. The cumulative effect is a state set apart from its society, in which 80 per cent of the population are at the margin.'[4]

Aké's central argument, however, is that the African élites absorbed the Western development paradigm, based on Western values and experience, and this is what has marginalized Africa, because this paradigm 'takes hardly any interest in Africa and its culture . . . African peoples, especially the rural people, and their culture are written off as being purely negative . . . enemies of progress.' The result is their total self-alienation. Aké, therefore, sees marginalization as 'precisely what Africa needs . . . improving the prospects of putting back development into the hands of Africans'. The African leaders, having marginalized their people, 'were obliged to look outside for aid, investment and technical assistance rather than tapping the energy of the people'. Such exogenous development not only neglected social needs and the social will of the people, but also, in effect, 'dehistoricized' development; it came to be believed that there was nothing to be learned from pre-colonial history.

Marginalization 'will not, of course, guarantee development', Aké concludes, 'but it will give it a chance; for a people develops itself or not at all . . . It will go a long way towards overcoming the problem posed by the difficulty of crystallizing a development agenda which expresses the aspirations of the people and can therefore elicit their support.'[5]

In this definition of 'marginalization' Claude Aké takes the side of Basil Davidson in the argument with Colin Leys, reviewed in the last chapter, about the value of understanding the past, the pre-colonial African experience, for Africans to find their own way into the future. But Leys himself calls upon history in his defence, citing Jean-François Bayart's interpretation of the history of the state in Africa. Bayart, writing in 1989, sees

Africans as having over the centuries always been subordinate players in relation to the outside world; but players nevertheless engaged in a process of 'extraversion', in which they sought to draw on resources or alliances available in the external environment in furtherance of their continuing internal competitions and conflicts. What we have now is only the latest version of this role . . . as members of the élites collaborate with each other to profit as best they can from their dealings with the outside world.[6]

Leys points out that this is a post-modernist view from which we can never know complex reality and which rejects all committed, practically oriented approaches. The African masses become an ironic chorus, whose passions are limited to those of Stendhal's peasant, who wished only 'not to be killed and for a good warm coat'. Leys is obviously not happy with all this, but regards it as a necessary corrective to what he sees as the Marxists' idealization of the masses and Davidson's supposedly romantic picture of pre-colonial Africa and of heroic national liberation struggles. He accuses Davidson of having no more answers to the African tragedy than Bayart, but confesses that he too does not know. In the meantime, he believes *pace* Davidson that 'the African state, for all its record of abuse, remains a potential line of defence for Africans against the depredations of the world economic and political system.'[7]

This is an astonishing assertion after all the evidence mounted by Davidson, but it follows from Leys's despair at the possibility of any progress being achievable within the world capitalist market system. All the obvious requirements for Africa's survival involve international cancellation of the debts, withdrawing support from kleptomaniac governments, strengthening the bargaining power of African exporters in world markets, changing World Bank policies and procedures to involve Africans themselves in their determination. But these are ruled out for Leys as totally impossible until the 'currently predominant ideology of the market' is in process of rejection.[8]

Working in and against the Market

There is no doubt that Colin Leys has correctly identified the main requirements for Africa's survival in the world economy. But do Africans have to wait for the ideology of the market to be rejected? In the upshot, Leys and Aké are in accord, in condemning Western ideology and the Western market. But, while Leys concludes with Marx's warning to all who would dream of avoiding the development in their lands of the capitalist mode of production – *de te fabula narratur* as it relates to you, or your turn next[9] – Aké believes that Africa can escape from the market in a 'second independence' for 'democratic endogenous development which ensures that the people of Africa are the means as well as the end of development, that power is held to account and public policy meets social needs'.[10]

The conclusion of this book follows the logic neither of Leys nor of Aké. It is that Africa cannot escape from the market, but can escape some of its ideology and some of its worst features. For this to happen, changes inside Africa, such as were discussed in earlier chapters, will have to be paralleled by changes outside, which are the subject of this chapter. These will need to involve Northern NGOs, Northern banks, Northern governments and the international financial institutions. Changes are already occurring and it is important that those of a like mind with Leys or Aké should recognize the fact. The North is becoming more aware of African differences and African strengths, Northern NGOs in particular, as was demonstrated in the last chapter.

There has to be some mutual understanding here. When some Northern NGOs and governments have been following the World Bank in imposing conditionality on the provision of aid and other support to meet Africa's needs, i.e. conditions of good governance, respect for human rights and protection of the environment, Aké is rightly enraged at the nerve of those whose record at home of fascist governments, of wholesale destruction of human life in two World Wars and most recently in the Gulf War and of oil tanker spillages, power-station emissions and pollution of rivers and seas is unequalled in the South.[11] And there is a further point to be made about such requirements of conditionality. The abuses in the South of which the North complains are the direct result of Northern actions – collection of debt and structural adjustment. These have made good governance impossible, undermined the economies, weakened the whole fabric of societies, so that violence and civil war are inevitable, and forced countries to exploit their resources, cutting down their forests and increasing the area of cash crops so as to meet the servicing of debt. Yet it has to be recognized that human rights and women's equality and conservation are important matters.

The changes that are occurring in Africa are to be seen in African government elections and in the general opening up of political life, but also in new forms of foreign and local NGO collaboration with governments. Active and practical measures of cooperation are likely to do much more than agreements on conditionality to move people in the North towards a greater understanding of African cultures and motivations. At the same time, self-reliance, if it were to mean isolation from the North, would hardly commend itself to most Africans. They are not likely to sacrifice the chance of having access to electricity and the telephone, and therefore to television and computers for E-mail and fax messages, or of having the capacity in their own manufacturing industry to make the tools and machinery and transport equipment for increasing productivity and reducing the burden of heavy labour – simply to ensure their immunity from Western ideas and ideology and so develop totally à l'africaine. It is not really necessary to welcome a marginalized autarky in order to avoid the development throughout Africa of the consumerism of the North.

Being in the world market does not, however, mean that any country cannot also be against the market. The success of the East Asian states in establishing their own manufacturing industries is that their governments managed the foreign market. They were able to do this largely because of Japan's preparedness to encourage them within the Japanese trading system and partly because their governments were prepared to reject completely all World Bank advice and intervene directly in industrial policy, controlling imports and subsidizing exports until they were competitive in world markets.[12]

Solidarity is not Enough: Openings for Alternative Trade

It is becoming very clear that what is required of people in the North in relation to Africa's development is not so much aid, apart from disaster relief, but a campaign against false policies, particularly those of the World Bank, and support for alternatives. Exposure of the faulty theory, which underpins all World Bank and market-centred solutions for Africa's problems, is regarded by some experts as the most important requirement of the North.[13] The theory at fault is that macro-economic policies of freeing economies to market forces can effectively establish their comparative advantage, even when such policies are pursued by the governments of small individual states in a world of transnational companies.

The fact is that in a globalized economy flows of goods and capital take place largely inside transnational companies and not between companies and individuals in the separate nation-states. As has been seen earlier, the World Bank's encouragement of nation-states to expand exports by devaluation of their currencies has simply led to beggar-my-neighbour competition; and this reduces the whole level of trade exchanges. Yet, despite the sequence of failures, now increasingly documented by economic writers,[14] the IMF and the World Bank continue to preach to the Third World the doctrine of free trade and salvation through the market.

Public response in the industrialized lands of the North to appeals for aid to victims of drought and disaster in Africa displays a noble sense of common humanity. Financial support for continuing help by voluntary organizations to the rebuilding of shattered communities and to the prevention of future disasters reveals some understanding of the long-term needs of people whose economic development has for so long been held back. Unfortunately such voluntary devotion is not carried over into support for much larger-scale national or international aid. National aid budgets have been steadily cut back during the world economic recession to the minimum needed to finance national exports.[15] International finance has taken the form of structural adjustment loans with all the attendant conditions of debt collection.

The further continuation of voluntary contributions and of government overseas development assistance has been questioned by Fowler and others. Fowler's conclusion can be summarized. It is that tied national government aid [i.e. tied to sales of goods from that nation] will continue to grow, but slowly. Government aid to NGOs will grow quite rapidly to account for at least a half of all NGO spending by the end of the century. Increasingly official aid will be supplied direct to local NGOs or indirectly through their Northern partners.[16]

He even raises the question whether Southern NGOs will be able to develop the institutional strengths to prevent their collapse under the weight of the projected growth of funds, and wonders how relations with governments for both local and Northern NGOs will avoid further strains arising from rivalry for receipt of outside funding.[17]

As far as opinion in the North has been consulted, the evidence of the polls is that almost all respondents believe that the Third World is exploited and they would prefer fairer trade to giving aid, while two-thirds would be prepared to pay extra for fairly traded Third World products.[18] When given the chance, shoppers have shown that they would pay a fair price for goods from the South, where it was guaranteed that a better price had been paid to the producers themselves. For a long time, such shopping was limited to charity shops like those of Oxfam and Traidcraft in the UK or to wholefood suppliers and their equivalents in other industrialized countries.

Today, in many advanced industrialized countries, alternative trade has penetrated the supermarkets. Coffee licensed by Max Havelaar (Netherlands) and Transfair (Germany) has begun to take 2 to 3 per cent of the market in these countries and Café Direct is selling similarly well in all the main UK chain stores. Advertisements in the press and on the billboards with a picture of Third World children tell you that 'you get excellent coffee and they get vaccines and schooling'. Prices are only a little above the norm; but because the supplies come direct from the producers, the producer gets a larger share of the final price.[19] And the shopper is also encouraging sustainable and environment-friendly production, since most small-scale producers produce organically, inter-cropping with food crops or other trees.

After coffee the alternative traders are moving into cocoa and tea, fruit and vegetables, and helping producers to add value to their products by processing coffee, chocolates, crunches, juices, jams and blended teas. They already sell honey, pecans and brazil nuts from the Amazon forests, so that the nut pickers do not have to cut down the trees or switch to growing coca to make a living. Alternative trade is exploiting a solidarity market in the North, and growers in Africa as well as elsewhere in the South are benefiting; but is this enough? The answer has, of course, to be 'No!' Even in the few products in which their members are dealing, the whole of the sales of alternative trade is to be measured in hundreds of millions of dollars, while Africa's total trade alone, small as it is, amounts to thousands of millions.[20]

Alternative trading should not be lightly dismissed because of the small scale of its sales. It has an importance for development in Africa and throughout the South that is greater than appears. It provides an alternative to a single buyer who sets the price; and it develops confidence – confidence among associations of small- and medium-scale producers in their competence to take on the power of the big companies and of governments, and to find ways to improve their condition; confidence also among people in the North that there is something positive that they can do about fair trading.[21]

An example of confidence raising that was also of considerable benefit for Third World producers was the founding of the Small Farmers' Cooperative Society. This is an association of small-scale coffee farmers, who came together in 1992 at a London conference organized by Twin Trading with financial support from Oxfam, Christian Aid and other agencies. Twenty-six coffee growing organizations attended, drawn from sixteen different countries in Latin America and the Caribbean and three in Africa, representing nearly a million families. Some of them were already supplying coffee to the alternative trade – brands like Max Havelaar, Transfair and Café Direct.

The newly formed society established an agency in London, called Twincafé, and proposed to have agencies elsewhere in Europe and North America to promote their coffees by ensuring a cooperative framework, within which they could compete for sales.[22] They succeeded well enough to reconvene in 1995. One result of this cooperation was that it led to all the world's coffee growers coming together in mid 1993 to agree on a scheme of stock retentions in order to try to lift the world price from the rock bottom levels to which it had sunk since 1989.[23] In this they had some success, although the biggest buyer in the world, Nestlé, argued that pushing up the price would only increase output and that would bring prices down again in the long run.[24] This was not really true; the main cause of the collapse in prices was the encouragement the World Bank had been giving to all coffee producers to expand exports to pay their debts and the large stocks that Nestlé and other big buyers were therefore able to draw on.[25] The sudden sharp rise in coffee prices as the result of frosts in Brazil in the spring of 1994, exaggerated by market speculation, revealed the absurdity of a commodity market system which brings prices so low as in the end to reduce production and new planting and then results in stocks running so low that they cannot cover a single bad crop.

This story reminds us that showing solidarity with Third World producers in our shopping habits is not enough. There are much bigger problems to be solved, that go beyond shopping and writing to show solidarity. It is nice, of course, to receive tributes from Africa such as the authors received for the book *Short Changed* on Africa and world trade. One lady from Uganda wrote:

It gives me pleasure to note that there are some Europeans who are on our side and see the wrong deeds of their fellow Europeans and point them out. Bravo! Therefore, it is from this stand that Africans should join hands and work as a team on a regional and international basis instead of fighting each other. They should create their own markets for their produce so that, in case they fail to sell their produce overseas, they know that there is a ready market at home.[26]

As the lady implies, there are wider complementary actions to be taken both inside and outside Africa. The position of African and other Third World producers will not be truly improved in world markets until people in Africa work together and people in the North succeed in several major actions that go beyond a mere show of solidarity.

The earlier chapters of this book suggested that these Northern actions would need to include:

* exposing and ending transfer pricing abuse by the transnational companies and their control over commodity markets;
* preventing GATT regulations from further weakening Third World countries' ability to defend themselves against subsidized food and other exports from the industrialized countries;
* requiring the World Bank to take account of African opinion and popular participation;
* forgoing the debt service charges owing to the North by the least developed countries in Africa.

We can take these one by one.

Challenging the Giant Companies

The very idea of challenging the giant companies' control over world trade and concealed internal transfers must appear at first sight to be a quite hopelessly utopian dream. But the giant IBM was brought down not by another giant but by smaller and more innovative companies. Stuart Holland, reporting to the European Commission, has called upon expert evidence to argue from new developments in modern technology that 'flexible production, combined with low wage costs, offers a potential competitive advantage to developing countries'.[27]

What the giant companies control is not any longer so much the means of production, whether in agriculture or industry, but the whole chain of commercialization between the original producer and the final consumer.[28] The capital costs of setting up production units, except in the case of assembly plants for motor vehicles and aircraft, are not large; and the parts for assembly come increasingly from a wide range of small plants. The control over commercialization is of course very powerful, but abuses are being exposed, as in the case of transfer pricing abuse by Alusuisse of the Sierra Leone bauxite exports.[29] The UN Centre for Transnational Corporations has expert advice available for any government wishing to check on the actual value it is receiving from transnational companies for its commodity exports.

A further weapon in the armoury of the developing countries dependent upon primary product exports is the UNCTAD Common Fund for Commodities. It was noted earlier that the Fund has a 'second window', which can be used by governments attempting to diversify and add value to their primary product exports. The key question is whether government ministers wish to challenge existing practices from which they may personally benefit. But, if they do, and if the recovery in commodity prices, which began in early 1994, continues, it should be possible to revive the working of the Common Fund itself.[30] It has to be recalled that the Fund is based on the spearate commodity agreements between producer and consumer countries, in which the outcome depends on the bargaining strength of the producers. This should be somewhat reinforced by the beginnings of an alternative trading system, which was described in the previous section, but it requires joint action of the producers.

Stuart Holland, in his further report for the European Commission, this time on alternatives for the global economy under a new Bretton Woods agreement, has taken the networking in alternative trade exchanges as a model of development for small- to medium-sized enterprises and especially for those in the smaller developing countries.[31] The strength of the giant multinational companies comes not only from the scale of their financial resources but from the wide range of facilities – research and development, design, processing, packaging, information, shipping, insurance, marketing, advertising – which they can call upon, and which individual small firms cannot afford to emulate. The solution Holland proposes is for small firms to come together in networks and joint ventures, both across the borders between neighbouring developing countries and with partners in the developed countries. He takes up some suggestions that I had made for the future of alternative trading,[32] and that Peter Cooke had made for environmental planning,[33] and elaborates them into a major concept of strategic alliances for the modernization of production structures in developing countries.[34]

Coping with GATT and the World Trade Organization

Adding value to primary production and diversifying exports are going to be hard tasks for any government of a developing country, particularly in Africa, under the provisions of the latest Uruguay Round agreements of GATT; and these are in future to be monitored strictly by the World Trade Organization. The overall calculation of the likely results of these agreements to free more trade, both in goods and services, suggests that the 15 per cent of the world's peoples in industrialized lands will get 67 per cent of the benefits from this freedom and the 85 per cent of the world's peoples in non-industrialized lands will get 33 per cent of the benefits and that sub-Saharan Africa, the poorest region of all, will get nothing and will probably actually suffer.[35]

The reason for this disparity is that most African countries at present lack any strong manufacturing base and still need protection for their infant manufacturing and service industries; they will lose their preferential treatment under the Lomé convention in Europe, the main market for their primary produce, and the cocoa and coffee growers will lose most heavily; they will not be able to take advantage of new market openings because many of these in the industrialized countries will remain closed to African products by quotas and non-tariff barriers and where production, for example of vegetable oils, beet sugar and corn syrup in Europe and North America, is subsidized; and many African farmers will not be able to compete with grains and other farm products from the North which will continue to receive Northern government subsidies. GATT remains, as an Indian delegate once dubbed it, a 'one way street' for the rich countries to go down, while the traffic is too heavy for the poor to make their way up.[36]

Apart from the outrageous double standards implied, GATT is based on a doctrine of international free trade and comparative advantage which a globalized world economy dominated by multi-national companies has rendered obsolete. There was in fact never any true mobility of factors of production to justify the law of comparative advantage. Labour is even less mobile than before, hedged around as it is by immigration controls. The 1992 UN Human Development Report estimated that *'under very conservative assumptions'* such controls deny developing countries at least $250 billion a year, that is about a fifth of their export earnings or enough to pay off their debts.[37] The proposed liberalization of the trade in services under GATT does not include labour services.

Capital was always the most mobile factor and it is capital mobility that has changed most in the globalization of economic activity. In the first place, flows of capital investment now lead trade flows instead of following them. According to the UN Center for Transnational Corporations, in the years between 1983 and 1989, foreign direct investment grew three times faster than the rate of growth of world trade and four times faster than the rate of growth of world output.[38] But the second change is that the direction of investment is increasingly concentrated inside the already developed countries. During the 1980s the developing countries' share of this worldwide investment fell from 26 to 17 per cent, Africa's from 3 to 2 per cent, and in 1992 Africa actually suffered a loss of investment. At least a third of all world trade takes place inside transnational companies, and 90 per cent of such companies are based in developed countries, none in sub-Saharan Africa. There are said to be 37,000 transnational companies in the world with 170,000 affiliates and the top 100 companies are said to own about a third of the worldwide foreign direct investment stock.[39]

What chance then does Africa's trade have now or in the future in face of such a concentration of power? The answer can only be that there is still two-thirds of the world's trade outside of the transnationals' internal exchanges and two-thirds of the investment outside of their control. There are plenty of opportunities for joint ventures and networking such as were proposed in the last section, if – and it is a big if – the exemptions remain under GATT for the least developed countries (mostly in Africa) to continue to protect their agriculture. But there will need also to be an early phasing out of the protection of their markets by the most developed countries, particularly in respect of textile and clothing imports from developing countries under the Multi-Fibres Arrangement.[40]

Such a proposal will raise at once deep fears among industrial producers in the developed countries of what is described as 'social dumping', that is selling goods produced with cheap and exploited labour and under conditions that would not be acceptable elsewhere on environmental as well as humane considerations. Such arguments can be employed to close the rich markets of the world to the products of all poor countries. For this reason it is essential that the aim of all should be to raise standards worldwide rather than to lower them. This should not be impossible. The three parties to the ILO, governments, employers and employee organizations, have agreed on certain minimum rights that should be observed – of the right to organize, non-discrimination, more equal remuneration, and the outlawing of forced labour and child labour. These should be observed; they make no unreasonable requirements such as a minimum wage unrelated to local conditions.[41]

It is well to recall here that the original intention of Keynes's proposals made on behalf of the British government for the Bretton Woods conference in 1944 was to create a framework for international cooperation to ensure full employment after the Second World War in place of the beggar-my-neighbour policies of the 1930s, which had led to slump and fascism and war. In the event, Keynes's proposed International Trade Organization, which was to have had this aim, was replaced at the United States' insistence by GATT with a purely free trade remit.[42] It is thus a matter of some importance that in the accord of December 1993, establishing a new World Trade Organization, the intention of Keynes's organization is repeated – that the parties to the agreement recognize that

their relations in the field of trade and economic endeavour should be conducted with a view to raising standards of living, ensuring full employment and a large and steady growing volume of real income and effective demand and expanding the production and trade in goods and services, while allowing for the optimal use of the world's resources in accordance with the objective of sustainable development, seeking both to protect and to preserve the environment and enhance the means for doing so in a manner consistent with their respective needs and concerns at different levels of economic development.[43]

It is a pretty large commitment, and leaves little or no room for lowering standards but much scope for relating standards to different levels of economic development.

Reforming Bretton Woods

Keynes's International Trade Organization was only one of his proposals which suffered a seachange at the hands of the United States' negotiators at Bretton Woods. His International Bank, being 'a purely technical, non-political instrument', was to issue its own world reserve currency *bancor*, backed by gold or national currencies, where short-term assistance was required by any government to support trade expansion. This became the IMF, which was virtually an arm of the US Treasury and treated the US dollar, backed at first by gold, as the world's reserve currency. After 1981, moreover, it was 'agreed that the Fund's financial assistance should be conditional on the adoption of adjustment policies'.[44]

Keynes's Development Fund was to have provided assistance to countries suffering from long-term disequilibria, drawing upon both taxes and borrowing on a scale necessary to maintain full employment and reduce inequalities between economies. This proposal for a Fund became, in part, the Marshall Plan, a system of grants which was limited to supporting recovery in Western Europe and Japan. In part it became the World Bank, which began only after the oil crisis of the early 1970s to play a major role in raising loans for developing countries. Once again, as with the IMF, loans came to be made on conditions involving structural adjustment.[45]

The Bank encouraged developing countries to borrow so as to recycle the oil money; and it then spawned a whole range of loan programmes to cover debt repayment, from the Structural Adjustment Facility to the Global Environment Facility, and of lending institutions from the private sector International Finance Corporation to the soft loan agency for the least developed countries, the International Development Association. Increasing the loan portfolio became, as we saw, the criterion of success, at least for the Bank's employees, whose numbers and salaries rose with each year that went past, doubling in numbers, earning salaries 50 per cent above other UN personnel. To house this army the Bank and IMF needed a new multi-million dollar office complex to be completed fifty years after the Bretton Woods agreement.[46]

'Fifty Years Is Enough' was the title of a voluntary agencies' campaign in the United States in 1994 to seek support for ending the rule of the Bretton Woods institutions over the world economy.[47] Nowhere has the impact of these institutions been more disastrous than in Africa, and the matter of their reform is of the greatest urgency for the African people. The G7 at its Naples meeting in 1994 agreed to discuss reform at its next meeting, but did not do so. In the meantime, a high-powered United States commission under the leadership of Mr Paul Volcker, former chairman of the US Federal Reserve Bank, recommended radical changes. In summary,

The IMF should concentrate on managing the global monetary system and play less of a role as a development agency. The Bank should focus on promoting growth of the private sector in Third World countries and improve its overall efficiency by rationalizing activities and cutting staff.[48]

What would this mean for Africa? As far as the IMF is concerned, there is no doubt that the global system needs managing. The dominant currency, the US dollar, continues its downward slide, only sustained by Japanese lending, with interest rates rising as the US economy booms. The oscillations in the dollar's value offer the speculators a field day and the ultimate in market worship is reached when world economic policy comes to be determined by the financial markets. As Keynes remarked, 'when capital development . . . becomes a by-product of the activities of a casino, the job is likely to be ill done.'[49] Mr Camdessus, the managing director of the IMF, has said that he 'yearns for more currency stability' but the member states resist taking the necessary common action.[50] These are the big members; the small members in Africa are not asked, but have to suffer from the impact on their own currencies.

As for the Bank, there is no doubt that it is overstaffed and exercises far too much power over governments, and that a 'leaner, greener' bank, as advocated by Mr Lewis Preston, as the Bank's president,[51] would be preferable to the Frankenstein monster which feeds on the children of the poor.[52] But concentrating on aid to the private sector in the Third World is apparently to abandon the public sector, which the Bank has laid waste throughout Africa, and to continue to neglect the strength of the mixed economy, as it has developed in East Asia.[53] Mr Preston, moreover, in a 'vision statement' still saw the Bank as the provider and mobilizer of capital resources, adviser on economic and development policy and key coordinator in addressing strategic global development problems.[54] Very few Africans are likely to trust the Bank in any of these roles after its manifest failures in each one of them.

So, what can be done to make real changes? Keynes made his proposals for Bretton Woods in the middle of the Second World War on the assumption that after the War there would be four or five major powers which would need to reach agrement on common policies of economic recovery – the USA, UK, France, the USSR, China and, in time, Germany and Japan. In the event there was only one major power; the rest were exhausted. The Bretton Woods institutions thus became an instrument of United States hegemony. But today this monopoly of power is under challenge; the military challenge of the USSR has failed, the UK and France have long lost their imperial reach, but the economic challenge of Germany and Japan and the growing power of China reproduce the scenario for which Keynes was prescribing. It could be that a major reform of Bretton Woods will become a possibility, which recognizes these changing power relations and returns more nearly to Keynes's vision.[55]

In the meantime, more modest measures of reform have been urged by the voluntary aid agencies, including those in the '50 Years Is Enough' campaign. Since Africa has been the main object of the World Bank's attention, such measures could have an important bearing on Africa's future if they could be pressed home. They are all concerned to reduce the unaccountable power of the Fund and the Bank and bring the developing countries themselves nearer to the decision-making development centre:

* the IDA (International Development Association) – the soft-loan programme aimed at the poorest countries – should be legally and financially separated from the Bank, and have a more open and democratic structure, related directly to the UN. As it is in part financed from taxation, it could have a grant programme to support the loans for health, education and social programmes and small producer projects;
* the GEF (Global Environmental Facility) should also be legally and financially separated from the Bank, and given an independent secretariat and a structure related to other UN agencies that ensures participation by NGOs and affected communities;
* the functions and funding of the IMF and the Bank should be further narrowed by:
  – restricting the IMF to technical assistance on fiscal and monetary policies and mobilizing capital and debt relief to support economic reform campaigns;
  – reducing the Bank's large-scale infrastructure projects to 10 per cent of the loan portfolio and expanding support for broad-based sustainable food production, incorporating environment-friendly practices;
* both the IMF and the Bank should pursue a more open information policy, with full publication of the documentation on project planning. Some progress has been made in information disclosure as a result of NGO complaints, but more needs to be made available;

* the inspection panel established as a result of outside pressure should be expanded to include independent members as well as those appointed by the Bank.[56]

Independent advisory bodies were stipulated in the Articles of Agreement of the IMF and of the Bank. These have never been made operational and could be instituted, if the will is there to make reforms:

* a Fund Council to give power to the Interim Committee, the Development Committee and the Committee of 24 in the IMF articles;
* a Bank Advisory Council, selected by the Board of Governors to include representatives of banking, commercial, industrial, labour and agricultural interests ... with as wide a national representation as possible;
* each loan committee of the Bank to 'include an expert selected by the Governor representing the member in whose territory the project is located'.[57]

When Mr Davidson L. Budhoo, a senior IMF consultant from Trinidad, resigned in protest at Fund policies, he wrote to his managing director a letter which he later expanded into a book entitled *Dear M. Camdessus – Enough is Enough*. In this he made a number of proposals for new organs to deal with the frequent and increasing conflicts between the international institutions and member governments, and to involve the people themselves, who were supposedly the object of assistance, more closely in what was being decided. These proposals included:

* an Advisory and Review Commission to deal with disputes and complaints;
* Regional Coordinating Committees composed of nationals of the region to review the implications for neighbouring states of the Bank's programmes designed for each single state;
* Programme Watch Committees, with wide representation from inside the countries where Bank programmes are in operation, to oversee the countries' interests;
* an Environmental Impact Assessment Committee, again composed of nationals of the region, to monitor the ecological impact of Bank programmes.[58]

If African governments were to unite in pressing for such reforms, other Third World countries could join with them and some progress might be made in reforming the Bretton Woods institutions.

Relieving the Burden of Debt

None of these reforms of the World Bank's mode of operation, however, will go far to advance the recovery of Africa, unless the problem of Africa's foreign debt is addressed. There need be no apology for repeating the words quoted earlier from the director general of the UN office in Vienna, the UN Under-Secretary General responsible for UN activities relating to social policy and development. In 1990 Margaret Joan Anstee gave the following warning:

Here it is sufficient to say unequivocally that, without significant alleviation of this burden [of the foreign debt], Africa will not be able to achieve the recovery and renewed growth, combined with improved living conditions for the poorer segment of its population, that it so desperately needs.[59]

Year after year during the 1980s, the foreign debts of the sub-Saharan African countries had grown, accumulating as a result of rescheduling and refinancing with new loans, to amount by 1993 to nearly US$200 billions.[60] Percy S. Mistry, formerly chief of staff in the Finance Complex of the World Bank, has provided the most up-to-date analysis of what has been happening.[61] Some $40 billion of the debt in 1994 consisted of short-term debt, mainly IMF debt and arrears on long-term debt servicing. Over a quarter of the debt was owed to the multilateral institutions – the IMF, World Bank and African Development Bank. The twenty-eight least developed countries of Africa accounted for a third of the total sub-Saharan debt and for twenty of these countries 40 per cent of their debt was multilateral, while for ten it was over 70 per cent. Arrears steadily increased from 1987 onwards, especially with official creditors, as the multilaterals pre-empted the debt-servicing payments.[62]

In other words, the IMF and the World Bank were themselves responsible for the net transfer of resources from Africa which for ten least developed countries amounted to over a fifth of their annual export earnings. It is indeed evident that 'enough is enough'. Mistry makes a number of proposals for relieving the debt, after dismissing all the arguments for making the Southern debtors pay up on moral grounds and for using bilateral grants (i.e. from individual Northern governments) to make good the arrears. When the cost of running the IMF and the World Bank is approximately $3.5 billion a year, and their new building is said to have cost nearly $1 billion, moral arguments hardly come into it. Tax payers of Northern countries, moreover, are hardly likely to wish to see their contributions to overseas development assistance going into paying off American lenders.[63]

Some of the debt relief, according to Mistry, could be quite simply achieved, by realizing the reserve assets in the hands of the institutions. The African Development Bank has very limited assets, but the other two – the IMF and the World Bank – are well insulated against default.

* The IMF could make an issue of SDRs (Special Drawing Rights) to OECD members for them to use to extinguish eligible countries' multilateral debt.

* The IMF has gold holdings, only 10–12 per cent of which would be adequate for it to write down the whole debt owed by low-income Africa.

* The World Bank has retained earnings, reserves and provisions amounting to respectively $17 billion and $5 billion which could be used to provide debt relief.

* The World Bank could cancel payments on loans and undisbursed balances of loans and credits made for projects which have proved unviable according to the Wappenhans report, subject to an independent tribunal to decide on the responsibility for project failure.

* Debt for equity swaps, already employed to reduce private and official debt, could be applied to multilateral debt, with the shareholder governments taking over the conversions to kick-start privatization schemes.

* Concessional finance (i.e. with a grant element) could be supplied to help the African Development Bank over its difficulties.[64]

Mistry is not very sanguine about the prospects of these steps being taken to relieve African countries' debts and supposes that both the IMF and the Bank will continue to operate structural adjustment programmes. In that case, Mistry has a number of recommendations to make: less rigid conditionality, larger loan size, more concessionality (i.e. a larger grant element), longer repayment periods, larger replenishments and a system of capital funding by the Bank from its reserves rather than from loans by donors.

The role of the IDA, the soft loan arm of the World Bank, will certainly need to be clarified.[65] It has become a lender of last resort, baling out the Bank with tax-payers' money, whereas it was originally intended to be a facility for the least developed countries to draw on for development programmes which would not be regarded as acceptable on ordinary commercial terms. It was because of this change of role that

NGOs, as we saw earlier, believe that the IDA should be separated legally and financially from the Bank.

Even with all these measures in place, it is Mistry's firm conviction that there will remain a huge and escalating problem of multilateral debt arrears for many low-income countries, and this is on top of the unilateral debts to private banks and governments. He concludes that the IMF and the Bank will have to depart from their insistence that they not only have preferential status in debt repayment but also exemption from default. They must be required to share responsibility with the borrowers for failed and unviable projects and programmes. It should then be easier to persuade the Paris Club of rich government donors themselves to move further towards the promise once made by a British Chancellor of the Exchequer of the forgiveness of all the least developed countries' debts.[66]

Conclusion

If we could just imagine that the four external obstacles to Africa's economic recovery and renewed development had been cleared – the ending of transfer price abuse and control over commodity markets by transnational companies, the modification of the GATT requirement of free markets in the North without a similar requirement from the South, the opening up of the international financial institutions to African opinion and African participation and the forgiveness of all foreign debts of the least developed countries, most of which are in Africa – then, it may well be asked, what could be done by Africans to take advantage of such an opportunity? Fortunately, the answer is not far to seek. The voices of Africans related throughout this book – from the grass roots of the rural areas, from the informal economy of the towns, from the cooperatives and producers' trading associations, from the pioneers of new and emerging technologies, from African writers, scientists and economists – have all at length come to be reflected in the political life of many African countries. But they need a wider focus than the narrow perspective of the nation-state.

Again, this is not lacking. The Africa-wide vision is already there – in the Lagos Plan of the Organization for African Unity (OAU) for an African Economic Community by the first decade of the new century, in the regional organizations of the north, south, east and west and in the Alternative Programme of the Economic Commission for Africa. The perspective and the proposals for action of these African bodies have been described at length in earlier chapters.[67] They have been ignored and subverted by the programmes imposed upon indebted African countries by the IMF and the World Bank. The time has come for a new start. What is needed is finance from the international institutions and national governments in the North to support regional and continent-wide initiatives. When the Bank moved from project lending – for dams and buildings – where assets would be created which would in time yield a return, to policy lending, where increased export earnings were to provide the return, it lost the right to refuse to provide loans unbacked by assets. What the Bank has now to do is to move from individual state programmes to multi-state, regional and continent-wide programmes, with joint government guarantees.

It will not happen without a great shove from public opinion in the North and united demands from the South. The statements from leading officials of the IMF and the Bank on the occasion of their fiftieth birthday revealed that they were aware of the rising tide of criticism against their high-handed, bureaucratic and secretive ways of working. The pressure has to be kept up. The financial institutions show no sign of recognizing the failure of their basic assumptions about the efficacy of the free market without extensive regulation and complementary provision by the public sector. They regret the fact that the health and education of children must suffer if their policies of reducing state power are rigorously applied, yet do not recognize that this must invalidate the whole exercise. They seem to be caught in a time warp with the doctrines and shibboleths of the Thatcher and Reagan era, which are now widely discredited. In their programmes they appear to have learnt nothing from the success in East Asia of demand and supply planning by government, within the framework of a mixed economy, despite the reports of the Bank's own technical consultants.[68]

Although Africa's crisis is grave indeed, the present conjuncture of events gives grounds for hope. Democratic forces are widely at work in Africa, bringing to an end the monopolization of power by autocrats and tyrants. Even the repulsive apartheid regime in South Africa is ended and a democratic republic is being born. There is everywhere in Africa support for new thinking about the mixed economy which rejects the old polarization of planning and the market.[69] New forms of cooperation are emerging in production and service industries.

Outside Africa, in the rich countries, there are many groups of people which are becoming frightened at the results of growing inequalities, in the outbreaks of violence and war, of terrorism and neo-fascism. They are worried also at the results of an unregulated market in the increase of pollution, the depletion of minerals and fuel resources, the destruction of the forests and the general disturbance of the planet's ecology.[70] At the same time, they are anxious to do something to respond to these developments through campaigning, green living and fair trading. There is a growing understanding that African ideas and customs are different but are equally valid, in African conditions superior, to those more familiar in Europe.

There is more to this conjuncture than fear and anxiety. The end of the cold war has loosened the restraints on radical actions and opened up minds to creative thinking. Those who thought that with the end of the arms race nothing need be changed – the market would solve everything – have found that they were wrong; those who thought that nothing could change unless everything was changed – the whole market ideology overturned – have seen that some things can be changed, even within the market. There is a place for self-reliance without isolation from the rest of the world. If regional groupings tend to give advantage to the leading country in each region, they need the counterbalance of an international order. The failure of Keynes's vision fifty years ago should not be cause for discouragement, but incentive to do better. The optimism of Chinua Achebe and his colleagues in the 'Beyond Hunger Project: Africa in 2057' has a firm philosophical foundation:

Contrary to the conventional wisdom which assumes a unilinear trend, the alternative future histories incorporate a dialectic movement, i.e. the notion that crisis and decline spur change and improvement.[71]

That is a lesson for us all to learn – in the North and in the South.

INTRODUCTION

1. Adebayo Adedeji, lecture in Kaduna, Nigeria, reported in *West Africa*, 11–17 November 1991.
2. Basil Davidson, *The Black Man's Burden: Africa and the Curse of the Nation-State*, James Currey, 1992.
3. *The Vampire State in Africa* is the title of J.H. Frimpong-Ansah's study of 'The Political Economy of Decline in Ghana', James Currey, 1992.
4. Dele Olowu, quoted in Davidson, *op. cit.*, p. 314.
5. Roland Oliver, *The African Experience*, Weidenfeld & Nicolson, 1991, p. 264.
6. Ralph G. Saylor, *The Economic System of Sierra Leone*, Duke University Press, North Carolina, 1967, and R.H. Green and S.H. Hymer, 'Cocoa in the Gold Coast: A Study in the Relations between African Farmers and Agricultural Experts', *Journal of Economic History*, XXVI (September 1966), both reviewed by Edward F. Douglass in FAO/FFHC, *Ideas and Action*, Rome, no. 112 (1976), pp. 16–20.
7. Ngugi wa Thiong'o, quoted in 'Culture and Rural Development', FAO/FFHC *Ideas and Action*, Rome, 1983, p. 28, and for similar stories see Preben Kaarsholm (ed.), *Culture and Development in Southern Africa*, James Currey, 1992.
8. Amilcar Cabral, 'The Role of Culture in Liberation Struggle', address to a UNESCO conference, Paris, 3–7 July, 1972, edited by LSM Information Centre.
9. M. Carnoy, *Education as Cultural Imperialism*, quoted in Ettore Gelpi (head of UNESCO's Lifelong Education Unit), *A Future for Lifelong Education*, trans. Ralph Ruddock, Manchester University Press 1979, pp. 28–9.
10. E.S. Ndione, *Le Don et le recours ressorts de l'économie urbaine*, ENDA, Dakar, 1992.
11. F.R. Mahieu, *Les Fondements de la crise économique en Afrique*, L'Harmattan, Paris, 1990.
12. Hassan Zaoual, 'The Economy and the Symbolic Sites of Africa', *South-North Network: Cultures and Development*, Interculture, Brussels, 27:122 (Winter 1994).

13. Ramgopal Agarwala, Preface to World Bank, Long-Term Perspective Study (LTPS) Background Papers, 1990.

14. This was published as M. Barratt Brown and Pauline Tiffen, *Short Changed: Africa and World Trade*, Pluto Press, 1992.

15. G.A. Cornia, R. van der Hoeven and T. Mkandawire, *Africa's Recovery in the 1990s*, Geneva, 1992.

16. Zafor Ahmed, in World Bank, LTPS, *Sub-Saharan Africa: From Crisis to Sustainable Growth*, (LTPS), Background Papers, vol. 3, Washington, 1989, p. 1.

17. Chinua Achebe et al. (eds), *Beyond Hunger in Africa: Africa 2057 – Conventional Wisdom and an African Vision*, James Currey, 1991.

18. UN Economic Commission for Africa, *African Alternatives to Structural Adjustment Programmes: a Framework for Transformation and Recovery*, Addis Ababa, 1989 p. 2.3.

19. See, for example, R. Cohen and H. Goulbourne (eds), *Democracy and Socialism in Africa*, Westview Press, 1991, and W. Sachs (ed), *The Development Dictionary*, Zed Books, 1992.

20. See Bill Rau, *From Feast to Famine: Official Cures and Grass roots Remedies to Africa's Food Crisis*, Zed Books, 1991.

21. See Basil Davidson, *Can Africa Survive?*, Little, Brown, 1974, and Laurence Cockcroft, *Africa's Way: Journey from the Past*, I.B. Taurus, 1991.

22. Quoted by Marc Nerfin, *IFDA Dossier*, Geneva, 13 September 1991.

23. See Dan Smith, 'Conflict and War' in Susan George, *The Debt Boomerang: How Third World Debt Harms US All*, Pluto Press, 1992.

24. Barratt Brown and Tiffen, *op. cit.*, Chapter 8.

25. M. Barratt Brown, *Fair Trade: Reforming the International Trading System*, Zed Books, 1993, Chapter 12.

26. See, for example, Olusegun Obasanjo, one-time president of Nigeria, quoted in *West Africa*, 7–13 May 1990.

27. Karl Marx and Friedrich Engels, *The Communist Manifesto*, 1848.

28. Barratt Brown and Tiffen, *op. cit.*, Chapter 2.

CHAPTER 1. HOW OLD IS AFRICA'S CRISIS?

1. Quoted in FAO/FFHC, *Ideas and Action*, Rome, no. 89 (1973).

2. Barratt Brown and Tiffen, *Short Changed, op. cit.*, pp. 2–3 and Table A.7.

3. Dr Alexander Yeats, *On the Accuracy of Observations: Do Sub-Saharan Statistics Mean Anything?*, quoted in Barratt Brown and Tiffen, *op. cit.*, p. 2.

4. Paul Harrison, *The Greening of Africa*, Paladin, 1987, pp. 33–4.

5. Lloyd Timberlake, *Africa in Crisis*, Earthscan, 1991, p. 76.

6. Barratt Brown and Tiffen, *op. cit.*, p. 24.

7. World Bank, *Sub-Saharan Africa: From Crisis to Sustainable Growth*, (LTPS), *op. cit.*, p. 3.

8. UN Economic Commission for Africa, *Statistics and Policies: ECA Preliminary*

Observations on the World Bank Report: Africa's Adjustment and Growth in the 1980s, quoted in Barratt Brown and Tiffen, *op. cit.*, p. 139.

9. See Bade Onimode, *A Political Economy of the African Crisis*, Zed Books, 1988, pp. 12–13.

10. Professor H.E. Egerton, *British Colonial Policy in the XXth Century*, quoted in Davidson, *Black Man's Burden*, *op. cit.*, p. 66.

11. Professor H.R. Trevor-Roper (Lord Dacre), quoted in Davidson, *op. cit.*, p. 92.

12. Basil Davidson, *Discovering Africa's Past*, Longman, 1978, p. 36.

13. Martin Bernal, *Black Athena: The Afro-Asiatic Roots of Classical Civilization*, Free Association Books, 1987.

14. Basil Davidson, *Discovering Africa's Past*, *op. cit.*, p. 113.

15. Rau, *From Feast to Famine*, *op. cit.*, Chapter 10.

16. Basil Davidson, *Black Man's Burden*, *op. cit.*, p. 58.

17. *ibid.*, p. 61.

18. Maya Jaggi, 'The Riddler Revealed', *Guardian*, 25 September 1993.

19. Davidson, *Black Man's Burden*, *op. cit.*, p. 86.

20. *ibid.*, p. 60.

21. Basil Davidson, *Black Mother: The African Slave Trade Revisited*, Little, Brown, 1980.

22. Mai Palmberg (ed.), *The Struggle for Africa*, Zed Books, 1983, p. 7.

23. Bade Onimode, *op. cit.*, p. 15.

24. Davidson, *Black Man's Burden*, *op. cit.*, Chapter 1.˙

25. *ibid.*, p. 88.

26. Rau, *op. cit.*, p. 31.

27. T.O. Ranger, 'African Initiatives and Resistance in the Face of Partition and Conquest' quoted in Rau, *op. cit.*, p. 32.

28. T.O. Ranger, 'The Invention of Tradition in Colonial Africa' in E.J. Hobsbawm, *The Invention of Tradition*, Cambridge, 1983.

29. Davidson, *Black Man's Burden*, *op. cit.*, p. 45.

30. *ibid.*, p. 39.

31. *ibid.*, p. 45.

32. *ibid.*, p. 103.

33. David Kimble, *Political History of Ghana: The Rise of Gold Coast Nationalism, 1850–1928*, quoted in Davidson, *Black Man's Burden*, *op. cit.*, p. 103.

34. E.A. Ayandele, *The Educational Elite in the Nigerian Society*, quoted in Davidson, *Black Man's Burden*, *op. cit.*, p. 168.

35. Lord Hailey, *An African Survey*, Oxford, 1945, pp. 1751–3.

36. Samir Amin, *Neo-Colonialism in West Africa*, Penguin, 1973, pp. xvi–xvii.

37. Davidson, *Black Man's Burden*, *op. cit.*, pp. 65–6.

38. E.H. Norman, *Japan's Emergence as a Modern State*, Institute of Pacific Relations, 1940.

39. Peter Madden, *A Raw Deal: Trade and the World's Poor*, Christian Aid, 1992, p. 41.

40. Barratt Brown and Tiffen, *op. cit.*, pp. 21–2.

41. Argiri Emmanuel, 'White Settler Colonialism and the Myth of Investor Imperialism' discussed in M. Barratt Brown, *Economics of Imperialism*, Penguin, 1974, pp. 197–8.

42. Samir Amin, 'Underdevelopment and Dependence in Black Africa: Origins and Contemporary Forms' quoted in Onimode, *op. cit.*, p. 324.

43. E.D. Morel, *Red Rubber: The Story of the Rubber Slave Trade which Flourished in the Congo for Twenty Years, 1890–1910*, quoted in Rau, *op. cit.*, pp. 36–7.

44. Rau, *op. cit.*, p. 40 and Basil Davidson, *In the Eye of the Storm: Angola's People*, Heinemann, 1972, *passim*.

45. Barratt Brown and Tiffen, *op. cit.* pp. 21ff. and Table A. 6.

46. *ibid.*, p. 23.

47. Dele Olowu and James S. Wunsch (eds), *The Failure of the Centralized State: Institutions and Self-Governance in Africa*, Westview Press, 1990, p. 35.

48. Barratt Brown and Tiffen, *op. cit.*, Table A. 1.

49. Davidson, *Black Man's Burden, op. cit.*, p. 180.

50. Elie Kedourie, *Nationalism*, Hutchinson, 1960, Chapter 2.

51. James M. Blaut, *The National Question*, Zed Books, 1987, p. 25.

52. Davidson, *Black Man's Burden, op. cit.*, p. 73.

53. *ibid.*, pp. 100–101.

54. Peter P. Ekeh, 'Social Anthropology and Two Contrasting Uses of Tribalism' quoted in Davidson, *op. cit.*, p. 226.

55. G. Lanning and M. Mueller, *Africa Undermined*, Penguin, 1979, pp. 61–3.

56. Olowu and Wunsch, *op. cit.*, p. 24.

57. Giovanni Arrighi and John S. Saul, *Essays on the Political Economy of Africa*, quoted in Olowu and Wunsch, *op. cit.*, p. 131.

58. Chris Allen et al., *Benin, The Congo, Burkina Faso*, quoted by Davidson, *op. cit.*, p. 206.

59. Olowu and Wunsch, *op. cit.*, p. 27.

60. *ibid.*, p. 31.

61. *ibid.*, pp. 66–7.

62. E.A. Wrigley, 'London's Importance, 1650–1750' quoted in M. Barratt Brown, *What Economics is About*, Weidenfeld & Nicolson, 1970, p. 66.

63. Frantz Fanon, *The Wretched of the Earth*, McGibbon and Kee, 1965, pp. 140ff.

64. Olowu and Wunsch, *op. cit.*, p. 67.

CHAPTER 2. ALTERNATIVE GROWTH MODELS IN THE POST-COLONIAL STATE

1. Quoted in Olowu and Wunsch, *The Failure of the Centralised State, op. cit.*, p. 246.

2. *ibid.* pp. 61 and 208.

3. Barry Munslow (ed.), *Africa: Problems in the Transition to Socialism*, Zed Books, 1986, pp. 31–3.

4. Olowu and Wunsch, *op. cit.*, p. 105.

5. *ibid.*, pp. 107ff.

6. Edward Marcus, 'The Economic Role of Government in Independent Tropical Africa' quoted in Olowu and Wunsch, *op. cit.*, p. 105.

7. *ibid.*, p. 45.

8. *ibid.*, pp. 107ff.

9. Munslow, *op. cit.*, p. 32.

10. J.F. Rweyemamu (ed.), *Industrialization and Income Distribution in Africa*, Zed, 1980, Tables on pp. 153 and 154.

11. Michael Lipton, *Why Poor People Stay Poor*, Temple Smith, 1977, p. 227 and Table 5.3.

12. Olowu and Wunsch, *op. cit.*, pp. 116–7.

13. International Labour Office, *First Things First: Meeting the Basic Needs of the People of Nigeria*, quoted in Olowu and Wunsch, *op. cit.*, p. 212.

14. Alkasum Abba et al., *The Nigerian Crisis: Causes and Solutions*, Academic Staff Union, Universities of Nigeria, Press Zaria, 1985, p. 27.

15. Olowu and Wunsch, *op. cit.*, p. 210.

16. Abba et al., *op. cit.*, p. 13.

17. *ibid.*, pp. 161–4.

18. W.W. Rostow, *The Stages of Economic Growth: A Non-Communist Manifesto*, Cambridge, 1960, pp. 1 and 106.

19. Wolfgang Sachs, Introduction, Sachs, *The Development Dictionary*, *op. cit.*

20. Rostow, *op. cit.*, p. 4.

21. Marx and Engels, *Manifesto of the Communist Party*, *op. cit.*, first edition, 1848, Part I, 'Bourgeois and Proletarians'.

22. Basil Davidson, *Can Africa Survive?*, *op. cit.*, p. 74.

23. Rostow, *op. cit.*, p. 112.

24. *ibid.*, pp. 7–8.

25. *ibid.*, p. 26.

26. *ibid.*, p. 39.

27. Basil Davidson, 'Africa: the Politics of Failure' in R. Miliband and L. Panitch, *The Socialist Register, 1992*, Merlin Press, 1992, p. 217.

28. World Bank, *Sub-Saharan Africa: From Crisis to Sustainable Growth*, (LTPS), *op. cit.*, Table 2.

29. Rostow, *op. cit.*, p. 8.

30. Issa G. Shivji, 'Tanzania: the Debate on Delinking' in Azzam Mahjoub (ed.), *Adjustment or Delinking*, Zed Books, 1990, p. 50.

31. *ibid.*, p. 51.

32. Issa G. Shivji, *Class Struggle in Tanzania*, Tanzania Publishing House, 1975, p. 79.

33. Phil Raikes, 'The Agricultural Sector' in Jannik Boesen et al. (eds),

Tanzania: Crisis and Struggle for Survival, Scandinavian Institute of African Studies, Uppsala, 1986, pp. 116ff.

34. Rune Skarstein, 'Growth and Crisis in the Manufacturing Sector' in Boesen, *op. cit.*, pp. 82–3.

35. Shivji, *op. cit.*, p. 79.

36. Julius K. Nyerere, *Freedom and Development*, Oxford, 1973, p. 277.

37. Skarstein, *op. cit.*, p. 82.

38. *ibid.*, p. 83.

39. Andrew Coulson, *Tanzania: A Political Economy*, Oxford, 1982, pp. 235ff.

40. Julius K. Nyerere, interview with *Third World Quarterly*, quoted in Olowu and Wunsch, *op. cit.*, p. 80.

41. P.J. Baran and E.J. Hobsbawm, reviewing Rostow, quoted in Davidson, *Can Africa Survive?, op. cit.*, p. 75.

42. Barratt Brown and Tiffen, *op. cit.*, Chapter 9, pp. 124ff.

43. Kwesi Krafona, Introduction, Kwesi Krafona (ed.), *Organization of African Unity: Twenty-five Years On, Essays in Honour of Kwame Nkrumah*, Afroworld, 1988.

44. Barratt Brown and Tiffen, *op. cit.*, pp. 4–5 and 17.

45. *ibid.*, Table 1.1, and UNCTAD *Statistical Pocket Book*, New York, 1989, Table 3.2.

46. Martyn A.R. Ngwenya, 'The African Debt Crisis' in Krafona, *op. cit.*, p. 29.

47. Barratt Brown and Tiffen, *op. cit.*, Table A.33.

48. *ibid.*, Table A.34.

49. Belinda Coote, *The Trade Trap*, Oxfam, 1992, Chapter 1.

50. Barratt Brown and Tiffen, *op. cit.*, Table A.40.

51. *ibid.*, pp. 51–2.

52. Unpublished paper by Robert Castley, Manchester University Institute for Development Policy and Management, and Ho Joon Chang, *The Political Economy of Industrial Policy*, Macmillan, 1993.

53. Barratt Brown, *Economics of Imperialism, op. cit.*, Table 3.

CHAPTER 3. REDISTRIBUTION AND BASIC NEEDS

1. Basil Davidson, *Can Africa Survive?, op. cit.*, p. 182.

2. UNCTAD, *Handbook of International Trade and Development Statistics, 1991*, Tables 6.1 and 6.2.

3. R. Jolly and G. Cornia, *The Impact of World Recession on Children*, Pergamon, 1984.

4. World Bank, *World Development Report, 1991*, Table 31, 'Urbanization'.

5. Ben Wisner, *Power and Need in Africa: Basic Human Needs and Development Policies*, Earthscan, 1988, p. 65.

6. *ibid.*, p. 63–4.

7. H. Chenery et al., *Redistribution with Growth*, Oxford, 1974.

8. Frances Stewart, *Technology and Underdevelopment*, Macmillan, 1977, p. 43.

9. International Labour Office, *Employment, Incomes and Equality: A Strategy for Increasing Productive Employment in Kenya*, Geneva, 1972.

10. UNCTAD, *op. cit.*, Table 6.10.

11. J. Grace and J. Laffin, *Africa since 1960*, Fontana, 1991, pp. 165–6.

12. Basil Davidson, *Africa in Modern History*, Allen Lane, 1978, p. 199.

13. Grace and Laffin, *op. cit.*, pp. 168–9.

14. Nicola Swainson, 'The Rise of a National Bourgeoisie in Kenya', Gavin Kitching, 'Modes of Production in Kenya and Dependency' and Stephen Langdon, 'The State and Capitalism in Kenya', in *Review of African Political Economy*, no. 8 (1977).

15. World Bank, *Recent Trends and Prospects for Agricultural Commodity Exports in Sub-Saharan Africa*, Working Paper S. 348, Washington, 1989, pp. 33–9.

16. Colin Leys, *Underdevelopment in Kenya: The Political Economy of Neo-Colonialism*, Heinemann, 1975, p. 220.

17. Wisner, *op. cit.*, p. 170 and ILO, *op. cit.*, pp. 345–53.

18. Leys, *op. cit.*, pp. 36ff.

19. Wisner, *op. cit.*, pp. 177ff.

20. Leys, *op. cit.*, p. 265.

21. ILO, *op. cit.*, pp. 11–12.

22. *ibid.*, p. 97.

23. *ibid.*, p. 25.

24. *ibid.*, pp. 62ff.

25. Leys, *op. cit.*, pp. 261–2.

26. *ibid.*, p. 262.

27. ILO, *op. cit.*, pp. 327–9.

28. Leys, *op. cit.*, p. 270, quoting the Kenyan government's Sessional Paper No. 10 of 1965.

29. *ibid.*, p. 274.

30. *ibid.*, p. 270.

31. ILO, *op. cit.*, p. 5.

32. *ibid.*, pp. 223ff.

33. Leys, *op. cit.*, p. 268.

34. ILO, *op. cit.*, p. 259 and Leys, *op. cit.*, p. 268 and for the critics see Nicola Swainson, *op. cit.*, pp. 40–14.

35. Wisner, *op. cit.*, p. 22.

36. *ibid.*, p. 23, taken from C. Haub et al., *World's Women Data Sheet*, UNICEF, 1980.

37. *ibid.*, pp. 33–4.

38. *ibid.*, p. 35.

39. R. Green, 'Basic Human Needs: Concept or Slogan, Synthesis or Smokescreen?', *IDS Bulletin*, 9:4 (June 1978), pp. 7–11 and R. King, 'Cooperative Policy and Village Development in Northern Nigeria' in J. Heyer et al. (eds),

Rural Development in Tropical Africa, St Martin's Press, New York, 1981, pp. 259–80.

40.   Frances Stewart, *Planning to Meet Basic Needs*, Macmillan, 1985.

41.   Wisner, *op. cit.*, p. 165.

42.   *ibid.*, p. 285.

43.   Judith Tendler, 'Turning Private Voluntary Organizations into Development Agencies: Questions for Evaluation', USAID Discussion Paper, April 1982.

44.   Wisner, *op. cit.*, p. 124.

45.   M. Hollsteiner, 'The Participatory Imperative in Primary Health Care', quoted in *ibid.*, p. 124.

46.   Quoted in *ibid.*, p. 125.

47.   J. Bugnicourt, 'Popular Participation in Development in Africa', quoted in *ibid.*, p. 125.

48.   G. Higgins et al., *Potential Population Supporting Capacities of Lands in the Developing Countries*, FAO, Rome, 1984.

49.   World Bank, *World Development Report, 1984*, Washington, 1984.

50.   J. Grant, *The State of the World's Children, 1984*, UNICEF, New York, 1985.

51.   J. Clark, *Democratic Development: The Role of Voluntary Organizations*, Earthscan, 1991, p. 120.

52.   Quoted in Wisner, *op. cit.*, p. 295.

53.   David Siddle and Ken Swindell, *Rural Change in Tropical Africa*, Blackwell, 1990, pp. 15–23.

CHAPTER 4. STRUCTURAL ADJUSTMENT – BY THE WORLD BANK

1.   Edward (Kim) Jaycox, reported in World Bank, *Africa Update*, quoted by Ben Turok in Bade Onimode (ed.), *The African Response: Adjustment or Transformation*, IFAA, 1992, p. 47.

2.   Paul Mosley et al., *Aid and Power: The World Bank and Policy-based Lending*, vol. 1, Routledge, 1991, p. 23.

3.   Robert Liebenthal, 'Adjustment in Low Income Africa, 1974–1978', quoted in Fantu Cheru, *The Silent Revolution in Africa*, Zed Books, 1989, p. 7.

4.   Samir Amin, 'A Critique of the World Bank Report, entitled "Accelerated Development in Sub-Saharan Africa"', *Africa Development*, Dakar, VII (1982).

5.   World Bank, *Accelerated Development in Sub-Saharan Africa: An Agenda for Action*, the Berg Report, Washington, 1981, Chapters 4 and 5.

6.   Mosley et al., *op. cit*, p. 299.

7.   Bjorn Beckman, 'Whose State? State and Capitalist Development in Nigeria' in *Review of African Political Economy*, no. 23 (1982), pp. 48–50.

8.   Barbara Dinham and Colin Hines, *Agribusiness in Africa*, Earth Resources Research, 258 Pentonville Road, London N1 9JY, Chapter 6.

9. UNCTAD, *Commodity Yearbook, 1991*, New York, 1992, Tables 1.7 and A.1.

10. Frances Moore Lappé and Joseph Collins, *Food First*, Abacus, 1982, Part 10.

11. FAO, *Yearbook: Production, 1990*, Rome, Table 1 and Crop Tables and for earlier years see Barratt Brown and Tiffen, *Short Changed, op. cit.*, p. 24.

12. UNCTAD, *Handbook, 1991, op. cit.*, Table 6.5.

13. N. Shanmugaratnam, 'Development and Environment: A View from the South', *Race and Class*, Jan–March 1989, p. 29.

14. Lipton, *Why Poor People Stay Poor, op. cit.*, Tables 5.1 and 5.2.

15. Annar Cassam, 'The Invisible Woman' in Mohamed Suliman (ed.), *Alternative Strategies for Africa, vol. 2, Environment and Women*, IFAA, 1991, pp. 113ff.

16. World Bank. *Annual Report, 1988*, Washington, p. 22.

17. Mosley et al., *op. cit.*, pp. 36–7.

18. Onimode, *A Political Economy of the African Crisis, op. cit.*, p. 288.

19. Bade Onimode, 'IMF and World Bank Programmes in Africa' in Bade Onimode (ed.), *The IMF, the World Bank and the African Debt, Vol. 1: The Economic Impact*, Zed Books, 1989.

20. John Toye, 'Ghana Case Study' in Mosley et al., *op. cit., Vol. 2: Case Studies*, pp. 158–9.

21. Laurence Cockcroft and Roger C. Riddell, *Foreign Direct Investment in Sub-Saharan Africa*, ODI, London, 1990, p. 17.

22. J.L.S. Abbey, 'Ghana's Experience with Structural Adjustment' in James Pickett and Hans Singer (eds), *Towards Economic Recovery in Sub-Saharan Africa*, Routledge, 1990, p. 32.

23. James Pickett and Hans Singer, 'Towards Economic Recovery in Sub-Saharan Africa', in Pickett and Singer, *op. cit.*, pp. 13–14.

24. Toye in Mosley et al., *op. cit.*, p. 151.

25. Frimpong-Ansah, *The Vampire State in Africa, op. cit.*, pp. 141–2 and p. 146.

26. *ibid.*, title page and p. 148.

27. Abbey in Hans and Singer, *op. cit.*, pp. 33–4.

28. Frimpong-Ansah, *op. cit.*, p. 146.

29. World Bank, Working Paper S (WPS). 348, *op. cit.*, pp. 35ff.

30. Frimpong-Ansah, *op. cit.*, p. 142 and Toye in Mosley et al., *op. cit.*, p. 168.

31. Frimpong-Ansah, *op. cit.*, p. 69.

32. *ibid.*, p. 66.

33. Kwame Nkrumah, *Africa Must Unite*, International Publishers, 1963, p. xiii.

34. Arthur Lewis, Colonial Economic Advisory Committee *Minutes*, quoted in Frimpong-Ansah, *op. cit.*, p. 26.

35.   *ibid.*, p. 27.

36.   Kwame Nkrumah, *Autobiography*, Panaf Books, 1973, p. 179.

37.   Eboe Hutchbull (ed.), *The IMF and Ghana: The Confidential Record*, Zed Books, 1987, p. 7 and pp. 145ff.

38.   Jitendra Mohan, 'Varieties of African Socialism' in R. Miliband and J. Savile, *The Socialist Register, 1965*, Merlin 1966, pp. 256ff.

39.   Frimpong-Ansah, *op. cit.*, p. 48.

40.   *ibid.*, p. 85.

41.   *ibid.*, p. 86.

42.   *ibid.*, pp. 110–11 and Toye in Mosley et al., *op. cit.*, p. 152.

43.   *ibid.*, p. 112.

44.   Zaya Yeebo, *Ghana: The Struggle for Popular Power*, New Beacon Books, 1992, pp. 74–5.

45.   *ibid.*, p. 79.

46.   *ibid.*, p. 81.

47.   UNCTAD, *op. cit.*, Table 6.2.

48.   Toye in Mosley et al., *op. cit.*, p. 157.

49.   *ibid.*, p. 168.

50.   Frimpong-Ansah, *op. cit.*, p. 151, quoting a paper by D.M. Newbery, given at the University of Warwick, April 1989.

51.   Frimpong-Ansah, *op. cit.*, p. 142.

52.   Toye in Mosley et al., *op. cit.*, pp. 174ff.

53.   *ibid.*, p. 169.

54.   *ibid.*, p. 193.

55.   *ibid.*, p. 187.

56.   Karl Marx's comment on Napoleon III, applied to Flight-Lieutenant Rawlings by Zaya Yeebo, *op. cit.*, p. 282.

57.   TWIN reports, 1993, available from 5–11 Worship Street, London EC2A 2BH.

58.   Quoted by Leslie Crawford, *Financial Times*, Ghana survey, 27 July 1993.

59.   *ibid.*

60.   *ibid.*

61.   UNCTAD, *op. cit.*, Table 5.14.

62.   Toye in Mosley et al., *op. cit.*, p. 167.

63.   *ibid.*, p. 192

64.   UNCTAD, *Commodity Yearbook, 1994*, New York Table A.1.

65.   Toye in Mosley et al., *op. cit.*, p. 196.

66.   Barratt Brown and Tiffen, *op. cit.*, especially Chapter 10.

67.   *ibid.*, Chapters 4 and 5.

68.   *ibid.*, Chapter 6.

69.   *ibid.*, p. iii.

70.   Cockcroft and Riddell, *op. cit.*, quoted in *ibid.*, p. 134.

71.   Mosley et al., *op. cit.*, vol.1., p. 199.

72. *ibid.*, p. 194.

73. World Bank, *Africa's Adjustment* and *Growth in the 1980s*, and UN Economic Commission for Africa, *Statistics and Policies: ECA Preliminary Observations on the World Bank Report, Africa's Adjustment and Growth in the 1980s*, quoted in Barratt Brown and Tiffen, *op. cit.*, p. 139.

74. 'Soak the Poor', *Economist*, London, 12 October 1991.

75. Onimode, *A Political Economy of the African Crisis, op. cit.*, Chapter 4.

76. Quoted in Timberlake, *Africa in Crisis, op. cit.*, p. 176.

CHAPTER 5. CRISIS MANAGEMENT: COMMODITY EXPORTS AND
DEBT

1. World Bank, *Africa's Adjustment and Growth in the 1980s*, Washington, 1989.

2. UN Secretary-General's Expert Group, *Africa's Commodity Problems: Towards a Solution* (the Fraser Report), New York, 1990.

3. S. Tomori, 'Towards a Solution to Africa's Commodity Problems: A Comment' in Onimode (ed.), *The African Response: Adjustment or Transformation, op. cit.*, p. 146.

4. Fraser Report, p. 36.

5. *ibid.*, p. 35.

6. *ibid.*, p. 30.

7. UNCTAD, *Handbook of International Trade and Statistics, 1993*, New York, Table 5.14.

8. Edward (Kim) Jaycox, quoted in Picket and Singer, *Towards Recovery in Sub-Saharan Africa, op. cit.*, p. 40.

9. Abbey in Pickett and Singer, *op. cit.*, p. 41.

10. 'Soak the Poor', *Economist*, 12 October 1991.

11. Fraser Report, *op. cit.*, pp. 83–7.

12. John Madeley, *Trade and the Poor: The Impact of International Trade on Developing Countries*, Intermediate Technology, 1992, p. 125.

13. Abbey in Pickett and Singer, *op. cit.*, pp. 40–1.

14. A.A. Dirar, 'The Fraser Report and the OAU Position' in Onimode (ed.), *The African Response, op. cit.*, p. 153.

15. Barratt Brown and Tiffen, *Short Changed, op. cit.*, p. 140, quoting from UN Centre on Transnational Corporations, *World Investment Report*, 1991, p. 28 and UN Centre on Transnational Corporations, *World Investment Report*, 1992, New York, 1992.

16. Cockcroft and Riddell, *Foreign Direct Investment, op. cit.*, pp. 14–15.

17. Fraser Report, *op. cit.*, p. 87.

18. *ibid.*, p. 31.

19. World Bank, *World Development Report, 1991*, Washington, p. 108.

20. World Bank, *World Development Report, 1992*, Washington, p. 308.

21. Magnus Blomstroem, *Transnational Corporations and Manufacturing Exports* *from Developing Countries*, UN Center on Transnational Corporations, New York, 1990, Table 3.1.

22. UNCTAD, *UNCTAD VIII: Analytical Report by the Secretariat to the Conference*, New York, 1992, p. 228.

23. World Bank, *Report, 1991*, p. 107.

24. *ibid.*, p. 106.

25. Barratt Brown and Tiffen, *op. cit.*, p. 27.

26. World Bank, *Adjustment in Africa: Reforms, Results and the Road Ahead*, Oxford, 1994, pp. 2, 3, 4 and 214.

27. World Bank, *Report, 1991*, *op cit.*, Table 24.

28. Percy S. Mistry, 'Africa's Adjustment and the External Debt Problem' in IMF, *Policies for African Development*, Washington, 1992, pp. 119–120

29. World Bank, *op. cit., 1991*, p. 125.

30. W. Wapenhans (ed.), *Report of a Task Force on Portfolio Management*, World Bank, Washington, 1992, pages of Report indicated in the text.

31. World Bank, *op. cit., 1991*, Debt Tables, pp. 240–8.

32. Percy Mistry, *op. cit.*, p. 121.

33. Jane Harrigan, 'Malawi' in Mosley et al., *Aid and Power, op. cit., vol. 2*, p. 201.

34. UNCTAD, *Handbook 1991, op. cit.*, Tables 5.14 and 6.1.

35. Harrigan in Mosley et al., *vol. 2, op. cit.* pp. 203ff.

36. *ibid.* p. 214.

37. UNCTAD, *op. cit., 1991*, Table 5.14.

38. Harrigan in Mosley et al., *vol. 2, op. cit.*, pp. 207 and 251.

39. *ibid.* pp. 216 and 215.

40. *ibid.*, pp. 228 and 234.

41. *ibid.*, p. 261.

42. *ibid.*, p. 239.

43. *Keesing's Record of World Events*, vol. 38 (1992), Reference Supplement, R. 15.

44. Barratt Brown and Tiffen, *op. cit.*, Table A.8.

45. Jean Drèze and Amartya Sen, *Hunger and Public Action*, Oxford, 1989, pp. 20ff.

46. Timberlake, *Africa in Crisis, op. cit.*, p. 165.

47. World Bank, *op. cit., 1991*, Table 31.

48. Roy A. Carr-Hill, *Social Conditions in Sub-Saharan Africa*, Macmillan, 1990, pp. 139ff.

49. David Siddle and Ken Swindell, *Rural Change in Tropical Africa, op. cit.*, p. 15.

50. Mark Duffield, *War and Famine in Africa*, Oxfam, 1991, p. 9.

51. Maureen Mackintosh, *Gender, Class and Rural Transition: Agribusiness and the Food Crisis in Senegal*, Zed Books, 1989, pp. 102ff.

52. Cassam, in Suliman, *Alternative Strategies for Africa, op. cit.*, p. 115.

53. Duffield, *op. cit.*, p. 26.

54. Akilagpa Sawyerr, 'The Politics of Adjustment Policy' in Adebayo Adedeji et al. (eds), *The Human Dimension of Africa's Persistent Economic Crisis*, Hans Zell for Economic Commission for Africa, 1990, p. 231.

55. J-M. Camdessus, Managing Director, IMF, quoted in UNICEF *Report, 1989*, pp. 17–18.

56. Duffield, *op. cit.*, p. 29.

CHAPTER 6. THE FOUR HORSEMEN OF THE APOCALYPSE

1. Quoted in Noam Chomsky, 'The Gulf Crisis', in *Third World War*, Spokesman, 1991, p. 11.

2. References in Dan Smith, 'Conflict and War' in George, *The Debt Boomerang, op. cit.*, pp. 141–2.

3. *ibid.*, pp. 145–8.

4. R.L. Sivard, *World Military and Social Expenditure*, quoted in Smith in George, *op. cit.*, p. 151.

5. M. Barratt Brown, 'How the Debt Broke up Yugoslavia', in Ken Coates (ed.), *Peace Register, 1993: Drawing the Peace Dividend*, Spokesman, 1993, pp. 105ff.

6. Ben Turok (ed.), *Alternative Strategies for Africa: Debt and Democracy*, IFAA, 1991, pp. 83.

7. Harrison, *The Greening of Africa, op. cit.*, pp. 17–19.

8. *ibid.*, pp. 32ff., quoting Sharon Nicholson, *The Sahel: A Climatic Perspective*.

9. *ibid.*, p. 207.

10. *ibid.*, p. 221.

11. Grace and Laffin, *Africa Since 1960, op. cit.*, p. 330.

12. Safwar Fanos, 'Sudan and the IMF, 1978–83' in Bade Onimode (ed.), *The IMF, the World Bank and the African Debt*, vol. 1, *op. cit.*, p. 124.

13. *ibid.*, p. 126.

14. *ibid.*, pp. 127–8.

15. T. Barnett and A. Abdelkarim (eds), *Sudan: State Capital and Transformation*, quoted in Simon Maxwell (ed.), *To Cure All Hunger: Food Policy and Food Security in Sudan*, Intermediate Technology, 1991, p. 12.

16. Fanos in Onimode, *op. cit.*, p. 126.

17. *ibid.*, p. 138.

18. Timberlake, *op. cit.*, p. 29.

19. Maxwell, *op. cit.*, p. 5.

20. Fanos in Onimode, *op. cit.*, p. 137.

21. Barbara Dinham and Colin Hines, *Agribusiness in Africa*, Earth Resources, 1983, pp. 83–4.

22. Maxwell, *op. cit.*, pp. 5–6.

23. *ibid.*, pp. 7–8.

24. Al Abdel Gadir Ali, 'Sudan' in Adedeji et al., *The Human Dimension of Africa's Persistent Economic Crisis, op. cit.*, p. 101.

25. Drèze and Sen, *Hunger and Public Action, op. cit.*, pp. 106–9.

26. Maxwell, *op. cit.*, p. 2.

27. René Dumont, *False Start in Africa*, Earthscan, 1988, p. 60.

28. Clive Robinson, *Hungry Farmers*, Christian Aid, 1989, Chapter 6.

29. J. Seaman and A. Holt, 'Markets and Famines in the Third World' quoted in Michael Watts, 'Entitlements or Empowerment? Famine and Starvation in Africa', in *Review of African Political Economy*, no. 51 (1991), p. 22.

30. Drèze and Sen, *op. cit.*, p. 71.

31. Watts, *op. cit.*, p. 23.

32. Timberlake, *Africa in Crisis, op. cit.*, p. 76.

33. *ibid.*, p. 78.

34. Michael Horowitz, quoted in Timberlake, *ibid.*

35. Revelation 6: 2–8.

36. Phil O'Keefe, 'Women, Food and the Flight to the Cities', quoted in Timberlake, *op. cit.*, p. 164.

37. Smith in George, *op. cit.*, pp. 152–4 and Krafona (ed.), *Organisation of African Unity, op. cit*, Annexe 3, Tables of Arms Suppliers and Recipient Countries, pp. 168–75.

38. Mohamed Omer Beshir, 'Conflict and Conflict Resolution in Africa – with Special Reference to Sudan', in Krafona, *Organization of African Unity, op. cit.*, p. 138.

39. World Bank, *Report, 1991*, Washington, p. 142.

40. Claude Aké, 'The Significance of Military Rule', quoted in Julius O. Ihonvbere, 'Structural Adjustment in Nigeria', in Turok, *op. cit.*, p. 92.

41. Mosley et al., *Aid and Power, op. cit.*, vol. 1, p. 153.

42. Deepak Lal, quoted in Mosley et al., *op. cit.*, p. 145.

43. Mark Gallagher, *Rent Seeking and Economic Growth in Africa*, summarized in Barratt Brown and Tiffen, *Short Changed, op. cit.*, pp. 131–2.

44. Drèze and Sen, *Hunger and Public Action, op. cit.*, p. 275.

45. Barratt Brown and Tiffen, *op. cit.*, p. 66 and Table A.36.

46. Ibbo Mandaza, 'Perspectives on Economic Cooperation and Autonomous Development in Southern Africa' in Samir Amin et al. (eds), *SADCC: Prospects for Disengagement and Development in Southern Africa*, Zed Books, 1987, p. 225.

47. Nancy Belliveau, 'Heading Off Zaire's Default', quoted in Susan George, *A Fate Worse than Debt*, Penguin, 1988, p. 117.

48. *ibid.*

49. *ibid.*, p. 118.

50. *Keesing's Record of World Events*, vol. 39 (1993), Annual Reference Supplement, R. 25.

51. Report of UN representative Margaret Anstee, Geneva, 3 June 1993, quoted in *Keesing's Record of World Events*, vol. 39 (1993), p. 39497.

52. Overseas Development Institute (ODI), London, evidence compiled for CAFOD and other British aid agencies, published in Ken Coates (ed), *The Third World War*, Spokesman, 1991, pp. 60–61.

53. David Seddon, 'The Gulf Crisis: Counting the Cost' in *Review of African Political Economy*, no. 51 (1991), p. 81.

54. ODI, *op. cit.*, pp. 56–7.

55. Smith in George, *op. cit.*, p. 167.

CHAPTER 7. AFRICA MUST UNITE: THE ALTERNATIVE VISION

1. Kojo Botsio in Krafona (ed.), *Organisation of African Unity, op. cit.*, p. 15.

2. Basil Davidson, *Which Way Africa?*, Penguin, 1964, p. 65.

3. *ibid.*, pp. 63–4.

4. Amilcar Cabral, 'The Role of Culture in the Liberation Struggle', speech to a UNESCO conference in Paris, 3–7 July, 1972, edited and published by Liberation Support Movement, California, USA, pp. 37–8.

5. Krafona in Krafona (ed.), *op. cit.*, p. 2.

6. Kwame Nkrumah, *Africa Must Unite*, quoted in Krafona (ed), *op. cit.*, p. 1.

7. Beshir in Krafona (ed.), *ibid.*, p. 134.

8. Kwame Nkrumah, *Neo-Colonialism: The Last Stage of Imperialism*, Nelson, 1965, p. 259.

9. Davidson, *op. cit.*, p. 64.

10. Grace and Laffin, *Africa since 1960, op. cit.*, p. 136.

11. W.H. Auden, 'In Time of War: Commentary' from *Journey to a War*, Faber and Faber, 1939.

12. Davidson, *op. cit.*, p. 70.

13. Philip Ndegwa, *Africa's Development Crisis*, James Currey, 1986, pp. 48–50.

14. Lanning and Mueller, *Africa Undermined, op. cit.*, pp. 438ff.

15. Beshir in Krafona (ed.), *op. cit.*, pp. 168–75.

16. Nzolonga Ntalaja, 'The Crisis in Zaire' in *Africa's Crisis*, IFAA, 1987, pp. 7ff., and see *Keesing's*, January 1993, p. 39257.

17. Ben Turok, *Africa: What Can be Done?*, Zed Books, 1987, p. 172 and Cheru, *The Silent Revolution in Africa, op. cit.*, p. 9.

18. Hailey, *An African Survey, op. cit.*, pp. 74ff.

19. Cabral, *op. cit.*, p. 38.

20. Michael Barratt Brown, *Anatomy of Underdevelopment*, Spokesman, 1974, pp. 11 and 56.

21. John Healey and Mark Robinson, *Democracy, Governance and Economic*

Policy: *Sub-Saharan Africa in Comparative Perspective*, Overseas Development Institute, 1992, p. 15.

22. Janet MacGaffey, 'Economic Disengagement and Class Formation in Zaire' in Donald Rothchild and Naomi Chazan (eds), *The Precarious Balance: State and Society in Africa*, Westview Press, 1989, p. 175.

23. Cheru, *op. cit.*, p. 12.

24. Beshir in Krafona (ed.), *op. cit.*, p. 139.

25. Cheru, *op. cit.*, p. 9.

26. Saadia Touval, *Partitioned Africa*, quoted in Beshir in Krafona (ed.), *op. cit.*, p. 137.

27. Healey and Robinson, *op. cit.*, p. 102.

28. Mark Gallagher, *Rent Seeking and Economic Growth in Africa*, Westview Press, 1991, pp. 122 and 133.

29. Healey and Robinson, *op. cit.*, p. 59.

30. D. Rothschild and M.W. Foley, 'African States and the Politics of Inclusive Coalitions' in Rothchild and Chazan, *op. cit.*, quoted in Healey and Robinson, *op. cit.*, p. 73.

31. Healey and Robinson, *op. cit.*, p. 75.

32. *ibid.*, p. 24.

33. A. Zolberg, *Creating Political Order: The Party-States of West Africa*, quoted in *ibid.*, p. 24.

34. *ibid.*, p. 145.

35. *ibid.*, p. 129.

36. *ibid.*, pp. 140ff.

37. *ibid.*, pp. 52ff.

38. Pickett and Singer, *Towards Economic Recovery in sub-Saharan Africa*, *op. cit.*, pp. 9–10.

39. Babacar Ndiaye, 'The African Development Bank Group and Economic Development in Africa' in Krafona (ed.), *op. cit.*, p. 65.

40. M. Barratt Brown, *After Imperialism*, Preface to the second edition, Merlin Press, 1970, pp. xviii–xix.

41. Rau, *From Feast to Famine*, *op. cit.*, p. 123.

42. Cheru, *op. cit.*, p. 8.

43. OAU, *The Lagos Plan of Action for the Economic Development of Africa, 1980–2000*, ILO, Geneva, 1981, p. 128.

44. Ndegwa, *op. cit.*, p. 82.

45. Bade Onimode, *A Future for Africa: Beyond the Politics of Adjustment*, Earthscan, 1992, p. 54.

46. OAU, *op. cit.*, p. 7, quoted in Rau, *op. cit.* p. 121.

47. OAU, *op. cit.*, p. 11, quoted in Rau, *op. cit.*, p. 122.

48. R.S. Browne and R.J. Cummings, *The Lagos Plan of Action vs. the Berg Report*, quoted in Cheru, *op. cit.*, p. 18.

49. Cheru *op. cit.*, p. 15.

50. Rau, *op. cit.*, pp. 123–4.

51. Cheru, *op. cit.*, p. 19.

52. Onimode, *A Political Economy of the African Crisis*, *op. cit.*, p. 295.

CHAPTER 8. REGIONAL GROUPINGS IN AFRICA

1. H.M.A. Onitiri, 'Rationalizing African Intergovernmental Organizations for Regional Cooperation' in World Bank, LTPS, Background Papers, vol. 4, Proceedings of a Workshop on Regional Integration and Cooperation, Washington, 1990, pp. 118–19.

2. Ndegwa, *Africa's Development Crisis*, *op. cit.*, pp. 49–50.

3. Mandaza, in Amin et al., 'Perspectives', *SADCC*, *op. cit., p. 212*.

4. Dan Nabudere, quoted by Mandaza, *ibid.*, p. 213, referring to papers published in Timothy Shaw and Yash Tandon (eds.), *Regional Development at the International Level: African and Canadian Perspectives*, vol. 2, AAPS/CPSA Publications, London, 1985.

5. *ibid.*, p. 214, referring to Shaw and Tandon.

6. Thandika Mkandawire, quoted by Mandaza, *ibid.*, p. 218, from Shaw and Tandon.

7. K. Jinadu, quoted by Mandaza, *ibid.*, p. 212, from Shaw and Tandon.

8. *ibid.*, pp. 214–15.

9. PTA, *Trade and Development Strategy*, Lusaka, 1992, p. 2.

10. Barratt Brown and Tiffen, *Short Changed*, *op. cit.*, pp. 14–15.

11. Onimode, *A Future for Africa*, *op. cit.*, p. 8.

12. Rau, *From Feast to Famine*, *op. cit.*, p. 129.

13. Chandra Hardy, 'Intra-regional Trade Growth in Africa' in Frances Stewart, Sanjaya Lall and Samuel Wangwe, *Alternative Development Strategies in Sub-Saharan Africa*, Macmillan, 1992, p. 440.

14. Ann Seidman, 'The State and Multinationals' in Turok, *op. cit.*, p. 167.

15. R.H. Green, 'Economic Integration and Coordination in Africa' in Pickett and Singer, *Towards Economic Recovery in Sub-Saharan Africa*, *op. cit.*, p. 107.

16. *ibid.*

17. Hardy in Stewart, Lall and Wangwe, *op. cit.*, p. 431.

18. Teshome Mulat, 'Intra-African Trade' in Pickett and Singer, *op. cit.*, p. 161.

19. Peter Robson, 'Economic Integration in Africa: A New Phase?' in Pickett and Singer, *op. cit.*, p. 135.

20. Hardy in Stewart, Lall and Wangwe, *op. cit.*, p. 430.

21. Mulat in Pickett and Singer, *op. cit.*, p. 163.

22. Robson in Pickett and Singer, *op. cit.*, pp. 134 and 140, and Hardy in Stewart, Lall and Wangwe, *op. cit.*, p. 431 and W. Zehender, *Regional Cooperation Through Trade and Industry*, quoted in Rau, *op. cit.*, p. 129.

23. J.H. Frimpong-Ansah, 'The Prospects for Monetary Union in ECOWAS' in World Bank, LTPS: Background Paper, no. 4, *op. cit.*, pp. 52ff.

24. Hardy in Stewart, Lall and Wangwe, *op. cit.*, p. 431.

25. Robson in Pickett and Singer, *op. cit.*, pp. 134–5.

26. Barratt Brown and Tiffen, *Short Changed, op. cit.*, Tables A.1 and A.8.

27. Green in Pickett and Singer, *op. cit.*, p. 108.

28. Dominic C. Mulaisho, 'SADCC: A New Approach to Integration' in World Bank, LTPS, Background Paper, no. 4. *op. cit.*, p. 40ff.

29. Barratt Brown and Tiffen, *op. cit.*, Table A.36.

30. Mandaza in Amin et al., *op. cit.*, p. 225.

31. *ibid.*, p. 21, quoting Sam Nujoma of SWAPO.

32. Simbarashi Makoni in *Africa Report*, quoted in Rau, *op. cit.*, p. 126.

33. Green in Pickett and Singer, *op. cit.*, pp. 117–8.

34. *Economist*, 15 May 1993.

35. *Keesing's Record of World Events*, Vol. 38. (1992), p. 39042.

36. Hardy in Stewart, Lall and Wangwe, *op. cit.*, pp. 435–6.

37. Green in Pickett and Singer, *op. cit.*, pp. 118–19.

38. D. Mbilima, 'Regional Organizations in Southern Africa' in Alan Whiteside (ed.), *Industrialization and Investment Incentives in Southern Africa*, James Currey, 1989, pp. 38–41.

39. R. Davies, D. Keet and M. Nkulu, *Reconstructing Economic Relations with the Southern African Region: Issues and Options for a Democratic South Africa*, MERG, University of the Western Cape, 1993.

40. Mbilima, in Whiteside, *op. cit.*, pp. 41–3.

41. John W.T. Otieno, 'The Experience of the African Development Bank in Financing Regional Integration Projects in Africa' in World Bank, LTPS, Background Papers, vol. 4, *op. cit.*, pp. 142–3.

42. Cheru, *op. cit.*, pp. 138–40.

43. Green in Pickett and Singer, *op. cit.*, pp. 127–8.

44. *ibid.*, p. 124.

45. Mulat in Pickett and Singer, *op. cit.*, p. 161.

46. Green in Pickett and Singer, *op. cit.*, p. 125.

47. Samuel Wangwe, 'A Comparative Analysis of the PTA and SADCC Approaches to Regional Economic Integration' in World Bank, LTPS, Background Papers, vol. 4, p. 37.

48. Hardy in Stewart, Lall and Wangwe, *op. cit.*, p. 442.

49. M. Barratt Brown, *Fair Trade, op. cit.*, pp. 128–9.

50. Barratt Brown and Tiffen, *op. cit.*, Chart 3.2.

51. Andreas Goseco, 'A Supplementary Payments Mechanism to Promote Trade among Developing Countries: A Proposal to the ECA, 1964', *Indian Journal for Agricultural Economics*, 19:2 (1967).

52. See Barratt Brown, *Fair Trade, op. cit.*, pp. 148–50.

CHAPTER 9. COMMON DEFENCE OF COMMON RESOURCES

1. Barratt Brown, *Anatomy of Underdevelopment*, op. cit., pp. 11 and 56.

2. *ibid.*, pp. 2–3.

3. *ibid.*, pp. 4–5.

4. Barratt Brown, *Fair Trade*. op. cit., pp. 79–84.

5. Gamani Corea, *Taming Commodity Markets: The Integrated Programme and the Common Fund in UNCTAD*, Manchester, 1992, pp. 27 and 35.

6. *ibid.*, pp. 36–41.

7. *ibid.*, pp. 90ff.

8. *ibid.*, p. 105.

9. *ibid.*, p. 86.

10. *ibid.*, p. 43.

11. *ibid.*, pp. 251–3.

12. Judith Hart, *Aid and Liberation*, Gollancz, 1973, pp. 273–6.

13. Barratt Brown, *Fair Trade*, op. cit., pp. 106–7.

14. Onimode, *A Future for Africa*, op. cit., pp. 140–1.

15. *ibid.*, pp. 46–7.

16. Corea, *op. cit.*, p. 147.

17. UNCTAD, *Prospects For The World Cocoa Market Until the Year 2005*, New York, 1991, p. 2.

18. Barratt Brown and Tiffen, *Short Changed*, op. cit., p. 50.

19. *ibid.*, pp. 44–5.

20. UNCTAD, *Commodity Yearbook, 1993*, Table A.1, and *Financial Times*, 12 March 1993.

21. Kenneth Dadzie, 'Introduction' to UNCTAD, *Trade and Development Report, 1989*, quoted in Barratt Brown, *Fair Trade*, op. cit., p. 94.

22. Editorial, *South*, June 1987.

23. UNCTAD, *International Agreement on Jute and Jute Products, 1989*, New York, 1990, Articles 1 and 22–24.

24. Barratt Brown, *op. cit.*, p. 56.

25. TWIN Reports received by author.

26. *Financial Times*, 16 September 1993.

27. J.W.F. Rowe, *Primary Commodities in International Trade*, Cambridge, 1965, pp. 134–6.

28. Private communication from Bert Beeckman of Max Havelaar.

29. Barratt Brown, *op. cit.*, pp. 180ff.

30. TWIN Reports.

31. Barratt Brown and Tiffen, *op. cit.*, pp. 114ff.

32. World Bank, *Cameroon Agricultural Sector Review*, quoted in Piet Konings, *Labour Resistance in Cameroon*, James Currey, 1993, pp. 183–4.

33. World Bank, *Strategy to Develop Agriculture in Sub-Saharan Africa and a Focus for the World Bank*, Washington, 1993, p. 79ff.

34.   Konings, *op. cit.*, p. 184.
35.   *ibid.*, p. 180.
36.   *ibid.*, p. 168.
37.   *ibid.*
38.   *ibid.*, pp. 175–6.
39.   *ibid.*, p. 183.
40.   Claude Aké, *Revolutionary Pressures in Africa*, Zed Books, 1978, p. 105.
41.   Onimode, *A Political Economy of the African Crisis, op. cit.*, p. 317.
42.   *ibid.*
43.   See Basil Davidson, *The Liberation of Guiné*, Penguin, 1969, pp. 49–51.

CHAPTER 10. TRANSFORMATION AND SELF-RELIANCE

1.   Onimode, *A Future for Africa, op. cit.*, pp. 74–5.
2.   Olusegun Obasanjo, speech at an OECD conference in Paris, reported in *West Africa*, 7–13 May 1990.
3.   ECA, *African Alternative to Structural Adjustment Programmes: A Framework for Transformation and Recovery*, Addis Ababa, 1989, p. 2.5.
4.   Adebayo Adedeji, lecture given in Kaduna, reported in *West Africa*, 11–17 November 1991.
5.   Adebayo Adedeji, review of Basil Davidson's *Black Man's Burden*, in ACDESS, Bulletin, July 1992.
6.   George Ayittey, 'Indigenous African Systems' in World Bank, LTPS, Background Papers, vol. 3, p. 27.
7.   Claude Aké, *Revolutionary Pressures in Africa, op. cit.*, p. 25.
8.   *ibid.*, taken from cover blurb and see p. 28.
9.   Claude Aké, 'Sustaining Development on the Indigenous' in World Bank, LTPS, Background Papers, vol. 3, p. 9.
10.   *ibid.*, p. 19.
11.   *ibid.*, p. 9.
12.   *ibid.*, p. 11.
13.   *ibid.*, p. 12.
14.   *ibid.*, p. 11.
15.   *ibid.*, p. 12, quoting from M. Cernea, 'Farmer Organizations and Institution Building for Sustainable Development'.
16.   *ibid.*, p. 12.
17.   *ibid.*, p. 14.
18.   *ibid.*, p. 15.
19.   *ibid.*, p. 9.
20.   *ibid.*, p. 18.
21.   *ibid.*, p. 19.
22.   *ibid.*
23.   World Bank, LTPS, Background Papers, vol. 3, p. v.

24. World Bank, *World Development Report, 1991*, p. 108.

25. ECA, *op. cit.*, p. 1.8.

26. *ibid.*, p. 2.3.

27. *ibid.*, pp. 5.01ff.

28. *ibid.*, Table 5.1.

29. Adebayo Adedeji, *The African Alternative*, Addis Ababa, 1990, pp. 62–5.

30. Onimode, *op. cit.*, p. 99.

31. ACDESS, *Bulletin*, July 1992, p. 1.

32. Onimode, *op. cit.*, pp. 43 and 99.

33. Rau, *From Feast to Famine, op. cit.*, p. 142.

34. World Bank, *Sub-Saharan Africa: From Crisis to Sustainable Growth*, (LTPS), *op. cit.*, pp. 1–2.

35. World Bank, LTPS, *Background Papers*, vols 1–4, *op. cit.*

36. Onimode, *op. cit.*, p. 100.

37. *ibid.*, p. 72.

38. Adedeji, *op. cit.*, p. 64.

39. James Pickett, 'The Low-income Economies of Sub-Saharan Africa' in Pickett and Singer, *Towards Economic Recovery in Sub-Saharan Africa, op. cit.*, p. 258.

40. *ibid.*, pp. 257–8.

41. *ibid.*, p. 258.

42. Pickett and Singer, *op. cit.*, Editorial, p. 22.

43. Pickett, in Pickett and Singer, *op. cit.*, p. 259, referring to Adam Smith, *Wealth of Nations*.

44. *ibid.*, p. 239, quoting Adam Smith, *op. cit.*

45. *ibid.*

46. *ibid.*, p. 219.

47. Steven Marglin, 'What Do Bosses Do' in Andre Gorz (ed.), *The Division of Labour*, Harvester Press, 1976, pp. 13ff.

48. Pickett, in Pickett and Singer, *op. cit.*, pp. 232–3.

49. *ibid.*, p. 234.

50. Pickett and Singer, *op. cit.*, p. 28.

51. Pickett, in Pickett and Singer, *op. cit.*, p. 261.

52. *ibid.*, p. 262.

53. *ibid.*, p. 241.

54. Pickett and Singer, *op. cit.*, p. 27.

55. Pickett, in Pickett and Singer, *op. cit.*, p. 258.

56. Basil Davidson, 'Africa: The Politics of Failure', in R. Miliband and L. Panitch (eds), *The Socialist Register – 1992*, Merlin Press, 1992, p. 217.

57. Adam Smith, *Theory of Moral Sentiments*, Henry Bohn, 1759, Oxford, 1976, vol. IV.i.10.

58. Onimode. *op. cit.*, pp. 117–8.

59. *ibid.*, p. 93.

60. *ibid.*, p. 114.

61. *ibid.*, p. 116.

62. *ibid.*, p. 136.

63. World Bank, *Sub-Saharan Africa: From Crisis to Sustainable Growth*, (LTPS), *op. cit.*, p. 194.

64. Adedeji, *op. cit.*, p. 54.

CHAPTER 11. AN AFRICAN MODEL OF INDUSTRIAL DEVELOPMENT

1. Stewart, Lall and Wangwe, *Alternative Development Strategies in Sub-Saharan Africa*, *op. cit.*, p. 14.

2. *ibid.*, p. 22, referring in particular to the Berg Report of 1981.

3. *ibid.*, pp. 34–5.

4. World Bank, *Sub-Saharan Africa: From Crisis to Sustainable Growth*, (LTPS), *op. cit.*, p. 13.

5. UNCTAD, *UNCTAD VIII*, New York, 1992, p. 228.

6. World Bank, *op. cit.*, p. 9.

7. Institute for African Alternatives, *The African Response*, IFAA, 1992.

8. *ibid.*, p. 3.

9. *ibid.*, pp. 4–5.

10. World Bank, *op. cit.*, p. 27.

11. *ibid.*

12. *ibid.*

13. Nzongola Ntalaja, quoted in Ben Turok, 'What Does the World Bank Mean by "Empowering Ordinary People"?' in IFAA, *op. cit.*, p. 54.

14. Samuel Wangwe, 'Building Indigenous Technological Capacity in African Idustry' in Stewart, Lall and Wangwe, *op. cit.*, p. 238.

15. Khetso Gordham, 'Industrial Development Strategies' in IFAA, *op. cit.*, p. 24.

16. Wangwe in Stewart, Lall and Wangwe, *op. cit.*, p. 239.

17. Dele Olowu, 'African Economic Performance: Current Programs and Future Failures' in Wunsch and Olowu, *The Failure of the Centralised State*, *op. cit.*, p. 106.

18. Harry Braverman, *Labor and Monopoly Capital*, Monthly Review Press, 1974, p. 12.

19. John Powell, quoted in Ian Smillie, *Mastering the Machine*, Intermediate Technology, 1991, p. 175.

20. Jacques Giri, 'Formal and Informal Small Enterprises in the Long-term Future of Sub-Saharan Africa' in World Bank, LTPS, Background Papers, vol. 2, *op. cit.*, p. 114.

21. Sanjaya Lall, 'Structural Problems of Industry in Sub-Saharan Africa' in World Bank, LTPS, Background Papers, vol. 2, *op. cit.*, p. 97.

22. Janardan Prasad Singh, 'Analysis of Project Costs in Sub-Saharan Africa in Selected Sectors', in World Bank, LTPS, Background Papers, vol. 2, *op. cit.*, pp. 25ff.

23. Robert Jungk quoted by Otto Ullrich, 'Technology' in Sachs, *Development Dictionary, op. cit.*, p. 283.

24. See, for example, Claude Alvares, 'Science' in Sachs, *op. cit.*, pp. 219ff.

25. Samuel Wangwe, 'Building Indigenous Technological Capacity: A Study of Selected Industries in Tanzania' in Stewart, Lall and Wangwe, *op. cit.*, p. 267.

26. *ibid.*, p. 268.

27. Roger C. Riddell (ed.), *Manufacturing Africa*, James Currey, 1990, pp. 18, 119 and 243.

28. Lall in World Bank, *op. cit.*, p. 103.

29. *ibid.*, p. 100.

30. Wangwe in Stewart, Lall and Wangwe, *op. cit.*, pp. 272ff.

31. *ibid.*

32. *ibid.*

33. M.S.D. Bagachwa and Frances Stewart, 'Rural Industries and Rural Linkages' in Stewart, Lall and Wangwe, *op. cit.*, p. 148.

34. Wangwe in Stewart, Lall and Wangwe, *op. cit.*, pp. 272ff.

35. Sanjaya Lall, 'Structural Problems of African Industry' in Stewart, Lall and Wangwe, *op. cit.*, p. 123.

36. Riddell, *op. cit.*, p. 52.

37. Sachs, *op. cit., passim.*

38. Barratt Brown and Tiffen, *Short Changed, op. cit.*, pp. 15ff. and see Lynn Mytelka, 'Ivorian Industry at the Crossroads' in Stewart, Lall and Wangwe, *op. cit.*, p. 260.

39. Stewart, Lall and Wangwe, *op. cit.*, p. 24.

40. John Nellis, 'Public Enterprise Management and Restructuring', World Bank Discussion Paper, reprinted in Gerald M. Meier and William F. Steel, *Industrial Adjustment in Sub-Saharan Africa*, World Bank, Oxford, 1989, pp. 235 and 237.

41. Lall in Stewart, Lall and Wangwe, *op. cit.*, p. 112.

42. Lall in World Bank, *op. cit.*, p. 95.

43. Stewart, Lall and Wangwe, *op. cit.*, pp. 24ff. and 42ff.

44. Lall in World Bank, *op. cit.*, p. 106.

45. Mytelka in Stewart, Lall and Wangwe, *op. cit.*, pp. 262-3.

46. World Bank, LTPS, *op. cit.*, p. 137.

47. *ibid.*, p. 191.

48. Lall in World Bank, *op. cit.*, pp. 96-7.

49. Adebayo O. Olukoshi, *The Politics of Structural Adjustment in Nigeria*, James Currey, 1992, pp. 71-2 and Tom Forrest, 'The Advance of African Capital: The Growth of Nigerian Enterprises', Queen Elizabeth House workshop, 11-13 December 1989, and Keith Marsden, *African Entrepreneurs: Pioneers of Development*, World Bank, 1990.

50. Carl Liedholm, 'Small-scale Industries in Africa' in Stewart, Lall and Wangwe, *op. cit.*, pp. 200ff.

51. Sanjaya Lall in Stewart, Lall and Wangwe, *op. cit.*, pp. 116ff.

52. Marsden, *op. cit.*

53. ILO, *African Employment Report, 1988*, Addis Ababa, 1989.

54. Marsden, *op. cit.*, p. 18.

55. *ibid.*, Introduction.

56. *ibid.*, pp. 23ff.

57. Sanjaya Lall, 'Industrial Structure and Exports' in Meier and Steel, *op. cit.*, p. 53.

58. C. Chamley, *Structural Adjustment in Côte d'Ivoire*, quoted in Riddell, *op. cit.*, p. 185.

59. Lall in Stewart, Lall and Wangwe, *op. cit.*, p. 112.

60. Riddell, *op. cit.*, p. 59.

61. *ibid.*, p. 52.

62. *ibid.*, p. 38.

63. *ibid.*, p. 61.

64. F. Baffoe, 'Lesotho: Investment Incentives as an Instrument for Industrialization' in Alan W. Whiteside (ed.), *Industrialization and Investment Incentives in Southern Africa*, James Currey, 1989, p. 78.

65. D. Mabiriizi, 'Democracy and "Another Development" in Lesotho' in Turok, *op. cit.*, p. 252.

66. Scott Tiffin and Fola Osotimehin, *New Technologies and Enterprise Development in Africa*, OECD, 1992, p. 8.

67. *ibid.*, p. 11.

68. *ibid.*, p. 16.

69. *ibid.*, pp. 12–13.

70. *ibid.*, p. 31.

71. *ibid.*, p. 43.

72. *ibid.*, p. 30.

73. *ibid.*, p. 39.

74. *ibid.*, p. 32.

75. *ibid.*, p. 33.

76. Wangwe in Stewart, Lall and Wangwe, *op. cit.*, p. 261.

77. Tiffin and Osotimehin, *op. cit.*, p. 43.

78. *ibid.*, pp. 47–8.

79. *ibid.*, pp. 71–3.

80. *ibid.*, pp. 151–3.

81. TWIN Reports.

82. Smillie, *op. cit.*

83. *ibid.*, pp. 127–8, 135–6, 149, 154–7, 173–5, 192–4.

84. *ibid.*, p. 240.

CHAPTER 12. THE INFORMAL, SECOND ECONOMY

1. Janet MacGaffey, *The Real Economy of Zaire*, James Currey, 1991; Ian Livingstone, 'A Reassessment of Kenya's Rural and Urban Informal Sector', mimeographed, University of East Anglia, 1990; Jacques Giri, 'Formal and Informal Small Enterprises in the Long-Term Future of Sub-Saharan Africa' in World Bank, LTPS, Background Papers, vol. 2., *op. cit.*, pp. 111ff.; and ILO, 'Impact of the Economic Crisis on Women' in Adedeji et al., *The Human Dimension of Africa's Persistent Economic Crisis*, *op. cit.*, p. 167.

2. Giri, *op. cit.*, p. 112.

3. Livingstone, *op. cit.*, p. 6.

4. Giri, *op. cit.*, p. 113; Sanjaya Lall, 'Achieving a More Ideal Structure' in Meier and Steel, *Industrial Adjustment in Sub-Saharan Africa*, *op. cit.*, p. 94; Riddell, *Manufacturing Africa*, *op. cit.*, pp. 10, 243, 261, 340; World Bank, LTPS, *op. cit.*, p. 139; Sanjaya Lall, 'Structural Problems of African Industry' in Stewart, Lall and Wangwe, *Alternative Development Strategies in Sub-Saharan Africa*, *op. cit.*, p. 116; D.R. Fraser Taylor and Fiona Mackenzie, *Development from Within: Survival in Rural Africa*, Routledge, 1992.

5. MacGaffey, *op. cit.*, pp. 10 and 38.

6. Basil Davidson, 'Africa: The Politics of Failure' in Miliband and Panitch, *Socialist Register – 1992*, *op. cit.*, p. 215.

7. T.L. Maliyamkono and M.S.D. Bagachwa, *The Second Economy in Tanzania*, James Currey, 1990, p. 49.

8. J-M. Servet in G. Henault and R. M'Rabat, *L'Entrepreneuriat en Afrique*.

9. Janet MacGaffey, 'Initiatives from Below' in Goran Hyden and Michael Bratton (eds), *Governance and Politics in Africa*, Lynne Rienner, 1991.

10. ILO survey quoted by MacGaffey, *The Real Economy of Zaire*, *op. cit.*, p. 38.

11. Giri, *op. cit.*, p. 113.

12. *ibid.*, p. 114.

13. *ibid.*, p. 115.

14. Smillie, *Mastering the Machine*, *op. cit.*, pp. 169 and 199.

15. World Bank, LTPS, *op. cit.*, p. 164.

16. *ibid.*, p. 113.

17. *ibid.*, p. 118.

18. *ibid.*, p. 116 and Lall in Stewart, Lall and Wangwe, *op. cit.*, p. 128; Riddell, *op. cit.*, pp. 38 and 61.

19. Keith Marsden, *African Entrepreneurs: Pioneers of Development*, World Bank, 1990.

20. Giri, *op. cit.*, p. 116.

21. ILO, in Adedeji et al., *op. cit.*, p. 169.

22.   Rau, *From Feast to Famine, op. cit.*, pp. 176–80; Taylor and Mackenzie, *op. cit.*, pp. 50, 189, 200; World Bank, LTPS, *op cit.*, p. 141.

23.   Giri, *op. cit.*, p. 117.

24.   Taylor and Mackenzie, *op. cit.*, pp. 9–10.

25.   A. Sena Gabianu, 'The Susu Credit Scheme' in World Bank, LTPS, Background Papers, vol. 2, *op. cit.*, pp. 123 and 124–5.

26.   *ibid.*, p. 123.

27.   Zaoual, 'The Economy and Symbolic Sites of Africa', *op. cit.*, p. 21.

28.   Henault and M'Rabat, *op. cit.*

29.   J-L. Lespes quoted in *ibid.*

30.   Katrine A. Saito et al. (eds), *Raising the Productivity of Women Farmers in Sub-Saharan Africa*, World Bank, 1994.

31.   Charles Magubre, 'When Credit is Not Due: Financial Services by NGOs in Africa', *Small Enterprise Development*, 4:4 (December 1993).

32.   *ibid.*

33.   Gabianu, *op. cit.*, p. 128.

34.   Giri, *op. cit.*, p. 119; Taylor and Mackenzie, *op. cit.*, pp. 200 and 250; Rau, *op. cit.*, pp. 178–9.

35.   Gabianu, *op. cit.*, pp. 125–6.

36.   Carl Liedholm, 'Small-scale Industries in Africa' in Stewart, Lall and Wangwe, *op. cit.*, pp. 192 and 210.

37.   UNCTAD, *Handbook, 1991, op. cit.*, Table 6.2.

38.   Livingstone, *op. cit.*, p. 12.

39.   Giri, *op. cit.*, p. 119.

40.   Livingstone, *op. cit.*, p. 3–4.

41.   Giri, *op. cit.*, p. 113 and Janet MacGaffey and Gertrud Windsperger, The Endogenous Economy' in World Bank, LTPS, Background Papers, vol. 3, *op. cit.*, p. 83

42.   Giri, *op. cit.*, p. 113.

43.   World Bank, LTPS, *op. cit.*, Statistical Tables 28 and 35, pp. 269 and 278.

44.   MacGaffey, *op. cit.*, p. 14.

45.   Liedholm, *op. cit.*, p. 189.

46.   *ibid.*, p. 210.

47.   Giri, *op. cit.*, p. 115.

48.   Taylor and Mackenzie, *op. cit.*, p. 6.

49.   Barratt Brown and Tiffen, *Short Changed, op. cit.*, p. 37.

50.   Taylor and Mackenzie, *op. cit.*, p. 7.

51.   MacGaffey, *op. cit.*, p. 13.

52.   *ibid.*

53.   Taylor and Mackenzie, *op. cit.*, p. 6–7.

54.   MacGaffey, *op. cit.*, p. 15.

55.   *ibid.* pp. 15–16.

56.   M.S.D. Bagachwa and Frances Stewart, 'Rural Industries and Rural

Linkages in Sub-Saharan Africa' in Stewart, Lall and Wangwe, *op. cit.*, Table 5.13.

57. J.F. Rweyemamu (ed.), *Industrialization and Income Distribution in Africa*, CODESRIA, Dakar, 1980, p. 9.

58. Makwala ma Mavambu ye Beda, 'Trade in Food Crops' in MacGaffey, *op. cit.*, p. 116.

59. MacGaffey, *op. cit.*, pp. 31–2.

60. Quoted by MacGaffey, *ibid.*, p. 37.

61. MacGaffey, *op. cit.*, p. 15.

62. Davidson in Miliband and Panitch, *op. cit.*, p. 220.

63. MacGaffey, *op. cit.*, map, p. 49.

64. Hardy in Stewart, Lall and Wangwe, *op. cit.*, pp. 437–8.

65. *ibid.*, p. 438.

66. Rukarangira wa Nkera, 'Unrecorded Trade in South-east Shaba' in MacGaffey, *op. cit.*, pp. 72–4.

67. *ibid.*, pp. 77–9.

68. *ibid.*, map on p. 73 and see map on p. 20 of MacGaffey, *op. cit.*

69. MacGaffey, *op. cit.*, pp. 17–19. (The text reads: '9000 kg of cobalt', but I am assured by dealers that it would be at least one hundred times that amount.)

70. *ibid.*, p. 16.

71. Janet MacGaffey, *Entrepreneurs and Parasites: the Struggle for Indigenous Capitalism in Zaire*, quoted in MacGaffey, *op. cit.*, p. 38.

72. Davidson in Miliband and Panitch, *op. cit.*, pp. 218–19.

73. Taylor and Mackenzie, *op. cit.*, p. 30.

74. World Bank, *Nigerian Industrial Sector Report, 1990*, quoted by Tony Hawkins, 'Industrialization in Africa' in Douglas Rimmer (ed.), *Africa Thirty Years On*, James Currey, 1991, p. 148.

75. Lall, World Bank, LTPS, Background Papers, vol. 2, *op. cit.*, p. 105.

76. UN Centre for Regional Development, *Reviving Local Self-Reliance: Challenges for Rural/Regional Development in Eastern and Southern Africa*, quoted in Taylor and Mackenzie, *op. cit.*, pp. 255–6 and 273.

77. Smillie, *op. cit.*, p. 169.

78. *ibid.*, p. 201.

79. Livingstone, *op. cit.*, p. 15.

80. Livingstone, *op. cit.*, pp. 3–4.

81. *ibid.*, p. 16.

82. MacGaffey and Windsperger, *op. cit.*, p. 87.

83. Marsden, *op. cit., passim*.

84. Tom Forrest, 'The Advance of African Capital: The Growth of Nigerian Private Enterprises' in Stewart, Lall and Wangwe, *op. cit.*, pp. 387–8.

85. Smillie, *op. cit.*, p. 201.

86. P. Dutkiewicz and R. Shenton, 'Debates' in *Review of African Political Economy*, no. 37 (1986), pp. 110–11.

87. Fiona Mackenzie in Taylor and Mackenzie, *op. cit.*, p. 30.

88. World Bank, LTPS, *op. cit.*, p. 191.

89. *ibid.*, p. xii.

90. Ben Turok, 'What Does the World Bank Mean by Empowering Ordinary People?' in IFAA, *The African Response*, *op. cit.*, p. 50.

91. Maxine Molyneux, 'Mobilization without Emancipation? Women's Interests, the State and Revolution in Nicaragua' quoted by Taylor and Mackenzie, *op. cit.*, p. 29.

92. Maliyamkono and Bagachwa, *op. cit.*, p. 35.

93. M. Bratton, 'Non-governmental Organizations in Africa: Can they Influence Public Policy?', *Development and Change*, 21, pp. 98–9.

94. Giri, *op. cit.*, p. 116.

95. Taylor and Mackenzie, *op. cit.*, p. 30.

96. D. Goulet, 'Participation in Development: New Avenues', *World Development*, 17:2, p. 172.

97. TWIN Reports, July 1993.

CHAPTER 13. LET THE WOMEN LEAD!

1. Cassam, in Suliman, *Alternative Strategies for Africa*, *op. cit.*, p. 113.

2. Emy Siganga, 'The LTPS and the Fraser Report on the Role of Women' in IFAA, *The African Response*, *op. cit.*, p. 58.

3. Paul Harrison, 'Sustainable Growth in African Agriculture' in World Bank, LTPS, Background Papers, vol. 2, *op cit.*, p. 69.

4. World Bank, *Sub-Saharan Africa: From Crisis to Sustainable Growth*, (LTPS), *op. cit.*, p. 103.

5. Siganga in IFAA, *op. cit.*, p. 58.

6. Barbara Rogers, *The Domestication of Women*, Kegan Paul, 1980, p. 181 and Saito, et al., *Raising the Productivity of Women Farmers in Sub-Saharan Africa*, *op. cit.*, p. 21.

7. George J.S. Dei, 'A Ghanaian Rural Community: Indigenous Responses to Seasonal Food Supply Cycles and the Socio-environmental Stresses of the 1980s' in Taylor and Mackenzie, *Development from Within*, *op. cit.*, pp. 71–3.

8. Richard Anker, 'Measuring Women's Participation in the African Labour Force' in Aderanti Adepoju and Christine Oppong, *Gender, Work and Population in Sub-Saharan Africa*, James Currey, 1994, pp. 67–8.

9. Noel A. Chavangi, 'Household-based Tree Planting Activities for Fuelwood Supply in Rural Kenya' in Taylor and Mackenzie, *op. cit.*, p. 164 and Timberlake, *Africa in Crisis*, *op. cit.*, pp. 194ff.

10. Rogers, *op. cit.*, pp. 188–9.

11. Adepoju and Oppong, *op. cit.*, pp. 59ff.

12. Barbara Böni, 'Women and Technology Transfer: Introduction of a Palm Oil Press in a Toura Village (Côte d'Ivoire)', *Bulletin BUROTROP*, 6 (1993).

13. Siganga in IFAA, *op. cit.*, p. 58.

14.   World Bank, LTPS, *op. cit.*, pp. 7 and 103.

15.   Harrison, in LTPS, Background Papers, vol. 2, *op. cit.*, p. 69.

16.   Axumite G. Egziabher, *Socio-economic Evaluation of Small-scale Village-based Irrigation in RADI/TWIN Projects in Senegal*, TWIN, 1990.

17.   Rogers, *op. cit.*, p. 183.

18.   Peter O. Ondiege, 'Local Coping Strategies in Machakos District, Kenya' in Taylor and Mackenzie, *op. cit.*, pp. 135-8.

19.   Harrison, *The Greening of Africa*, *op. cit.*, pp. 121-3.

20.   Harrison in LTPS, Background Papers, vol. 2, *op. cit.*, p. 69.

21.   Marjorie Mbilinyi et al., 'Women's Initiatives in the United Republic of Tanzania', in Linda Mayoux (ed.), *All Are Not Equal: African Women in Cooperatives*, IFAA, 1988, p. 70.

22.   Margaret Joan Anstee, 'Social Development in Africa' in Pickett and Singer, *Towards Economic Recovery in Sub-Saharan Africa*, *op. cit.*, p. 203.

23.   Mary Bosede Ayo-Bello, 'Cooperative Development for Women in Nigeria' in Mayoux, *op. cit.*, pp. 61-2 and pp. 84-5.

24.   Harrison in LTPS, Background Papers, vol. 2, *op. cit.*, p. 70.

25.   Saito et al., *op. cit.*, p. 79.

26.   Dei in Taylor and MacKenzie, *op. cit.*, p. 73.

27.   *ibid.*, p. 61.

28.   John English, Mary Tiffen and Michael Mortimore, *Land Resource Management in Machakos District, Kenya, 1930-1990*, World Bank Environment Paper, no. 5, 1994, pp. 55-6.

29.   ECA, *African Socio-economic Indicators, 1990-91*, Addis Ababa, 1991, Tables 12 and 13.

30.   World Bank, LTPS, *op cit.*, Table 32.

31.   Brigit Brock-Utne, 'Schooling Prospects of Tanzanian Female Students in a Situation of Economic Crisis' in Suliman, *op. cit.*, p. 172.

32.   Alice Nkhoma-Wamunza, 'The Informal Sector: A Strategy for Survival in Tanzania' in Taylor and Mackenzie, *op. cit.*, p. 210.

33.   Ondiege in Taylor and Mackenzie, *op. cit.*, pp. 135-6.

34.   Jacob Songsore, 'The Cooperative Credit Movement in North-Western Ghana: Development Agent or Agent of Incorporation?' in Taylor and Mackenzie, *op. cit.*, p. 93.

35.   Nkhoma-Wamunza in Taylor and Mackenzie, *op. cit.*, pp. 206-10.

36.   Taylor, in Taylor and Mackenzie, *op. cit.*, p. 250.

37.   MacGaffey, *The Real Economy of Zaire*, op. cit., p. 35.

38.   *ibid.*

39.   Joseph Houyoux, Kinavwuidi Niwembo and Okita Onya, *Budgets des Ménages, Kinshasa 1986*, BEAU, Kinshasa, 1986.

40.   Walu Engundu and Brooke Grundfest Schoepf, 'Women's Trade and Contributions to Household Budgets in Kinshasa' in MacGaffey, *op. cit.*, pp. 124ff.

41.   *ibid.*, p. 126ff.

42.   *ibid.*, Table 6.1.

43.   *ibid.*, p. 131.

44.   Vwakanakazi Mukohya, 'Import and Export in the Second Economy in North Kivu' in MacGaffey, *op. cit.*, p. 58.

45.   B.C. Koda and C.K. Omari, 'Crisis in the Household Economy: Women's Strategies in Dar es Salaam' in Suliman, *op. cit.*, p. 122.

46.   Aili Mari Tripp, 'Deindustrialization and the Growth of Women's Economic Associations and Networks in Urban Tanzania' in UNU/WIDER, *Empowering Women in the Casualized Trades*, UNU, Helsinki, 1990, p. 6.

47.   Aili Mari Tripp, 'Defending the Right to Subsist: the State Versus the Urban Informal Economy in Tanzania', paper presented to the African Studies Association Annual Meeting, Chicago, 1988, p. 11, quoted in Mac-Gaffey, *op. cit.*, p. 39.

48.   Engundu in MacGaffey, *op. cit.*, p. 149.

49.   Brooke G. and Claude Schoepf, 'Zaire's Rural Development in Perspective' in *The Role of US Universities in International Rural and Agricultural Development*, Tuskegee, 1981, p. 250.

50.   Engundu in MacGaffey, *op. cit.*, p. 148.

51.   Tripp in UNU/WIDER, *op. cit.*, pp. 25–6.

52.   Engundu and Schoepf in MacGaffey, *op. cit.*, p. 139.

53.   Tripp in UNU/WIDER, *op. cit.*, p. 20.

54.   Ondiege in MacGaffey, *op. cit.*, pp. 135–8.

55.   *ibid.*, pp. 141–5.

56.   Gloria Thomas-Emeagwali, 'Perspectives on Women and the Development of Agricultural Cooperatives in Nigeria' in Suliman, *op. cit.*, p. 150.

57.   *ibid.*, p. 148.

58.   Kingston Kajese, 'Decolonizing African NGOs', paper given to a seminar of SCIAF and the Centre for African Studies, University of Edinburgh, reproduced in *Quid Pro Quo*, 3:8/9 (1990), p. 19 and see Luke Mhlaba, 'Local Cultures and Development in Zimbabwe' in Kaarsholm, *Culture and Development in Southern Africa*, *op. cit.*

59.   Linda Mayoux, Introduction in Mayoux, *op. cit.*, p. 8.

60.   Fiona Mackenzie, 'The Struggle to Survive' in Taylor and Mackenzie, *op. cit.*, p. 28.

61.   Mayoux, Introduction in Mayoux, *op. cit.*, p. 19, quoting cases in Kenya and Gambia.

62.   Rosaria Pacavira, 'Prospects for Cooperative Development for Women in Angola', Esther Moepi, 'Women in Cooperatives: the Case of Botswana', and Anneke Mulder, 'The Participation of Women in the Agricultural Cooperatives in Maputo, Mozambique' in Mayoux, *op. cit.*, respectively pp. 31, 34 and 59.

63.   Personal communication from Victoria Bawtree.

64.   Celina Cossa, 'Peasant Cooperatives in Mozambique: The Experience of the União General of Maputo' in Mayoux, *op. cit.*, pp. 55–6 and see Stephanie Urdang, *And Still They Dance*, Earthscan, 1989, pp. 140–50.

65. Joyce B. Endely, 'Strategies and Programmes for Women in Africa's Agricultural Sector', in Suliman, *op. cit.*, p. 135.

66. Rau, *From Feast to Famine. op. cit.*, p. 182; but see also Lionel Cliffe, 'Zimbabwe's Agricultural "Success" and Food Security', *Review of African Political Economy*, no. 43 (1988), p. 21.

67. Mbilinyi in Mayoux, *op. cit.*, p. 70 and Restie Jolly Katusiime, 'Problems Faced by Women's Cooperatives in Uganda' in Mayoux, *op. cit.*, p. 73.

68. Lovemore M. Zinyama, 'Local Farmer Organizations and Rural Development in Zimbabwe' in Taylor and Mackenzie, *op. cit.*, pp. 23–7.

69. *ibid.*, pp. 51–2.

70. Kate McCalman, 'Zimbabwe: Women Speak Out' in FAO, *Ideas and Action*, no. 158 (1984), p. 29ff.

71. Timberlake, *op. cit.*, pp. 184–5.

72. Sithembesi Nyoni, 'The ORAP Concept of *Zenzele*', Discussion Paper 1, ORAP Tenth Anniversary Reflection Workshop, 4–6 September 1991.

73. Endely in Suliman, *op. cit.*, pp. 135–6.

74. *ibid.*, p. 134.

75. Fatima Babiker Mahmoud, 'African Women and Feminist Schools of Thought' in Suliman, *op. cit.*, p. 146.

76. Linda Mayoux, 'Women-only Cooperatives: The Case of FEDEV Mali' in Mayoux, *op. cit.*, p. 50.

77. Saito et al., *op. cit.*, pp. 73ff.

78. *ibid.*, pp. 66–7.

79. *ibid.*, pp. 79–80.

80. Mayoux, Introduction in Mayoux, *op. cit.*, p. 16.

81. Ann Waters-Bayer, 'Soybean Daddawa: an innovation by Nigerian Women', quoted in Rau, *op. cit.*, p. 152.

82. Phyllis Kaberry, *Women of the Grassfields*, cited in Kathryn S. March and Rachelle L. Taqqu, *Women's Informal Associations* in *Developing Countries*, Westview, 1986, p. 57, quoted in Rau, *op. cit.*, p. 171.

83. Mabel C. Milimo, 'Chikuni Fruit and Vegetable Producers' Cooperative Society, Zambia, a Case Study' in ILO, *Rural Development and Women: Lessons from the Field*, vol. 1., 1985, pp. 21–36, quoted in Rau, *op. cit.*, p. 177–8.

84. Paul Richards, *Indigenous Agricultural Revolution*, quoted in Rau, *op. cit.*, pp. 149–50.

85. Mackintosh, *Gender, Class and Rural Transition, op. cit.*, pp. 102ff and Philip Woodhouse and Ibrahima Ndiaye, *Structural Adjustment and Irrigated Food Farming in Africa: The 'Disengagement' of the State in the Senegal River Valley*, Open University (Development Policy and Practice) Working Papers, 1990, *passim*.

86. Soon Young Youn of UNICEF, in Timberlake, *op. cit.*, pp. 185–6.

87. Saito et al., *op. cit.*, p. 63.

88. Timberlake, *op. cit.*, pp. 151 and 193.

89. Almaz Eshete, 'Women and Cooperatives: the Ethiopian Experience' in Mayoux, *op. cit.*, p. 37.

90.   Axumite G. Egziabher, 'Urban Agriculture as a Coping Strategy: Agricultural Cooperatives in Addis Ababa', Ph.D. thesis, University of London, 1993.

91.   James Firebrace and Stuart Holland, *Never Kneel Down*, Spokesman, 1984, pp. 36–7 and Basil Davidson, Lionel Cliffe and Bereket Habte Selassie, *Behind the War in Eritrea*, Spokesman, 1980, pp. 108ff.

92.   Carolyn Baylies and Janet Bujra, 'Challenging Gender Inequalities in Africa' in *Review of African Political Economy*, no. 56 (1993), p. 8.

93.   Ekei Umo Etim, 'ECA and its Women's Programme: What Went Wrong?' in Mayoux, *op. cit.*, p. 30.

94.   *Keesing's Record of World Events*, vol. 39 (1993), Annual Reference Supplement, R. 11.

95.   Johannes N.S. Mutanyatta, 'Women in Development: The Case of Botswana' in Suliman, *op. cit.*, p. 164 and Moepi in Mayoux, *op. cit.*, pp. 33–5.

96.   Marga Holness, Introduction, Organization of Angolan Women, *Angolan Women Building the Future*, tr. Marga Holness, Zed Books, 1984, pp. 15ff.

97.   Pacavira in Mayoux, *op. cit.*, p. 31.

98.   Mulder in Mayoux, *op. cit.*, p. 57.

99.   Hussaina Abdullah, '"Transition Politics" and the Challenge of Gender in Nigeria' in *Review of African Political Economy*, no. 56 (1993), p. 31.

100.   Baylies and Bujra, *op. cit.*, p. 3.

101.   Bjorn Beckman, quoted by Rau, *op. cit.*, pp. 153–4.

102.   Elizabeth A. Eames, 'Why the Women Went to War' in Gracia Clark (ed.), *Traders versus State*, Westview, 1988, pp. 81–97.

103.   Catherine Newberry, 'Ebutumwa Bw'Emiogo', quoted in Rau, *op. cit.*, p. 155.

104.   *Keesing's*, *op. cit.*, R. 11.

105.   Pekka Hussi et al., *The Development of Rural Cooperatives and Other Rural Organizations: The Role of the World Bank*, World Bank, 1993, p. 8.

106.   Avishay Braverman et al., *Promoting Rural Cooperatives in Developing Countries: The Case of Sub-Saharan Africa*, World Bank Discussion Paper, no. 12, 1991 and see Judith Tendler, see reference 43, Chapter 3 above.

107.   Taylor in Taylor and Mackenzie, *op. cit.*, p. 254.

108.   World Bank, LTPS, *op. cit.*, p. 103.

109.   *ibid.*, p. 75.

110.   *ibid.*, p. 169.

111.   Mackenzie in Taylor and Mackenzie, *op. cit.*, pp. 23–7.

CHAPTER 14. DEVELOPING HUMAN RESOURCES

1.   Achebe et al., *Beyond Hunger in Africa. op. cit.*

2.   *ibid.*, p. 15.

3.   *ibid.*, p. 6.

4.   *ibid.*, p. 23.

5. Adedeji et al., *The Human Dimension of Africa's Persistent Economic Crisis, op. cit.*, p. 380.

6. *ibid.*, p. 378.

7. *ibid.*, p. ix.

8. Aderanti Adepoju (ed.), *The Impact of Structural Adjustment on the Population of Africa*, James Currey, 1993, p. 6.

9. *ibid.*, p. 4.

10. Anstee in Pickett and Singer, *Towards Economic Recovery in Sub-Saharan Africa, op. cit.*, p. 200.

11. Barratt Brown and P. Tiffen, *Short Changed, op. cit.*, pp. 12–13.

12. Anstee in Pickett and Singer, *op. cit.*, p. 212.

13. Quoted by Venkatash Seshamani in 'Zambia' in Adedeji et al., *op. cit.*, p. 120.

14. *Keesing's Record of World Events*, vol. 39 (1993), Annual Reference Supplement, R. 26.

15. Seshamani in Adedeji et al., *op. cit.*, pp. 105 and 119.

16. *ibid.*, p. 120.

17. *ibid.*

18. Akilagpa Sawyerr, 'The Politics of Adjustment Policy' in Adedeji et al., *op. cit.*, p. 231.

19. *ibid.*, p. 232.

20. *ibid.*, p. 228.

21. E.K. Tapsoba (FAO) 'Structural Adjustment, Food Production and Rural Poverty' in Adedeji et al., *op. cit.*, p. 284.

22. UNICEF, 'The State of Africa's Children: Priorities of Action' in Adedeji et al., *op. cit.*, p. 197.

23. Adepoju, *op. cit.*, p. 6.

24. Ismail Serageldin (World Bank), 'The Human Dimension of Structural Adjustment Programmes: The World Bank's Perspective' in Adedeji et al., *op. cit.*, pp. 254–5.

25. ECA, *African Alternative Framework, op. cit.*, pp. 5.13–14.

26. Seshamani in Adedeji et al., *op. cit.*, p. 121.

27. *ibid.*, quoting from J. Levi and A.M. Mwanza, 'Zambia Case Study: Agricultural Policy Issues', draft report for the Economic Development Institute, World Bank, 1986.

28. Saito et al., *Raising Productivity of Women Farmers in Sub-Saharan Africa, op. cit.*, pp. 46ff.

29. Harrison, *The Greening of Africa, op. cit.*, p. 59.

30. *ibid.*, p. 313.

31. *ibid.*, p. 59.

32. F. Ajayi et al., 'Tools of the Trade: Do Farmers Have the Right Ones?', *African Farmer*, no. 5, pp. 5–13.

33. Harrison, *op. cit.*, p. 57.

34. *ibid.*, p. 92.

35. Lionel Cliffe, 'Zimbabwe's "Agricultural Success" and Food Security' in *Review of African Political Economy*, no. 43 (1988), pp. 13–14.

36. Harrison, *op. cit.*, p. 95.

37. Saito et al., *op. cit.*, pp. 6off.

38. Harrison, *op. cit.*, pp. 267–9.

39. See Salihu Bappa, 'The Maska Project (popular theatre) in Nigeria' in FAO, *Ideas and Action*, no. 152 (1983), pp. 34–5; and Ndumbe Eyoh, 'Improvization and Traditional African Theatre' in FAO, *Ideas and Action*, no. 165 (1985), pp. 12–18.

40. *ibid.*, p. 13 and see Kimani Gecau in Kaarsholm, *Culture and Development in Southern Africa*, *op. cit.*

41. Harrison, *op. cit.*, p. 270.

42. *ibid.*, pp. 334–5.

43. The Khartoum Declaration, para. 24 as in the Appendix to Adedeji et al., pp. 381–2.

44. Tsatsu Tsikata, in Adedeji et al., *op. cit.*, pp. 156ff.

45. Adepoju, *op. cit.*, p. 4.

46. *ibid.*, p. 5.

47. World Bank, *Sub-Saharan Africa: From Crisis to Sustainable Growth*, (LTPS), *op. cit.*, p. 67.

48. ECA, *African Socio-Economic Indicators, 1990/91*, Addis Ababa, 1991, Table 9.

49. Achebe et al., *op. cit.*, pp. 43–4.

50. World Bank, *op. cit.*, p. 66 and Norman Miller and Richard Rockwell, *AIDS in Africa*, Edwin Melles, Lewiston, NY, 1988.

51. Harrison, *op. cit.*, p. 121.

52. *ibid.*, p. 271.

53. Achebe et al., *op. cit.*, p. 59.

54. UNCTAD, *The Least Developed Countries: 1993–4, Report*, New York, 1994, pp. 102–107.

55. *ibid.*, p. 59.

56. Crispin Grey-Johnson (ECA), 'An Enabling Environment to Retain Africa's High-Level Manpower' in Adedeji et al., *op. cit.*, p. 296.

57. Achebe et al., *op. cit.*, pp. 97.

58. *ibid.*, pp. 96–7.

59. *ibid.*, p. 99.

60. *ibid.*, pp. 99 and 133.

61. Adedeji et al., *op. cit.*, Appendix, p. 378.

62. Tony Killick, 'Explaining Africa's Post-Independence Development Experiences', Working Paper no. 60, ODI, London, 1992, Table 1.

63. Edward Jaycox, 'The Benefits of Adjustment', FAO, *Ceres* (Sept–Oct 1993), p. 21.

64. Killick, *op. cit.*

65. World Bank, *World Development Report, 1993*, Oxford, 1993, Table 2.1.

66.   World Bank, *World Development Report, 1994*, Oxford, 1994, Table 30.

67.   Serge Latouche, *In the Wake of the Affluent Society*, Zed Books, 1993 and 'Standard of Living' in Sachs, *The Development Dictionary, op. cit.*, pp. 256–7.

68.   Wolfgang Sachs, Introduction in Sachs, *op. cit.*

69.   UNDP, 'Short-, Medium- and Long-term Support for the Human Dimension: The Role of International Organizations' in Adedeji et al., *op. cit.*, pp. 331ff.

70.   UNICEF, 'Monitoring Human and Social Indicators in the Adjustment Process', in Adedeji et al., *op. cit.*, p. 276.

71.   See Table 3.1., 'Basic Needs Indicators' in Chapter 3 above and see Killick, *op. cit.*, Table 3.

72.   ECA *Survey of Economic and Social Conditions in Africa, 1989–90*, New York, 1992, p. 112.

73.   WHO and World Food Programme, 'Structural Adjustment, Health, Nutrition and Food Aid in Africa' in Adedeji et al., *op. cit.*, p. 295.

CHAPTER 15. RURAL DEVELOPMENT FROM THE GRASS ROOTS

1.   Quoted in Bertrand Schneider, *The Barefoot Revolution: Report to the Club of Rome*, IT Publications, 1988, p. 141.

2.   Julius Nyerere, 'Socialism and Rural Development' in J.K. Nyerere, *Freedom and Socialism*, Oxford, 1968, pp. 340–41.

3.   René Dumont, *False Start in Africa*, Editions du Seuil, 1962 and Earthscan, 1988, pp. 215ff.

4.   *ibid.*, p. 224.

5.   David Siddle and Ken Swindell, *Rural Change in Tropical Africa*, Blackwell, 1990, pp. 159ff.

6.   Bernard Lecomte, 'Senegal: The Young Farmers of Walo and the New Agricultural Policy' in *Fenix*, no. 2 (1990), available from Victoria Bawtree, viale Glorioso 8, 00153 Roma, Italy.

7.   Idrian N. Resnick, 'The Long Transition: Building Socialism in Tanzania', *Monthly Review*, 1981, p. 23.

8.   Lionel Cliffe, 'Nationalism and the Reaction to Enforced Agricultural Change in Tanganyika During the Colonial Period', quoted in Resnick, *op. cit.*, p. 23.

9.   Alf Carlsson, *Cooperatives and the State: Partners in Development? A Human Resource Perspective*, KOOPI, 1992, available from Box 20063, 10460 Stockholm.

10.   Fred Howarth, reviewing Alf Carlsson's book in the Cooperative College house magazine, Stanford Hall, Loughborough, 1992, p. 54.

11.   Resnick, *op. cit.*, p. 67.

12.   Arusha Declaration, 1967, reproduced in Andrew Coulson, *Tanzania: A Political Economy*, Oxford, 1982, pp. 176ff.

13.   Coulson, *ibid.*, pp. 323ff. and see Carlsson, *op cit.*, *passim*.

14. Resnick, *op. cit.*, pp. 98 and 108.

15. Carlsson, *op. cit.*, p. 231.

16. TWIN reports.

17. Manzi Bakaramutsa, 'Why Do Our Cooperatives Fail?', FAO/FFHC, *Ideas and Action*, Rome, 146 (1982/3), pp. 4ff.

18. Siddle and Swindell, *Rural Change in Tropical Africa*, *op. cit.*, pp. 98–100.

19. Avishay Braverman et al., *Promoting Rural Cooperatives in Developing Countries: The Case of Sub-Saharan Africa*, World Bank Discussion Paper, no. 121, Washington, 1994.

20. *ibid.*, pp. 28–9.

21. *ibid.*, p. 14.

22. *ibid.*, p. 19.

23. Nana Frimpong-Ansah, Kuapa Kokoo, Ghana, TWIN reports.

24. Pekka Hussi et al., *The Development of Cooperatives and Other Rural Organizations: The Role of the World Bank*, World Bank, 1993.

25. *ibid.*, pp. 8 and 24.

26. *ibid.*, p. 12.

27. *ibid.*, p. 84.

28. *ibid.*, p. 81.

29. Quoted in Rau, *From Feast to Famine*, *op. cit.*, p. 32.

30. Nzongola-Ntalaja, *Revolution and Counter-Revolution in Africa*, Zed Books, 1987, pp. 100ff.

31. Basil Davidson, *The People's Cause*, Longman, 1981, *passim*, but especially quoting Cabral, p. 167.

32. Schneider, *op. cit.*, pp. 46–7.

33. Rau, *op. cit.*, pp. 155–8.

34. Resnick, *op. cit.*, pp. 159–60.

35. Rau, *op. cit.*, p. 154.

36. *ibid.*, p. 155.

37. *ibid.*, p. 154.

38. *ibid.*, p. 157.

39. Lecomte, *op. cit.*, *passim*.

40. Siddle and Swindell, *op. cit.*, p. 172.

41. *ibid.*, p. 171.

42. Onimode, *A Political Economy of the African Crisis*, *op. cit.*, p. 317.

43. Aké, *Revolutionary Pressures in Africa*, *op. cit.*, pp. 99 and 105.

44. Mahmood Mamdani, 'Class, Democracy and Uganda' in Peter Anyang' Nyong'o (ed.), *Popular Struggles for Democracy in Africa*, Zed Books, 1987, p. 94.

45. Schneider, *op. cit.*, pp. 78 and 221–3.

46. Aubrey Williams, 'A Growing Role for NGOs in Development', *Finance and Development*, December 1991.

47. *ibid.*

48. Siddle and Swindell, *op. cit.*, pp. 92ff. and 176–7.

49. *ibid.*, pp. 96 and 103.

50. *ibid.*, pp. 205-6.

51. FAO reports from Malawi, Sierra Leone, Ghana, Senegal, Nigeria, Gambia, Madagascar, Mozambique, Sudan, Ethiopia and Cameroon collated by B. Mulugettaa and others and made available to me by Professor Lionel Cliffe of University of Leeds.

52. Bernard J. Lecomte, *Project Aid: Limitations and Alternatives*, OECD, Paris, 1986.

53. Peter Oakley, *Projects with People: The Practice of Participation in Rural Development*, ILO, Geneva, 1991.

54. Schneider, *op. cit.*

55. Robin Poulton and Michael Harris, *Putting People First*, Macmillan, 1988.

56. Daniel Descendre, *L'Autodétermination paysanne en Afrique: solidarité ou tutelle des ONG partenaires?*, l'Harmattan, Paris, 1991.

57. Pierre Pradervand, *Une Afrique en Marche: la révolution silencieuse des paysans africans*, Plon, Paris, 1989.

58. FAO reports, *op. cit.*

59. *ibid.*

60. Adama Dieng, 'Self-Reliant Development in Senegal: Myth or Reality?' in FAO/FFHC, *Ideas and Action*, Rome, 160 (1985), pp. 4ff.

61. *ibid.*, p. 9.

62. *ibid.*, p. 7.

63. Nora McKeon, 'Sierra Leone: Helping Local Groups to Organize Themselves' in FAO/FFHC, *Ideas and Action*, Rome, 167 (1986), pp. 3ff.

64. *ibid.*, p. 7.

65. *ibid.*

66. FAO reports, *op. cit.*

67. Schneider, *op. cit.*, p. 206, reporting from the UN Environmental Programme and see Harry Underhill, *Small-scale Irrigation in Africa*, FAO and Cranfield College, 1986.

68. Descendre, *op. cit.*, p. 18.

CHAPTER 16. URBANIZATION AND WORKERS' ORGANIZATIONS

1. Carl K. Eicher, 'African Agricultural Development Strategies' in Stewart, Lall and Wangwe, *Alternative Development Strategies in Sub-Saharan Africa*, *op. cit.*, p. 81 and see Clive Robinson, *Hungry Farmers*, Christian Aid, 1989, pp. 77-8.

2. Achebe et al., *Beyond Hunger in Africa*, *op. cit.*, p. 45.

3. World Bank, *Sub-Saharan Africa: From Crisis to Sustainable Growth*, *op. cit.*, Table 35, 'Urbanization', pp. 278-9.

4. John Block, former US Secretary of Agriculture, quoted by Kevin Watkins, *Fixing the Rules: North-South Issues in International Trade and the GATT Uruguay Round*, CIIR, 1992, p. 2.

5. World Bank, *The East Asian Miracle: Economic Growth and Public Policy*, Oxford, 1993, pp. 32–3.

6. Lipton, *Why Poor People Stay Poor. op. cit.*, p. 13.

7. Carr-Hill, *Social Conditions in Sub-Saharan Africa, op. cit.*, pp. 135–6 and John Weekes, *Development Strategy and the Economy of Sierra Leone*, Macmillan, 1992, p. 59.

8. Carr-Hill, *op. cit.*, p. 138.

9. World Bank, *World Development Report, 1993*, Oxford, 1993, Table 31.

10. A.T. Salau, 'The Urban Process in Africa', *African Urban Studies*, vol. 4 (1979), pp. 27–34.

11. Olowu and Wunsch, *The Failure of the Centralized State, op. cit.*, pp. 33 and 66.

12. Charles M. Becker, Andrew M. Hamer and Andrew R. Morrison, *Beyond Urban Bias in Africa: Urbanization in an Era of Structural Adjustment*, James Currey, 1994, p. 49 and pp. 189ff.

13. Barratt Brown, *Fair Trade. op. cit.*, pp. 120–2 and G. Maasdorp, 'Overview: Regional Prospects and Rapid Technological Change' in Whiteside, *Industrialization and Investment Incentives in Southern Africa, op. cit.*, p. 208.

14. Steve Akin and Carole Collins, 'External Collusion with Kleptocracy: Can Zaire Recapture its Stolen Wealth?' in *Review of African Political Economy*, no. 57 (1993), p. 83.

15. *ibid.*, p. 84.

16. World Bank, *Sub-Saharan Africa: From Crisis to Sustainable Growth*, (LTPS), *op. cit.*, Table 1.

17. *ibid.*

18. World Bank, *Beyond Adjustment: Towards Sustainable Growth with Equity in Sub-Saharan Africa*, Technical Report, Washington, 1988, Table 1.5.

19. Akin and Collins, *op. cit.*, p. 81.

20. *ibid.*

21. UNCTAD, *Handbook, 1991, op. cit.*, Table 5.14.

22. Avishay Braverman et al., *Promoting Rural Cooperatives in Developing Countries*, World Bank Discussion Paper, no. 12, Washington 1991, p. 3.

23. Salau, *op. cit.*, quoted in Roy A. Carr-Hill, *op. cit.*, pp. 128–9.

24. Malcolm Harper, *Their Own Idea: Lessons from Workers' Cooperatives*, IT Publications, 1992, pp. 42–3 and pp. 141–2.

25. *ibid.*, pp. 129–33.

26. *ibid.*

27. Ian Livingstone, 'A Reassessment of Kenya's Rural and Urban Informal Sector', *World Development*, 19:6 (1991), pp. 651–70.

28. Becker, Hamer and Morrison, *op. cit.*, pp. 227–8.

29. Carl Liedholm and Donald C. Mead, 'The Small-Scale Sector and Entrepreneurship' in Meier and Steel, *Industrial Adjustment in Sub-Saharan Africa, op. cit.*, pp. 186–7.

30. Carl Liedholm, 'Small-scale Industries in Africa' in Stewart, Lall and Wangwe, *Alternative Development Strategies in Sub-Saharan Africa, op. cit.*, p. 189.

31. *ibid.*, p. 190.

32. M.D. Bagachwa and Frances Stewart, 'Rural Industries and Rural Linkages in Sub-Saharan Africa: A Survey' in Stewart, Lall and Wangwe, *op. cit.*, pp. 147–8.

33. Mohamed L. Gakou, *The Crisis in African Agriculture*, Zed Books, 1987, p. 84.

34. Rhoda Howard, 'Third World Trade Unions as Agencies of Human Rights: The Case of Commonwealth Africa' in Roger Southall (ed.), *Trade Unions and the New Industrialization*, Zed Books, 1988, pp. 240ff.

35. Basil Davidson, *Africa in Modern History, op. cit.*, pp. 217–18.

36. Ben Turok, *Africa: What Can Be Done?, op. cit.*, p. 86.

37. Davidson, *op. cit.*, p. 217.

38. Turok, *op. cit.*, p. 87.

39. *ibid.*

40. J. Crisp, *The Story of an African Working Class*, quoted in Turok, *op. cit.*, p. 90.

41. Howard, *op. cit.*, p. 239.

42. Richard Sandbrook, *The Politics of Basic Needs*, Toronto University Press, 1982, p. 138.

43. Wogu Ananaba, *The Trade Union Movement in Africa*, Hurst, 1979, p. 6.

44. Nicholas Van Hear, 'Recession, Retrenchment and Military Rule: Nigerian Labour in the 1980s' in Southall, *op. cit.*, p. 158.

45. Yasuf Bangura, 'The Recession and Workers' Struggles in Vehicle Assembly Plants: Steyr-Nigeria' in *Review of African Political Economy*, no. 39 (1987), pp. 19–20.

46. Adebayo Olukoshi, 'Impact of IMF–World Bank Programmes on Nigeria' in Onimode, *The IMF, the World Bank and African Debt, op. cit.*, p. 227.

47. World Bank, *Ghana: Policies and Program for Adjustment*, Washington, 1983, quoted by Jeff Haynes in 'Inching Towards Democracy: The Ghanaian "Revolution", the IMF and the Politics of the Possible' in Cohen and Goulbourne, *Democracy and Socialism in Africa, op. cit.*, pp. 155–6.

48. Haynes, *op. cit.*, p. 156.

49. Renee Pittin, 'Women, Work and Ideology in Nigeria' in *Review of African Political Economy*, no. 52 (1991), pp. 38ff.

50. *ibid.*, p. 49.

51. *Keesing's Record of World Events*, July 1994.

52. Robin Cohen, 'Socialism or Democracy: Socialism and Democracy' in Cohen and Goulbourne, *op. cit.*, pp. 11–12.

53. Piet Konings, 'The Political Potential of Ghanaian Miners: A Case Study of the AGC Workers at Obuasi' quoted in Konings, *Labour Resistance in*

Cameroon, op. cit., pp. 178–9.

54. Sandbrook, *op. cit.*, p. 209.

55. Konings, *op. cit.*, p. 182.

56. *ibid.*, p. 180.

57. *ibid.*, pp. 183–4.

58. *ibid.*

59. Onimode, *A Political Economy of the African Crisis, op. cit.*, pp. 104ff. and p. 124; and see Michael Chege, 'The State and Labour in Kenya' in Nyong'o, *Popular Struggles for Democracy in Africa, op. cit.*, p. 248.

60. Fanon, *The Wretched of the Earth, op. cit.*, p. 47.

61. Konings, *op. cit.*, p. 181.

62. Quoted by A. Nwafor, 'Imperialism and Revolution in Africa', *Monthly Review*, April 1975 and see Robin Cohen, 'Marxism in Africa: The Groundings of a Tradition' in Munslow, *Africa: Problems in the Transition to Socialism, op. cit.*, pp. 48ff.

63. Konings, *op. cit.*, p. 180.

64. Ben Turok, *Mixed Economy in Focus: Zambia*, IFAA, 1989, pp. 23–4.

65. Don Thompson, *Trade Union Solidarity for Survival*, Spokesman, 1989, pp. 19–20. But note that the OATUU recovered by 1992 to organize a joint regional conference with ECA on 'Popular Participation in AAF–SAP' in Addis Ababa; see Onimode, *A Future for Africa, op. cit.*, p. 116.

66. Peter Lawrence, 'Economic Democracy, Socialism and the "Market"' in Cohen and Goulbourne, *op. cit.*, p. 33.

67. Wilbert B.L. Kapinga, 'State Control of the Working Class through Labour Legislation' in Issa G. Shivji (ed.), *CODESRIA Bulletin*, Dakar, 1986, p. 93.

68. Chris Allen, 'Gender, Participation, and Radicalism in African Nationalism: Its Contemporary Significance' in Cohen and Goulbourne, *op. cit.*, p. 212.

69. Daryl Glaser, 'Discourses of Democracy in the South African Left: A Critical Commentary' in Cohen and Goulbourne, *op. cit.*, pp. 114ff.

70. Amilcar Cabral, 'Brief Analysis of the Social Structure of Guinea-Bissau', in P. Gutkind and P. Waterman (eds), *African Social Studies: A Reader*, Monthly Review Press, 1977, p. 230.

71. *ibid.*

72. Kole Ahmed Shettima, 'Structural Adjustment and the Student Movement in Nigeria', *Review of African Political Economy*, no. 56 (1993), p. 83.

73. Cabral quoted in Robin Cohen, 'Marxism in Africa: the Grounding of a Tradition' in Munslow, *op. cit.*, p. 51.

74. Nyong'o, *op. cit.*, pp. 22–4.

75. *ibid.*, p. 21.

76. Peter Anyang' Nyong'o, 'Popular Alliances and the State of Liberia, 1980–85' in Nyong'o, *op. cit.*, p. 246.

77. *ibid.*, p. 226.

78. *ibid.*, p. 244.

79. Grace and Laffin, *Africa Since 1960, op. cit.*, p. 183.

80. Mahmood Mamdani, 'Contradictory Class Perspectives on the Question of Democracy in the Case of Uganda' in Nyong'o, *op. cit.*, p. 93.

81. *ibid.*, p. 94.

82. TWIN reports.

83. TWIN reports.

CHAPTER 17. COOPERATION ON THE GROUND

1. UNESCO, theme for a research programme of the South–North Network 'Culture and Development' on 'Entrepreneurship and African Cultures', *Courier*, no. 15 (1993), p. 22.

2. Proposed by Gustavo Esteva, 'Development' in Sachs, *The Development Dictionary, op. cit.*, pp. 6–25.

3. Explored by Serge Latouche, *La Planète des naufragés*, La Découverte, Paris, 1991; English translation, *In the Wake of the Affluent Society*, Zed Books, 1993, Preface and pp. 220ff.

4. See Michael Barratt Brown, *European Union: Fortress or Democracy?*, Spokesman, 1991, pp. 86ff.

5. Anthony Giddens, *A Contemporary Critique of Historical Materialism*, Macmillan, 1981, pp. 135ff. and see Kimani Gecau, 'Culture and the Tasks of Development in Africa' in Kaarsholm, *Culture and Development in Southern Africa, op. cit.*, pp. 91–2.

6. Barratt Brown and Tiffen, *Short Changed, op. cit., passim*, especially pp. 141–2.

7. Alex Comfort, *Man and Society*, Joy of Knowledge Library, Mitchell Beazley, 1976, pp. 16–19.

8. Mackintosh, *Gender, Class and Rural Transition, op. cit.*, 1989, pp. 30ff and 150ff.

9. Healey and Robinson, *Democracy, Governance and Economic Policy, op. cit.*

10. Colin Leys, 'Confronting the African Tragedy', *New Left Review*, no. 204 (March–April 1994).

11. Davidson, *Black Man's Burden, op. cit.*, pp. 27ff.

12. Leys, *op. cit.*, p. 45.

13. Goran Hyden, 'The Changing Context of Institutional Development in Sub-Saharan Africa' in World Bank, LTPS, Background Papers, vol. 3, *op. cit.*, pp. 45ff.

14. Milton and Rose Friedman, *Free to Choose*, Penguin, 1980, pp. 44ff.

15. Adam Smith, *Theory of Moral Sentiment*, Henry Bohn, 1759.

16. Adam Smith, *The Wealth of Nations*, Ward Lock, 1776, 1812 reprint, p. 356.

17. Tim Lang and Colin Hines, *The New Protectionism*, Earthscan, 1993, pp. 126ff.

18. Robin Murray, 'Underdevelopment, International Firms and the International Division of Labour' in Jan Tinbergen (ed.), *Toward a New World Economy*, Rotterdam University Press, 1972, pp. 203ff.

19. Peter L. Berger, *The Capitalist Revolution,* Wildwood House, 1987, pp. 162ff.

20. World Bank, *Sub-Saharan Africa: From Crisis to Sustainable Development,* (LTPS), *op. cit.*, p. 14.

21. Barratt Brown, *op. cit.*, Chapter 7.

22. *ibid.*, pp. 96–7.

23. 'FAVDO Statutes: Article 21' in *Echoes of FAVDO*, no. 4 (June 1993), p. 28.

24. Zimbabwe Women's Resource Centre and Network, *Women's Income Generating Projects and Empowerment*, Harare, September 1992.

25. Joseph Songsore, 'The Cooperative Credit Union in North-western Ghana: Development Agent or Agent of Incorporation?' in Taylor and Mackenzie, *Development from Within, op. cit.*, pp. 82ff.

26. D.R.F. Taylor, 'Survival in Rural Africa' in Taylor and Mackenzie, *op. cit.*, pp. 253ff.

27. World Bank, *Sub-Saharan Africa: From Crisis to Sustainable Development,* (LTPS), *op. cit.*, p. 182.

28. Mark Duffield, *War and Famine in Africa*, Oxfam, 1991, p. 26.

29. Alan Fowler, 'Distant Obligations: Speculations on NGO Funding and the Global Market', *Review of African Political Economy*, no. 55 (1992), p. 15.

30. Yash Tandon, 'Foreign NGOs, Uses and Abuses: An African Perspective', IFDA *Dossier*, Geneva, no. 81 (1991), pp. 68ff.

31. George B. Baldwin, 'NGOs and African Development: An Inquiry' in World Bank, LTPS, Background Papers, vol. 3, *op. cit.*, p. 91.

32. Charles Mabugre, 'When Credit is not Due: Financial Services by NGOs in Africa', *Small Enterprise Development*, no. 4 (December 1993).

33. Baldwin, *op. cit.*, p. 93.

34. Yash Tandon, *op. cit.*, p. 75.

35. Mark Nerfin, *The Relationship, NGOs – UN Agencies – Governments: Challenges, Possibilities and Prospects*, IFDA, Geneva, 1990.

36. TWIN, *Fair Trade: A Rough Guide for Business*, Twin Trading, 1994.

37. Peter Oakley, *Projects with People: The Practice of Participation in Rural Development*, ILO, 1991.

38. World Bank, 'The Bank and NGOs: Recent Experience and Emerging Trends', draft paper, 1990, quoted in Fowler, *op. cit.*, pp. 19–22.

39. Quoted in Timberlake, *Africa in Crisis, op. cit.*, p. 188.

40. Timberlake, *ibid.*, p. 189.

41. Barratt Brown and Tiffen, *op. cit.*, p. 141–2 and see Ibre Hutchful, '"Smoke and Mirrors": The World Bank's Social Dimensions of Adjustment (SDA) Programme', *Review of African Political Economy*, no. 62 (1994), pp. 582–3.

42. Akilagpa Sawyerr, 'The Politics of Adjustment Policy' in Adedeji et al., *The Human Dimension of Africa's Persistent Economic Crisis, op. cit.*, p. 228.

43. Bernard Lecomte, *Project Aid: Limitations and Alternatives*, OECD, Paris, 1986, Annexe 2, case study, 'The 6S Association in French-Speaking West Africa'.

44. *ibid.*

45. *ibid.*

46. TWIN, *op. cit.*

47. Healey and Robinson, *op. cit.*, pp. 14 ff.

48. Fowler, *op. cit.*, p. 26.

49. Goran Hyden, 'Creating an Enabling Environment' in World Bank, LTPS, Background Paper, vol. 3, *op. cit.*, pp. 79–80.

50. Baldwin, *op. cit.*, p. 91.

51. Hyden, 'The Changing Context', in World Bank, *op. cit.*, p. 53.

52. Hyden, 'Creating an Enabling Environment', *op. cit.*, p. 73.

53. *ibid.*, p.79.

54. *ibid.*

55. *ibid.*

56. OECD, *International Cooperation in Institutional Development of NGOs in Africa*, OECD Development Cooperation Directorate Documents, DCD/88.14, Paris, 1988.

57. John Clark, *Democratizing Development: The Role of Voluntary Organizations*, Earthscan, 1991.

58. Leys, *op. cit.*, p. 46.

59. Editorial, 'Democracy, Civil Society and NGOs', *Review of African Political Economy*, no. 55 (1992), p. 3.

60. TWIN Reports.

61. Healey and Robinson, *op. cit.*, p. 129.

62. Editorial, 'Surviving Democracy', *Review of African Political Economy*, no. 54 (1992), p. 7.

63. *ibid.*

64. Healey and Robinson, *op. cit.*, pp. 147–8.

65. J. Herbst, 'Structural Adjustment Politics in Africa', *World Development*, 18:7 (1990), pp. 949–58.

66. Healey and Robinson, *op. cit.*, p. 145.

67. Timberlake, *op. cit.*, pp. 190–91.

68. Kate Wellard and James G. Copestake (eds), *NGOs and the State in Africa: Rethinking Roles in Sustainable Agricultural Development*, Routledge, 1994.

69. John Farrington and Anthony Bebbington with Kate Wellard and David J. Lewis, *Reluctant Partners? Non-Governmental Organizations, the State and Sustainable Agricultural Development*, Routledge, 1993, p. 183.

CHAPTER 18. AFRICA IN THE WORLD ECONOMY

1. World Bank, *Development Report 1994*, Washington, 1994.
2. Claude Aké, 'The Marginalization of Africa: Notes on a Productive Confusion', paper prepared for the Council on Foreign Relations African Studies seminar, New York, 18 February 1994, p. 10.
3. *ibid.*, p. 15.
4. Adebayo Adedeji, 'Marginalization and Marginality' in Adebayo Adedeji (ed.), *Africa Within the World: Beyond Dispossession and Dependence*, Zed Books, 1993, p. 8.
5. Aké, *op. cit.*, p. 19.
6. Jean-François Bayart, *The State in Africa: The Politics of the Belly*, Paris, 1989, Longman, 1992, quoted in Leys, 'Confronting the African Tragedy', *op. cit.*, p. 42.
7. Leys, *op. cit.*, p. 46.
8. *ibid.*
9. *ibid.*, p. 47.
10. Aké *op. cit.*, p. 39.
11. *ibid.*, p. 38.
12. World Bank, *The East Asian Miracle. op. cit.*, pp. 5ff.
13. Jacques Polak, *The Changing Nature of IMF Conditionality*, quoted in Stuart Holland, *Towards a New Bretton Woods: Alternatives for the Global Economy*, Spokesman, pp. 124ff.
14. See Paul Ormerod, *The Death of Economics*, Faber and Faber, 1994, pp. 3ff. and for Africa, S.M. Shafaeddin, *The Impact of Trade Liberalization on Export and GDP Growth in Least Developed Countries*, UNCTAD Discussion Paper No. 85, July 1994, pp. 15ff.
15. Oxfam, *Africa – Make or Break: Action for Recovery*, Oxford, 1993.
16. Alan Fowler, 'Distant Obligations: Speculations on NGO Funding and the Global Market', *Review of African Political Economy*, no. 55 (November 1992), pp. 16–17.
17. *ibid.*, p. 27.
18. National opinion poll, November 1993, conducted for Christian Aid, quoted in TWIN, *Fair Trade: A Rough Guide for Business*, *op. cit.*, p. 2.
19. TWIN Reports.
20. Barratt Brown, *Fair Trade*, *op. cit.*, pp. 158ff.
21. TWIN, *Fair Trade*, *op. cit.*, p. 12.
22. TWIN Reports.
23. Deborah Hargreaves, 'Fight over a Hill o'Beans', *Financial Times*, 1 October 1993.
24. Miguel Garronté, Nestlé spokesman, reported by Reuters, 1 November 1993.
25. Barratt Brown and Tiffen, *Short Changed*, *op. cit.*, pp. 44–45.
26. Letter to the author, at TWIN Ltd, April 1993.

27. Holland, *op. cit.*, p. 236.

28. Barratt Brown, *op. cit.*, pp. 69ff.

29. Peter Madden, *A Raw Deal: Trade and the World's Poor*, Christian Aid, 1992, pp. 77–8.

30. Gamani Corea, *Taming the Commodity Markets: The Integrated Programme and the Common Fund of UNCTAD*, Manchester University Press, 1992, Chapter 11.

31. Holland, *op. cit.*, pp. 241ff.

32. Barratt Brown, *op. cit.*, pp. 169ff.

33. Peter Cooke, 'Flexible Integration, Scope Economies and Strategic Alliances', *Environment and Planning*, vol. 6 (1988).

34. Holland, *op. cit.*, p. 242.

35. Peter Madden and John Madeley, *Winners and Losers: The Impact of the GATT Uruguay Round on Developing Countries*, Christian Aid, 1993, pp. 2–3 and p. 23.

36. Barratt Brown, *op. cit.*, pp. 8off.

37. Madden and Madeley, *op. cit.*, p. 21.

38. UN Centre for Transnational Corporations (UN CTC), *World Investment Report, 1991: The Triad in Foreign Investment*, New York, 1991, pp. 4–10 and UN CTC *Investment Report, 1993: Transnational Corporations and Integrated International Production*, New York, 1993, p. 45.

39. UN CTC, *1993, ibid.*, pp. 19–23.

40. Barratt Brown and Tiffen, *op. cit.*, pp. 25ff. and Table A.40.

41. James Avery Joyce, *World Labor Rights and their Protection*, ILO, New York, 1980.

42. Michael Barratt Brown, 'Towards a New Bretton Woods', *European Labour Forum*, no. 9 (1993).

43. Quoted in Holland, *op. cit.*, p. 102.

44. Holland, *op. cit.*, pp. 121ff.

45. *ibid.*, pp. 136ff. and Oxfam, *op. cit.*, pp. 22ff.

46. Michael Irwin, *Inside the World Bank*, IFAA, London, 1990 and Michael Prowse, 'Interview with Lewis Preston, World Bank President', *Financial Times*, 18 July, 1994.

47. The Development-GAP, *BankCheck*, no. 8, June 1994.

48. Quoted by Michael Prowse, 'IMF and World Bank Must Adapt', *Financial Times*, 7 July, 1994.

49. John Maynard Keynes, *The General Theory of Employment, Interest and Money*, Macmillan, 1936, p. 159.

50. Quoted by John Williamson, 'Rules Needed for a New Age', *Financial Times*, 8 July 1994.

51. Quoted by Michael Prowse, 'A Leaner, Greener Bank', *Financial Times*, 20 July 1994.

52. Michael Barratt Brown, 'The Modern Frankenstein', *European Labour Forum*, no. 10 (1993), pp. 35ff.

53. Robert Wade, 'The Mixed Economy and Export-Led Growth: Lessons from (Capitalist) East Asia', paper quoted by Holland, *op. cit.*, p. 174.

54. World Bank, *Learning from the Past: Embracing the Future*, quoted by Michael Prowse, *op. cit.*

55. Michael Barratt Brown, 'Money, Debt and Slump, the Lessons of the Thirties', *European Labour Forum*, no. 9, 1993.

56. 'Fifty Years Is Enough' campaign, *op. cit.*

57. Quoted in Bade Onimode, *A Future for Africa: Beyond the Politics of Adjustment*, Earthscan, 1992, p. 164.

58. *ibid.*, p. 165.

59. Margaret Joan Anstee, 'Social Development in Africa: Perspective, Reality and Promise', in Pickett and Singer, *Towards Economic Recovery in Sub-Saharan Africa*, *op. cit.*, p. 212.

60. World Bank, *World Debt Tables, 1993–4*, vol. 1, Washington, 1993.

61. Percy S. Mistry, *Multilateral Debt: An Emerging Crisis?*, Fondad, The Hague, 1994.

62. *ibid.*, Box 1, p. 20.

63. *ibid.*, p. 40.

64. *ibid.*, pp. 40–44 and see Kevin Watkins, 'Debt Relief for Africa', *Review of African Political Economy*, no. 62 (1994), pp. 599–609.

65. *ibid.*, pp. 50–55.

66. Holland, *op. cit.*, pp. 226ff.

67. Chapters 7–10.

68. See Barratt Brown and Tiffen, *op. cit.*, pp. 15–16.

69. Benedict S. Mongula, 'Development Theory and Changing Trends in Sub-Saharan African Economies, 1965–1989' in Ulf Himmelstrand et al. (eds), *African Perspectives on Development*, James Currey, 1994.

70. Miles Litvinoff, *The Earthscan Action Handbook for People and Planet*, Earthscan, 1990.

71. Achebe et al., *Beyond Hunger in Africa*, *op. cit.*, p. 22.

INDEX

Discover more about our forthcoming books through Penguin's FREE newspaper...

Penguin
Quarterly

It's packed with:

- exciting features
- author interviews
- previews & reviews
- books from your favourite films & TV series
- exclusive competitions & much, much more...

Write off for your free copy today to:
Dept JC
Penguin Books Ltd
FREEPOST
West Drayton
Middlesex
UB7 0BR
NO STAMP REQUIRED

READ MORE IN PENGUIN

In every corner of the world, on every subject under the sun, Penguin represents quality and variety – the very best in publishing today.

For complete information about books available from Penguin – including Puffins, Penguin Classics and Arkana – and how to order them, write to us at the appropriate address below. Please note that for copyright reasons the selection of books varies from country to country.

In the United Kingdom: Please write to *Dept. JC, Penguin Books Ltd, FREEPOST, West Drayton, Middlesex UB7 OBR.*

If you have any difficulty in obtaining a title, please send your order with the correct money, plus ten per cent for postage and packaging, to *PO Box No. 11, West Drayton, Middlesex UB7 OBR*

In the United States: Please write to *Consumer Sales, Penguin USA, P.O. Box 999, Dept. 17109, Bergenfield, New Jersey 07621-0120.* VISA and MasterCard holders call 1-800-253-6476 to order all Penguin titles

In Canada: Please write to *Penguin Books Canada Ltd, 10 Alcorn Avenue, Suite 300, Toronto, Ontario M4V 3B2*

In Australia: Please write to *Penguin Books Australia Ltd, P.O. Box 257, Ringwood, Victoria 3134*

In New Zealand: Please write to *Penguin Books (NZ) Ltd, Private Bag 102902, North Shore Mail Centre, Auckland 10*

In India: Please write to *Penguin Books India Pvt Ltd, 706 Eros Apartments, 56 Nehru Place, New Delhi 110 019*

In the Netherlands: Please write to *Penguin Books Netherlands bv, Postbus 3507, NL-1001 AH Amsterdam*

In Germany: Please write to *Penguin Books Deutschland GmbH, Metzlerstrasse 26, 60594 Frankfurt am Main*

In Spain: Please write to *Penguin Books S. A., Bravo Murillo 19, 1° B, 28015 Madrid*

In Italy: Please write to *Penguin Italia s.r.l., Via Felice Casati 20, I–20124 Milano*

In France: Please write to *Penguin France S. A., 17 rue Lejeune, F–31000 Toulouse*

In Japan: Please write to *Penguin Books Japan, Ishikiribashi Building, 2–5–4, Suido, Bunkyo-ku, Tokyo 112*

In Greece: Please write to *Penguin Hellas Ltd, Dimocritou 3, GR–106 71 Athens*

In South Africa: Please write to *Longman Penguin Southern Africa (Pty) Ltd, Private Bag X08, Bertsham 2013*

READ MORE IN PENGUIN

BUSINESS AND ECONOMICS

North and South David Smith

'This authoritative study ... gives a very effective account of the incredible centralization of decision-making in London, not just in government and administration, but in the press, communications and the management of every major company' – *New Statesman & Society*

I am Right – You are Wrong Edward de Bono

Edward de Bono expects his ideas to outrage conventional thinkers, yet time has been on his side, and the ideas that he first put forward twenty years ago are now accepted mainstream thinking. Here, in this brilliantly argued assault on outmoded thought patterns, he calls for nothing less than a New Renaissance.

Lloyds Bank Small Business Guide Sara Williams

This long-running guide to making a success of your small business deals with real issues in a practical way. 'As comprehensive an introduction to setting up a business as anyone could need' – *Daily Telegraph*

The *Economist* Economics Rupert Pennant-Rea and Clive Crook

Based on a series of 'briefs' published in the *Economist* , this is a clear and accessible guide to the key issues of today's economics for the general reader.

The Rise and Fall of Monetarism David Smith

Now that even Conservatives have consigned monetarism to the scrap heap of history, David Smith draws out the unhappy lessons of a fundamentally flawed economic experiment, driven by a doctrine that for years had been regarded as outmoded and irrelevant.

Understanding Organizations Charles B. Handy

Of practical as well as theoretical interest, this book shows how general concepts can help solve specific organizational problems.

READ MORE IN PENGUIN

BUSINESS AND ECONOMICS

The Affluent Society   John Kenneth Galbraith

Classical economics was born in a harsh world of mass poverty, and it has left us with a set of preoccupations hard to adapt to the realities of our own richer age. Our unfamiliar problems need a new approach, and the reception given to this famous book has shown the value of its fresh, lively ideas.

Lloyds Bank Tax Guide   Sara Williams and John Willman

An average employee tax bill is over £4,000 a year. But how much time do you spend checking it? Four out of ten never check the bill – and most spend less than an hour. Mistakes happen. This guide can save YOU money. 'An unstuffy read, packed with sound information' – *Observer*

Trouble Shooter II   John Harvey-Jones

The former chairman of ICI and Britain's best-known businessman resumes his role as consultant to six British companies facing a variety of problems – and sharing a new one: the recession.

Managing on the Edge   Richard Pascale

Nothing fails like success: companies flourish, then lose their edge through a process that is both relentless and largely invisible. 'Pascale's analysis and prescription for "managing on the edge" are unusually subtle for such a readable business book' – *Financial Times*

The Money Machine: How the City Works   Philip Coggan

How are the big deals made? Which are the institutions that really matter? What causes the pound to rise or interest rates to fall? This book provides clear and concise answers to a huge variety of money-related questions.

READ MORE IN PENGUIN

HISTORY

The Making of Europe   Robert Bartlett

'Bartlett does more than anyone before him to bring out the way in which medieval Europe was shaped by [a] great wave of internal conquest, colonization and evangelization. He also stresses its consequences for the future history of the world' – *Guardian*

The Somme Battlefields   Martin and Mary Middlebrook

This evocative, original book provides a definitive guide to the cemeteries, memorials and battlefields from the age of Crécy and Agincourt to the great Allied sweep which drove the Germans back in 1944, concentrating above all on the scenes of ferocious fighting in 1916 and 1918.

Ancient Slavery and Modern Ideology   M. I. Finley

Few topics in the study of classical civilization could be more central – and more controversial – than slavery. In this magnificent book, M. I. Finley cuts through the thickets of modern ideology to get at the essential facts. 'A major creative achievement in historical interpretation' – *The Times Higher Education Supplement*

The Penguin History of Greece   A. R. Burn

Readable, erudite, enthusiastic and balanced, this one-volume history of Hellas sweeps the reader along from the days of Mycenae and the splendours of Athens to the conquests of Alexander and the final dark decades.

The Laurel and the Ivy   Robert Kee

'Parnell continues to haunt the Irish historical imagination a century after his death ... Robert Kee's patient and delicate probing enables him to reconstruct the workings of that elusive mind as persuasively, or at least as plausibly, as seems possible ... This splendid biography, which is as readable as it is rigorous, greatly enhances our understanding of both Parnell, and of the Ireland of his time' – *The Times Literary Supplement*

READ MORE IN PENGUIN

HISTORY

A History of Wales   John Davies

'Outstanding . . . Dr Davies casts a coolly appraising eye upon myths, false premises and silver linings . . . He is impartial. He grasps the story of his country with immense confidence and tells it in vigorous and lucid prose . . . Its scope is unique. It is the history Wales needed' – *Daily Telegraph*

Daily Life in Ancient Rome   Jerome Carcopino

This classic study, which includes a bibliography and notes by Professor Rowell, describes the streets, houses and multi-storeyed apartments of the city of over a million inhabitants, the social classes from senators to slaves, and the Roman family and the position of women, causing *The Times Literary Supplement* to hail it as a 'thorough, lively and readable book'.

The Anglo-Saxons   Edited by James Campbell

'For anyone who wishes to understand the broad sweep of English history, Anglo-Saxon society is an important and fascinating subject. And Campbell's is an important and fascinating book. It is also a finely produced and, at times, a very beautiful book' – *London Review of Books*

Customs in Common   E. P. Thompson

Eighteenth-century Britain saw a profound distancing between the culture of the patricians and the plebs. E. P. Thompson explains why in this series of brilliant essays on the customs of the working people, which, he argues, emerged as a culture of resistance towards an innovative market economy. 'One of the most eloquent, powerful and independent voices of our time' – *Observer*

The Habsburg Monarchy 1809–1918   A J P Taylor

Dissolved in 1918, the Habsburg Empire 'had a unique character, out of time and out of place'. Scholarly and vividly accessible, this 'very good book indeed' (*Spectator*) elucidates the problems always inherent in the attempt to give peace, stability and a common loyalty to a heterogeneous population.

READ MORE IN PENGUIN

HISTORY

Citizens Simon Schama

The award-winning chronicle of the French Revolution. 'The most marvellous book I have read about the French Revolution in the last fifty years' – Richard Cobb in *The Times*

To the Finland Station Edmund Wilson

In this authoritative work Edmund Wilson, considered by many to be America's greatest twentieth-century critic, turns his attention to Europe's revolutionary traditions, tracing the roots of nationalism, socialism and Marxism as these movements spread across the Continent creating unrest, revolt and widespread social change.

The Tyranny of History W. J. F. Jenner

A fifth of the world's population lives within the boundaries of China, a vast empire barely under the control of the repressive ruling Communist regime. Beneath the economic boom China is in a state of crisis that goes far deeper than the problems of its current leaders to a value system that is rooted in the autocratic traditions of China's past.

The English Bible and the Seventeenth-Century Revolution
Christopher Hill

'What caused the English civil war? What brought Charles I to the scaffold?' Answer to both questions: the Bible. To sustain this provocative thesis, Christopher Hill's new book maps English intellectual history from the Reformation to 1660, showing how scripture dominated every department of thought from sexual relations to political theory ... 'His erudition is staggering' – *Sunday Times*

Private Lives, Public Spirit: Britain 1870–1914 Jose Harris

'Provides the most convincing – and demanding – synthesis yet available of these crowded and tumultuous years' – *Observer* Books of the Year. 'Remarkable ... it locates the origins of far-reaching social change as far back as the 1880s [and] goes on to challenge most of the popular assumptions made about the Victorian and Edwardian periods' – *Literary Review*

READ MORE IN PENGUIN

ARCHAEOLOGY

Breaking the Maya Code Michael D. Coe

Over twenty years ago, no one could read the hieroglyphic texts carved on the magnificent Maya temples and palaces; today we can understand almost all of them. The inscriptions reveal a culture obsessed with warfare, dynastic rivalries and ritual blood-letting. 'An entertaining, enlightening and even humorous history of the great searchers after the meaning that lies in the Maya inscriptions' – *Observer*

The Ancient Economy M. I. Finley

One of M. I. Finley's most influential contributions to ancient history, this study examines the structure, character and operation of the ancient economy, illustrating, for example, that the Roman Empire was for centuries a single political unit operating within a 'common cultural-psychological framework'.

The Pyramids of Egypt I. E. S. Edwards

Dr Edwards offers us the definitive work on these gigantic tombs, drawing both on his own original research and on the work of the many archaeologists who have dug in Egypt. This revised edition includes recent discoveries and research.

Lucy's Child Donald Johanson and James Shreeve

'Superb adventure ... *Lucy's Child* burns with the infectious excitement of hominid fever ... the tedium and the doubting, and the ultimate triumph of an expedition that unearths something wonderful about the origins of humanity' – *Chicago Tribune*

Archaeology and Language Colin Renfrew
The Puzzle of Indo-European Origins

'The time-scale, the geographical spaces, the questions and methods of inquiry ... are vast ... But throughout this teeming study, Renfrew is pursuing a single, utterly fascinating puzzle: who are we Europeans, where do the languages we speak really stem from?' – *Sunday Times*

READ MORE IN PENGUIN

POLITICS AND SOCIAL SCIENCES

National Identity Anthony D. Smith

In this stimulating new book, Anthony D. Smith asks why the first modern nation states developed in the West. He considers how ethnic origins, religion, language and shared symbols can provide a sense of nation and illuminates his argument with a wealth of detailed examples.

The Feminine Mystique Betty Friedan

'A brilliantly researched, passionately argued book – a time-bomb flung into the Mom-and-Apple-Pie image . . . Out of the debris of that shattered ideal, the Women's Liberation Movement was born' – Ann Leslie

Faith and Credit Susan George and Fabrizio Sabelli

In its fifty years of existence, the World Bank has influenced more lives in the Third World than any other institution yet remains largely unknown, even enigmatic. This richly illuminating and lively overview examines the policies of the Bank, its internal culture and the interests it serves.

Political Ideas Edited by David Thomson

From Machiavelli to Marx – a stimulating and informative introduction to the last 500 years of European political thinkers and political thought.

Structural Anthropology Volumes 1–2 Claude Lévi-Strauss

'That the complex ensemble of Lévi-Strauss's achievement . . . is one of the most original and intellectually exciting of the present age seems undeniable. No one seriously interested in language or literature, in sociology or psychology, can afford to ignore it' – George Steiner

Invitation to Sociology Peter L. Berger

Sociology is defined as 'the science of the development and nature and laws of human society'. But what is its purpose? Without belittling its scientific procedures Professor Berger stresses the humanistic affinity of sociology with history and philosophy. It is a discipline which encourages a fuller awareness of the human world . . . with the purpose of bettering it.

READ MORE IN PENGUIN

POLITICS AND SOCIAL SCIENCES

Conservatism Ted Honderich

'It offers a powerful critique of the major beliefs of modern conservatism, and shows how much a rigorous philosopher can contribute to understanding the fashionable but deeply ruinous absurdities of his times' – *New Statesman & Society*

The Battle for Scotland Andrew Marr

A nation without a parliament of its own, Scotland has been wrestling with its identity and status for a century. In this excellent and up-to-date account of the distinctive history of Scottish politics, Andrew Marr uses party and individual records, pamphlets, learned works, interviews and literature to tell a colourful and often surprising account.

Bricks of Shame: Britain's Prisons Vivien Stern

'Her well-researched book presents a chillingly realistic picture of the British sytstem and lucid argument for changes which could and should be made before a degrading and explosive situation deteriorates still further' – *Sunday Times*

Inside the Third World Paul Harrison

This comprehensive book brings home a wealth of facts and analysis on the often tragic realities of life for the poor people and communities of Asia, Africa and Latin America.

'Just like a Girl' Sue Sharpe
How Girls Learn to be Women

Sue Sharpe's unprecedented research and analysis of the attitudes and hopes of teenage girls from four London schools has become a classic of its kind. This new edition focuses on girls in the nineties – some of whom could even be the daughters of the teenagers she interviewed in the seventies – and represents their views and ideas on education, work, marriage, gender roles, feminism and women's rights.

READ MORE IN PENGUIN

PHILOSOPHY

What Philosophy Is   Anthony O'Hear

'Argument after argument is represented, including most of the favourites
... its tidy and competent construction, as well as its straightforward style,
mean that it will serve well anyone with a serious interest in philosophy'
– *Journal of Applied Philosophy*

Montaigne and Melancholy   M. A. Screech

'A sensitive probe into how Montaigne resolved for himself the age-old
ambiguities of melancholia and, in doing so, spoke of what he called the
"human condition"' – *London Review of Books*

Labyrinths of Reason   William Poundstone

'The world and what is in it, even what people say to you, will not seem
the same after plunging into *Labyrinths of Reason* ... He holds up the
deepest philosophical questions for scrutiny and examines their relation to
reality in a way that irresistibly sweeps readers on' – *New Scientist*

I: The Philosophy and Psychology of Personal Identity
Jonathan Glover

From cases of split brains and multiple personalities to the importance of
memory and recognition by others, the author of *Causing Death and
Saving Lives* tackles the vexed questions of personal identity.

Philosophy and Philosophers   John Shand

'A concise and readily surveyable account of the history of Western
philosophy ... it succeeds in being both an illuminating introduction to the
history of philosophy for someone who has little prior knowledge of the
subject and a valuable source of guidance to a more experienced student'
– *The Times Literary Supplement*

Russian Thinkers   Isaiah Berlin

As one of the most outstanding liberal intellects of this century, the author
brings to his portraits of Russian thinkers a unique perception of the social
and political circumstances that produced men such as Herzen, Bakunin,
Turgenev, Belinsky and Tolstoy.